A must read for a mathematical programming practitioner. Masterfully done, Professor Li takes an end-to-end approach for the modeling of supply chain and logistics problems, providing a comprehensive and accessible treatment of building and solving optimization models to address data-driven decision problems in supply chain management. Professor Li is the best mathematical optimization modeler I know.

Cipriano (Pano) Santos
former Distinguished Technologist from HP Labs

This is an exceptional book. It is the first to comprehensively integrate a broad range of important concepts and innovations from optimization into the treatment of supply chain management. The outcome is not merely informative but provides a perspective that significantly enriches the literature on supply chains.

The preface and first chapter by themselves give a sense of the relevance of optimization modeling to supply chain management that goes beyond discussions found in previous treatments of these topics. The author, Haitao Li, exposes fundamental concepts in a clear and unpretentious way, and then progressively builds on them in multiple contexts to create a comprehensive set of principles for applying optimization modeling effectively in the supply chain setting. As a bonus, the book also covers new developments that are influencing the direction of supply chain applications, including a special chapter on models that are attracting attention in quantum computing.

The book is packed with examples and illustrations. The value of this treatment for understanding goes well beyond the value of commonly encountered treatments that leave the reader with little appreciation of the concrete details of practical applications.

Haitao Li's *Optimization Modeling for Supply Chain Applications* is an essential part of the toolkit for anyone who wants to have a well-grounded and accessible introduction to this important area.

Dr. Fred Glover
Distinguished Professor, University of Colorado
& Chief Technology Officer, OptTek Systems

This book contains the complete suite of prescriptive analytic tools necessary to practice supply chain analysis in 2023. Over time surely more techniques will be discovered, but at this point in time, this is the bible.

Dr. Keith Womer
Professor Emeritus, University of Missouri – St. Louis

Optimization Modeling for Supply Chain Applications by Professor Haitao Li is the most-comprehensive text I have seen that combines the art and fundamentals of mathematical programming modeling with applications in supply chain management. The breadth and depth of the mathematical modeling and the various applications from network design to production scheduling and inventory control make this an excellent text for technical undergraduate majors in supply chain management, as well as for master's degree students in analytics or supply chain management.

Dr. Jeffrey Camm
Inmar Presidential Chair in Analytics,
Wake Forest University School of Business

Optimization Modeling for Supply Chain Applications

Optimization Modeling for Supply Chain Applications

Haitao Li
University of Missouri-St Louis, USA

World Scientific

EW JERSEY • LONDON • SINGAPORE • BEIJING • SHANGHAI • HONG KONG • TAIPEI • CHENNAI • TOKYO

Published by

World Scientific Publishing Co. Pte. Ltd.
5 Toh Tuck Link, Singapore 596224
USA office: 27 Warren Street, Suite 401-402, Hackensack, NJ 07601
UK office: 57 Shelton Street, Covent Garden, London WC2H 9HE

Library of Congress Cataloging-in-Publication Data
Names: Li, Haitao, 1976– author.
Title: Optimization modeling for supply chain applications / Haitao Li, University of Missouri-St Louis, USA.
Description: USA : World Scientific, 2023. | Includes bibliographical references and index.
Identifiers: LCCN 2022022458 | ISBN 9789811259685 (hardcover) | ISBN 9789811260520 (ebook) | ISBN 9789811260537 (ebook other)
Subjects: LCSH: Business logistics. | Business logistics--Mathematical models. | Business logistics--Technological innovations.
Classification: LCC HD38.5 .L495 2023 | DDC 658.70285--dc23/eng/20220513
LC record available at https://lccn.loc.gov/2022022458

British Library Cataloguing-in-Publication Data
A catalogue record for this book is available from the British Library.

For any available supplementary material, please visit
https://www.worldscientific.com/worldscibooks/10.1142/12930#t=suppl

Desk Editors: Soundararajan Raghuraman/Lum Pui Yee

Typeset by Stallion Press
Email: enquiries@stallionpress.com

To my caring parents Fuqiong Cheng and Anquan Li, loving wife Liuqing Mai and three precious children, Hannah, Rachel and Grace.

Preface

The fast advancement of technologies and growing availability of data create new opportunities for data-driven decision-support using Optimization (also known as Prescriptive Analytics). The recent development in mathematical programming and the commercially available solvers, e.g., Gurobi, IBM CPLEX, and Xpress, etc. have shortened the learning curve of optimization and made it more accessible for students, researchers and practitioners.

Given the wide scope of the general field of *optimization*, we have to draw a line between the approaches using calculus, variational inequality and optimal control in Economics, versus mathematical programming based approaches, i.e., linear programming, integer programming/combinatorial optimization in Operations Research (OR). This text focuses on mathematical programming modeling due to its prominent role in real life decision-making, diverse practical applications, and the growing needs for data-driven optimization.

Among various application domains of optimization modeling, this text focuses on the applications in Supply Chain Management, a critical business function that encompasses the entire end-to-end operations of purchasing/procurement, production, logistics, transportation and delivery. It is also a rich arena for the development and application of various optimization models, including but not limited to: supply chain network design, production planning, material requirement planning (MRP), machine/project scheduling, and vehicle routing.

This text provides a systematic, comprehensive and accessible treatment of building optimization models to address data-driven decision problems in supply chains. From the methodological perspective, it introduces various modeling techniques, including mathematical programming (linear programming, network optimization and integer programming), and constraint programming that originated in Artificial Intelligence (AI). From the application perspective, in addition to the traditional supply chain related topics as mentioned above, it also covers some emerging applications such as supply chain configuration and supply chain finance. A state-of-the-art optimization modeling software, IBM's OPL CPLEX Studio (free academic license is available through IBM's Academic Initiative program), is used for implementing and solving the mathematical programming and constraint programming models.

To make the text accessible to readers with the knowledge of no more than basic linear algebra, the theory and technical details of optimization have been purposely kept minimal in the Appendices for the purpose of understanding and interpreting solutions. Just like the use of statistical software, one does not necessarily need to master all the technical details of statistical models and procedures to apply statistical analysis, but would definitely need to know how to build and specify statistical models. This is the premise and main learning goal of the text: To be able to build an optimization model of your own tailored to your problem at hand, and then implement and solve it using optimization software. Additional notes and references are provided at the end of each chapter to refer reader to a plethora of literature on the theories and technical details of the corresponding topics.

This text is suitable for a one-semester upper-level Undergraduate or Master/MBA level course in Business or Data Analytics. It can also be chosen by students in Economics, Industrial Engineering, Computer Science and Applied Math who are interested in optimization modeling and its applications in supply chains. It can also be used by practitioners or business consultants who are interested to be "Citizen Data Scientists" who bridge the gap between supply chain professionals and pure data scientists.

Haitao Li
St. Louis, Missouri, USA
January 2023

About the Author

Haitao Li is Professor and Chair of the Supply Chain & Analytics Department, College of Business Administration, and founding Director of Laboratory of Advanced Supply Chain Analytics (LASCA), at the University of Missouri — St. Louis. He holds his Ph.D. degree in Operations Management (2005) and Master of Arts in Economics (2002) from the University of Mississippi and Bachelor of Engineering in Foreign Trade in Industry with a minor in Aeronautical Engineering from Beijing University of Aeronautics and Astronautics, P.R. China (2000). Dr. Li's research focuses on optimization modeling and algorithm design in the application areas of supply chain optimization, project scheduling, and resource allocation, among others. He worked as a Statistical Analyst at the Naval Personnel Research, Study and Technology (NPRST) in Millington, TN, in 2004, a Visiting Scholar at the Hewlett-Packard Laboratory (HPL) in Palo Alto, CA, in 2005, and Research Consultant for HP Enterprises from 2010–2016. Dr. Li currently serves as Associate Editor of the *Journal of the Operational Research Society* and *Transportation Journal*, and Editorial Board member of the *International Journal of Project Management*.

Contents

List of Figures

List of Tables

Part I
Modeling Methodologies

Chapter 1

Introduction and Overview

1.1 Introduction to Optimization Modeling

People often need to make feasible and best decisions for complex decision problems. A decision problem is *complex* when there are numerous solutions to choose from, many requirements and conditions to satisfy, and often an objective to optimize.[a] For instance, finding the shortest route to visit each of n cities once and only once, well-known as the Traveling Salesman Problem (TSP), amounts to $n!$ possible routes. Choosing facilities among n candidate locations for shipping goods to a set of warehouses with minimum transportation cost, known as the Facility Location Problem (FLP), amounts to 2^n possible network configurations.

Feasible means that a solution is implementable, i.e., satisfying all requirements, conditions and limits, which are called *constraints* in a decision problem. For example, the TSP requires a *Hamiltonian tour*[b] to ensure all the cities are visited once and only once *and* the salesman must return to the original city she departs from. In the FLP, the designed network must meet warehouse demands without exceeding facility capacities.

---

[a]Formal definition and proof of NP-hardness in combinatorial optimization and complexity theory is beyond the scope of this text.

[b]In Graph Theory, a Hamiltonian tour is a cycle that visits every vertex exactly once.

Finding the *best* solution concerns searching and finding one or multiple solutions, among the set of all feasible solutions, that *optimize* a problem-specific objective, e.g., minimizing the total travel distance in the TSP, or minimizing the total facility setup and transportation costs in the FLP. A naïve enumeration or trial-and-error search approach is often intractable for solving such decision problems with a large feasible solution space.

Finding an optimal solution to a complex decision problem calls for optimization-based decision-support. The first step is to build an *optimization model*, as an abstraction of the problem at hand, with three structured components: decision variables, objective function, and constraints. A *decision variable* represents the decision to be made or the action to be taken by a decision-maker.[c] An *objective function* represents the decision-maker's goal, expressed as a mathematical function of decision variables, either to be maximized or minimized. It provides a quantifiable criterion for what it means by "best" or "optimal" solution. *Constraints* specify the requirements, conditions or limits to be satisfied, which are expressed as equalities ($=$) and/or inequalities ($\leq, \geq$), often with functions of decision variables at the left-hand-side (LHS), and a constant parameter at the right-hand-side (RHS). Mathematically, these equalities and inequalities confine the *feasible region* where all feasible solutions to the model must lie in. Two examples are provided below for a verbal description of an optimization model with the three components.

Example 1.1 (TSP). In a standard TSP, the decision variables represent a *permutation* of cities, i.e., the order to visit the cities; the objective function is to minimize the total travel distance; and the constraints include: (i) a city must be visited once and only once; and (ii) the salesman must return to the origin, i.e., one and only one tour may exist in a feasible solution.

Example 1.2 (FLP). In a single-sourcing uncapacitated FLP, the decision variables represent whether to open a facility or not, plus assignment of facilities to warehouses; the objective function is to minimize the total facility setup and transportation costs; and the constraints include: (i) a warehouse must be served by one facility

[c]It is also called control variable in the Optimal Control Theory.

(single-sourcing), and (ii) a facility cannot serve any warehouse if it is not opened.

The purpose of this book is to provide a systematic coverage on the techniques and recipes to build mathematical model formulations for optimization problems. It guides one on how to translate the verbal description of an optimization model to its mathematical form using algebraic notations, functions and equality/inequality relationships. By grasping these modeling techniques, one will be equipped with the skills and toolbox needed to build their own models for new and innovative optimization problems in real life applications.

It is important to note that being able to identify and define an optimization problem for real-world decision-support is a skill by itself, which is often not a trivial task. It often requires domain knowledge to define and articulate the decisions to be made, the objective to optimize, and the constraints to be satisfied. This can be a learning process where one may gain domain experience and knowledge over time.

In addition, while optimization modeling is a *science* with mathematical rigor, it is also an *art*. The art of modeling balances complexity and tractability of a model. On one hand, a model can be complex and sophisticated enough to be as close as to the reality; on the other hand, a highly complex model may hamper one's ability of obtaining optimal or near-optimal solutions, which may defeat the original purpose of such sophistication. By getting enough exposure to a variety of optimization models, and by understanding the connections and relationships among their variations and extensions, one would grow his/her artistic skills of modeling. For example, the basic TSP can be extended to numerous variants with more complexity and computational challenge, e.g., TSPs with side constraints, and a myriad of Vehicle Routing Problems (VRPs). The single-sourcing uncapacited FLP can also be extended to the multi-sourcing, capacited versions, and those in a multi-tier network and/or multi-period setting.

1.2 Optimization Using Mathematical Programming

Among a variety of optimization approaches and methods, we shall focus on the category of techniques known as Mathematical

Programming, which has its root in Operations Research (OR), originated in the World War II and later in the field of Management Science in the 1980s. Note that the term *programming* here carries a different meaning from that in computer programming: it refers to (i) a model formulation to represent an optimization problem; and (ii) an algorithmic method to obtain optimal (or near optimal) solutions to a model formulation.

Mathematical programming also belongs to the realm of Prescriptive Analytics, which, along with Descriptive and Predictive Analytics, forms the *three pillars* of modern Business Analytics with a wide range of applications in manufacturing, services, agriculture, healthcare and military.

Figure 1.1 shows the Three Pillars of Business Analytics, their roles, and relationships. Descriptive Analytics is usually a first step in data analysis to describe and understand *what happened in the past*, using descriptive statistics and modern data visualization techniques. Going one step further is the use of Predictive Analytics to predict/forecast *what will happen in the future*. To prescribe *what to do and how to react* calls for Prescriptive Analytics, or data-driven optimization, for which mathematical programming is a powerful tool. Note that the Three Pillars serve different purposes, but do overlap and synergize with each other for solving many of today's challenging real life problems.[d]

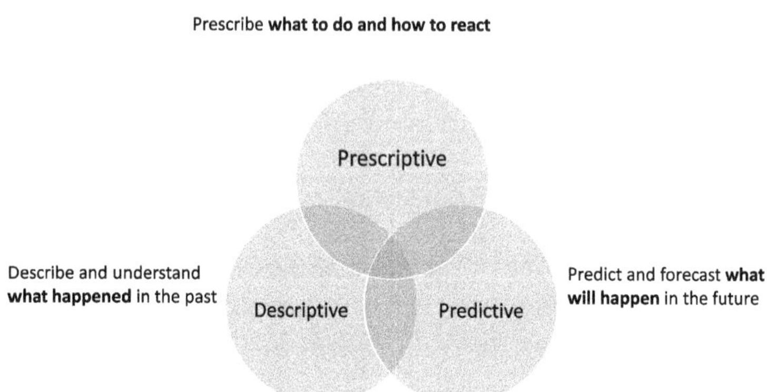

Figure 1.1. Three pillars of business analytics.

[d]Synthesizing different analytical techniques requires in-depth knowledge of solution methods in both deterministic and stochastic optimization, which goes beyond the scope of this text.

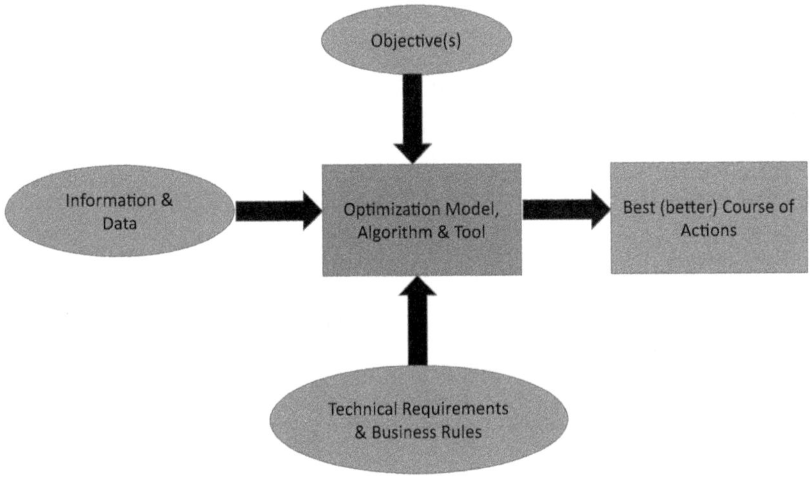

Figure 1.2. A conceptual sketch of prescriptive analytics (data-driven optimization) approach.

Figure 1.2 provides a conceptual sketch of a prescriptive analytical, or data-driven optimization, approach. The core is an optimization model and its solution algorithm, built upon the objective(s) to be optimized and various technical requirements/business rules to be satisfied. Knowledge and information about the optimization problem take some form of data, serving as inputs to the model. This approach prescribes the best course of decision or action for the decision-maker to take.

A generic mathematical programming model can be written as follows:

$$\text{Minimize } g(\boldsymbol{a},\boldsymbol{x}) \tag{1.1}$$

Subject to:

$$\boldsymbol{f}(\boldsymbol{b},\boldsymbol{x}) \geq \boldsymbol{d} \tag{1.2}$$

$$\boldsymbol{x} \geq 0 \tag{1.3}$$

where $\boldsymbol{x}$ is a $n \times 1$ vector of decision variables, $\boldsymbol{a}$ is a $1 \times n$ vector of coefficients in the objective function $g(\cdot)$, $\boldsymbol{b}$ is an $m \times n$ matrix of coefficients in the LHS of m constraints $\boldsymbol{f}(\cdot)$, and $\boldsymbol{d}$ is an $m \times 1$ vector of RHS constants in the constraints. Depending on the domain of $\boldsymbol{x}$ and the form of both $g(\cdot)$ and $\boldsymbol{f}(\cdot)$, the generic mathematical programming model above can be categorized into different classes, as elaborated in Table 1.1.

Table 1.1. Characterization of different mathematical programming models.

	Domain of x	Form of $g(\cdot)$	Form of $f(\cdot)$
Linear program (LP)	$\mathbb{R}^n$	Linear	Linear
Integer linear program (ILP)	$\mathbb{Z}^n$	Linear	Linear
Binary integer program (BIP)	$\mathbb{B}^n$	Linear or nonlinear	Linear or nonlinear
Mixed-integer linear program (MILP)	$\mathbb{R}^n \cup \mathbb{Z}^n$	Linear	Linear
Nonlinear program (NLP)	$\mathbb{R}^n$	At least one function is nonlinear	
Mixed-integer nonlinear program (MINLP)	$\mathbb{R}^n \cup \mathbb{Z}^n$	At least one function is nonlinear	

In addition to mathematical programming, we shall also introduce constraint programming (CP) as a useful modeling approach. CP was originated in the artificial intelligence (AI) area, which differs significantly from mathematical programming in modeling constructs and solution methods. CP proves to be effective for certain classes of optimization problems, including various scheduling and sequencing problems in supply chains.

1.3 Optimization Applications in Supply Chains

Supply chain provides a rich arena for mathematical programming. Supply chain management (SCM) has evolved from various isolated business functions, including demand management, purchasing/procurement, production, inventory management, warehousing and transportation, into an integrated systematic paradigm to manage all of the above functions. It intersects with multiple disciplines including Operations Management, Marketing, Information Systems, and Industrial Engineering.

The hierarchy of supply chain optimization decisions can be depicted by Figure 1.3. The strategic level decisions are those having long-term impact, usually more than three years, e.g., supply

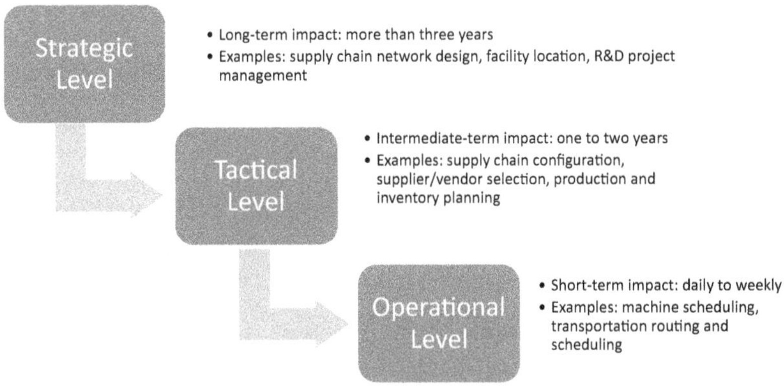

Figure 1.3. The hierarchy of optimization decisions in supply chains.

chain network design, capacity planning. Next at the tactical level are intermediate-term decisions, usually one to two years in scope, including supplier/vendor selection, safety stock placement, production and inventory planning, among others. The operational level decisions can be as frequent as weekly or daily, such as machine scheduling, transportation routing, etc.

Table 1.2 outlines the supply chain optimization models covered in this text with their corresponding modeling techniques, positioning in the hierarchy, and example application industries.

Figure 1.4 provides a sample path to cover the topics in this text. One starts with Chapter 2 on the basic modeling approach using LP. Appendix 2 can be accompanied to refresh students' knowledge of the LP solution methods: the graph method and the Simplex method. One may then proceed to Chapter 3 on modeling building in integer programming, with supplement on the branch-and-bound and cutting-plane methods in Appendix 3. Appendix 1 on using the CPLEX Studio to implement and solve the LP and MILP models can be covered after Chapters 2 and 3. Next, one may proceed with Chapter 4 on a special class of LP models for network flow optimization, followed by Chapter 6 on CP with supplement of CP solving methods in Appendix 4. Chapter 5 introduces a special modeling technique via quadratic unconstrained binary programming (QUBO), which facilitates the use of quantum computing technology.

After completing the above modeling techniques in Part I, one continues with Part II on supply chain applications. While

Table 1.2. Outline of optimization models covered.

Models	Techniques	Positioning	Application industry
Network flow	LP	Tactical	Agriculture, Manufacturing
Supply chain network design	MILP	Strategic	Agriculture, Manufacturing, Energy, Healthcare, Transportation
Master production scheduling (MPS)	MILP	Tactical	Food, Manufacturing
Material requirement planning (MRP)	MILP	Tactical	Food, Manufacturing
Labor strategy optimization	MILP	Strategic	Manufacturing, Professional service
Resource matching	BIP	Tactical	Professional service, Healthcare
Project portfolio optimization	MILP	Tactical	Manufacturing, R&D, professional service
Supply chain configuration	MINLP	Tactical	Food, Manufacturing, Energy
Machine scheduling	MILP and CP	Operational	Manufacturing, Healthcare
Resource-constrained project scheduling	MILP and CP	Operational	Construction, Manufacturing, R&D, Professional service, Healthcare
TSPs	MILP	Operational	Food, Manufacturing, Transportation, Healthcare
VRPs	MILP	Operational	Food, Manufacturing, Transportation, Healthcare

each chapter in Part II covers a self-contained topic, it is recommended to follow some intrinsic logic and sequence for Chapters 7 (Network Design), 10 (Supply Chain Configuration), 12 (TSPs) and 14 (VRPs) from decision-making at the strategic level to the tactical and operational levels. On the path of topics on production and operations, one is suggested to start with Chapter 8 (Production Planning), followed by Chapter 11 (Machine Scheduling) and Chapter 12 (Resource-Constrained Project Scheduling). Chapters 9

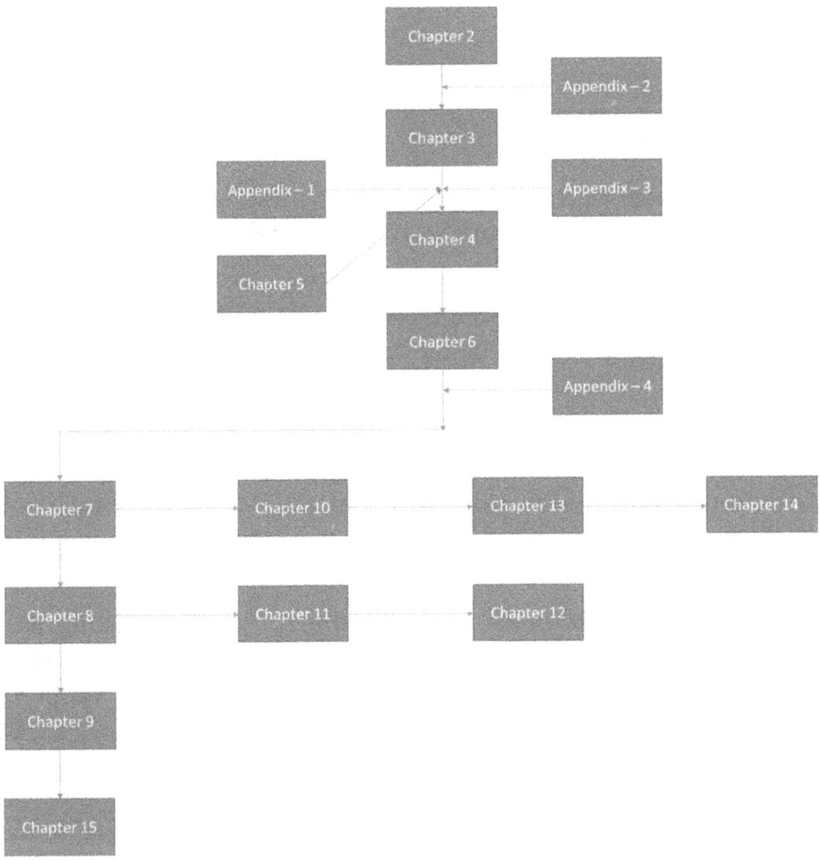

Figure 1.4. A sample path to cover the topics in this text.

(Resource Planning) and 15 (Supply Chain Finance) are relatively independent topics, which an instructor may choose to cover with his/her discretion.

1.4 Additional Notes

Getting some domain knowledge in SCM is helpful for learning supply chain modeling. We refer to [1–3] for a systematic and conceptual coverage on the broad topic of SCM. More technical treatment of operations and SCM are available in [4–6].

Exercises

1.1. What are the three components of an optimization model? What are their roles in the model? Describe an example of an optimization problem and conceptually describe its optimization model.

1.2. Comparing optimization modeling (prescriptive analytics) to statistics (descriptive and predictive analytics), what are their differences and connections?

1.3. Conceptually describe the three components in an optimization model for a standard FLP. Show and discuss one real world application of FLP. (*Hint*: in industries such as food and agriculture, manufacturing, healthcare, energy, telecommunication, logistics and transportation, etc.)

1.4. Conceptually describe the three components in an optimization model for a standard TSP. Show and discuss one real world application of TSP.

1.5. Identify and elaborate characteristics from the modeling perspective for the following decision scenarios, including the level in the decision hierarchy (strategic, tactical or operational), scope of decision (long-term, mediate-term or short-term), and the best-fit optimization model (LP, BIP, MILP or CP):

- A farm manager needs to determine which and how much crops to grow in the upcoming year.
- A brewery needs to plan for its delivery to serve the local bars, restaurants, and grocery stores.
- A non-for-profit health organization is planning to setup a vaccine delivery network in a developing country.
- A music box (audio system) manufacturer needs to plan for the production of a mixture of models and styles to produce in the upcoming year.
- A pharmaceutical company is selecting most beneficial and promising drug development projects among a set of opportunities.

1.6. A utility company has its routine maintenance, repairing and operations to serve a region with millions of residents. It needs to keep proper amount of inventories for thousands of parts, materials and equipment to achieve high service levels. Identify and elaborate the strategic, tactical and operational decisions the company might be facing to address.

1.7. An indoor farming company is considering to expand its operations to better serve its customers (grocery stores and restaurants) in the region. The expansion involves building up to three new indoor farming facilities, with more growing capacity and better technologies. Identify and elaborate the strategic, tactical and operational decisions the company might be facing to address.

1.8. A construction company has just been awarded multiple building contracts. With limited availability of budget, equipment and labor, the company needs to properly schedule the construction projects and allocated the limited resources. Conceptually describe an optimization model for this purpose, elaborating its decision variables, objective function and constraints.

Chapter 2

Linear Programming

2.1 Introduction to Linear Programming

Linear Programming (LP) is the foundation of mathematical programming. It not only has numerous applications by itself, but also serves as the building block of various integer programming models, i.e., ILP, BIP and MILP. There are five key assumptions required for an LP model: proportionality, additivity, divisibility, certainty and non-negativity.

Proportionality means that the contribution of a decision to an objective function and the LHS of a constraint is proportional to the value/magnitude of the decision.

Example 2.1 (Proportionality). The production cost of manufacturing x units can be computed as cx, where c is the cost/unit of the product. The transportation cost of shipping y miles can be computed as cy, where c is the cost/mile. The revenue of selling z units of goods equals pz, where p is the price/unit of the goods.

Additivity means that the total contribution of multiple actions is the summation of the contribution of each individual action.

Example 2.2 (Additivity). The total production cost of manufacturing x_1 units of product 1 and x_2 units of product 2 equals $c_1x_1 + c_2x_2$, where c_1 and c_2 are the unit production cost of product 1 and 2, respectively. The total transportation cost of shipping y_1 miles to destination 1 and y_2 miles to destination 2 equals $c_1y_1 + c_2y_2$, where c_1 and c_2 are cost/mile of shipping to destination 1 and 2, respectively.

Divisibility means that decision variables may take fractional values, i.e., they are not required to be integral. Satisfaction of this assumption depends largely on problem settings and applications.

Example 2.3 (Divisibility). Acres of land to grow a crop can take fractional value. Number of employees to hire at a large firm may take fractional value, but can be an integral value for a small firm. Tons of beer to produce in a month takes fractional value, whereas units of aircrafts to manufacture in a month is better to take integral value.

Certainty means that all the required data (input parameters) to a model are known and constant, with no uncertainty or randomness. Thus, LP is a *deterministic* optimization approach. In practice, "certainty" of a random parameter is assumed by using its point estimates (mean). Although it is prone to the flaw-of-average, sensitivity analysis or post-optimality analysis is available in LP to examine the effect of change of parameter on the optimal solution and objective value.

Non-negativity means that all the decision variables must be no less than zero, which is the case in almost all business applications.

2.2 Steps to Formulate an LP Model

Step 0: The first step is to understand and conceptually define the optimization problem on hand: its setting, scope and how decisions are made.

Step 1: Define decision variables: use math notations to represent the decisions to be made.

Step 2: Identify and write the objective function: use the decision variables in Step 1 to write a mathematical expression of the objective function to be optimized (minimized or maximized).

Step 3: Identify and write the constraints. These are usually requirements, restrictions, and/or limits that constrain the feasible solutions to the optimization problem.

Step 0 is a crucial step to start with, especially for a real world application. It often requires domain knowledge of a subject matter expert to identify and define the right optimization problem to address.

2.3 A Generic LP Formulation

Let $x_1, x_2, \ldots, x_n$ be n decision variables. A generic formulation of LP model with n decision variables and m constraints can be written as below.

$$\text{Maximize or Minimize } Z = c_1x_1 + c_2x_2 + \ldots + c_nx_n$$

Subject to:

$$\begin{aligned} a_{11}x_1 + a_{12}x_2 + \ldots + a_{1n}x_n &\leq b_1 \\ a_{21}x_1 + a_{22}x_2 + \ldots + a_{2n}x_n &\geq b_2 \\ &\vdots \\ a_{m1}x_1 + a_{m2}x_2 + \ldots + a_{mn}x_n &= b_m, \end{aligned}$$

where Z is the linear objective function, and the system of constraints consists of both inequalities and equalities. $c_1, c_2, \ldots, c_n$ are the coefficients of decision variables in the objective function; $b_1, b_2, \ldots, b_m$ are the RHS constants in the m constraints; and a_{ij} is the coefficient of decision variable x_j in the i-th constraint.

Example 2.4 (Product Mix Problem). ABC Inc. needs to determine the quantity and mix of its digital cameras to be produced next year. The company produces two popular models, the Max and the Multimax. The average profit of Max and Multimax is \$400 and \$800 per unit, respectively. Fabrication and assembly are needed for manufacturing the two models. Both have limited available capacity. Each Max model requires 3 hours of fabrication and 1 hour of assembly; and each Multimax model requires 5 hours of fabrication and 4 hours of assembly. There are maximum of 5,000 hours of fabrication and 3,000 hours of assembly available each monthly. How many units of each model should be manufactured each month to maximize the total profit?

Step 1. Define decision variables
x_1: units of model Max to be produced
x_2: units of model Multimax to be produced

Step 2. Objective function

$$\text{Maximize } 400x_1 + 800x_2 \tag{2.1}$$

Step 3. Constraints

Subject to:

$$3x_1 + 5x_2 \leq 5{,}000 \tag{2.2}$$

$$x_1 + 4x_2 \leq 3{,}000 \tag{2.3}$$

$$x_1,\ x_2 \geq 0 \tag{2.4}$$

The objective function (2.1) maximizes the total profit of producing the two products. Constraint (2.2) ensures that the total required fabrication hours does not exceed the available 5,000 hours. Constraint (2.3) makes sure that the total required assembly hours does not exceed 3,000. Constraint (2.4) states the non-negativity requirement.

Example 2.5 (Ingredient Mix Problem). The ABC Farm would like to determine the best way to blend ingredients for its cattle feeds. The feeds must meet the following nutrition requirements: calcium — at least 0.6% but no more than 1.4%, protein — at least 20%, and fiber — at most 6%. The costs of three ingredients: rice hall, corn and wheat, and their nutrition contributions are provided in the following table.

	Calcium (g/kg)	**Protein (g/kg)**	**Fiber (g/kg)**	**Unit cost (cents/kg)**
Rice hulls	0.34	0	0	12
Corn	0.003	0.08	0.04	32
Wheat	0.004	0.48	0.12	86

Step 1. Define decision variables

x: proportion of rice hulls in 1 kg of feeds
y: proportion of corn in 1 kg of feeds
z: proportion of wheat in 1 kg of feeds

Step 2. Objective function

$$\text{Minimize } 12x + 32y + 86z \tag{2.5}$$

Step 3. Constraints

Subject to:

$$0.34x + 0.003y + 0.004z \geq 0.006 \tag{2.6}$$

$$0.34x + 0.003y + 0.004z \leq 0.014 \tag{2.7}$$

$$0.08y + 0.48z \geq 0.2 \tag{2.8}$$

$$0.04y + 0.12z \leq 0.06 \tag{2.9}$$

$$x + y + z = 1 \tag{2.10}$$

$$x, y, z \geq 0 \tag{2.11}$$

The objective function (2.5) minimizes the total costs of mixing the three ingredients to get 1 kg feed. Constraints (2.6) and (2.7) satisfy the minimum and maximum requirements of calcium, respectively. Constraint (2.8) meets the minimum requirement of protein. Constraint (2.9) ensures fiber does not exceed the maximum threshold. Constraint (2.10) imposes the total proportion of the three ingredients adds up to 100%. Constraint (2.11) specifies the non-negativity requirement.

The model formulations presented in this section require all the input parameters (data) to be explicitly identified and expressed with the model components: decision variables, objective function and constraints. While it is intuitive and facilitates the use of Excel Solver, such *explicit formulation* has several drawbacks: (i) it is impractical for large-size problems with thousands of decision variables and constraints; and (ii) it is not general and flexible as all input data must be explicitly mingled with model formulation. Using the explicit formulation is a good starting point to learn mathematical programming modeling, but a more general, compact and rigorous way of model formulation is needed. This is called the algebraic formulation to be introduced next.

2.4 Algebraic Formulation for Math Programming Models

An *algebraic formulation* consists of the following components in a structured way. Different from the explicit formulation, here we use math notations instead of the actual numbers in the formulation.

- *Sets and Indexes*: notations to define the scope and domain of the decisions to be made and the data needed.
- *Parameters*: notations to define the input data for the model.
- *Decision variables*: notations to describe the decisions to be made.
- *Objective function*: mathematical expression as a function of the defined parameters and decision variables.
- *Constraints*: equations and inequalities using the defined parameters and decision variables.

A *set* is a mathematical term to represent a collection of elements with the same nature or characteristics, e.g., a set of products, a set of geographical locations, and a set of machines, etc. The elements in a set are unordered, unlike the elements in an *array* which are often ordered. An *index* can be used to reference an element in a set.

Example 2.6 (Set and index). Define I as a set of facilities, and $i \in I$ denotes a facility in I (does not matter which specific one). $\in$ is a mathematical operator that reads "belong to", which is used to indicate the membership of an element in a set. Let P denote a set of products, then $i \in P$ denotes the product i in P. Define S as a set of resources, then $s \in S$ refers to the resource s in S.

When defining a parameter or a decision variable, we often use *subscript* or *double-subscript* to reference an element in a set. For instance, unit prices of a set P of products can be written as $\pi_1, \pi_2, \ldots, \pi_{|P|}$, where π_i denotes the price of product $\forall i \in P$. $|P|$ is the cardinality of set P, i.e., the number of elements in P. $\forall$ is a mathematical notation that reads "for all", which is used to reference every element in a set. As another example, the unit cost of s in a set S of resources can be denoted by $c_s \; \forall \; s \in S$.

Example 2.7 (Double-subscript). Define I as a set of facilities, and J as a set of customers. Then we may denote c_{ij} as the transportation cost of serving customer $j \in J$ by facility $i \in I$. If there are two facilities and three customers, c_{ij} is a compact and convenient way to represent $c_{11}, c_{12}, c_{13}, c_{21}, c_{22}, c_{23}$. Similarly, we may define x_{ij} as a decision variable to represent the amount of goods to be shipped from facility $i \in I$ to customer $j \in J$.

Another useful notation is Σ (reads "sigma"), which is the summation of a set of parameters or decision variables. Adding n terms of decision variables $x_1 + x_2 + \cdots + x_n$ can be conveniently written as $\sum_{i=1}^{n} x_i$. Note it is important to indicate the "range" of a summation, and in this case, x_i is summed with i ranging from 1 to n. The range for summation can also be indicated as a set. For instance, we may define a set $V = \{1, 2, \ldots, n\}$, then $\sum_{i \in V} x_i$ is equivalent to $\sum_{i=1}^{n} x_i$.

Example 2.8 (Summation). Consider a set A of products $1, 2, \ldots, n$. Each product $i \in A$ has a selling price of p_i per unit. If the units of product i sold is x_i, the total revenue $p_1x_1 + p_2x_2 + \cdots + p_nx_n$ can be compactly written as $\sum_{i=1}^{n} p_ix_i$. Consider a set I of warehouses and a set J of customers. The transportation cost from warehouse $i \in I$ to customer $j \in J$ is c_{ij} per truckload. If the number of truckloads shipped from i to j is denoted by x_{ij}, the total transportation cost can be conveniently written as $\sum_{i \in I} \sum_{j \in J} c_{ij}x_{ij}$.

We now use the algebraic formulation approach for the two examples presented in Section 2.3. The algebraic formulation of the LP model for Example 2.4 Product Mix Problem can be written as below.

Sets

P: set of products
R: set of resources

Parameters

π_i: Unit profit of product $i \in P$
k_j: maximum capacity of resource $j \in R$
r_{ij}: capacity of resource j required by product i

Decision variables

$x_i \geq 0$: amount of product $i \in P$ to produce

Objective function

$$\text{Maximize} \sum_{i \in P} \pi_i x_i \tag{2.12}$$

Constraints

$$\sum_{i \in P} r_{ij} x_i \leq k_j, \quad \forall j \in R \tag{2.13}$$

$$x_i \geq 0, \quad \forall i \in P \tag{2.14}$$

The objective function (2.12) serves the same role as (2.1) to maximize the total profit. Constraint (2.13) reads: "for each resource $j \in R$, the total required amount cannot exceed the maximum capacity of j", which achieves the role of (2.2) and (2.3), but with only one row in the algebraic formulation.

The algebraic formulation of the LP model for Example 2.5 Ingredient Mix Problem can be written as below.

Sets

S: set of different ingredients
G: set of different nutrition elements

Parameters

c_i: cost per kg of ingredients $i \in S$
r_j: minimum requirement of nutrition $j \in G$ in 1 kg of feed
l_j: maximum requirement of nutrition $j \in G$ in 1 kg of feed
a_{ij}: amount of nutrition j provided by 1 kg of ingredient i

Decision variables

$x_i \geq 0$: proportion (percentage) of ingredient $i \in S$ to blend 1 kg of feed

Objective function

$$\text{Minimize} \sum_{i \in S} c_i x_i \tag{2.15}$$

Constraints

$$\sum_{i \in S} a_{ij} x_i \geq r_j, \quad \forall j \in G \tag{2.16}$$

$$\sum_{i \in S} a_{ij} x_i \leq l_j, \quad \forall j \in G \tag{2.17}$$

$$\sum\nolimits_{i \in S} x_i = 1, \tag{2.18}$$

$$x_i \geq 0 \qquad \forall i \in S \tag{2.19}$$

The objective function (2.15), minimizing the total cost of ingredient mix, is more compact than (2.5). Constraint (2.16) satisfies the minimum requirement of each nutrition, which replaces (2.6) and (2.8); while Constraint (2.17) meets the maximum limit of each nutrition, which replaces (2.7) and (2.9). Constraint (2.18) ensures the total percentage adds up to 1, which is equivalent to (2.10).

2.5 More LP Formulation Examples

2.5.1 *Advertising-Mix Problem*

ABC company is promoting its new product through various advertising media. The Marketing department has collected historical data on the effectiveness of media about its exposure and cost on two types of budgets: the advertising budget and the planning budget. The data is provided in the following table.

	TV Commercial	Magazine Ad	Sunday Ad
Ad budget	\$300,000	\$150,000	\$100,000
Planning budget	90,000	30,000	40,000
Expected number of exposures	1,300,000	600,000	500,000

The company has \$4,000,000 Ad budget and \$1,000,000 planning budget available. There are a maximum of 5 TV spots available. What is ABC's optimal advertising mix?

This problem is similar to the Product-Mix example in that it optimizes the *mix* of advertising media given limited available budgets (resources). The decision to be made is the number of advertising spots for each media, with the objective of maximizing the total expected exposure. The main constraint is the limited budget of each type, with an additional side constraint restricting an upper limit on the number of TV spots. The algebraic formulation of the mathematical programming model can be written as below.

<u>Sets</u>

A : set of advertising media
B : set of different types of budgets

<u>Parameters</u>

e_i : expected number of exposures of advertising media $i \in A$
k_b : limit of budget type $b \in B$
c_{ib} : cost of budget type b per spot of advertising media $i \in A$
N_i: maximum number of spots of advertising media $i \in A$ available

<u>Decision variables</u>

$x_i \geq 0$ and integer, number of spots of advertising type $i \in A$

<u>Objective function</u>

$$\text{Maximize} \sum_{i \in A} e_i x_i \tag{2.20}$$

<u>Constraints</u>

$$\sum_{i \in A} c_{ib} x_i \leq k_b, \quad \forall b \in B \tag{2.21}$$

$$x_i \leq N_i, \quad \forall i \in A \tag{2.22}$$

$$x_i \in Z^+, \quad \forall i \in A \tag{2.23}$$

Objective function (2.20) maximizes the total expected exposure. Constraint (2.21) ensures that the required fund of each budget type does not exceed the available budget. Constraint (2.22) limits the number of advertising of each media not to exceed the maximum number of available spots. The decision variables must take integers here as in (2.23), which makes the model to be an integer programming model (to be introduced in Chapter 3). Note that only TV commercial has a maximum limit, thus one may assume an arbitrarily large number for N_i with i referring to the other media: magazine and Sunday newspaper.

2.5.2 *Diet Problem*

ABC Hospital applies optimization to determine the diet menu for patients. On one hand, the hospital would like to provide the essential nutrition so as to help with patients' rehab and recovery process. On the other hand, the hospital would like to achieve this in the least costly way. A nutritionist at the hospital provides the following estimates of nutrition provided by three foods: milk, beans and oranges and their costs per unit of food. How should the hospital prepare the meal for its patients?

	Milk (gallons)	**Navy beans (cups)**	**Oranges (large Calif. Valencia)**	**Minimum daily requirement**
Niacin (mg)	3.2	4.9	0.8	13.0
Thiamine (mg)	1.12	1.3	0.19	1.5
Vitamin C (mg)	32	0	93	45
Cost ($/unit)	2.00	0.20	0.25	

This problem is similar to the Ingredient Mix example, as it attempts to mix multiple food items to meet some nutrition requirements while minimizing the total cost. It also belongs to the more general cost-benefit analysis to optimize decisions that lead to tradeoffs in cost and benefit, i.e., the nutrition provided in food items. Its LP formulation can be written as below.

Sets

F: set of food items
N: set of nutrition elements

Parameters

c_i: cost of per unit (gallon for milk, cup for beans, etc.) of food item $i \in F$
R_n: minimum requirement (in mg) of nutrition $n \in N$
a_{in}: amount (in mg) of nutrition n provided by one unit of $i \in F$

Decision variables

$x_i \geq 0$: units of food item $i \in F$ in the diet

Objective function

$$\text{Minimize} \sum_{i \in F} c_i x_i \tag{2.24}$$

Constraints

$$\sum_{i \in F} a_{in} x_i \geq R_n \quad \forall n \in N \tag{2.25}$$

$$x_i \geq 0 \qquad \forall i \in F \tag{2.26}$$

Objective function (2.24) minimizes the total cost of the menu. Constraint (2.25) satisfies the minimum nutrition requirement of each type. Constraint (2.26) specifies the domain of decision variables.

2.5.3 *Transportation Problem*

ABC Foods Inc. produces a novel protein food in its three canneries located in Bellingham, Eugene and Albert Lea. Its main warehouses are located in Sacramento, Salt Lake City, Rapid City and Albuquerque.

Each cannery has its maximum supply available to be distributed to meet the demand at the four markets. The supply capacities at the three canneries, the demand at the four warehouses, and the unit transportation cost per truckload are listed in the following table.

	Sacramento	Salt Lake City	Rapid City	Albuquerque	Supply (truck load)
Bellingham	$464	$513	$654	$867	75
Eugene	352	416	690	791	125
Albert Lea	995	682	388	685	100
Demand (truck load)	80	65	70	85	

How should the company distribute its products to minimize the total transportation cost?

This is a standard transportation problem widely applied in transportation and logistics. It can be schematically depicted by the following diagram. It has a simple and distinctive structure with two sets of nodes, e.g., canneries (supply nodes) and warehouses (demand nodes), in this example. The decision to be made determines how many truckloads of products are to be shipped from a supply node to a demand node. The objective is to minimize the total shipping costs. There are two main constraints: (i) the available capacity at each supply node cannot be exceeded; and (ii) the demand at each demand node must be satisfied. The LP model for the problem can be written as follows.

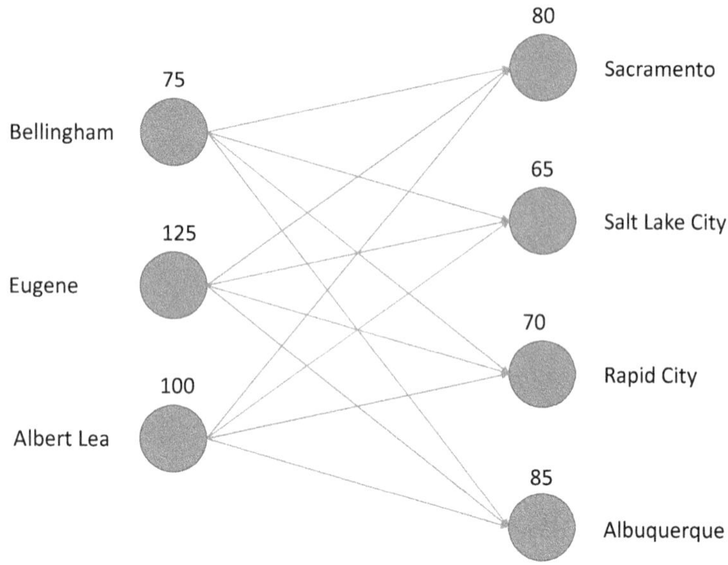

Sets

S: set of supply nodes
T: set of demand nodes

Parameters

d_j: truckloads of demand at demand node $j \in T$
k_i: truckloads of capacity at supply node $i \in S$
c_{ij}: transportation cost per truckload shipped from supply node $i \in S$ to demand node $j \in T$

Decision variables

$x_{ij} \geq 0$: truckloads of products shipped from $i \in S$ to $j \in T$

Objective function

$$\text{Minimize} \sum_{i \in S} \sum_{j \in T} c_{ij} x_{ij} \tag{2.27}$$

Constraints

$$\sum_{i \in S} x_{ij} \geq d_j \quad \forall j \in T \tag{2.28}$$

$$\sum_{j \in T} x_{ij} \leq k_i \quad \forall i \in S \tag{2.29}$$

$$x_{ij} \geq 0 \quad \forall i \in S, j \in T \tag{2.30}$$

Objective function (2.27) minimizes the total transportation costs. Constraint (2.28) satisfies the demand d_j at each demand node $j \in T$. Its LHS adds up the number of truckloads shipped from all supply nodes $i \in S$ *into* node j. Constraint (2.29) ensures that the supply capacity at each supply node $i \in S$ cannot be exceeded. Its LHS adds up the number of truckloads shipped from node i to all demand nodes $j \in T$. Constraint (2.30) specifies the domain of all decision variables.

This formulation has $|S| \times |T|$ decision variables, where $|S|$ and $|T|$ are the cardinality (number of elements) of the sets S and T, respectively. In this example, $|S| = 3$ and $|T| = 4$, thus there are a total of 12 decision variables.

2.5.4 *Personnel Scheduling*

ABC Inc. is a call center that provides 24-hour online banking and credit card services for its customers. It aims to utilize its employees to meet its staffing needs in the most efficient way. The number of agents needed for each time period is shown in the table below. A new shift starts every 4 hours with the first shift starting at 12 am. A union contract requires that all employees work 8 consecutive hours. How should the company staff the shifts in an optimal way?

Time period	Number of agents needed
12 am–4 am	11
4 am–8 am	15
8 am–12 pm	31
12 pm–4 pm	17
4 pm–8 pm	25
8 pm–12 am	19

A key to understand this problem is to realize that the number of agents in a *shift* must meet the demand of agents in a *period* that can be "covered" by the shift. According to the definition of shift and the business rule, the set of shifts include: 12 am–8 am, 4 am–12 pm, 8 am–4 pm, 12 pm–8 pm and 4 pm–12 am. We may come up with the following cover matrix with 0–1 entries to indicate which time periods can be covered by each shift. For instance, the two entries of 1 in the Shift 2 column indicate that Shift 2 (4 am–12 pm) covers both time periods of 4 am–8 am and 8 am–12 pm.

	Shift 1: 12 am–8 am	Shift 2: 4 am–12 pm	Shift 3: 8 am–4 pm	Shift 4: 12 pm–8 pm	Shift 5: 4 pm–12 am
12 am–4 am	1				
4 am–8 am	1	1			
8 am–12 pm		1	1		
12 pm–4 pm			1	1	
4 pm–8 pm				1	1
8 pm–12 am					1

The decision is to determine how many agents to staff in each shift. The objective function is to minimize the total number of agents needed, thus the total staffing cost. The main constraint is to meet the number of agents needed in each time period. This problem has the flavor of the general set covering problem, which is elaborated in Chapter 3.

Sets

S : set of shifts
T : set of time periods

Parameters

a_{st} = 1 if time period $t \in T$ is covered by shift $s \in S$; and 0 otherwise. It can be obtained by the information in the table and the fact that all employees work eight consecutive hours. For instance, $a_{12} = 1$ because shift 1 covers time period 2.
D_t : number of agents required at time t

Decision variables

$x_s \geq 0$: number of employees in shift $s \in S$

Objective function

$$\text{Minimize} \sum_{s \in S} x_s \tag{2.31}$$

Constraints

$$\sum_{s \in S: a_{st}=1} x_s \geq D_t \quad \forall t \in T \tag{2.32}$$

$$x_s \geq 0 \quad \forall s \in S \tag{2.33}$$

The objective function (2.31) minimizes the total number of agents to be staffed. Constraint (2.32) ensures that the demand D_t in each period $t \in T$ must be satisfied. Note that its LHS sums the number of agents staffed in the shifts that cover period t. The colon : (reads "such that") is used to specify the condition for summing over elements in a set. In this case, the condition is $a_{st} = 1$, meaning that it adds up only those shift s that covers period t. An alternative way to write (2.32) is $\sum_{s \in S} a_{st} \cdot x_s \geq D_t$. Constraint (2.33) specifies the domain of decision variables.

2.6 Additional Notes

Expressing a mathematical programming formulation in an explicit format is amenable to spreadsheet implementation using Excel Solver, but has a major drawback in its generality and flexibility. Because an explicit formulation mingles model components with data, it makes the model to be dependent upon a particular instance of the input data, but lacks generality. More importantly, this hampers the ease and flexibility of applying the model in a changing environment where the input data need to be changed/updated (without changing the model formulation).

The algebraic formulation overcomes the above limitations of an explicit formulation. In an algebraic formulation, the modeling components (decision variables, objective function and constraints) are clearly separated from the input data (parameters), making the formulation general enough to be applicable for different instances of the input parameters. It also facilitates the use of state-of-the-art optimization solvers, such as IBM CPLEX, Gurobi, and Xpress, among others, which are more powerful than Excel Solver for solving industry strength optimization models. A hands-on coverage of implementing optimization models using CPLEX OPL Studio is provided in Appendix 1.

Appendix 2 provides a concise introduction to the solution methods for LP, including the graph method and the Simplex method. We refer to [7–9] for a systematic treatment of LP, and [10] for a comprehensive coverage on optimization methods in OR.

Exercises

2.1. ABC Brewery in St. Louis, Missouri, USA produces three crafted beers: White Lager, Brown Ale and Oatmeal Stout to serve its local market. Their profit margins are White Lager — $10/gallon, Brown Ale — $14/gallon and Oatmeal Stout — $18/gallon. The company's weekly supply is limited by its capacities of ingredients and processing time: 1,000 pounds of malt, 200 pounds of Caramunich, and 600 hours of processing time. To produce 5 gallons of White Lager, 6 pounds of malt, 1 pound of Caramunich and 3 hours of processing time are needed; 5 gallons of Brown Ale requires 8 pounds of malt, 0.7 pounds of Caramunich and 2 hours of processing time; 5 gallons of Oatmeal Stout requires 6.5 pounds of malt, 1.2 pound of Caramunich and 4 hours of processing time. What is the optimal product mix for ABC Brewery to maximize its total profit?

2.2. ABC Construction Corp. is a medium-size construction company for private residences, commercial buildings and healthcare facilities. Every year, the company's senior management team reviews new project opportunities and determines the best portfolio of projects to engage in the coming year. A list of project opportunities is shown in the following table with their expected NPV (in $million), first-year investment (in $million), workforce FTE needed, and type of construction. The company has a $10 million budget and 100 FTEs available. Assume partial investment in a project is possible, and the NPV and FTE requirement of a project are proportional to the percentage of investment for the project. The company's Board of Directors requires the company invests at least 25% of its total investments to healthcare facilities, and at most 40% to commercial buildings. What is the optimal project portfolio for ABC Construction Corp.?

Project opportunities	Expected NPV	First-Year investment	FTE needed	Construction type
1	0.2	0.4	8	Residence
2	0.5	0.8	12	Residence
3	0.6	1	10	Residence
4	5	2.5	25	Commercial
5	4	2	20	Commercial
6	1	2	18	Healthcare
7	0.8	1.5	16	Healthcare
8	0.6	1.2	15	Healthcare
9	0.8	1.2	12	Residence
10	3.5	1.5	18	Commercial

2.3. The ABC Nutrition Inc. provides customized weight-control meal plan services for adults. Building a weight-control weekly meal plan involves selecting the proper amount of food items to meet certain nutrition requirements. The list of items with their categories, prices, and nutrition ingredients per pound, i.e., calories, protein, calcium, and vitamins, is provided in the following table.

Item	Category	Price ($/lb.)	Calories/lb.	Protein (g/lb.)	Calcium (mg/lb.)	Vitamins (mg/lb.)
Whole Milk	Diary	0.42	300	16	560	100
Skim Milk	Diary	0.40	170	14	600	105
Yogurt	Diary	1.75	270	48	550	20
Bread	Grain	1.31	1,200	45	1,250	40
Bagel	Grain	6.50	1,100	48	100	25
Cereal	Grain	5.50	1,600	28	500	30
Beef	Meat	5.60	1,000	140	100	320
Pork	Meat	3.20	1,250	130	90	350
Fish	Meat	4.60	800	110	70	350
Chicken	Meat	2.68	1,200	130	75	243
Apple	Fruit	2.89	250	1.5	28	115
Orange	Fruit	2.56	245	4.5	180	180
Banana	Fruit	1.45	400	5.5	22	358
Grape	Fruit	2.86	330	3	68	191
Lettuce	Vegies	1.85	75	7	120	141
Potato	Vegies	0.75	420	10	28	500
Cauliflower	Vegies	1.86	125	9.5	100	303
Green bean	Vegies	2.13	150	9	160	209

The minimum weekly intake of calories, protein, calcium and vitamins depends on the age, gender, and personal preference, which is provided in the following table. What is the optimal weekly meal plan for different age-gender groups?

Age group	Gender	Calories	Protein (g)	Calcium (mg)	Vitamins (mg)	Max. meat (%)	Min. vegetable (%)
19–30	Male	18,200	980	7,700	1,050	20	20
19–30	Female	14,000	840	7,700	980	18	20
31–59	Male	16,800	910	7,000	1,140	18	24
31–59	Female	12,600	770	8,400	1,050	16	24

2.4. Transportation Problem. ABC Electronics headquartered in Southwest China has three manufacturing plants in Hebei, Sichuan and Guangdong provinces serving four market regions: Northeast, East, Southwest and South. The supply capacity (in truckloads) at each plant, the demand in each region (truckloads), and the shipping distances (in km), are provided in the following table. The transportation cost is $1.8/truckload/mile. What is the optimal shipping plan for ABC Electronics?

	Northeast	East	Southwest	South	Supply
Hebei	400	800	1,000	1,200	1,000
Sichuan	1,500	750	200	1,300	1,300
Guangdong	1,800	700	1,200	400	1,300
Demand	600	1,000	800	1,200	

2.5. Workforce Planning. ABC Consulting Inc. in London, UK conducts business consulting in four areas for its clients worldwide: Data Integration, Software Development, Business Analytics and Change Management. To meet the revenue target of next year, the company projects the need for a total of at least 1,000 FTEs of skilled professionals. The company recruits talents (both full-time employees and contractors) worldwide, onshore and offshore, for its service delivery. The average costs of acquiring workforce resources vary by geographical location and workforce type, which are provided in the table below ($/FTE). Each source of workforce is limited to a maximum capacity, which is due to the existing skill mix of workforce in the short-term, competitive labor market and high attrition. Based on historical data, the HR team estimates the minimum threshold (in %) of FTEs in each skill area for successful service delivery. For instance, a minimum of 10% of Solution Architects and 25% of Business Analysts are required in the total FTEs. What is an optimal workforce plan for ABC Consulting Inc.?

	Solution Architecture	**Data Integration**	**Software Development**	**Business Analytics**	**Max. FTEs**
Fulltime-Onshore	140,000	120,000	130,000	150,000	200
Fulltime-Offshore	100,000	80,000	70,000	120,000	100
Contractor-Onshore	180,000	140,000	160,000	180,000	400
Contractor-Offshore	140,000	100,000	110,000	130,000	600
Min %	10%	20%	30%	25%	

2.6. Shift Scheduling. ABC Bank needs to have a shift schedule for its weekly operations. Their full-time employees work on three 8-hour shifts: 8 am–4 pm, 12 pm–8 pm, and 4 pm-midnight. Their part-time employees can be flexibly scheduled as needed. The table below shows the minimum FTEs needed for the 2-hour intervals from 8 am to midnight. The hourly wage for a full-time employee is $30. The hourly wage for a part-time employee varies by time as shown in the table. The company requires minimum 75% of its staffing to be full-time employees. How should ABC Bank optimally staff for its operations?

Time periods	**Minimum FTEs**	**Part-time hourly wage**
8 am–10 am	5	20
10 am–noon	8	20
Noon–2 pm	12	20
2 pm–4 pm	9	20
4 pm–6 pm	12	25
6 pm–8 pm	8	25
8 pm–10 pm	6	30
10 pm–midnight	3	30

Chapter 3

Integer Programming

3.1 The Use of Integer Decision Variables

There are four general types of use with integer decision variables. The first type simply requires decisions to be *indivisible*, i.e., they must take integral values. For instance, number of aircrafts to manufacture, number of facilities to build, etc. Sometimes deciding whether a decision variable need to be integral is an "art", depending upon the real life scenario. Table 3.1 shows examples where decision variables can be either integral or continuous in different settings.

The second type of use, and perhaps the most important one, is for the *binary*, i.e., 0–1 decision variables. Table 3.2 shows examples of binary variables with their basic application settings.

The third type of use is the so-called "indicator" variable, which is to indicate/track the status of a decision variable. Consider a continuous decision variable $x \geq 0$, and suppose one would like to know/control whether x is zero or positive. Introduce a binary decision variable y such that x can be positive, i.e., $x > 0$, only if $y = 1$. In other words, if $y = 0$, x must be zero. We need a constraint to establish such relationship between x and y.

Since $y = 0 \rightarrow x = 0$, it is satisfied by $x \leq y$. Note, however, this inequality suggests $x \leq 1$ when $y = 1$, which is not necessarily true. To ensure no upper bound is imposed to x when $y = 1$, we introduce a large positive number M, such that:

$$x \leq My \tag{3.1}$$

Table 3.1. Examples of decision variable that can be integral or continuous.

Decision	Integral	Continuous
Number of people to hire	Small firm, monthly	Large firm, yearly
Truckloads of goods to ship	Small trucking company, daily	Large trucking company, weekly
Number of vehicles to manufacture	Small auto-manufacturer, daily	Large auto-manufacturer, monthly
Starting time of service	Accuracy is needed	Approximate timing is ok

Table 3.2. Examples of binary decision variables.

Purpose of use	Basic problem setting	Example explanation	Applications
Assignment	Assignment Problem	Whether a worker is assigned to a job	Workforce planning, Rostering, Resource planning
Sequencing	Traveling salesman, Vehicle routing	Whether one travels from one city to the other	Transportation planning, fleet scheduling
Scheduling	Machine scheduling, project scheduling	Whether a job is performed right before the other	Manufacturing, transportation
Classification	Set partitioning	Whether a customer belongs to a certain category	Data mining, machine learning
Selection	Knapsack problem, bin packing problem	Whether a facility or project is selected	Network design, portfolio optimization

Inequality (3.1) is called *big-M* constraint/formulation in math programming. To see how it works, plugging in $y = 0$ makes $x \leq 0$, thus x must be zero since it is non-negative; plugging in $y = 1$ leads to $x \leq M$, which allows x to take any positive value as long as M is large enough. In case one knows an upper bound on x, M can be replaced by the upper bound.

Example 3.1. In a typical supplier/vendor selection problem, a supplier cannot provide any goods unless it is selected. To model this requirement, we define x to represent the quantity of products provided by a supplier, and a binary decision variable $y = 1$ if the supplier is selected, and 0 otherwise. The big-M constraint to be satisfied can be written as: $x \leq My$, where M is a large positive number.

Example 3.2. Suppose a company requires that if a supplier is selected, it must provide a non-zero amount of goods. To model this requirement, we define x to represent the amount provided by a supplier, and a binary decision variable $y = 1$ if the supplier is selected, and 0 otherwise. But we now need a "small-m" constraint to be satisfied: $x \geq my$, where m is a small positive number, or a known lower bound for x.

In the fourth use case, a binary decision variable can be used to control whether a constraint needs to be satisfied or not. Now consider a general linear constraint with the form:

$$\sum_{i=1}^{n} a_i x_j \leq b. \tag{3.2}$$

One would like to track/control whether this constraint needs to be satisfied. We may introduce a binary decision variable y, such that (3.2) needs to be satisfied if and only if $y = 1$. That is, when $y = 0$, (3.2) does not need to be satisfied. Since $1-y = 0 \rightarrow \sum_{i=1}^{n} a_i x_j - b \leq 0$, we have $\sum_{i=1}^{n} a_i x_j - b \leq 1 - y$. However, when $y = 0$, it restricts $\sum_{i=1}^{n} a_i x_j - b \leq 1$, which is not necessary. To fix this, we employ the big-M constraint:

$$\sum_{i=1}^{n} a_i x_j - b \leq M(1 - y), \tag{3.3}$$

where M is a large positive number.

Using (3.3) one may track and control how a general set of m constraints should be satisfied. Given m inequalities in the form:

$$\sum_{j=1}^{n} a_{ij}x_j \leq b_j, \quad \forall j = 1, \ldots, m \tag{3.4}$$

To require that *at least* k out of the m constraints must be satisfied, one may define a binary variable y_j corresponding with each constraint $j = 1, \ldots, m$, such that if $y_j = 1$, constraint j must be satisfied; and if $y_j = 0$, constraint j need not be satisfied. We need both (3.5) and (3.6) to hold:

$$\sum_{j=1}^{n} a_{ij}x_j - b_j \leq M(1 - y_j), \qquad \forall j = 1, \ldots, m \tag{3.5}$$

$$\sum_{j=1}^{m} y_j \geq k, \tag{3.6}$$

To require that *at most* k out of the m constraints must be satisfied, we need (3.5) and (3.7):

$$\sum_{j=1}^{m} y_j \leq k, \tag{3.7}$$

Example 3.3. Given the following three constraints:

$$x_1 + 3x_2 + x_3 \leq 10$$
$$2x_1 + x_2 + x_3 \leq 8$$
$$3x_1 + 2x_2 + 2x_3 \leq 14.$$

To ensure exactly two of them are satisfied, we define three binary decision variables y_1, y_2 and y_3, such that:

$$x_1 + 3x_2 + x_3 - 10 \leq M(1 - y_1)$$
$$2x_1 + x_2 + x_3 - 8 \leq M(1 - y_2)$$
$$3x_1 + 2x_2 + 2x_3 - 14 \leq M(1 - y_3).$$

Then we also require:

$$y_1 + y_2 + y_3 = 2.$$

3.2 Some Classical Combinatorial Optimization Problems

Combinatorial optimization is a sub-area in mathematics that studies the optimization problems involving *combination* or *permutation* of discrete elements. These problems are often amenable to be modeled and solved by integer programming. There are several motivations for studying the classical combinatorial optimization problems. First, from the modeling perspective, they often serve as building blocks for more complex optimization problems. Being familiar with formulations of classical problems facilitates the modeling of more complex problems that are either generalizations or extensions of some basic combinatorial optimization problems. Secondly, from the algorithmic perspective, efficient exact and heuristic algorithms often exist for classical combinatorial optimization problems, which may shed light on the algorithm design for their generalizations, although this goes beyond the scope of this text.

3.2.1 *Knapsack Problem*

Consider a hiker who is about to start her next adventure and needs to determine what items to be packed into her backpack. Her goal is to pack as many useful and essential items as possible, but not to exceed the weight limit of her backpack. The hiker's problem is intuitively known as the *knapsack problem*. Formally, there are n items to be packed into a knapsack. Each item $i = 1, \dots, n$ has a value of v_i and a weight of w_i. The total weight of items in the knapsack cannot exceed W. The decision-maker needs to determine how many copies of each item i to pack so as to maximize the total value of all the packed items.

Example 3.4. Three items A, B and C can be packed into a knapsack. Their values are 60, 75, 90, and their weights are 2, 3, 4, respectively. The maximum weight of the knapsack is 5. Packing two copies of A is a feasible solution, but not optimal. An optimal solution is to pack A and B with a maximum value of 135.

Define $x_i \in Z^+$, i.e., $x_i \geq 0$ and being integer, as the number of copies of item $i = 1, \dots, n$ to be packed. Now we write an integer programming formulation for the knapsack problem:

$$\text{Maximize} \sum_{i=1}^{n} v_i x_i \tag{3.8}$$

Subject to:

$$\sum_{i=1}^{n} w_i x_i \leq W \tag{3.9}$$

$$x_i \in Z^+ \tag{3.10}$$

The objective function (3.8) maximizes the total value of the knapsack. Constraint (3.9) ensures that the total weight of the knapsack does not exceed the maximum capacity. Constraint (3.10) specifies the domain of the decision variables.

An alternative model formulation for the knapsack problem is a binary integer program. Suppose each item i has m_i copies available. Then if we treat each copy of an item as an independent item, there are a total of $M = m_1 + m_2 + \cdots + m_n$ items to packed, each of which can be packed at most once. Define binary decision variables $x_i \in \{0, 1\}$, such that $x_i = 1$ means item i is packed and 0 otherwise. An alternative BIP formulation for the knapsack problem can be written as follows.

$$\text{Maximize} \sum_{i=1}^{M} v_i x_i \tag{3.11}$$

Subject to:

$$\sum_{i=1}^{M} w_i x_i \leq W \tag{3.12}$$

$$x_i \in \{0, 1\} \tag{3.13}$$

3.2.2 *Set Covering Problem*

A tooling company is selecting its suppliers to procure a set of parts. Each supplier may provide a certain set of parts, if not all the parts. The company needs to ensure that all its parts can be sourced from *at least* one supplier by selecting minimum number of suppliers.

The company's supplier selection problem can be modeled as a *set covering* problem. Formally, consider a set of elements $S = \{1, 2, \ldots, m\}$ and a set of subsets of S denoted by $\bar{S}$. Each subset has a cost. In a set covering problem, one seeks to select the subsets in $\bar{S}$ with the minimum cost, so that every element in S is covered at least once.

Example 3.5 (Supplier Selection). A tooling company has five parts $S = \{1, 2, \ldots, 5\}$ to be procured from six potential suppliers. Each supplier is able to provide a certain subset of the parts, which is given by $\bar{S} = \{\{1, 2\}, \{1, 3, 5\}, \{2, 4, 5\}, \{3\}, \{1\}, \{4, 5\}\}$. For instance, Supplier 1 is able to provide Part 1 and 2, Supplier 5 is only able to provide Part 1, etc. The company could choose Supplier 1, 2 and 3, which is feasible, but not optimal. An optimal solution for this example is to choose Supplier 2 and 3, which "covers" all the parts with only two suppliers.

Define $x_i = 1$ if the i-th supplier in $\bar{S}$ is selected and 0 o.w. An explicit formulation for this supplier selection problem can be written as:

$$
\begin{array}{lllllllll}
\text{Minimize} & x_1 & + x_2 & + x_3 & + x_4 & + x_5 & + x_6 & \\
\text{s.t.} & x_1 & + x_2 & & & + x_5 & & \geq 1 \\
& x_1 & & + x_3 & & & & \geq 1 \\
& & x_2 & & + x_4 & & & \geq 1 \\
& & & x_3 & & & + x_6 & \geq 1 \\
& & x_2 & + x_3 & & & + x_6 & \geq 1 \\
& x_i \in \{0, 1\} & & & & & &
\end{array}
$$

We now present a general algebraic formulation for the set covering problem.

Sets and parameters

S: set of elements to be covered
$\bar{S}$: set of subsets of S
c_i: cost of subset $i \in \bar{S}$

Decision variables

$x_i = 1$ if the i-th subset in $\bar{S}$ is selected and 0 o.w.

Objective function

$$\text{Minimize} \sum_{i \in \bar{S}} c_i x_i \tag{3.14}$$

Constraints

$$\sum_{i \in \bar{S}: j \in \bar{S}_i} x_i \geq 1 \ \forall j \in S \tag{3.15}$$

$$x_i \in \{0, 1\} \tag{3.16}$$

The objective function (3.14) minimizes the total cost for the "cover". Constraint (3.15) ensures that each element j in the set S is covered at least once. Its LHS adds up the selection decision variables x_i of only those subset i that covers element j. If one defines a parameter $a_{ij} = 1$ if subset $i \in \bar{S}$ covers element j, then (3.16) can also be written as: $\sum_{i \in \bar{S}: a_{ij}=1} x_i \geq 1$ or $\sum_{i \in \bar{S}} a_{ij} x_i \geq 1$, which is similar to (2.32) in the Personnel Scheduling example.

3.2.3 *Set Packing Problem*

An antique gallery has a set of items to sell to a group of potential buyers. Each buyer submits a bid for a certain subset of the items with its bidding price. The gallery selects the best set of buyers to maximize its total revenue, while making sure each item can be sold to *at most* one buyer. Formally, consider a set of elements $S = \{1, 2, \ldots, m\}$ and a set of subsets of S denoted by $\bar{S}$. Each subset has a value. In a set packing problem, one seeks to select subsets in $\bar{S}$ with the maximum value, so that every element in S is covered at most once.

Example 3.6 (Combinatorial Auction). An antique gallery has six items $S = \{1, 2, \ldots, 6\}$ to be sold to five potential buyers. Each buyer is interested to bid a certain subset of the items, which is given by $\bar{S} = \{\{1, 2, 5\}, \{1, 3\}, \{2, 4\}, \{3, 6\}, \{2, 3, 6\}\}$. For instance, Buyer 1 wants to buy Item 1, 2 and 5; Buyer 4 is interested to buy Item 3 and 6. The buyers' bids have the following corresponding values: $\{8, 4, 3, 5, 7\}$. The gallery would like to sell its items to maximize its total revenue. Selecting Buyer 1 and 4 is feasible, but selecting Buyer 1 and 3 is not, because Item 2 would be sold twice.

Define $x_i = 1$ if the i-th subset in $\bar{S}$ is selected and 0 o.w. An explicit formulation for the combinatorial auction problem can be written as:

$$
\begin{array}{llllllll}
\text{Maximize} & 8x_1 + 4x_2 + 3x_3 + 5x_4 + 7x_5 & & & & & & \\
\text{s.t.} & x_1 + x_2 & & & & & & \leq 1 \\
 & x_1 & & + x_3 & & & x_5 & \leq 1 \\
 & & x_2 & & + & x_4 + & x_5 & \leq 1 \\
 & & & x_3 & & & & \leq 1 \\
 & x_1 & & & & & & \leq 1 \\
 & & & & & x_4 + & x_5 & \leq 1 \\
 & x_i \in \{0, 1\} & & & & & &
\end{array}
$$

The general algebraic formulation for the set packing problem can be written as below.

Sets and parameters

S: set of elements to be covered
$\bar{S}$: set of subsets of S
v_i: value of subset $i \in \bar{S}$

Decision variables

$x_i = 1$ if the i-th subset in $\bar{S}$ is selected and 0 o.w.

Objective function

$$\text{Maximize} \sum_{i \in \bar{S}} v_i x_i \tag{3.17}$$

Constraints

$$\sum_{i \in \bar{S}: j \in \bar{S}_i} x_i \leq 1 \ \forall j \in S \tag{3.18}$$

$$x_i \in \{0, 1\} \tag{3.19}$$

The objective function (3.17) maximizes the total value of selected subsets (winning bids). Constraint (3.18) ensures that each item $j \in S$ cannot be packed (selected) more than once. Its LHS adds up the selection decision variables of only those subset i that contains element j. Constraint (3.19) specifies the domain of the decision variables.

3.2.4 *Set Partitioning Problem*

A typical set partitioning problem can be described as below. Given a set of items $S = \{1, 2, \ldots, m\}$ and a set $\bar{S}$ of subsets of S. One needs to partition all the elements in S using minimum number of subsets in $\bar{S}$, so that an element belongs to one and only one subset. Its algebraic formulation can be written as below.

Sets and parameters

S: set of elements to be covered
$\bar{S}$: set of subsets of S

Decision variables

$x_i = 1$ if the i-th subset in $\bar{S}$ is selected and 0 o.w.

Objective function

$$\text{Minimize} \sum_{i \in \bar{S}} x_i \tag{3.20}$$

Constraints

$$\sum_{i \in \bar{S}: j \in \bar{S}_i} x_i = 1, \ \forall j \in S \tag{3.21}$$

$$x_i \in \{0, 1\} \tag{3.22}$$

The objective function (3.20) minimizes the total number of selected subsets. Constraint (3.21) partitions each element $j \in S$ to exactly one subset i that contains j, i.e., $j \in \bar{S}_i$. Constraint (3.22) specifies the domain of decision variables.

Table 3.3 summarizes and compares the characteristics of the set covering, bin packing and set partitioning problems.

3.2.5 *Generalized Assignment Problem*

A manufacturer has m jobs to be assigned to n machines. Each job is assigned to exactly one machine and requires a certain amount of capacity on the machine. A machine can be assigned with multiple jobs as long as its maximum capacity is not exceeded.

Table 3.3. Characteristics of set covering, bin packing and set partitioning problems.

	Set covering problem	Bin packing problem	Set partitioning problem
Objective function	Minimization	Maximization	Minimization
Constraints	$\geq$	$\leq$	$=$
RHS constants	All 1	All 1	All 1
LHS coefficients	0 or 1	0 or 1	0 or 1

Each assignment generates a revenue. The manufacturer's objective is to maximize its total revenue. How should the job-machine assignment be made? This can be addressed by the well-known generalized assignment problem (GAP).

Example 3.7 (Resource Planning). ABC Inc. is a professional consulting firm offering software development services. It has six upcoming projects to be assigned to five employees: Adam, Brian, Clark, Daniel and Emily. A job requires exactly one employee and may take a different amount of time, depending on the skill set and proficiency of the assigned employee. Each assignment has a fitness score measured by the employees' preferences and skill set. An employee has a maximum number of working hours that cannot be exceeded. All the needed data is provided below.

Fitness scores of assignments.

	Adam	Brian	Clark	Daniel	Emily
Project 1	3	5	7	9	8
Project 2	4	8	5	3	5
Project 3	7	9	8	2	6
Project 4	9	3	6	5	4
Project 5	6	4	5	4	8
Project 6	8	2	6	3	9

Number of hours of assignments and available capacity of employees.

	Adam	Brian	Clark	Daniel	Emily
Project 1	160	120	100	90	100
Project 2	170	100	150	190	160
Project 3	80	60	70	120	80
Project 4	50	80	65	70	80
Project 5	70	90	80	90	50
Project 6	100	160	140	150	80
Max capacity	320	200	240	320	240

We first present an explicit formulation for this example. Define $x_{ij} = 1$ if Project i is assigned to Employee j and 0 otherwise (o.w.), for $i = 1, 2, \ldots, 6$ and j = Adam, Brian, ..., Emily. The objective function is to maximize the total fitness scores:

$$\text{Maximize} \quad \begin{aligned} &3x_{1,Adam} + 5x_{1,Brian} + 7x_{1,Clark} + 9x_{1,\,Daniel} + 8x_{1,Emily} + \\ &4x_{2,Adam} + 8x_{2,Brian} + 5x_{2,Clark} + 3x_{2,\,Daniel} + 5x_{2,Emily} + \\ &\ldots \\ &8x_{6,Adam} + 2x_{6,Brian} + 6x_{6,Clark} + 3x_{6,\,Daniel} + 9x_{6,Emily} \end{aligned}$$

Subject to:

$$\begin{aligned} \text{Job 1 assignment:}\quad & x_{1,Adam} + x_{1,Brian} + x_{1,Clark} + x_{1,\,Daniel} \\ & + x_{1,Emily} = 1 \\ \text{Job 2 assignment:}\quad & x_{2,Adam} + x_{2,Brian} + x_{2,Clark} + x_{2,\,Daniel} \\ & + x_{2,Emily} = 1 \\ & \ldots \\ \text{Job 6 assignment:}\quad & x_{6,Adam} + x_{6,Brian} + x_{6,Clark} + x_{6,\,Daniel} \\ & + x_{6,Emily} = 1 \\ \text{Adam's capacity:}\quad & 160x_{1,Adam} + 170x_{2,Adam} + 80x_{3,Adam} \\ & + 50x_{4,\,Adam} + 70x_{5,Adam} + 100x_{6,Adam} \leq 320 \end{aligned}$$

$$\text{Brian's capacity: } 120x_{1,Brian} + 100x_{2,Brian} + 60x_{3,Brian}$$
$$+ 80x_{4,\,Brian} + 90x_{5,Brian}$$
$$+ 160x_{6,Bian} \leq 200$$

$$\ldots$$

$$\text{Emily's capacity: } 100x_{1,Emily} + 160x_{2,Emily} + 80x_{3,Emily}$$
$$+ 80x_{4,\,Emily} + 50x_{5,Emily}$$
$$+ 80x_{6,Emily} \leq 240$$

Apparently, it is tedious to write the explicit formulation even for this small instance. The algebraic formulation for the GAP can be written as below.

Sets

I: set of projects
J: set of employees

Parameters

p_{ij}: fitness score of assigning project i to employee j
w_{ij}: amount of capacity of employee j required by project i
k_j: maximum capacity of employee j

Decision variables

$x_{ij} = 1$ if project $i \in I$ is assigned to employee $j \in J$; and 0 o.w.

Objective function

$$\text{Maximize} \sum_{i \in I} \sum_{j \in J} p_{ij} x_{ij} \tag{3.23}$$

Constraints

$$\sum_{j \in J} x_{ij} = 1, \ \forall i \in I \tag{3.24}$$

$$\sum_{i \in I} w_{ij} x_{ij} \leq k_j, \ \forall j \in J \tag{3.25}$$

$$x_{ij} \in \{0, 1\} \tag{3.26}$$

The objective function (3.23) maximizes the total fitness scores of all assignments. Constraint (3.24) assigns a project to exactly one employee. Constraint (3.25) ensures that the maximum capacity of each employee is not exceeded. Constraint (3.26) specifies the domain of all the decision variables. Note the compactness, conciseness and clarity of the algebraic formulation compared to the explicit formulation.

3.2.6 *Bin Packing Problem*

A typical bin packing problem can be described as below. A set of items with different sizes is to be packed into bins with a constant maximum capacity. The goal is to use minimum number of bins to pack all the items.

Example 3.8 (Truck Loading). A third-party logistics (3PL) company needs to plan for nine loads with its available trucks. Each truck has a maximum weight capacity of 1. And each load has its weight as a percentage of the truck capacity as shown below.

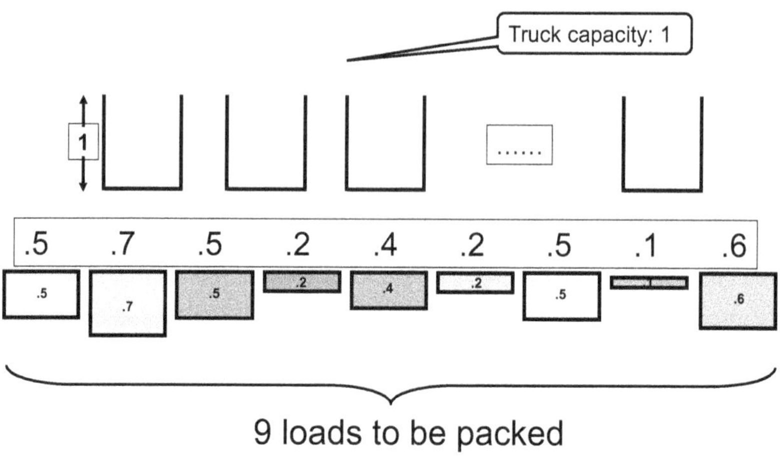

A minimum of 4 trucks are needed with the following packing plan:

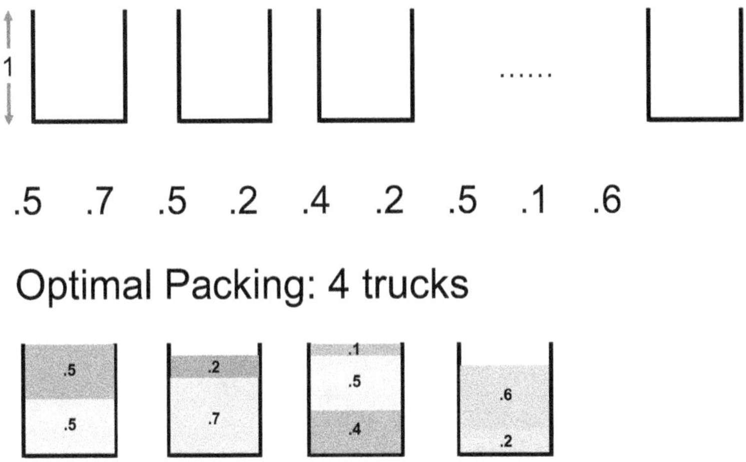

Two decisions are made in the bin packing problem: how many bins to use *and* how to pack each (used) bin. In order to determine how many and which bins to use, we need binary decision variables to track whether a bin is used or not; and to determine the packing plan, we need the assignment-type binary decision variables to indicate if an item is assigned to a bin. An algebraic formulation for the bin packing problem can be written as below.

Parameters

N: number of items to be packed
M: upper bound on the number of bins needed
W: maximum number of items that can be packed into each bin

Decision variables

$x_j = 1$ if bin $j = 1, 2, \ldots, M$ is used; and 0 o.w.
$y_{ij} = 1$ if item $i = 1, 2, \ldots, N$ is packed (assigned) to bin $j = 1, 2, \ldots, M$; and 0 o.w.

Objective function

$$\text{Minimize} \sum_{j=1}^{M} x_j \tag{3.27}$$

Constraints

$$\sum_{j=1}^{M} y_{ij} = 1, \ \forall i = 1, 2, \ldots, N \tag{3.28}$$

$$\sum_{i=1}^{N} y_{ij} \leq W, \ \forall j = 1, 2, \ldots, M \tag{3.29}$$

$$y_{ij} \leq x_j, \ \forall i = 1, 2, \ldots, N; j = 1, 2, \ldots, M \tag{3.30}$$

$$x_j, y_{ij} \in \{0, 1\} \tag{3.31}$$

Objective function (3.27) minimizes the number of bins used. Constraint (3.28) packs (assigns) each item to exactly one bin. Constraint (3.29) guarantees that each bin's maximum capacity is not exceeded. Constraint (3.30) ensures that if a bin is not used, no item can be packed in it. Constraint (3.31) specifies the domain of all the decision variables.

3.3 Additional Notes

Integer programming is a general and powerful approach for dealing with various combinatorial optimization problems in discrete mathematics [11], many of which are NP-hard [12], meaning that there is no polynomial algorithm available to obtain optimal solutions. We refer to [13] for a systematic treatment of model building in mathematical programming. A comprehensive coverage on the theory of integer programming is available in [14–16].

There are two general solution approaches to solve integer programming models: *exact* and *heuristic*. Appendix 3 provides a concise introduction to two exact methods for integer programming: branch-and-bound method and cutting-plane method. To obtain quality solutions for large-scale NP-hard problems often calls for the use of various heuristic methods, including custom-designed approximation algorithms which are often problem-dependent [17], and a rich variety of metaheuristics [18].

Exercises

3.1. ABC Inc. needs to optimize its portfolio of projects to be selected for the next fiscal year. Define decision variables and write constraints to model the following requirements:

- If Project 1 is chosen, Project 2 must be chosen.
- Only one of Project 1 and Project 2 can be chosen.
- One of Project 1 and Project 2 must be chosen.
- Project 2 cannot be chosen unless Project 1 is chosen.
- Three projects out of Projects $1, 2, \ldots, 5$ must be chosen.

3.2. A facility can manufacture a product at a marginal cost unit of c. There is a setup cost of S to open the facility. Define decision variables to represent the total cost of operating the facility. Write the constraint needed for your decision variables.

3.3. In a diet problem (ingredient mix problem), if ingredient a is included in the diet, ingredient b must also be included. Define decision variables and write constraints to model this.

3.4. Define decision variable and write constraints to model whether the following constraint is imposed: $2x_1 + 3x_2 \leq 1$, where $0 \leq x_1, x_2 \leq 1$.

3.5. Model the requirement that at least two of the following constraints must be satisfied.

$$2x_1 + 3x_2 \leq 5$$

$$x_1 + 2x_2 \leq 4$$

$$2x_1 + 5x_2 \leq 9$$

3.6. ABC Inc. is considering some capital investment opportunities. Each project is either invested or not, but partial investment is not allowed. The NPV and capital requirement (in \$million) of each project is provided below:

	1	**2**	**3**	**4**	**5**	**6**	**7**
NPV	10	4	12	18	8	10	7
Capital	35	26	32	42	20	26	20

The total amount of available capital is \$80 million. Projects 2 and 3 are mutually exclusive, meaning that they cannot be both selected. Projects 5 and 7 are also mutually exclusive. Neither Project 5 nor 6 can be chosen unless one of the first two projects are chosen. The objective is to maximize the total NPV of the selected project. Formulate a BIP model for this problem.

3.7. Production with Setup Cost. Innovation Foods is an indoor farming start-up company with the mission to provide fresh and nutritious vegetables for its local markets and consumers. After a consumer survey of the local markets, the company narrows down to four candidate specialty crops to produce: Okra, Romaine Lettuce, Tomatoes, and Lima Beans. Some substantial initial setup cost is needed for any produce due to their different biological traits and the corresponding growing methods needed. The table provides the sales price per unit, the initial setup cost and the yield of each produce.

Produce	**Sales price (\$/lb)**	**Setup cost (\$)**	**Yield (lb/sq. foot)**
Okra	1.75	200	8.75
Romaine Lettuce	0.33	100	11.85
Tomatoes	1.43	150	12.90
Lima Beans	0.54	120	10.52

Innovation Foods' current indoor farming facility has a limited space of 2,000 sq. feet and would like to produce no more than three vegetables. The company would like to determine the best production plan to maximize its total net profit.

(a) Formulate an MILP model to help Innovation Foods make such production planning decision.
(b) The company has an option of an alternative technology that is able to achieve higher yields (lb/sq. foot) for some produce, but lower yields for others: Okra — 10.52, Romaine Lettuce — 8.65, Tomatoes — 10.20, Lima Beans — 12.42. What new constructs (decision variables) and constraints are needed to take this into consideration.

3.8. ABC Inc. is a 3PL (third-party logistic) company who provides last-mile deliver services locally. Since most of its customers need less-than-truckload service, the parcels are loaded onto its transportation fleet for the same-day delivery in the service region, according to the geographical locations of destinations. The company employs a Route Dispatcher software to provide decision-support for dispatching its three trucks. Based on the delivery locations entered each morning, the software first generates a set of possible and attractive routes, then selects three best routes that minimize the total delivery time. In one morning, eight possible routes to serve five destinations with the travel and service times (in hours) are listed below.

	Candidate Routes							
Destination	1	2	3	4	5	6	7	8
A	1			2		2		
B		1			1	2	2	
C	2		3		3			1
D		2		2		3		3
E		3	2		2		2	
F	2		1	1				
Total time	5	6	6	5	6	7	4	4

Formulate a BIP model to select the best routes. Is your model set packing, set partitioning, or setting covering, and why?

Chapter 4

Network Optimization

4.1 Introduction to Network Optimization

A manufacturer needs to plan for its flow of goods to minimize the total distribution cost. A mountain hiker would like to travel via the shortest path from an origin to a destination. A city planner designs a road system with limits on traffic flow, so that the maximum amount of traffic can be sent from an origin to a destination. A warehouse manager determines the proper order quantity and frequency to meet the demand in multiple periods with minimum total sourcing and inventory holding cost.

The above decision scenarios share a common feature in their underlying setting, i.e., they can be modeled as a *network* of nodes (vertices) and arcs (edges). A *node* may represent a physical location (e.g., plant, warehouse, distribution center, retail store), raw material, a part or component required to produce a product (as in its bill-of-materials (BOMs)), *or* a time point when a decision is to be made. Its specific definition depends on the corresponding application. An *arc* denotes an activity connecting a pair of nodes in general. Again, depending on a specific application, it may represent production and transportation flow of goods, and carrying of inventory from one period to the next, etc.

There are several motivations to study network optimization problems. First, they are often amenable for the use of a special network diagram, known as a NETFORM, to describe the model. Using visualization via a NETFORM provides an intuitive and accessible way to present and communicate the modeling approach with practitioners who may not have the technical background in mathematical programming. Secondly and more importantly, due to the special network structure and its mathematical property,[a] many network optimization problems can be solved by linear programming (LP) or special-purpose algorithms with better efficiency. In addition, many real-life optimization problems can be complex enough to include certain network optimization problems as special cases, which may serve as sub-problems in a more sophisticated model. In this text, we shall focus on the first motivation to show how to formulate the NETFORM for various network flow optimization problems, and delineate the correspondence between the NETFORM and an LP formulation.

4.2 Modeling a Pure Network

A *pure network* is a network in which flows are *conserved*, i.e., with no gain nor loss, when passing through every node in the network. More precisely, it means that for each node, the total inflow into the node equals the total outflow from the node. The following building blocks are needed for a typical pure network model via a NETFORM representation.

4.2.1 *Modeling Input and Output*

We use a triangle pointing toward a node with a directed arc (shown as an arrow) to represent the *supply* of the node; and a directed arc leading from a node to a triangle pointing away from the node to denote the *demand* of the node. As shown in Figure 4.1(a), there are five units of supply for the node A; and there are five units of demand for node B as in Figure 4.1(b).

Sometimes the supply or demand may not be a fixed amount, but can be a range. For example, the maximum supply of a node may be 100, and the demand of a node may be between 50 and 100. In this case, one may use a parenthesis (lb, ub) identifying a lower bound

[a]The unimodularity property of a pure network model: One does not need the integral requirements to guarantee integral solutions. That is, a pure network model requiring integral solutions can be modeled and solved as an LP.

(a) 5 units of input (supply) (b) 5 units of output (demand)

Figure 4.1. Modeling input and output in NETFORM.

(a) range of input (supply) (b) range of output (demand)

Figure 4.2. Modeling input and output with a range in NETFORM.

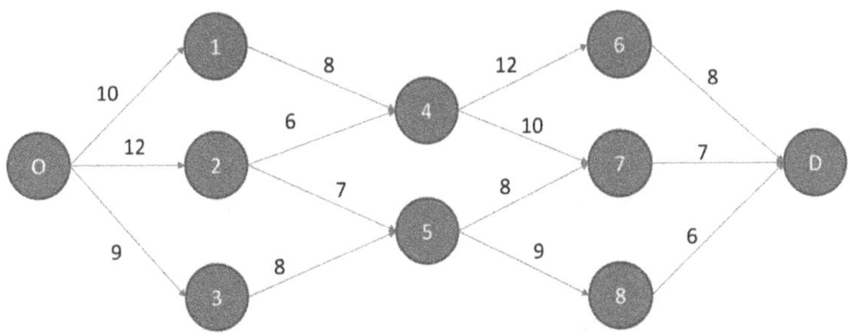

Figure 4.3. An example of modeling connecting activities with arcs.

(lb) and an upper bound (ub) to specify the range of the supply or demand. As shown in Figure 4.2(a), node A has a supply no more than 200; and in Figure 4.2(b) node B has a demand no less than 60 and no more than 100.

4.2.2 *Modeling Connecting Activities*

An arc between a pair of nodes models a connecting activity. Figure 4.3 shows the activities of grain shipping between Warehouse A and Customer 1, and between Warehouse A and Customer 2. We observe that the arc into node A with bounds (50, 50) to indicate the available supply gives a more general type of representation than in Figure 4.1 where triangles are used to identify fixed supplies and demands.

Depending on the problem context and definition of the nodes, an arc may carry different meanings as shown in Table 4.1. As we will

Table 4.1. The use of arcs in NETFORM to model connecting activities.

Problem context	Definition of nodes	Meaning of arcs
Shipping and transportation	Facilities (warehouses, distribution centers)	Flow of goods
Production and inventory planning	Facilities and time periods	Flow of goods
Financial planning	Time periods	Cash flow
Manufacturing	Nodes in the BOMs: parts, components	Flow of goods
Public transportation	Locations	Flow of passengers

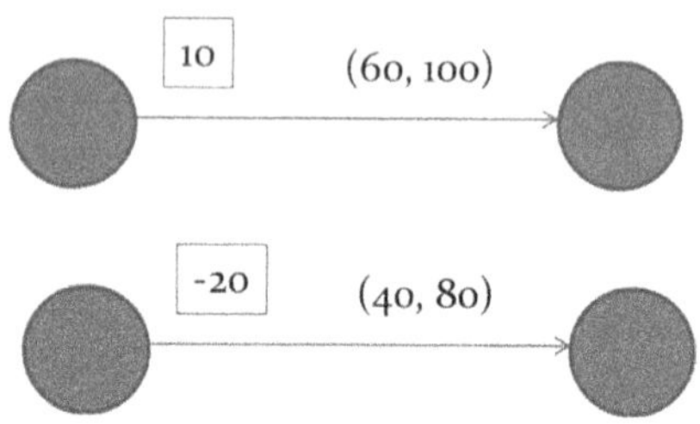

Figure 4.4. Modeling cost of activities in the objective function.

show later, each arc in the NETFORM except those having equal lower and upper bounds represents a decision variable in its mathematical programming (LP) formulation.

4.2.3 *Modeling Objective Function*

A connecting activity usually incurs a cost, e.g., the cost of production, shipping or inventory carrying. This can be modeled by putting a box on an arc with the cost per unit of flow on the corresponding arc. The top diagram in Figure 4.4 shows an arc with \$10 per unit of flow, with a lower bound of 60 and an upper bound of 100 on its flow. Sometimes, a connecting activity generates revenue, e.g., sales of goods, deposit of cash, etc., which can be represented as a negative number in the box on an arc. The bottom diagram in Figure 4.4 shows a revenue of \$20 per unit of flow, with a lower bound of 40 and an upper bound of 80 on its flow. The reason for having a negative

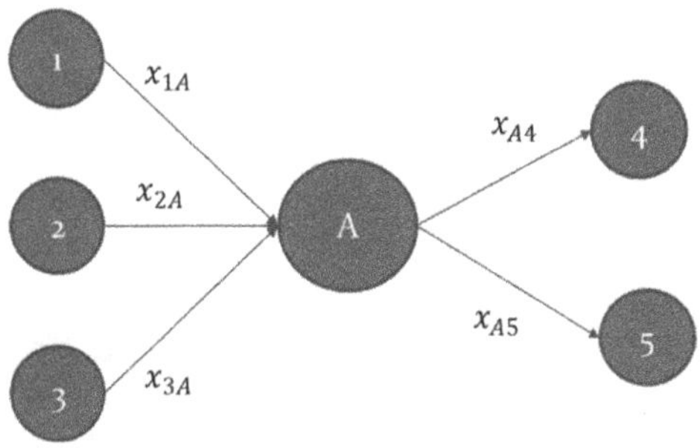

Figure 4.5. Modeling flow conservation in a pure network.

value for revenue is to accommodate a generic LP formulation, with a minimization objective function, for the NETFORM to be presented next.

4.2.4 *Modeling Flow Conservation*

Flow conservation, or flow balancing, is the most important characteristic of a pure network. It simply means that the total inflow into a node equals the total outflow from the node. As shown in Figure 4.5, the flow conservation constraint at node A requires that the total flow into A (from nodes 1, 2, and 3) equals the total flow out of A (into nodes 4 and 5). Mathematically, we write: $x_{1A} + x_{2A} + x_{3A} = x_{A4} + x_{A5}$.

4.3 Minimum Cost Flow Problem

We now present a concrete example of minimum cost flow problem (MCFP) with its NETFORM model and algebraic LP model formulations. We shall identify and elaborate the connections between the two formulations. We choose the MCFP as an example for this purpose because it is general enough to include a number of other network optimization problems as special cases.

Example 4.1 (MCFP). ABC Inc. is a company located in St. Louis, Missouri that distributes grains from its two warehouses to two customers located in the Midwest. Each ton of grain shipped from Warehouse B costs \$300; each ton of grain sold to Customer 1 brings a revenue of \$400. Each ton of grain shipped from Warehouse

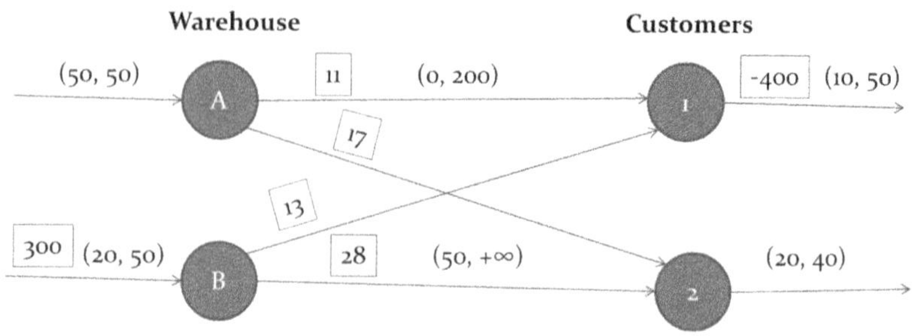

Figure 4.6. NETFORM for ABC's grain distribution (MCFP).

A to Customer 2 costs \$17, from Warehouse A to Customer 1: \$11, from Warehouse B to Customer 1: \$13, and from Warehouse B to Customer 2: \$28. The supply at Warehouse A is fixed at 50 tons; the supply at Warehouse B is in the range of [20, 50]. The shipment from Warehouse A to Customer 1 cannot exceed 200 tons, and the shipment from Warehouse B to Customer 2 cannot be less than 50 tons. ABC seeks to plan its grain distribution with minimum total transportation cost.

The NETFORM model for ABC's grain distribution problem is shown in Figure 4.6.

Since the supply of node B and the demands of nodes 1 and 2 are part of the decision, sometimes dummy nodes are created to emphasize that the associated arcs, currently appearing as "half arcs" (either without a from node or a to node) identify variables that enter into the decision process. For example, we may introduce a dummy source node S and a dummy destination node T as shown in Figure 4.7. We have also renumbered the other nodes to be 1, 2, 3, 4 for the convenience of referencing the nodes.

Define $x_{ij} \geq 0$ as the flow of grains from node i to node j. With the dummy source defined, the supply into node B can be denoted as x_{S2}. Similarly, with the dummy destination node defined, the demand at node 3 can be denoted by x_{3T}. The objective function minimizes the total shipping cost:

$$\text{Minimize} \quad 300x_{S2} + 11x_{13} + 17x_{14} + 13x_{23} + 28x_{24} - 400x_{3T}$$

Note that the coefficient of x_{3T} in the objective function of minimization is negative, since the corresponding flow generates a revenue. Constraints of the LP formulation, corresponding with all the nodes

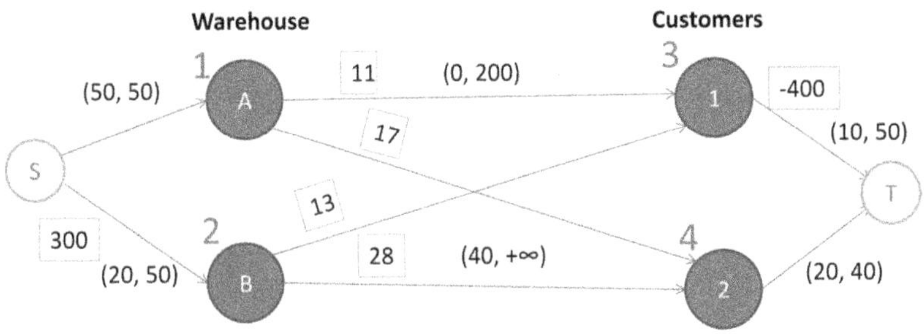

Figure 4.7. NETFORM for ABC's grain distribution with dummy nodes.

in Figure 4.7, can be written as below. The first four maintain the flow conservation at the four nodes: 1, 2, 3 and 4. The remaining constraints specify bounds on the flows.

Flow conservation at node 1:	$x_{13} + x_{14} = x_{S1}$
Flow conservation at node 2:	$x_{23} + x_{24} = x_{S2}$
Flow conservation at node 3:	$x_{13} + x_{23} = x_{3T}$
Flow conservation at node 4:	$x_{14} + x_{24} = x_{4T}$
Flow from S to node 1:	$x_{S1} = 50$
Flow from S to node 2:	$20 \leq x_{S2} \leq 50$
Flow from node 1 to node 3:	$x_{13} \leq 200$
Flow from node 2 to node 4:	$x_{24} \geq 40$
Flow from node 3 to node T:	$10 \leq x_{3T} \leq 50$
Flow from node 4 to node T:	$20 \leq x_{4T} \leq 40$
Non-negativity:	$x_{ij} \geq 0$

Rearranging terms of the first four constraints, we have

$$\begin{array}{lllllllll} x_{S1} & & -x_{13} & -x_{14} & & & & & = 0 \\ & x_{S2} & & & -x_{23} & -x_{24} & & & = 0 \\ & & x_{13} & & +x_{23} & & & -x_{3T} & = 0 \\ & & & x_{14} & & +x_{24} & -x_{4T} & & = 0 \end{array}$$

This illustrates an important property of a pure network model, i.e., the *unimodularity property*. To identify this property, pay attention to the coefficients of the decision variables at the LHS of the constraints, which are either 0, +1 or −1. Unimodularity guarantees an optimal solution to be integral (without explicitly requiring the decision variables to be integral), as long as the LHS parameters of the model are all integral.

4.4 Generic LP Formulation for NETFORM

We now present a generic LP formulation for any pure network that can be represented as a NETFORM. The general rule of formulating the LP model for the NETFORM is:

(1) Each arc in the NETFORM identifies a decision variable; and
(2) Each node in the NETFORM identifies a constraint.

Sets

V: set of all nodes
S: set of supply nodes
D: set of demand nodes
A: set of arcs, with $(i, j) \in A$ representing arc (i, j)

Parameters

c_{ij}: cost of flow per unit of goods on arc (i, j), i.e., from node i to node j
s_i: supply capacity of node $i \in S$
d_i: demand of node $i \in D$ (need $d_i \leq 0$)
k_{ij}: maximum flow capacity on arc (i, j)
l_{ij}: minimum flow on arc (i, j)

Decision variable

$x_{ij} \geq 0$ as the flow from node i to j

Objective function

$$\text{Minimize total cost} = \sum_{(i,j)\in A} c_{ij}x_{ij} \tag{4.1}$$

Constraints

Supply capacity:

$$\sum_{j:(i,j)\in A} x_{ij} = s_i, \quad \forall i \in S \tag{4.2}$$

Demand capacity:

$$-\sum_{i:(i,j)\in A} x_{ij} = d_j, \quad \forall j \in D \tag{4.3}$$

Transshipment node (flow conservation):

$$\sum_{j:(i,j)\in A} x_{ij} - \sum_{j:(j,i)\in A} x_{ji} = 0, \quad \forall i \in V\backslash S\backslash D \tag{4.4}$$

Flow capacity:

$$x_{ij} \le k_{ij}, \quad \forall (i,j) \in A \tag{4.5}$$

Minimum flow:

$$x_{ij} \ge l_{ij}, \quad \forall (i,j) \in A \tag{4.6}$$

Non-negativity:

$$x_{ij} \ge 0 \tag{4.7}$$

The objective function (4.1) minimizes the total shipping cost. Constraint (4.2) states that the total shipment out of a supply node $i \in S$ must equal its supply s_i. Constraint (4.3) ensures that the total flow into a demand node $j \in D$ must equal its demand d_j. The negative sign — at the LHS is consistent with the convention that the demand value must be negative in the NETFORM. In Constraint (4.4), for a *transshipment node* i that is neither a supply node nor a demand node, i.e., $i \in V\backslash S\backslash D$, the flow conservation constraint must hold, such that the total outflow from i computed as $\sum_{j:(i,j)\in A} x_{ij}$ subtracting the total inflow into i computed as $\sum_{j:(j,i)\in A} x_{ji}$ must equal zero. Constraint (4.5) imposes the upper bound of flow on arc $(i,j) \in A$. Constraint (4.6) specifies the non-negativity of the decision variables.

Note that Constraints (4.2) and (4.3) are special cases of the flow conservation constraint, in that the total inflow of a supply node is the supply quantity in Constraint (4.2), and the total outflow of a demand node is the demand quantity in Constraint (4.3). In a NETFORM representation where supply and demand arcs are included with bounds on the arcs, the constraints of (4.2) and (4.3) become instances of the constraint (4.4).

The above LP formulation is feasible when the total supply equals the total demand, i.e., $\sum_{i\in S} s_i = \sum_{j\in D} d_i$, which is called a *balanced* problem. If the problem is *unbalanced*, Constraints (4.2) and/or (4.3) can be modified to be inequalities to maintain feasibility, which can be represented in a natural way with a NETFORM by putting bounds on an arc into a supply node and/or out of a demand node. In those cases where a lower bound equals an upper bound, the NETFORM that puts supplies and demands in triangles is commonly used.

4.5 Special Cases of Minimum Cost Flow Problem

In this section, we show that the MCFP can be reduced to various other network optimization problems via the NETFORM.

4.5.1 *Transportation Problem*

The standard Transportation Problem is a special case of MCFP where there are only two sets (or two tiers in the supply chain) of nodes: supply nodes and demand nodes. Figure 4.8 shows a transportation problem with four supply nodes and four demand nodes. Each supply node i has a capacity of s_i, and each demand node j has a demand of d_j.

4.5.2 *Transshipment Problem*

The *transshipment problem* is a special case of the MCFP where there are at least three sets (tiers) of nodes: supply, transshipment and demand. Figure 4.9 shows a transshipment problem with four supply nodes (set I), two transshipment nodes (set K) and four demand nodes (set J). The shipping cost between the supply nodes and transshipment nodes can be denoted by c_{ik} for $i \in I$, $k \in K$, and the shipping cost between the transshipment nodes and demand nodes can be denoted by c_{kj} for $k \in K, j \in J$.

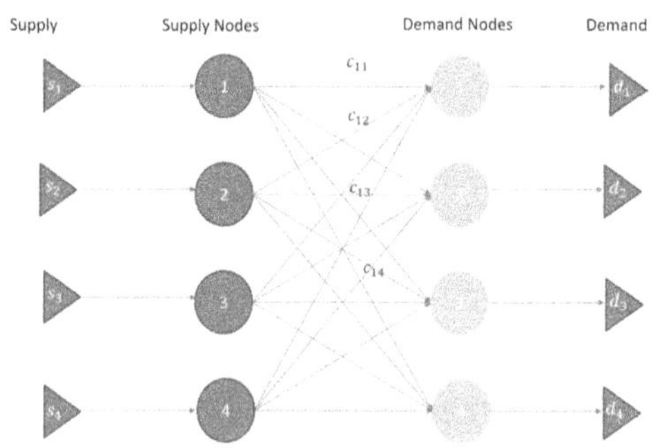

Figure 4.8. NETFORM for the transportation problem.

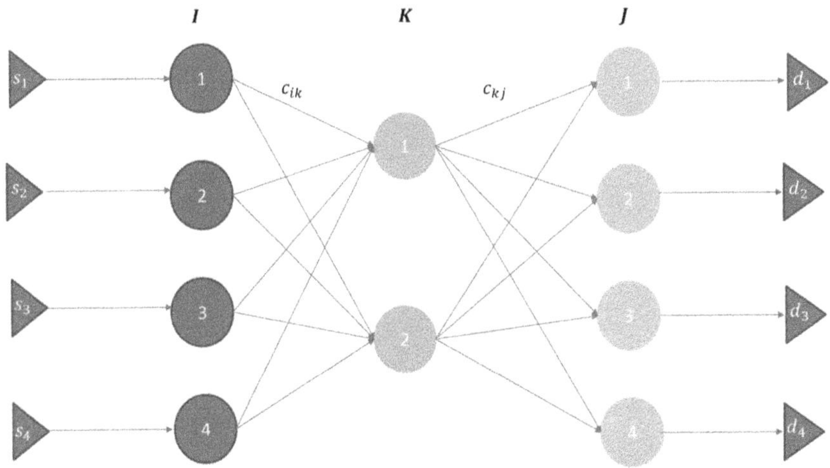

Figure 4.9. NETFORM for the transshipment problem.

4.5.3 *Shortest Path Problem*

The *shortest path problem* seeks to find a path with the shortest distance (or cost) from the source to the destination through a network. The example in Figure 4.10(a) shows a shortest path problem with nine nodes, starting from node 1 (the source) to node 9 (the destination). The distance of an arc (i, j) is a constant d_{ij}. To transform it to an MCFP, we send 1 unit of supply into the source node, and impose 1 unit of demand out of the destination node, as shown in Figure 4.10(b).

4.5.4 *Maximum Flow Problem*

The *maximum flow problem* seeks to find a feasible flow through a (capacitated) network that maximizes the total throughput flow. As shown in Figure 4.11(a), each arc(i, j) has a maximum capacity k_{ij} that cannot be exceeded. For instance, a maximum k_{24} units of flow can be sent from node 2 to node 4. It can be transformed into an MCFP by sending a variable supply into the source node, and imposing a variable demand out from the destination node. As shown in Figure 4.11(b), a supply denoted by $Z \geq 0$ is sent into the source node 1, and a demand of $-Z$ is at the destination node 9. The objective function is to maximize the through flow Z.

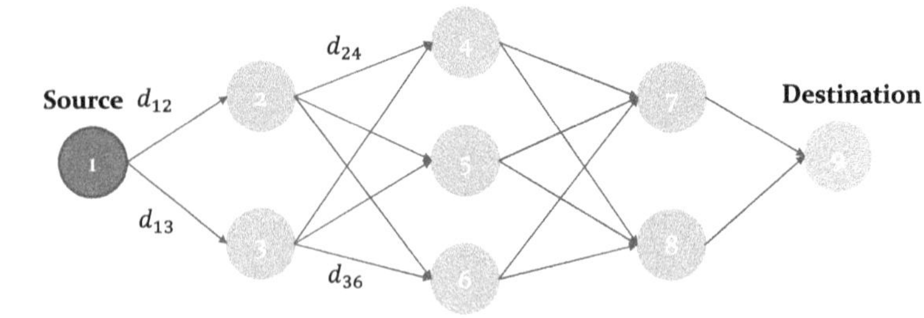

(a) An example of shortest path problem

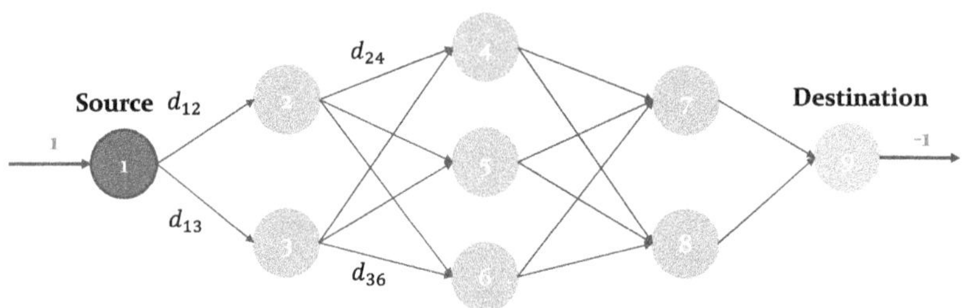

(b) NETFORM for the shortest path problem

Figure 4.10. Shortest path problem and its NETFORM transformation.

4.5.5 *Assignment Problem*

A standard *assignment problem* seeks to assign a set of tasks to a set of machines, so that each task is assigned to exactly one machine, and each machine is assigned exactly one task. The objective is to minimize the total assignment cost (or to maximize some measure of reward or benefit). The problem is a special case of the transportation problem (and consequently of the minimum cost flow problem), where the capacity of a supply node is 1, and the demand of a demand node is also 1. The NETFORM for assignment problem is shown in Figure 4.12.

4.6 Modeling Complex Networks

A real-world logistics and transportation network often consists of many facilities: plants, warehouses, distribution centers and retailers in multiple stages, which can be well-represented by NETFORM.

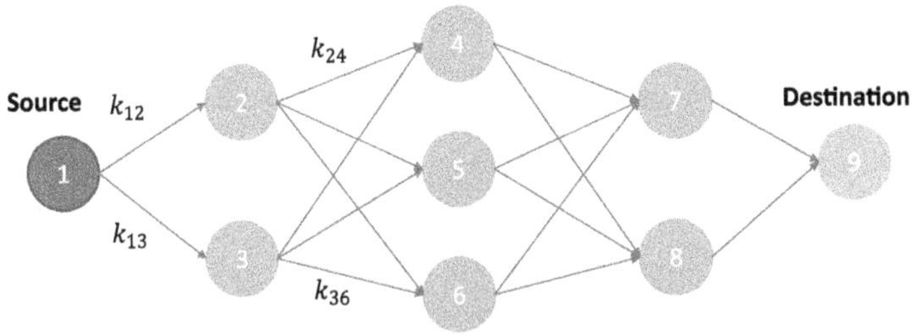

(a) An example of the maximum flow problem

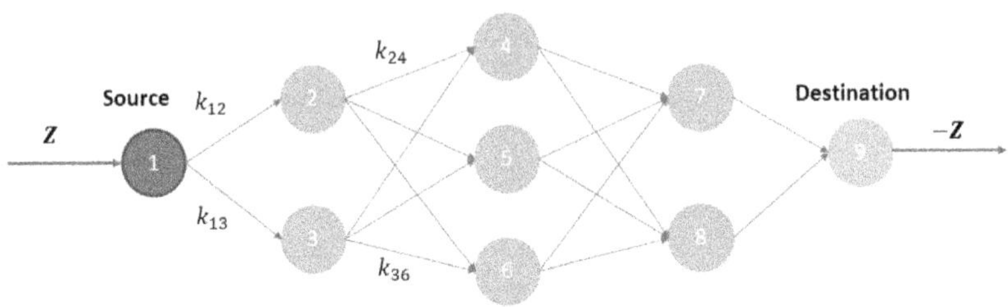

(b) NETFORM for maximum flow problem

Figure 4.11. Maximum flow problem and its NETFORM transformation.

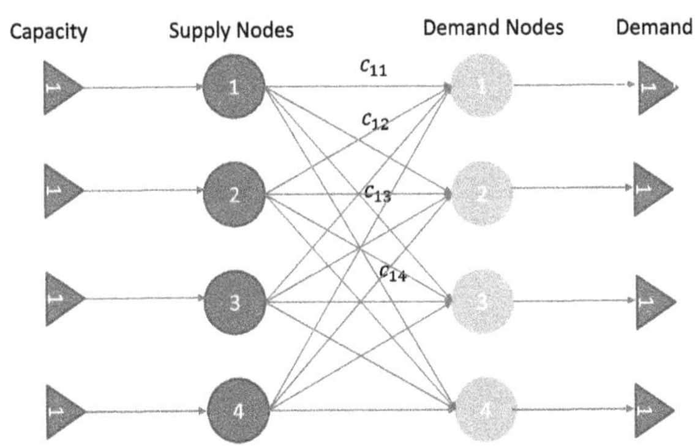

Figure 4.12. NETFORM for an assignment problem.

A schematic illustration of a multi-stage network is shown in Figure 4.13.

Each stage may contain multiple facilities (nodes), and activities (arcs) may exist between an arbitrary pair of nodes. For instance, raw materials are shipped from a supplier to a manufacturer; finished

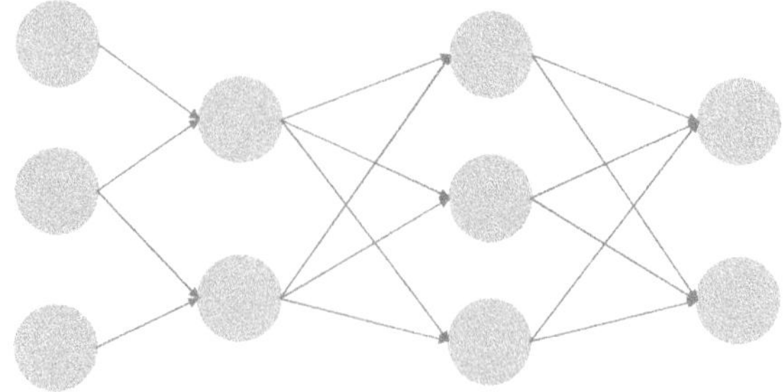

Figure 4.13. A schematic view of multi-stage network.

products are transported from a manufacturer to a distribution center, then to a retailer. The principle of flow conservation applies in most real-world scenarios where the flow of physical goods does not gain or lose during transit. The NETFORM provides a general and powerful framework for modeling the network flow type of problems.

Another dimension of complexity arises in a transportation network with multiple products. The way to model a multi-product network as a NETFORM is to create nodes to represent different products separately. An example of a two-tier supply chain with three types of products is shown in Figure 4.14. Three products are produced at two plants and shipped to two DCs. A plant does not produce all three products, but all three products are shipped to each DC. The arcs into node P1 represent the total combined quantity of both products 1 and 2 produced at Plant-1. The two arcs from node P1 to two manufacturing nodes 1 and 2 represent the quantity of products 1 and 2 made at Plant-1, respectively. (Note that product 3 is not produced at this plant.) Similarly, products 1 and 3 are produced at P2.

4.7 Dynamic NETFORM Models

The NETFORM models we have shown so far represent a one-time view of a network, i.e., a *static* network. Many real-world applications involve flow of goods or decisions to be made over multiple time

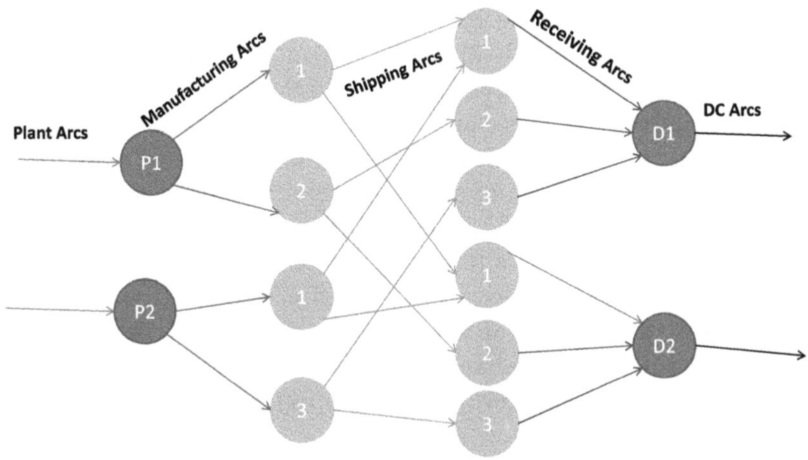

Figure 4.14. An example of a three-tier supply chain network with three product types.

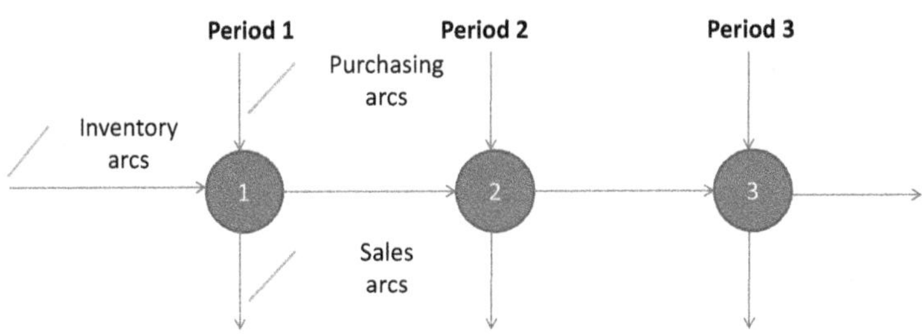

Figure 4.15. The fundamental framework of a dynamic NETFORM.

periods or decision stages in a *dynamic* fashion. The assumption of flow conservation may still hold if the flow has no gain or loss over time. The fundamental structure of a dynamic NETFORM can be depicted in Figure 4.15.

Each time period is represented by a node, where some inflow (purchase, production) increases the stock (inventory) of the current time period, and some outflow (sales, consumption) decreases its stock. Any remaining stock is carried over to the next time period as *inventory*. Thus the flow conversation constraint takes a special form in the dynamic setting:

$$\text{Inventory in } t + \text{ Purchase in } t = \text{ Sales in } t + \text{ Inventory in } (t+1)$$

Example 4.2 (Purchase Planning). A corn distributor buys corns from farms and sells directly to local markets or stores it for sales in the future. The distributor's purchasing price, sales price, maximum limit to purchase and maximum limit to sell in three time periods of the planning horizon are available in the table below. Note that the market demand and price vary significantly over time, which creates an incentive to hold inventory. The maximum quantity that can be stored as inventory from one period to the next is 700 tons. The distributor's storage cost is \$0.6 per ton. The distributor has 400 tons already in inventory at the start of period one. It would like to have at least 300 tons on hand at the end of period three (to hedge against some possible uncertainty of supply).

Time periods	**1**	**2**	**3**
Purchase price (\$/ton)	2.2	3.1	2.8
Selling price (\$/ton)	3.2	4.3	3.7
Max quant. to purchase	1600	2000	1800
Max quant. to sell	1200	2400	2600

The NETFORM for the problem is as follows.

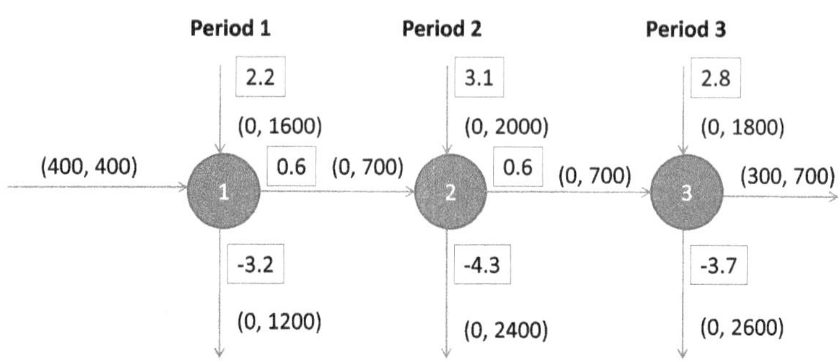

Its corresponding LP formulation can be written as.

<u>Sets</u>

T: set of time periods: $1, 2, \ldots, |T|$

Parameters

π_t: selling price in period $t \in T$
c_t: purchase price in period $t \in T$
K_t: maximum quantity to purchase in period $t \in T$
D_t: maximum quantity to sell in period $t \in T$
a_t: minimum inventory level in each period $t \in T$
b_t: maximum inventory level in each period $t \in T$
I_0: the initial inventory

Decision variables

x_t: the purchasing quantity in period $t \in T$
y_t: the sale quantity in period $t \in T$
I_t: the inventory level at the end of period $t \in T$, and define $I_0 = 0$.

Objective function

$$\text{Maximize} \sum_{t \in T} (\pi_t y_t - c_t x_t) \tag{4.8}$$

Constraints

Flow conservation:

$$I_{t-1} + x_t = y_t + I_t, \quad \forall t \in T \tag{4.9}$$

Max quant to purchase:

$$x_t \leq K_t, \quad \forall t \in T \tag{4.10}$$

Max quant to sell:

$$y_t \leq D_t, \quad \forall t \in T \tag{4.11}$$

Min inv. level:

$$I_t \geq a_t, \quad \forall t \in T \tag{4.12}$$

Max inv. level:

$$I_t \leq b_t, \quad \forall t \in T \tag{4.13}$$

Non-negativity:

$$x_i, y_t, I_t \geq 0 \tag{4.14}$$

The objective function (4.8) maximizes the total profit of the distributor. Constraint (4.9) maintains the flow conservation for each

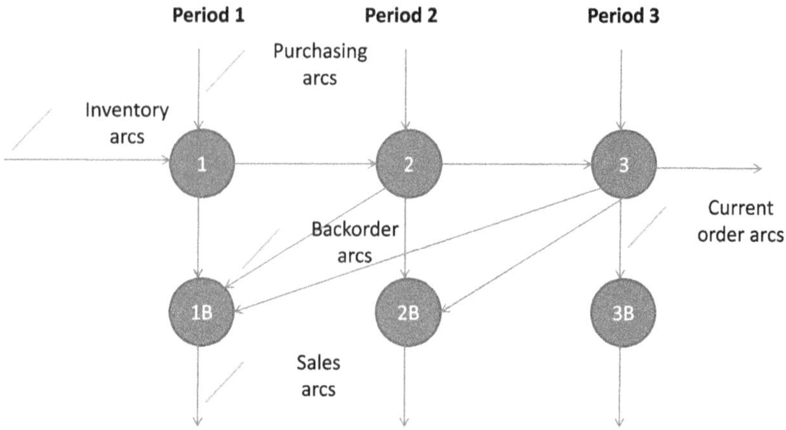

Figure 4.16. Modeling backorders with a NETFORM.

time period. Note that I_0 needs to be defined as zero or any initial inventory for (4.9) to work. Constraints (4.10) and (4.11) satisfy the upper and lower bounds of purchasing, respectively. Constraints (4.12) and (4.13) specify the upper and lower bounds on the inventory carried in each period, respectively.

In real-world applications, it is often not possible, or cost-effective, to satisfy current demands out of inventories and purchases. Analogously, in financial settings, it may not always be best to pay off all debts and financial liabilities precisely when they come due. In such cases, effective planning and management must allow for options of meeting current demands out of future resources, which is called *backordering*.

Figure 4.16 shows an example of modeling backordering in NETFORM. A new layer of nodes can be created to represent backorder occurred in each time period: 1B, 2B and 3B, etc. Red arcs between node 2 and 1B indicate fulfilling the order in period 1 by the purchase in period 2; similarly, the order in period 1 can be met by the purchase in period 3. The length or lag of backorder can be firm-specific and customized as needed.

As an expansion of complexity, NETFORMs can be employed to model multiple supply chain stages in a dynamic setting. Multiple layers of nodes can be created to represent purchase, production, warehousing and/or sales. As shown in Figure 4.17, nodes 1, 2 and 3 represent the purchase of raw materials, whereas nodes 1P, 2P and

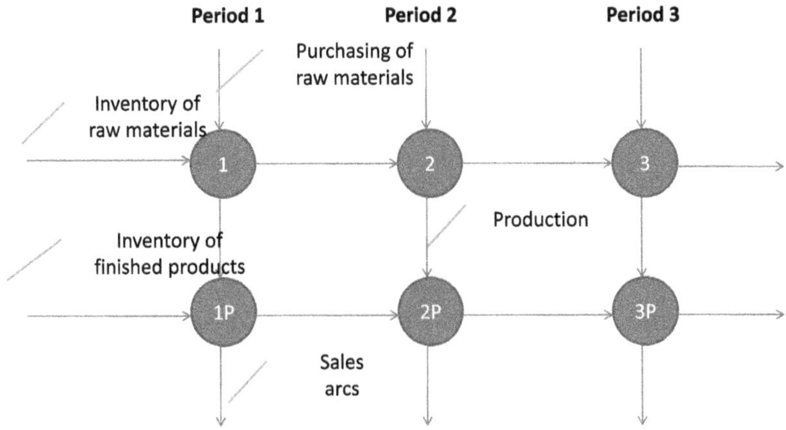

Figure 4.17. Modeling multiple stages with a NETFORM.

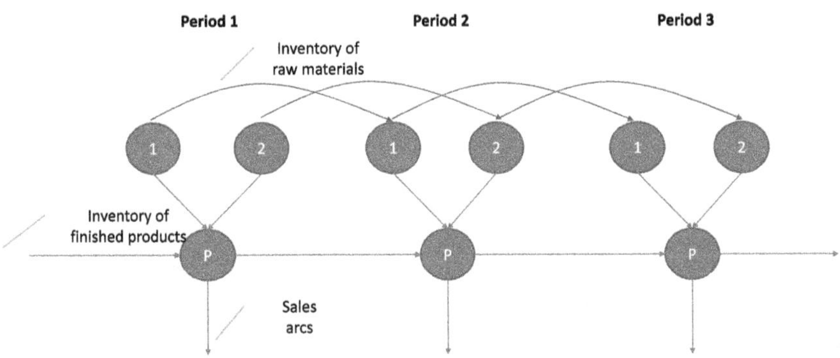

Figure 4.18. Modeling a time-spatial network with a NETFORM.

3P represent production. Both the purchasing and production stages may carry inventory.

A real-world supply chain often involves external operations and activities of a firm, e.g., suppliers/vendors and 3PLs. A variant of the example above is to model supply chain activities with different geographical locations in the so-called *time-spatial network*. Figure 4.18 shows a supply chain network with two suppliers of raw materials represented by nodes 1 and 2, and one manufacturer denoted by node P. The manufacturer may carry finished goods inventory and the two suppliers may keep inventory of raw materials. Such a time-spatial network is flexible enough to integrate decisions on both the flow of goods through the physical network and the inventory across multiple time periods.

4.8 Generalized Network Models

The NETFORM models introduced so far all assume no gain or loss of flow, i.e., flow conservation. In real-world operations, this assumption does not always hold. We show three scenarios where flows do not meet the flow conservation assumption, where they can either achieve a gain or suffer a loss during transit, in a *generalized network*. The gain or loss factor can be modeled as a *multiplier* in a triangle on an arc: where a multiplier greater than 1 indicates gain, and a multiplier less than 1 indicates loss. Arcs without multipliers, as in the previous examples, implicitly have a multiplier of 1. Without flow conservation, the unimodularity property no longer holds. Nevertheless, the NETFORM representation offers an intuitive way to present and visualize a generalized network model.

The first scenario is for the conversion of different measurements for the flow through a network. For instance, packaging table grapes (in pounds) into boxes (in units) requires a conversion ratio. If a box contains 5 pounds of table grapes, then the conversion ratio for placing these grapes into a single box would be 0.2 for the outgoing arc from the table grape node (or the incoming arc into the box node).

Example 4.3 (Passenger Transport). An airline at City A has incoming flights from different cities. Each flight has a capacity of 200. The operating cost is $800 per flight, and the airline schedules 4 to 10 flights per day. The company would like to understand the number of passengers it can transport to different destinations per day. This problem can be depicted by the following NETFORM in Figure 4.19. A multiplier of 200 is imposed on the arc between node A and Z to convert the outflow from A (in a number of planes) to the inflow to Z (in a number of passengers).

The asterisk (*) attached to the arc is a notation used in NETFORM representations to indicate that the flow on the arc must be an integer amount, since planes only occur in integer quantities. A NETFORM model containing integer flow restrictions is an

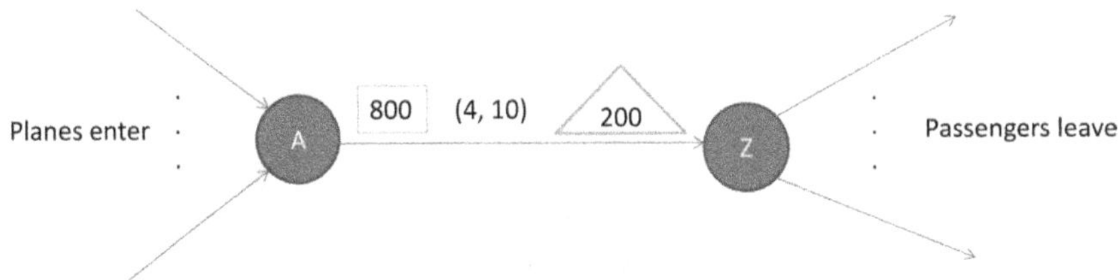

Figure 4.19. Example of passenger transport with multipliers.

instance of an integer programming problem, as described in Chapter 3.

It may be observed that passengers also come only in integer quantities, but if the arc (A, Z) for the planes only contains integer flows then the passengers leaving the planes will automatically be in integer amounts when treated by standard integer programming methods.

To allow for the possibility that a plane may carry fewer than 200 passengers, one of the arcs leaving node Z can be a dummy passenger arc whose flow corresponds to passengers that were not carried on the planes. In the presence of arc multipliers, such integer flow restrictions and dummy arcs can be used to model a wide range of practical applications.

In a second scenario, we consider a problem widely encountered in food transportation and supply chains with *perishable* foods, such as fruits, vegetables, fresh meat, seafood and dairy. Due to the perishable nature of these food items, their quantity may suffer loss during transit or storage, and their quality (value) may deteriorate. Coping with food waste and loss is one of the grand challenges in our economy. Modeling food transportation and distribution often requires taking account of the food loss through the network.

Example 4.4 (Perishable Food Network). Consider a distribution network of fresh table grapes with a 4% loss rate from one period to the next as shown in Figure 4.20. To capture this, we impose a multiplier of 0.96 on the inventory arcs between two time periods.

In the foregoing example, we are not concerned with integer restrictions on the arcs because a fractional number of grapes in a final solution can simply be rounded down with no significant effect on the outcome. A variety of other problems can disregard attaching

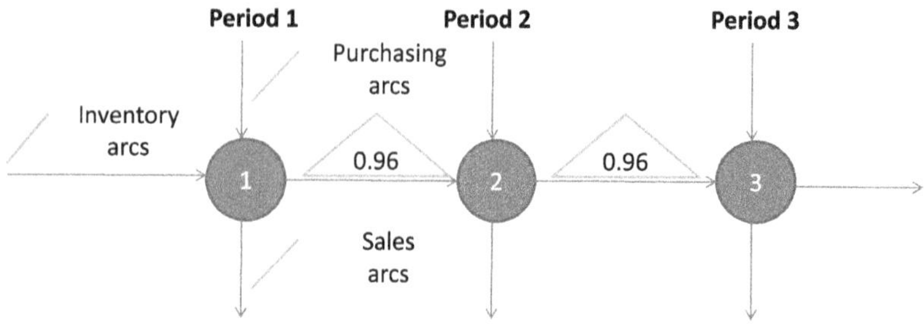

Figure 4.20. Example of shipping perishable foods with multiplier.

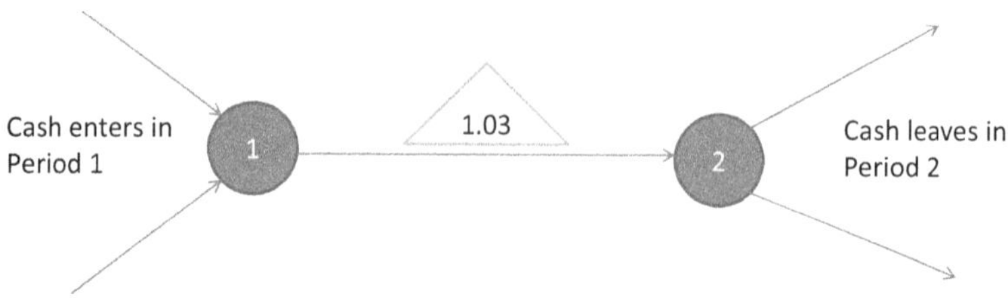

Figure 4.21. Example of cash flow with multiplier.

integer restrictions to arcs for similar reasons. In a network with no multipliers on the arcs (other than an implicit multiplier of 1), LP solutions produced by customary methods will automatically yield integer flows.

As a last scenario, we consider an application in financial planning on cash flow over multiple time periods. There, the flow of cash naturally generates interests over time, with the interest rate being the multiplier.

Example 4.5 (Cash Flow Network). Assuming the interest rate is 3%, we impose a multiplier of 1.03 on the cash savings (inventory) carried from one period to the next as in Figure 4.21.

4.9 Additional Notes

We refer to Glover *et al.* [19] for a systematic and accessible treatment of NETFORMs and their applications. The comprehensive theory and algorithmic aspects of network optimization are well covered by Ahuja *et al.* [20].

Exercises

4.1. Transportation Problem. ABC Metal Company engages in the recycling and reuse of scrap metals. It sources from three pits located in A, B and C and ships the scrap metals to its three processing factories in locations 1, 2 and 3 through a truckload shipping service from a 3PL on a weekly basis. The weekly available supplies of scrap metals at A, B and C are 20, 30, and between 25 and 35 (denoted by [25, 35]) truckloads, respectively. The weekly demands at factories 1, 2 and 3 are [20, 30], 25, [20, 25] truckloads, respectively. The shipping cost ($/truckload) between an OD (origin-destination) pair is provided below.

	1	**2**	**3**
A	200	300	250
B	150	250	300
C	180	200	275

(a) Draw a NETFORM to optimize the shipping plan.
(b) Write the corresponding LP formulation of the NETFORM.

4.2. Assignment Problem. ABC Law Firm handles cases in four specialty areas: M&A (merger & acquisition), Insurance, Medical and Civil, which requires different skill sets and expertise. To achieve efficiency and customer satisfaction, the firm opts to assign attorneys having the most experience and expertise to these cases. The company tracks the record of time (in weeks) spent by its four attorneys A, B, C, D for handling these different types of cases as indicated in the following table.

	M&A	**Insurance**	**Medical**	**Civil**
A	10	8	9	7
B	8	7	9	8
C	12	6	8	9
D	14	5	7	10

(a) Draw a NETFORM to optimize the assignment of attorneys to types of cases.
(b) Write the corresponding LP formulation of the NETFORM.

4.3. Shortest Path Problem. A mountain explorer would like to hike part of the Rocky Mountain from departing location O to destination D. He estimates the time (in hours) of using all trails and possible paths given the known distance information and difficulty level based on his experience. The network of trails and paths from O to D is illustrated below.

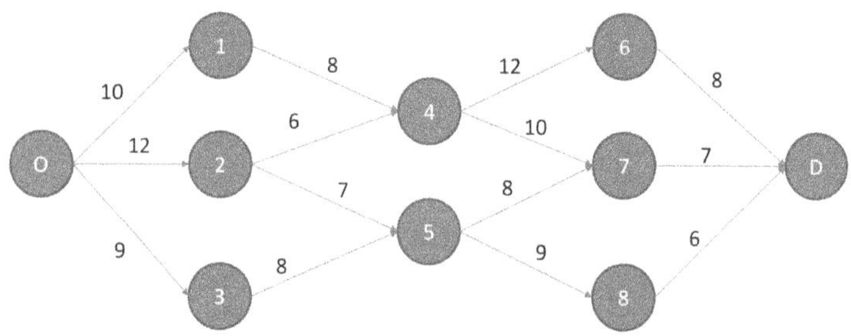

(a) Draw a NETFORM to minimize the total travel time from O to D.
(b) Write the corresponding LP formulation of the NETFORM.

4.4. Maximum Flow Problem. The Department of Public Health needs to send vaccines to a remote region to cope with the spread of an infectious disease. Due to the tight cold-chain requirement for transporting the vaccine and the poor transportation infrastructure in the region, the amount of vaccines transported weekly between locations is limited through the network linking the national depot (O) and the regional vaccine storage facility (D). The table below shows the maximum amount (in liters) of vaccines through a pair of transshipment locations 1, 2, 3 and 4 in the network.

(a) Draw a NETFORM to allow maximum flow from O to D.
(b) Write the corresponding LP formulation of the NETFORM.

4.5. Transshipment Problem. Innovation Foods is an indoor farming start-up company with the mission to provide fresh and nutritious vegetables for its local markets and consumers. The company would like to optimize its supply network consisting of three

	To				
From	1	2	3	4	D
O	80	120	–	–	–
1	–	–	60	40	–
2	–	–	50	45	–
3	–	–	–	–	35
4	–	–	–	–	45

indoor farming facilities F1, F2 and F3, two warehouses W1 and W2 and three customers (C1, C2 and C3).

The maximum supply (in truckloads) at each facility and the shipping cost ($/truckload) between facilities and warehouses are provided below.

	Warehouse		
Facility	**W1**	**W2**	**Supply**
F1	100	90	100
F2	130	120	140
F3	110	105	120

The demand at each customer and the shipping cost between warehouses and customers are provided below.

	Customer		
Warehouse	**C1**	**C2**	**C3**
W1	50	70	80
W2	75	80	60
Demand	90	130	120

Each facility must produce at least 50 truckloads to maintain economies of scale. The company would like to come up with a shipping plan that minimizes the total transportation cost.

(a) Draw a NETFORM to optimize the shipping plan.
(b) Write the corresponding LP formulation of the NETFORM.

4.6. Multi-product Distribution Planning. ABC Company manufactures three best-selling models of mowers: Basic, Standard and Premium. These models are made at two production plants: P1 and P2, and then distributed to two regional markets: M1 and M2. Each plant has a specified capacity for producing a model, and there is an overall combined capacity for all the models that cannot be exceeded. The monthly production capacities (Cap) and costs at each plant are shown in the following table.

	Basic		**Standard**		**Premium**		
	Cap	**Cost ($)**	**Cap**	**Cost ($)**	**Cap**	**Cost ($)**	**All Combined**
P1	800	1,200	1,200	1,650	–	–	1,500
P2	400	1,400	1,000	1,800	700	2,600	1,800

Using the historical market data, the company estimates the minimum monthly demands (Min) of each model in each market and the sales price in the following table.

	Basic		**Standard**		**Premium**		
	Min	**Price ($)**	**Min**	**Price ($)**	**Min**	**Price ($)**	**All Combined**
M1	300	4,800	900	5,400	300	7,300	1,600
M2	500	4,900	700	5,900	200	7,100	1,500

Shipping costs ($/mower) between a plant-market pair are provided as follows.

	M1	**M2**
P1	180	250
P2	230	200

ABC Company would like to come up with a production-distribution plan to maximize its monthly profit.

(a) Draw a NETFORM to optimize the distribution plan.
(b) Write the corresponding LP formulation of the NETFORM.

4.7. Multi-period Purchasing Planning. ABC Inc. is a major food distributor serving a region of 2 million population. It purchases grain from local growers and farm corporates, then sells it to wholesalers and retailers. Due to the seasonality of production and fluctuation of grain price, the company finds it necessary to perform a careful planning for the upcoming quarters for efficient operations. The purchasing cost ($/bushel) and supply capacity (thousand bushels) of two main growers G1 and G2 in the next three quarters are provided in the following table.

	Quarter 1		**Quarter 2**		**Quarter 3**	
	Cost	Cap	Cost	Cap	Cost	Cap
G1	4.5	5	3.9	7	4.7	6
G2	4.8	10	4.3	12	5.2	10

Using historical data, the company projects the minimum demand in the upcoming three quarters to be 12,000, 14,000 and 15,000 bushels, respectively. The ending inventory in the third quarter must be no less than 3,000 bushels. Due to limited warehouse space, the maximum amount of inventory carried in any quarter cannot exceed 6,000 bushels. The inventory holding cost per quarter is $7,200 per 1,000 bushels.

(a) Draw a NETFORM to optimize the purchasing plan.
(b) Write the corresponding LP formulation of the NETFORM.

4.8. Sales Planning with Backorders. ABC Costume is an online retailer selling festival costumes. Due to significant seasonality of festival costumes, the company often needs to utilize a backorder strategy to plan for its sales. For any customer who is willing to wait for the product to be available in one month, a $10 discount is offered; while a $15 discount is offered for those who would wait for two months. (The Batman costume set, for instance, is a product that experiences high seasonality of demand and limited supply, for which backorders often occur.) The sales department estimates the demand to be 200, 150 and 120 sets in the next three months; while the purchasing department reports that a maximum of 150 sets will be available in each month. The purchasing cost is \$25/set, while sales prices vary and are projected to be \$150, \$135, \$120 in the next three months. The inventory carrying cost is \$2 per set per month.

(a) Draw a NETFORM to optimize the sales and purchasing plan.
(b) Write the corresponding LP formulation of the NETFORM.

Chapter 5

Quadratic Unconstrained Binary Optimization (QUBO) Modeling

5.1 Introduction to QUBO

In this section, we introduce a special modeling approach known as quadratic unconstrained binary optimization (QUBO). A QUBO model has all its decision variables binary (0–1). And unlike the mathematical programming models we have seen so far, a QUBO model has a nonlinear (quadratic) objective function with no constraints. Below we introduce a generic formulation of QUBO to show its characteristics.

Let $\boldsymbol{Q}$ be an $n \times n$ matrix, and $\boldsymbol{c}^{\mathrm{T}} = (c_1, c_2, \ldots, c_n)$ be a row vector of constants in $\mathbb{R}^n$. The set of decision binary variables is a row vector $\boldsymbol{x}^{\mathrm{T}} = (x_1, x_2, \ldots, x_n)$ in $\mathbb{B}^n$. A generic mathematical programming formulation for a QUBO model can be written as:

$$\text{Minimize} \quad \boldsymbol{x}^{\mathrm{T}}\boldsymbol{Q}\boldsymbol{x} + \boldsymbol{c}^{\mathrm{T}}\boldsymbol{x} \tag{5.1}$$

Subject to:

$$\boldsymbol{x} \in \{0, 1\}^n \tag{5.2}$$

Note that the objective function (5.1) may in general include both a quadric term and a linear term. But since $x_i^2 = x_i$ for $i = 1, 2, \ldots, n$, the linear term can be embedded in the quadratic term. Specifically, each coefficient c_i for $i = 1, 2, \ldots, n$ can be added to q_{ii} of the $\boldsymbol{Q}$ matrix, where q_{ii} is the diagonal element in the ith row and ith column of $\boldsymbol{Q}$. Thus, (5.2) can also be written as:

$$\text{Minimize} \quad \boldsymbol{x}^{\mathrm{T}}\boldsymbol{Q}\boldsymbol{x} \tag{5.3}$$

To put the above definitions and generic formulation into context, consider the following numerical example.

$$\begin{aligned} \text{Minimize} \quad & -10x_1 - 8x_3 - 4x_4 + 5x_1^2 - x_2^2 \\ & + 6x_1x_2 + 10x_1x_3 + 2x_3x_2 + 8x_3x_4, \end{aligned}$$

where x_i is binary for $i = 1, 2, 3, 4$.

The objective function is in the form of (5.1) with both quadratic and linear terms. Since $x_i^2 = x_i$, the linear part is equivalent to: $-10x_1^2 - 8x_3^2 - 4x_4^2$. Merging with the other squared terms yields the following objective function with only quadratic terms:

$$\text{Minimize} \quad -5x_1^2 - x_2^2 - 8x_3^2 - 4x_4^2 + 6x_1x_2 + 10x_1x_3 + 2x_3x_2 + 8x_3x_4$$

The coefficients of squared terms appear in the diagonal of the $\boldsymbol{Q}$ matrix. For instance, $q_{11} = -5$ and $q_{33} = -8$. The coefficients of cross product terms appear in the non-diagonal part of $\boldsymbol{Q}$. For instance, $q_{12} = 6$ and $q_{32} = 2$. The $\boldsymbol{x}^{\mathrm{T}}\boldsymbol{Q}\boldsymbol{x}$ form of the objective function can be written as:

$$[x_1\ x_2\ x_3\ x_4] \begin{bmatrix} -5 & 6 & 10 & 1 \\ 0 & -1 & 0 & 0 \\ 0 & 2 & -8 & 8 \\ 0 & 0 & 0 & -4 \end{bmatrix} \begin{bmatrix} x_1 \\ x_2 \\ x_3 \\ x_4 \end{bmatrix}$$

Since $x_ix_j = x_jx_i$, one may assume that $\boldsymbol{Q}$ is in *upper triangular form* without loss of generality. For $j > i$, replace q_{ij} by $q_{ij} + q_{ji}$ and set all q_{ij} for $j < i$ to be 0. The upper triangular form of the original $\boldsymbol{x}^{\mathrm{T}}\boldsymbol{Q}\boldsymbol{x}$ of the example can be written as below:

$$[x_1\ x_2\ x_3\ x_4] \begin{bmatrix} -5 & 6 & 10 & 0 \\ 0 & -1 & 2 & 0 \\ 0 & 0 & -8 & 8 \\ 0 & 0 & 0 & -4 \end{bmatrix} \begin{bmatrix} x_1 \\ x_2 \\ x_3 \\ x_4 \end{bmatrix}$$

It is often common to work with the *symmetric form* of $\boldsymbol{Q}$: for $i \neq j$, replace q_{ij} by $(q_{ij} + q_{ji})/2$.

Some combinatorial optimization problems can be naturally formulated as a QUBO model.

Example 5.1 (Number Partitioning Problem). A set of numbers is partitioned into two subsets such that the difference between the sum of numbers in each subset is minimized. A binary decision variable is defined to identify the membership of a number in a subset. The objective function minimizes the *squared difference* between the sum of the two subsets, which is a quadratic function. The Number Partitioning Problem can be modeled as QUBO since all three conditions are met: (i) all decision variables are binary; (ii) the objective function is quadratic; (iii) no constraint is needed.

Example 5.2 (Maximum-Cut Problem). Given an undirected graph, one partitions the set of nodes into two subsets. The set of edges connecting the two subsets is called a *cut*. The Maximum-Cut Problem seeks to find a cut with the maximum cardinality, i.e., number of edges in the cut. A binary decision variable is defined to identify whether a node is in a subset or not. Using the binary decision variable, the status of an edge in the cut or not can be expressed as a quadratic function. The objective function maximizes the cardinality of the cut. The Maximum-Cut Problem can be modeled as QUBO since all three conditions are met: (i) all decision variables are binary; (ii) the objective function is quadratic; (iii) no constraint is needed.

Many combinatorial optimization problems have constraints, thus do not have a natural QUBO formulation, but they can be transformed or reformulated as QUBO. These include the knapsack problem, the set covering problem, the set packing problem, the set partitioning problem, the generalized assignment problem, the bin-packing problem covered in Section 3.2, and many others in supply chains to be introduced in Part II of the book. One motivation of such reformulation is the mathematical structure of QUBO, which is amenable to efficient computational algorithms. For instance, many local search based metaheuristics may take advantage of binary decision variables and the unconstrained nature of QUBO to perform efficiently.[a]

---

[a]The suite of metaheuristics widely applied for QUBO include simulated annealing, tabu search, and scatter search, among others. Technical details on the design

The most exciting motivation of applying QUBO for optimization problems comes from the emerging use of quantum computing. Quantum annealing computers such as those developed by D-Wave systems give a natural foundation for QUBO implementations. In addition, other forms of quantum and quantum-inspired computing being developed by groups like IBM, Microsoft and Fujitsu have an important though not exclusive involvement with QUBO models. Quantum annealing approaches to an optimization problem operate by a form of search that drives the process to reach low-energy solutions. The *quantum bit*, or *qubit*, is a basic unit of quantum information which quantum computing is built upon. Differing from the classical *binary bit* in two states (0 or 1), a qubit can be in a superposition of both states simultaneously. Superposition is the fundamental property of quantum computing that enables its promise of superior computational efficiency when quantum computers achieve a *breakthrough maturity* where they outperform classical computers on a significant range of practical applications, envisioned to occur within the next decade. In the meantime, highly refined algorithms designed to bridge the classical/quantum gap are providing importance advances that can be implemented on classical and hybrid quantum-classical systems. This is a fast growing area with numerous applications in computational finance, information systems, life sciences, and supply chains.

In this chapter, we introduce a systematic and unified approach to reformulate BIPs to QUBO. Application examples are presented to show applicability of this approach for various supply chain optimization applications.

5.2 Building QUBO Formulations

We start with the principle of reformulating a constrained BIP model to QUBO, followed by recipes for handling BIPs with some special types of constraints, then present a unified approach to reformulate general BIPs to QUBO.

---

and implementation of metaheuristics for combinatorial optimization problems go beyond the scope of this book.

5.2.1 *Principle of Reformulation*

Consider a general BIP model below with $\boldsymbol{x}$ being a column vector of n binary decision variables, and $\mathbf{c}^{\mathrm{T}}$ being a row vector of n constants. $\boldsymbol{A}_1$, $\boldsymbol{A}_2$ and $\boldsymbol{A}_3$ are $m_1 \times n$, $m_2 \times n$ and $m_3 \times n$ matrices, respectively. And $\boldsymbol{b}_1$, $\boldsymbol{b}_2$ and $\boldsymbol{b}_3$ are column vectors of constants with dimensions of m_1, m_2 and m_3, respectively.

$$\text{Minimize} \quad \mathbf{c}^{\mathrm{T}}\boldsymbol{x} \tag{5.4}$$

Subject to:

$$\boldsymbol{A}_1\boldsymbol{x} = \boldsymbol{b}_1 \tag{5.5}$$

$$\boldsymbol{A}_2\boldsymbol{x} \leq \boldsymbol{b}_2 \tag{5.6}$$

$$\boldsymbol{A}_3\boldsymbol{x} \geq \boldsymbol{b}_3 \tag{5.7}$$

$$\boldsymbol{x} \in \{0, 1\}^n \tag{5.8}$$

The objective function minimizes a linear function $\mathbf{c}^{\mathrm{T}}\boldsymbol{x}$. Constraints (5.5) are m_1 equality constraints. Two types of inequality constraints includes m_2 type-$\leq$ (5.6) and m_3 type-$\geq$ constraints (5.7). There is a total of $m_1 + m_2 + m_3$ constraints in the above formulation.

To transform the BIP in (5.4)–(5.8) to a QUBO formulation, one seeks to obtain a proper *penalty function* $\Lambda_l(\boldsymbol{x})$ for each constraint $l = 1, 2, \ldots, m_1+m_2+m_3$, which penalizes violation of the constraint. For our purpose of reformulation, $\Lambda_l(\boldsymbol{x})$ is required to be quadratic. The resulting QUBO model can be written as:

$$\text{Minimize} \quad \mathbf{c}^{\mathrm{T}}\boldsymbol{x} + \sum_{l=1}^{m_1+m_2+m_3} \Lambda_l(\boldsymbol{x}) \tag{5.9}$$

As shown in Section 5.1, (5.9) can be represented in the $\boldsymbol{x}^{\mathrm{T}}\boldsymbol{Q}\boldsymbol{x}$ form once all the penalty functions are given.

5.2.2 *Reformulation of Constraints with Known Penalties*

For some special types of constraints, the penalty functions are known and can be used directly to transform a constrained model to QUBO. Following Glover *et al.* [21], a list of constraints with their corresponding penalty functions are elaborated below. In all the penalty functions, P is a sufficiently large positive scalar.

$x + y \leq 1 \rightarrow P \cdot (xy)$: The original constraint effectively prevents both x and y to be 1, which is equivalent to minimizing the penalty function $P \cdot (xy)$.

$x + y \geq 1 \rightarrow P \cdot (1 - x - y + xy)$: The original constraint requires at least one of x and y to be 1, which can be achieved by minimizing the penalty function $P \cdot (1 - x - y + xy)$.

$x + y = 1 \rightarrow P \cdot (1 - x - y + 2xy)$: The original constraint requires exactly one of x and y to be 1, which can be achieved by minimizing $P \cdot (1 - x - y + 2xy)$.

$x \leq y \rightarrow P \cdot (x - xy)$: The original constraint prevents the solution $x = 1$, $y = 0$, which is equivalent to minimizing $P \cdot (x - xy)$.

$x = y \rightarrow P \cdot (x + y - 2xy)$: The original constraint requires x and y to be equal to each others (being either 0 or 1), which can be achieved by minimizing $P \cdot (x + y - 2xy)$.

$x_1 + x_2 + x_3 \leq 1 \rightarrow P \cdot (x_1x_2 + x_1x_3 + x_2x_3)$: The original constraint prevents more than one of x_1, x_2 and x_3 to be 1, which is equivalent to minimizing $P \cdot (x_1x_2 + x_1x_3 + x_2x_3)$.

Remark 5.1. Keeping the penalty function to be zero is a sufficient and necessary condition for the corresponding original constraint to be satisfied.

Remark 5.2. The choice of the penalty scalar P is not unique. A penalty value that is too large can distort the information about the original objective function, making it difficult to find an optimal solution; while a penalty value that is too small can lead to an infeasible solution. A proper choice of P may vary by problem, and by constraints in the same problem. Domain knowledge about the problem at hand is often helpful to tune the value. As a rule of thumb, setting P between 75% to 150% of an estimate of the original objective value is often a good starting point [21].

Example 5.3. Transform the following BIP to a QUBO formulation.

$$\text{Minimize} \quad 2x_1 + 5x_2 + 3x_3 + 6x_4$$

Subject to:

$$x_1 + x_3 \leq 1$$
$$x_1 + x_4 \geq 1$$
$$x_2 \geq x_3$$
$$x_1, x_2, x_3, x_4 \in \{0, 1\}$$

All the three constraints have known penalty functions which can be directly applied as follows:

$$x_1 + x_3 \leq 1 \rightarrow P \cdot (x_1 x_3)$$
$$x_1 + x_4 \geq 1 \rightarrow P \cdot (1 - x_1 - x_4 + x_1 x_4)$$
$$x_2 \geq x_3 \rightarrow P \cdot (x_3 - x_2 x_3)$$

Then the objective function in the $\boldsymbol{x}^{\mathrm{T}}\boldsymbol{Q}\boldsymbol{x}$ formulation can be written as:

$$\begin{aligned} \text{Minimize} \quad & 2x_1 + 5x_2 + 3x_3 + 6x_4 + P \cdot x_1 x_3 \\ & + P \cdot (1 - x_1 - x_4 + x_1 x_4) + P \cdot (x_3 - x_2 x_3) \end{aligned}$$

A straightforward upper bound of the objective function value in the original BIP is 16. Taking 75% of the upper bound yields 12 for the penalty scalar P. Thus the objective function of the $\boldsymbol{x}^{\mathrm{T}}\boldsymbol{Q}\boldsymbol{x}$ formulation becomes:

$$\begin{aligned} \text{Minimize} \quad & 12 - 10x_1 + 5x_2 + 15x_3 - 6x_4 + 12 \cdot x_1 x_3 \\ & + 12x_1 x_4 - 12x_2 x_3 \end{aligned}$$

Dropping the constant of 12, the corresponding $\boldsymbol{x}^{\mathrm{T}}\boldsymbol{Q}\boldsymbol{x}$ can be written as:

$$[x_1 \; x_2 \; x_3 \; x_4] \begin{bmatrix} -10 & 0 & 12 & 12 \\ 0 & 5 & -12 & 0 \\ 0 & 0 & 15 & 0 \\ 0 & 0 & 0 & -6 \end{bmatrix} \begin{bmatrix} x_1 \\ x_2 \\ x_3 \\ x_4 \end{bmatrix}$$

Solving it yields an optimal solution $x_1 = 1$ and $x_2 = x_3 = x_4 = 0$ with an objective value of -10. Adding it with the constant of 12 yields 2, which is the optimum objective value of the original problem.

5.2.3 *Reformulation of General BIPs*

While it is convenient to use the known penalty functions for QUBO reformulation, constraints involved in many combinatorial optimization problems and real world applications do not have known penalty functions, which would require a general reformulation approach.

Consider a *standard* BIP with n binary decision variables and m equality constraints as described as follows.

$$\text{Minimize} \quad \sum_{j=1}^{n} c_j x_j \tag{5.10}$$

Subject to:

$$\sum_{j=1}^{n} a_{ij} x_j = b_i, \quad \forall i = 1, 2, \ldots, m \tag{5.11}$$

Its QUBO equivalent can be obtained by penalizing the squared violation of constraint (5.11) in the objective function. Specifically,

$$\text{Minimize} \quad \sum_{j=1}^{n} c_j x_j + P \cdot \sum_{i=1}^{m} \left(b_i - \sum_{j=1}^{n} a_{ij} x_j \right)^2 \tag{5.12}$$

Example 5.4 (Set Partitioning Problem). Consider an instance of the set partitioning problem introduced in Section 3.2.4. Given a set of items $S = \{1, 2, 3, 4\}$ and a set $\bar{S}$ of subsets of S: $\{1, 3\}$, $\{2, 3, 4\}$, $\{2, 4\}$, $\{1\}$, $\{3, 4\}\}$, one partitions all the items in S using the minimum number of subsets in $\bar{S}$, so that an element belongs to exactly one subset. Define $x_i = 1$ if the ith subset in $\bar{S}$ is selected and 0 otherwise. An explicit BIP formulation can be written as follows.

$$\text{Minimize} \quad x_1 + x_2 + x_3 + x_4 + x_5 \tag{5.13}$$

Subject to:

$$x_1 + x_4 = 1 \tag{5.14}$$

$$x_2 + x_3 = 1 \tag{5.15}$$

$$x_1 + x_2 + x_5 = 1 \tag{5.16}$$

$$x_2 + x_3 + x_5 = 1 \tag{5.17}$$

$$x_i \in \{0, 1\}, \quad \forall i = 1, 2, \ldots, 5 \tag{5.18}$$

Constraints (5.14) and (5.15) have known penalty functions, while Constraints (5.16) and (5.17) do not but can use the general penalty function in (5.12). The QUBO equivalent formulation can be written as:

$$\begin{aligned}\text{Minimize} \quad & x_1 + x_2 + x_3 + x_4 + x_5 + P \cdot (1 - x_1 - x_4 + 2x_1x_4) \\ & + P \cdot (1 - x_2 - x_3 + 2x_2x_3) + P \cdot (1 - x_1 - x_2 - x_5)^2 \\ & + P \cdot (1 - x_2 - x_3 - x_5)^2 \end{aligned} \tag{5.19}$$

Assuming $P = 5$ and arranging terms, (5.19) becomes:

$$\begin{aligned}\text{Minimize} \quad & 20 - 9x_1^2 - 14x_2^2 - 9x_3^2 - 4x_4^2 - 9x_5^2 + 10x_1x_2 \\ & + 10x_1x_5 + 10x_1x_4 + 20x_2x_3 + 20x_2x_5 + 10x_3x_5 \end{aligned} \tag{5.20}$$

Dropping the constant of 20, the corresponding $\boldsymbol{x}^{\mathrm{T}}\boldsymbol{Q}\boldsymbol{x}$ of (5.20) can be written as:

$$[x_1 \; x_2 \; x_3 \; x_4 \; x_5] \begin{bmatrix} -9 & 10 & 0 & 10 & 10 \\ 0 & -14 & 20 & 0 & 20 \\ 0 & 0 & -9 & 0 & 10 \\ 0 & 0 & 0 & -4 & 0 \\ 0 & 0 & 0 & 0 & -9 \end{bmatrix} \begin{bmatrix} x_1 \\ x_2 \\ x_3 \\ x_4 \\ x_5 \end{bmatrix}$$

Solving it yields the solution $x_1 = x_3 = 1$ and $x_2 = x_4 = x_5 = 0$, with an minimum objective of -18.[b] Adding the constant of 20 yields 2, which is the optimum objective value of the original problem.

Now consider the following BIP with inequality constraints, assuming a_{ij} and b_i are all integers.

$$\text{Minimize} \quad \sum_{j=1}^{n} c_j x_j \tag{5.21}$$

Subject to:

$$\sum_{j=1}^{n} a_{ij} x_j \leq b_i, \quad \forall i = 1, 2, \ldots, m \tag{5.22}$$

The inequality constraints (5.22) can be converted to equality constraints by adding slack variables $s_i \in Z^+$ for $i = 1, 2, \ldots, m$, which leads to:

$$\sum_{j=1}^{n} a_{ij} x_j + s_i = b_i, \quad \forall i = 1, 2, \ldots, m \tag{5.23}$$

An obvious upper bound for s_i is b_i. Then the binary number system can be used to represent s_i as a function of new binary decision variables.

The similar approach can be applied for a BIP model with $\geq$-type inequality constraints as shown below:

$$\text{Minimize} \quad \sum_{j=1}^{n} c_j x_j \tag{5.24}$$

Subject to:

$$\sum_{j=1}^{n} a_{ij} x_j \geq b_i, \quad \forall i = 1, 2, \ldots, m \tag{5.25}$$

The inequality constraints (5.25) can be converted to equality constraints by subtracting slack variables $s_i \in Z^+$ for $i = 1, 2, \ldots, m$,

[b]An alternative optimal solution to the problem is: $x_2 = x_4 = 1$ and $x_1 = x_3 = x_5 = 0$.

which leads to:

$$\sum_{j=1}^{n} a_{ij}x_j - s_i = b_i, \quad \forall i = 1, 2, \ldots, m \tag{5.26}$$

Example 5.5 (Multi-Knapsack Problem). A hiker is packing her backpack for an upcoming adventure. She considers the following list of five items with different utility values, weights, and space requirements. The backpack has a maximum weight limit of 10 and a maximum space limit of 20. Which items should the hiker include in her backpack to maximize the total utility value?

Item	Value	Weight	Space Requirement
1	3	3	6
2	4	4	8
3	5	3	7
4	4	2	9
5	3	4	6

Compared to the Knapsack Problem in Example 3.4, this problem has more than one-type of capacity constraint to satisfy, which is called the multi-knapsack problem. Define $x_i = 1$ if item i is selected and 0 o.w. for $i = 1, 2, \ldots, 5$. An explicit BIP formulation can be written as:

$$\text{Maximize} \quad 3x_1 + 4x_2 + 5x_3 + 4x_4 + 3x_5$$

Subject to:

$$3x_1 + 4x_2 + 3x_3 + 2x_4 + 4x_5 \leq 10$$

$$6x_1 + 8x_2 + 7x_3 + 9x_4 + 6x_5 \leq 20$$

$$x_i \in \{0,\ 1\}$$

Adding two integer slack variables s_1 and s_2 to the two inequality constraints yields:

$$3x_1 + 4x_2 + 3x_3 + 2x_4 + 4x_5 + s_1 = 10$$

$$6x_1 + 8x_2 + 7x_3 + 9x_4 + 6x_5 + s_2 = 20$$

Obvious upper bounds for s_1 and s_2 are 10 and 20, respectively. However, better (tighter) better bounds can be obtained. For the first equality constraint, observe that at least two items can be selected without violating the original constraint, and the least left-hand-side value with two items selected is 5, thus a better upper bound for s_1 is 5; In a similar way for the second equality constraint, a better upper bound of 8 can be obtained for s_2. Therefore we have: $s_1 \leq 5$ and $s_2 \leq 8$. We now introduce new binary decision variables $x_6, x_7, \ldots, x_{12}$ to express s_1 and s_2, using the binary number system:

$$s_1 = 1x_6 + 2x_7 + 4x_8$$
$$s_2 = 1x_9 + 2x_{10} + 4x_{11} + 8x_{12}$$

Written in the standard BIP in (5.10) and (5.11), the original formulation becomes:

$$\text{Maximize} \quad 3x_1 + 4x_2 + 5x_3 + 4x_4 + 3x_5$$

Subject to:

$$3x_1 + 4x_2 + 3x_3 + 2x_4 + 4x_5 + 1x_6 + 2x_7 + 4x_8 = 10$$
$$6x_1 + 8x_2 + 7x_3 + 9x_4 + 6x_5 + 1x_9 + 2x_{10}$$
$$+ 4x_{11} + 8x_{12} = 20$$
$$x_i \in \{0, 1\}$$

Using (5.12), the $\boldsymbol{x}^{\mathrm{T}}\boldsymbol{Q}\boldsymbol{x}$ equivalent is:

$$\begin{aligned} \text{Maximize} \quad & 3x_1 + 4x_2 + 5x_3 + 4x_4 + 3x_5 - P \cdot (10 - 3x_1 - 4x_2 \\ & - 3x_3 - 2x_4 - 4x_5 - 1x_6 - 2x_7 - 4x_8)^2 \\ & - P \cdot (20 - 6x_1 - 8x_2 - 7x_3 - 9x_4 - 6x_5 - 1x_9 \\ & - 2x_{10} - 4x_{11} - 8x_{12})^2 \end{aligned}$$

Note that since the objective is maximization, the penalty terms should be subtracted from the original objective function. Setting $P = 10$ and arranging terms generate the following $\boldsymbol{Q}$ matrix:

$$\begin{bmatrix} 2533 & -1200 & -1020 & -1200 & -960 & -60 & -120 & -240 & -120 & -240 & -480 & -960 \\ 0 & 3204 & -1360 & -1600 & -1280 & -80 & -160 & -320 & -160 & -320 & -640 & -1280 \\ 0 & 0 & 2825 & -1380 & -1080 & -60 & -120 & -240 & -140 & -280 & -560 & -1120 \\ 0 & 0 & 0 & 3144 & -1240 & -40 & -80 & -160 & -180 & -360 & -720 & -1440 \\ 0 & 0 & 0 & 0 & 2683 & -80 & -160 & -320 & -120 & -240 & -480 & -960 \\ 0 & 0 & 0 & 0 & 0 & 190 & -40 & -80 & 0 & 0 & 0 & 0 \\ 0 & 0 & 0 & 0 & 0 & 0 & 360 & -160 & 0 & 0 & 0 & 0 \\ 0 & 0 & 0 & 0 & 0 & 0 & 0 & 640 & 0 & 0 & 0 & 0 \\ 0 & 0 & 0 & 0 & 0 & 0 & 0 & 0 & 390 & -40 & -80 & -160 \\ 0 & 0 & 0 & 0 & 0 & 0 & 0 & 0 & 0 & 760 & -160 & -320 \\ 0 & 0 & 0 & 0 & 0 & 0 & 0 & 0 & 0 & 0 & 1440 & -640 \\ 0 & 0 & 0 & 0 & 0 & 0 & 0 & 0 & 0 & 0 & 0 & 2560 \end{bmatrix}$$

Solving it yields the solution $x_1 = x_3 = x_5 = 1$, $x_2 = x_4 = 0$, with an objective value of 5011. Subtracting the constant of 5000 yields 11, which is the optimum objective value for the original problem.

5.3 QUBO for Supply Chain Applications

In this section, we show how to apply the QUBO approach for some well-known supply chain applications. For each application, we present its algebraic formulation and the equivalent QUBO reformulation followed by a numerical example.

5.3.1 *Shortest Path Problem*

Consider a network $G(N, A)$ consisting of a set N of nodes and a set A of arcs. The node set N consists of a source node s, a destination node t, and n intermediary nodes. Each arc $(i, j) \in A$ has a constant distance d_{ij}. The shortest path problem finds a path from s to t with the minimum distance. Using its NETFORM introduced in Section 4.5.3, a BIP formulation for the shortest path problem can be written as follows:

Decision Variables

$x_{ij} = 1$ if arc (i, j) is on the shortest path; and 0 otherwise

Objective Function

$$\text{Minimize} \sum_{(i,j)\in A} d_{ij} x_{ij} \tag{5.27}$$

Subject to:

$$\sum_{j:(s,j)\in A} x_{s,j} = 1, \tag{5.28}$$

$$-\sum_{j:(i,t)\in A} x_{i,t} = -1, \tag{5.29}$$

$$\sum_{j:(i,j)\in A} x_{ij} - \sum_{j:(j,i)\in A} x_{ji} = 0, \quad \forall i \in V \backslash \{s,t\} \tag{5.30}$$

$$x_{ij} \in \{0,1\}, \tag{5.31}$$

Since this formulation contains only equality constraints, one may use (5.12) to reformulate it to QUBO, which leads to:

$$\begin{aligned}\text{Minimize} \quad & \sum_{(i,j)\in A} d_{ij}x_{ij} \\ & + P\cdot\left(1-\sum_{j:(s,j)\in A} x_{s,j}\right)^2 + P\cdot\left(1-\sum_{j:(i,t)\in A} x_{i,t}\right)^2 \\ & + P\cdot\sum_{i\in V\backslash\{s,t\}}\left(\sum_{j:(i,j)\in A} x_{ij} - \sum_{j:(j,i)\in A} x_{ji}\right)^2 \end{aligned} \tag{5.32}$$

Example 5.6 (Shortest Path Problem). Consider the following network consisting of nine nodes with Node 1 and Node 9 being the source and destination node, respectively.

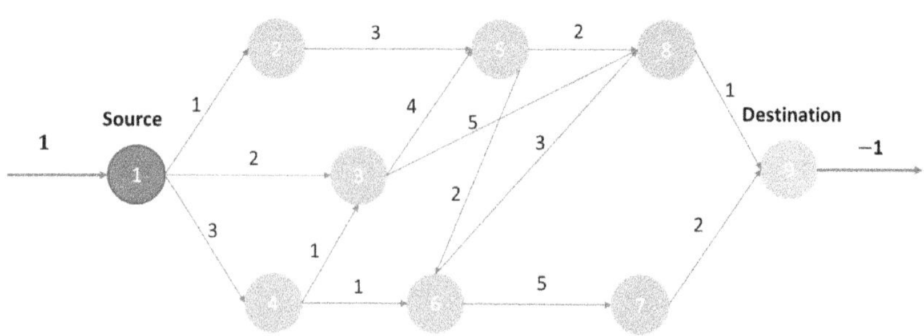

An extended BIP formulation of (5.27)–(5.30) for this instance can be written as:

$$\begin{aligned}\text{Minimize}\quad & 1x_{12} + 2x_{13} + 3x_{14} + 3x_{25} + 4x_{35} + 5x_{38} + 1x_{43} + 1x_{46}\\ & + 2x_{56} + 2x_{58} + 5x_{67} + 3x_{68} + 2x_{79} + 1x_{89}\end{aligned}$$

Subject to:

$$x_{12} + x_{13} + x_{14} = 1$$

$$-x_{79} - x_{89} = -1$$

$$x_{25} - x_{12} = 0$$

$$x_{35} + x_{38} - x_{13} - x_{43} = 0$$

$$x_{43} + x_{46} - x_{14} = 0$$

$$x_{56} + x_{58} - x_{25} - x_{35} = 0$$

$$x_{67} + x_{68} - x_{46} - x_{56} = 0$$

$$x_{79} - x_{67} = 0$$

$$x_{89} - x_{38} - x_{58} - x_{68} = 0$$

Using (5.12) and choosing P to be 10, one obtains the following $\boldsymbol{x}^{\mathrm{T}}\boldsymbol{Q}\boldsymbol{x}$ equivalent with the $\boldsymbol{Q}$ matrix as follows:

$$\begin{bmatrix}
1 & 10 & 10 & -10 & 0 & 0 & 0 & 0 & 0 & 0 & 0 & 0 & 0 & 0\\
10 & 2 & 10 & 0 & -10 & -10 & 10 & 0 & 0 & 0 & 0 & 0 & 0 & 0\\
10 & 10 & 3 & 0 & 0 & 0 & -10 & -10 & 0 & 0 & 0 & 0 & 0 & 0\\
-10 & 0 & 0 & 23 & 10 & 0 & 0 & 0 & -10 & -10 & 0 & 0 & 0 & 0\\
0 & -10 & 0 & 10 & 24 & 10 & -10 & 0 & -10 & -10 & 0 & 0 & 0 & 0\\
0 & -10 & 0 & 0 & 10 & 25 & -10 & 0 & 0 & 10 & 0 & 10 & 0 & -10\\
0 & 10 & -10 & 0 & -10 & -10 & 21 & 10 & 0 & 0 & 0 & 0 & 0 & 0\\
0 & 0 & -10 & 0 & 0 & 0 & 10 & 21 & 10 & 0 & -10 & -10 & 0 & 0\\
0 & 0 & 0 & -10 & -10 & 0 & 0 & 10 & 22 & 10 & -10 & -10 & 0 & 0\\
0 & 0 & 0 & -10 & -10 & 10 & 0 & 0 & 10 & 22 & 0 & 10 & 0 & -10\\
0 & 0 & 0 & 0 & 0 & 0 & 0 & -10 & -10 & 0 & 25 & 10 & -10 & 0\\
0 & 0 & 0 & 0 & 0 & 10 & 0 & -10 & -10 & 10 & 10 & 23 & 0 & -10\\
0 & 0 & 0 & 0 & 0 & 0 & 0 & 0 & 0 & 0 & -10 & 0 & 2 & 10\\
0 & 0 & 0 & 0 & 0 & -10 & 0 & 0 & 0 & -10 & 0 & -10 & 10 & 1
\end{bmatrix}$$

Solving it yields the solution: $x_{12} = x_{25} = x_{58} = x_{89} = 1$, and all the other decision variables are zero, with the objective value of −83. Adding the constant of 90 yields the optimum objective of 7 for the original problem.

5.3.2 *Uncapacitated FLP*[c]

Consider a set I of candidate locations to build facilities to meet the demand at a set J of customers. Each customer must be served by one facility. A facility can serve a customer only if it is selected. A facility $i \in I$, if selected, incurs a fixed cost of f_i. The cost for facility $i \in I$ to serve customer $j \in J$ is c_{ij}. The objective of the uncapacitated facility location problem (UFLP) is to minimize the total operational costs consisting of the total fixed cost and the total cost of serving all customers. A BIP formulation for this problem can be written as:

Decision Variables

$y_i = 1$ if facility is located at site $i \in I$; and 0, otherwise
$x_{ij} = 1$ if customer $j \in J$ is served by facility $i \in I$; and 0, otherwise

Objective Function

$$\text{Minimize} \quad \sum_{i\in I} f_i y_i + \sum_{i\in I}\sum_{j\in J} c_{ij}x_{ij} \tag{5.33}$$

Subject to:

$$\sum_{i\in I} x_{ij} = 1, \quad \forall j \in J \tag{5.34}$$

$$x_{ij} \le y_i, \quad \forall i \in I, j \in J \tag{5.35}$$

$$x_{ij}, \quad y_i \in \{0,1\} \tag{5.36}$$

Observe that (5.34) is an equality constraint, for which (5.12) can be applied for the reformulation. Constraint (5.35) has known penalty

[c]The uncapacitated facility location problem will be covered with more detail in Section 7.2.2.

function as shown in Section 5.2.2. Thus the QUBO formulation for the UFLP can be written as:

$$\text{Minimize} \quad \sum_{i\in I} f_i y_i + \sum_{i\in I}\sum_{j\in J} c_{ij}x_{ij} + P\cdot\sum_{j\in J}\left(1-\sum_{i\in I} x_{ij}\right)^2 + P\cdot\sum_{i\in I}\sum_{j\in J}(x_{ij}-x_{ij}y_i) \tag{5.37}$$

Example 5.7 (UFLP). Consider three candidate facilities to serve four customer locations. The fixed operating costs of facilities and the costs of facilities serving customer locations are provided in the following table (in $ thousand).

Facility	Fixed Cost	Customer 1	Customer 2	Customer 3	Customer 4
1	100	35	40	60	60
2	125	40	55	50	60
3	125	40	30	45	50

The extended BIP formulation of (5.33)–(5.35) for this instance can be written as:

$$\begin{aligned}\text{Minimize} \quad & 100y_1 + 125y_2 + 125y_3 + 35x_{11} + 40x_{12} + 60x_{13} \\ & + 60x_{14} + 40x_{21} + 55x_{22} + 50x_{23} + 60x_{24} + 40x_{31} \\ & + 30x_{32} + 45x_{33} + 50x_{34}\end{aligned}$$

Subject to:

$$\begin{aligned} x_{11} + x_{21} + x_{31} &= 1 \\ x_{12} + x_{22} + x_{32} &= 1 \\ x_{13} + x_{23} + x_{33} &= 1 \\ x_{14} + x_{24} + x_{34} &= 1 \\ x_{11} &\le y_1 \\ x_{12} &\le y_1 \end{aligned}$$

$$x_{13} \leq y_1$$

$$x_{14} \leq y_1$$

$$x_{21} \leq y_2$$

$$x_{22} \leq y_2$$

$$x_{23} \leq y_2$$

$$x_{24} \leq y_2$$

$$x_{31} \leq y_3$$

$$x_{32} \leq y_3$$

$$x_{33} \leq y_3$$

$$x_{34} \leq y_3$$

Applying (5.37) and choosing P to be 250, the $\boldsymbol{x}^{\mathrm{T}}\boldsymbol{Q}\boldsymbol{x}$ formulation for this instance has the following $\boldsymbol{Q}$ matrix:

$$\begin{bmatrix}
100 & 0 & 0 & -250 & -250 & -250 & -250 & 0 & 0 & 0 & 0 & 0 & 0 & 0 & \\
0 & 125 & 0 & 0 & 0 & 0 & 0 & -250 & -250 & -250 & -250 & 0 & 0 & 0 & 0 \\
0 & 0 & 125 & 0 & 0 & 0 & 0 & 0 & 0 & 0 & 0 & -250 & -250 & -250 & -250 \\
0 & 0 & 0 & 35 & 0 & 0 & 0 & 500 & 0 & 0 & 0 & 500 & 0 & 0 & 0 \\
0 & 0 & 0 & 0 & 40 & 0 & 0 & 0 & 500 & 0 & 0 & 0 & 500 & 0 & 0 \\
0 & 0 & 0 & 0 & 0 & 60 & 0 & 0 & 0 & 500 & 0 & 0 & 0 & 500 & 0 \\
0 & 0 & 0 & 0 & 0 & 0 & 60 & 0 & 0 & 0 & 500 & 0 & 0 & 0 & 500 \\
0 & 0 & 0 & 0 & 0 & 0 & 0 & 40 & 0 & 0 & 0 & 500 & 0 & 0 & 0 \\
0 & 0 & 0 & 0 & 0 & 0 & 0 & 0 & 55 & 0 & 0 & 0 & 500 & 0 & 0 \\
0 & 0 & 0 & 0 & 0 & 0 & 0 & 0 & 0 & 50 & 0 & 0 & 0 & 500 & 0 \\
0 & 0 & 0 & 0 & 0 & 0 & 0 & 0 & 0 & 0 & 60 & 0 & 0 & 0 & 500 \\
0 & 0 & 0 & 0 & 0 & 0 & 0 & 0 & 0 & 0 & 0 & 40 & 0 & 0 & 0 \\
0 & 0 & 0 & 0 & 0 & 0 & 0 & 0 & 0 & 0 & 0 & 0 & 30 & 0 & 0 \\
0 & 0 & 0 & 0 & 0 & 0 & 0 & 0 & 0 & 0 & 0 & 0 & 0 & 45 & 0 \\
0 & 0 & 0 & 0 & 0 & 0 & 0 & 0 & 0 & 0 & 0 & 0 & 0 & 0 & 50
\end{bmatrix}$$

Solving it yields the solution $y_3 = 1$, $x_{31} = x_{32} = x_{33} = x_{34} = 1$, and all the other variables being 0, with an objective value of -710. Adding the constant of 1000, one obtains the optimum objective value of 290 for the original problem.

5.3.3 *Job Assignment Problem*

Consider the problem of assigning a set I of jobs to a set J of machines. Each job is assigned to one machine, and each machine can be assigned with one job. The cost of job $i \in I$ processed by machine $j \in J$ is c_{ij}. The objective is to minimize the total cost of processing all jobs. This is an assignment problem, which can be modeled in NETFORM as shown in Section 4.5.5 with is BIP formulation below.

Decision Variables

$x_{ij} = 1$ if job $i \in I$ is assigned to machine $j \in J$; and 0, otherwise

Objective Function

$$\text{Minimize} \quad \sum_{i\in I}\sum_{j\in J} c_{ij}x_{ij} \tag{5.38}$$

Subject to:

$$\sum_{j\in J} x_{ij} = 1, \quad \forall i \in I, \tag{5.39}$$

$$\sum_{i\in I} x_{ij} = 1, \quad \forall j \in J, \tag{5.40}$$

$$x_{ij} \in \{0,\ 1\} \tag{5.41}$$

Since this formulation contains only equality constraints, the reformulation approach in (5.12) can be directly applied to obtain its QUBO equivalent as shown below:

$$\text{Minimize} \quad \sum_{i\in I}\sum_{j\in J} c_{ij}x_{ij} + P\cdot\sum_{i\in I}\left(1-\sum_{j\in J}x_{ij}\right)^2 + P\cdot\sum_{j\in J}\left(1-\sum_{i\in I}x_{ij}\right)^2 \tag{5.42}$$

Example 5.8 (Job Assignment). A set of thee jobs is assigned to three machines with the processing costs shown in the following table.

Job	Machine 1	Machine 2	Machine 3
1	5	11	7
2	10	7	8
3	12	8	9

The extended BIP formulation of (5.38)–(5.40) for this instance can be written as:

$$\begin{aligned}\text{Minimize}\quad & 5x_{11} + 11x_{12} + 7x_{13} + 10x_{21} + 7x_{22} + 8x_{23} \\ & + 12x_{31} + 8x_{32} + 9x_{33}\end{aligned}$$

Subject to:

$$\begin{aligned}x_{11} + x_{12} + x_{13} &= 1 \\ x_{21} + x_{22} + x_{23} &= 1 \\ x_{31} + x_{32} + x_{33} &= 1 \\ x_{11} + x_{21} + x_{31} &= 1 \\ x_{12} + x_{22} + x_{32} &= 1 \\ x_{13} + x_{23} + x_{33} &= 1\end{aligned}$$

Applying (5.42) and choosing P to be 20, the $\boldsymbol{x}^{\mathrm{T}}\boldsymbol{Q}\boldsymbol{x}$ formulation for this instance has the following $\boldsymbol{Q}$ matrix:

$$\begin{bmatrix} -35 & 40 & 40 & 40 & 0 & 0 & 40 & 0 & 0 \\ 0 & -29 & 40 & 0 & 40 & 0 & 0 & 40 & 0 \\ 0 & 0 & -33 & 0 & 0 & 40 & 0 & 0 & 40 \\ 0 & 0 & 0 & -30 & 40 & 40 & 40 & 0 & 0 \\ 0 & 0 & 0 & 0 & -33 & 40 & 0 & 40 & 0 \\ 0 & 0 & 0 & 0 & 0 & -32 & 0 & 0 & 40 \\ 0 & 0 & 0 & 0 & 0 & 0 & -28 & 40 & 40 \\ 0 & 0 & 0 & 0 & 0 & 0 & 0 & -32 & 40 \\ 0 & 0 & 0 & 0 & 0 & 0 & 0 & 0 & -31 \end{bmatrix}$$

Solving it yields the solution $x_{11} = x_{22} = x_{33} = 1$, and all the other variables being 0, with an objective of -99. Adding the constant of

120, one obtains the optimum objective value of 21 for the original problem.

5.3.4 *Crew Scheduling Problem*

A typical crew scheduling problem considers a set S of crews who serve a set J of flight legs. The set of flight legs that can be served by crew $s \in S$ is denoted by J_s, which is a subset of J, i.e., $J_s \subseteq J$. Each crew $s \in S$ has an operating cost c_s. The objective is to select crews with minimum total operating cost, so that each flight leg must be served by at least one crew.

The above crew scheduling problem can be modeled as a set covering problem introduced in Section 3.2.2 with its BIP formulation as follows:

Decision Variables

$x_s = 1$ if crew $s \in S$ is selected; and 0, otherwise

Objective Function

$$\text{Minimize} \quad \sum_{s \in S} c_s x_s \tag{5.43}$$

Subject to:

$$\sum_{s \in S: j \in J_s} x_s \geq 1, \quad \forall j \in J, \tag{5.44}$$

$$x_s \in \{0, 1\} \tag{5.45}$$

This formulation contains $\geq$ constraints, which would generally require subtracting slack variables on the left-hand-side as shown in (5.26). For special cases where only two decision variables appear on the left-hand-side, known penalty functions are available.

Example 5.9 (Crew Scheduling). ABC Airline is scheduling its five crews to serve six flight legs. The set of flight legs that can be covered each crew and the crew operating cost (in $ thousand) are provided in the following table. An entry of 1 indicates that the corresponding flight leg can be covered by the corresponding crew. For instance, Crew 1 is able to cover Flight Legs 1, 4 and 6. Due to efficiency considerations, the airline would like to operate no more than three crews.

Flight Legs	**Crew 1**	**Crew 2**	**Crew 3**	**Crew 4**	**Crew 5**
1	1			1	
2		1	1		
3			1	1	1
4	1	1		1	
5		1			1
6	1		1		
Operating Cost	2	4	4	3	2

Following the BIP in (5.43)–(5.44), and adding a side constraint limiting the maximum number of crew selected, the extended formulation for this instance can written as:

$$\text{Minimize} \quad 2x_1 + 4x_2 + 4x_3 + 3x_4 + 2x_5$$

Subject to:

$$x_1 + x_4 \geq 1 \tag{5.46}$$

$$x_2 + x_3 \geq 1 \tag{5.47}$$

$$x_3 + x_4 + x_5 \geq 1 \tag{5.48}$$

$$x_1 + x_2 + x_4 \geq 1 \tag{5.49}$$

$$x_2 + x_5 \geq 1 \tag{5.50}$$

$$x_1 + x_3 \geq 1 \tag{5.51}$$

$$x_1 + x_2 + x_3 + x_4 + x_5 \leq 3 \tag{5.52}$$

Note that Constraints (5.46), (5.47), (5.50) and (5.51) all have known penalty functions in Section 5.2.2.

For (5.48) and (5.49) with $\geq$ constraints, we convert them to equality constraints by subtracting slack variables as in (5.26). Thus

(5.48) and (5.49) become:

$$\begin{aligned} x_3 + x_4 + x_5 - s_1 &= 1 \\ x_1 + x_2 \quad + x_4 \quad - s_2 &= 1 \end{aligned}$$

where s_1, $s_2 \in Z^+$ and $s_1 \leq 2$, $s_2 \leq 2$. Then s_1 and s_2 can be expressed as functions of new binary decision variables x_6, x_7, x_8 and x_9: $s_1 = x_6 + 2x_7$, $s_2 = x_8 + 2x_9$.

For (5.52) with a $\leq$ constraint, we convert it to an equality constraint by adding one slack variable as in (5.23). Thus (5.52) becomes:

$$x_1 + x_2 + x_3 + x_4 + x_5 + s_3 = 3$$

where $s_3 \in Z^+$ and $s_3 \leq 3$. Then s_3 can be expressed as a function of new binary decision variables x_{10} and x_{11}: $s_3 = x_{10} + 2x_{11}$.

With all the above reformulation recipes, the QUBO formulation for this instance can be written as:

$$\begin{aligned} \text{Minimize} \quad & 2x_1 + 4x_2 + 4x_3 + 3x_4 + 2x_5 + P \cdot (1 - x_1 - x_4 + x_1x_4) \\ & + P \cdot (1 - x_2 - x_3 + x_2x_3) + P \cdot (1 - x_2 - x_5 + x_2x_5) \\ & + P \cdot (1 - x_1 - x_3 + x_1x_3) + P \cdot (1 - x_3 - x_4 - x_5 \\ & + x_6 + 2x_7)^2 + P \cdot (1 - x_1 - x_2 - x_4 + x_8 + 2x_9)^2 \\ & + P \cdot (3 - x_1 - x_2 - x_3 - x_4 - x_5 - x_{10} - 2x_{11})^2 \end{aligned}$$

Choosing P to be 10, the $\boldsymbol{Q}$ matrix can be obtained as below:

$$\begin{bmatrix} -78 & 40 & 30 & 50 & 20 & 0 & 0 & -20 & -40 & 20 & 40 \\ 0 & -76 & 30 & 40 & 30 & 0 & 0 & -20 & -40 & 20 & 40 \\ 0 & 0 & -76 & 40 & 40 & -20 & -40 & 0 & 0 & 20 & 40 \\ 0 & 0 & 0 & -77 & 40 & -20 & -40 & -20 & -40 & 20 & 40 \\ 0 & 0 & 0 & 0 & -68 & -20 & -40 & 0 & 0 & 20 & 40 \\ 0 & 0 & 0 & 0 & 0 & 30 & 40 & 0 & 0 & 0 & 0 \\ 0 & 0 & 0 & 0 & 0 & 0 & 80 & 0 & 0 & 0 & 0 \\ 0 & 0 & 0 & 0 & 0 & 0 & 0 & 30 & 40 & 0 & 0 \\ 0 & 0 & 0 & 0 & 0 & 0 & 0 & 0 & 80 & 0 & 0 \\ 0 & 0 & 0 & 0 & 0 & 0 & 0 & 0 & 0 & -50 & 40 \\ 0 & 0 & 0 & 0 & 0 & 0 & 0 & 0 & 0 & 0 & -80 \end{bmatrix}$$

Solving it yields the solution $x_1 = x_2 = x_5 = x_8 = 1$, and all the other variables being zero, with an objective value of -142. Adding the constant of 150 obtains the objective value of 8, which is the optimum for the original problem.

5.4 Additional Notes

A systematic treatment on the theory, algorithms, and applications of QUBO is available in [22]. We refer to [21] for an up-to-date tutorial on the QUBO approach, which includes a comprehensive list of QUBO applications for various combinatorial optimization problems. Notable recent applications of QUBO using quantum annealing include deep space network scheduling [23], job shop scheduling [24], supply chain network design [25], and machine learning [26], among others.

Exercises

5.1. Write a QUBO formulation for the following BIP.

$$\text{Minimize} \quad 2x_1 + 3x_2 + 5x_3 + 4x_4 + 2x_5$$

Subject to:

$$x_1 + x_5 \leq 1$$

$$x_3 + x_4 \geq 1$$

$$x_3 \geq x_5$$

$$x_4 = x_5$$

$$x_1,\ x_2,\ x_3,\ x_4,\ x_5 \in \{0,\ 1\}$$

5.2. Write a QUBO formulation for the following BIP.

$$\text{Maximize} \quad 4x_1 + 3x_2 + 6x_3 + 4x_4$$

Subject to:

$$2x_1 + 3x_2 + 3x_3 + 2x_4 \leq 6$$

$$3x_2 + 4x_2 + 2x_3 + 3x_4 \geq 4$$

$$x_1 + 2x_2 + x_3 + x_4 = 3$$

$$x_1, x_2, x_3, x_4 \in \{0,\ 1\}$$

5.3. Number Partitioning Problem. Given a set of numbers 20, 8, 12, 28, 40, 15, 19, 10}, partition it into two subsets such that the subset sums are as close to each other as possible. Write a QUBO formulation and solve it to obtain your solution.

5.4. Max-Cut Problem. Consider the following undirected graph with six vertices and eight edges. Partition the six vertices into two subsets such that the number of edges between the two subsets, i.e., the edges severed by the cut, is as large as possible. Write a QUBO formulation and solve it to obtain your solution.

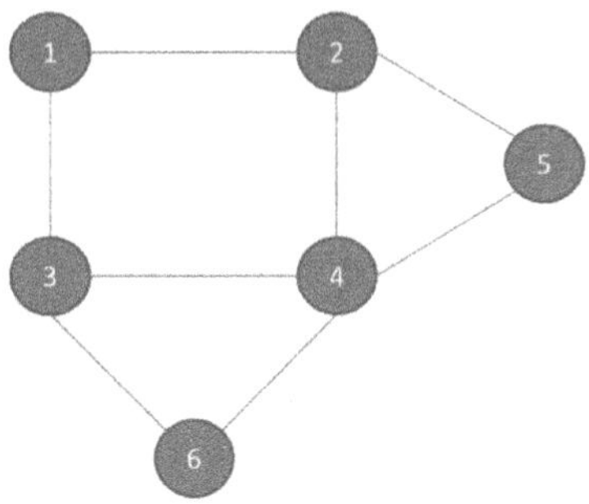

5.5. Max 2-SAT Problem. The satisfiability (SAT) problem originated in the computer science and AI fields. It seeks to assign values to binary *literals* (true or false) so that as many *clauses*, expressed as functions of literals, as possible are satisfied. The notation $\bar{x}$ denotes the complement of x, which equals $1 - x$. In a two-SAT problem, each clause consists of two literals and it is satisfied if at least one of the two literals is true. For instance, $x \vee y$ reads "x or y" which is satisfied if either x or y or both are true. Write a QUBO formulation for the following 2-SAT problem with seven clauses, solve it to find your solution.

$$x_1 \vee x_2$$
$$x_1 \vee \bar{x}_2$$
$$\bar{x}_1 \vee \bar{x}_2$$
$$x_2 \vee \bar{x}_3$$
$$x_2 \vee x_4$$
$$x_3 \vee x_4$$
$$\bar{x}_2 \vee \bar{x}_4$$

5.6. Project Selection. Reconsider Exercise 3.6 and reformulate its BIP formulation as a QUBO model. Then solve it to find your solution.

5.7. Critical Path Problem. ABC Manufacturer is planning for its equipment installation project. A list of activities and their predecessors are provided in the following table. The project manager needs to estimate the project makespan, i.e., how long it will take to complete all the activities, which can be addressed by finding a critical path of the project. Build a BIP model to find a critical (longest) path of the project. Reformulate the BIP as a QUBO model and solve it to find your solution.

Activity	Description	Immediate Predecessors	Duration (Weeks)
A	Procure parts and components	–	2
B	Modify roof and floor layout	–	4
C	Construct foundation platform	A	3
D	Install framework and pour concrete	A, B	4
E	Build high-capacity burner	C	5
F	Install hazard material control device	C	3
G	Install air pollution control system	D, E	5
H	Inspect and test	F, G	3

5.8. Facility Layout. ABC Warehousing would like to redesign its layout to improve operational efficiency. It has three categories of stock keeping units (SKUs): home appliances, electronics, and hardware to be positioned in three areas in the warehouse, so that the total operating cost is minimized. Due to the nature of the SKUs and the complementary demand among them, there is more traffic between certain categories of SKUs than others. For instance, customers who need appliances often need hardware, thus there is often more traffic between the location of appliances and the location of hardware. In general, the operating cost between a SKU of type i in location k and SKU of type j in location l is a function of the traffic f_{ij} between SKU i and j and the distance d_{kl} between location k and l. The f_{ij} between all pairs of SKU types and d_{kl} between all pairs of locations are provided below.

Traffic Frequency	**Home Appliances**	**Electronics**	**Hardware**
Home Appliances	0	2	4
Electronics	2	0	3
Hardware	4	3	0

Distance (meters)	**Area 1**	**Area 2**	**Area 3**
Area 1	0	50	150
Area 2	50	0	100
Area 3	150	100	0

Build a BIP model for ABC Warehouse's facility layout problem. Reformulate it as a QUBO model and solve it to find your solution.

Chapter 6

Constraint Programming

6.1 Introduction to Constraint Programming

Eugene C. Freuder wrote in his 1997 paper published in Constraints: *Constraint programming represents one of the closest approaches computer science has yet made to the Holy Grail of programming: the user states the problem, the computer solves it.* Dr. Freuder's exceptional advocacy for constraint programming (CP) motivated its numerous applications in optimization during the past two decades.

Different from mathematical programming, CP originated from Logic Programming in Computer Science and Artificial Intelligence (AI) for solving the so-called constraint satisfaction (SAT) problem. The SAT problem aims to find a feasible solution that satisfies a system of constraints, without the need to seek optima. A distinctive feature of CP is its expressive and declarative nature that facilitates model building. The formulation of a CP model is often intuitive to understand. With some special constructs available in a CP modeling tool such as ILOG OPL Studio, one can use CP to model certain complex optimization problems with significantly fewer decision variables and constraints than possible using mathematical programming.

Example 6.1 (A First CP Example). Each of the following letters represents a number between 0 and 9. Find an assignment of numerical values to the letters to satisfy the equation expressed by the following riddle: SEND + MORE = MONEY. The CP model for solving this riddle can be written as below:

$$1{,}000S + 100E + 10N + D + 1{,}000M + 100O + 10R + E$$
$$= 10{,}000M + 1{,}000O + 100N + 10E + Y,$$

where $S, M \in \{1, 2, \ldots, 9\}$, and $E, N, D, O, R, Y \in \{0, 1, \ldots, 9\}$. This algebraic equation is obtained by explicitly converting the verbal riddle into an arithmetic equation, which demonstrates the intuitive and expressive nature of CP. Note that since S and M appear in the first digit of the character number, they cannot be zero. One solution for the riddle is:

$$S = 0,\ E = 0,\ N = 0,\ D = 0,\ M = 1,\ O = 0,\ R = 0,\ Y = 0.$$

There are two solution techniques in CP: *constraint propagation* and *search*. Constraint propagation, also called domain reduction, seeks to reduce the domains of decision variables. The term "propagation" refers to the mechanism that operates when the domain of one decision variable is modified (reduced) to cause the domain of all variables related to the decision variable through the constraints to be modified (reduced).

Ideally, one would like to reduce the domain of each decision variable to a singleton, i.e., leaving only one value in the reduced domain, which would mean that the problem is solved. However, reducing a domain to a singleton is often computationally intractable, and consequently a search procedure is needed to obtain a solution. Constraint propagation and search are further explained in Appendix 4.

6.2 CP for Constraint Satisfaction Problems

A Constraint Satisfaction Problem (CSP), which may be addressed either by CP or mathematical programming, seeks a feasible solution to a system of constraints. We show two examples in this section to demonstrate the declarative nature of CP for conveniently representing certain CSPs that can be non-intuitive for mathematical programming to model.

Example 6.2 (The N-Queens Problem). How can one place n queens in an $n \times n$ chess board, such that no pair of queens are able to attack each other? (According to the rule of chess, a queen may

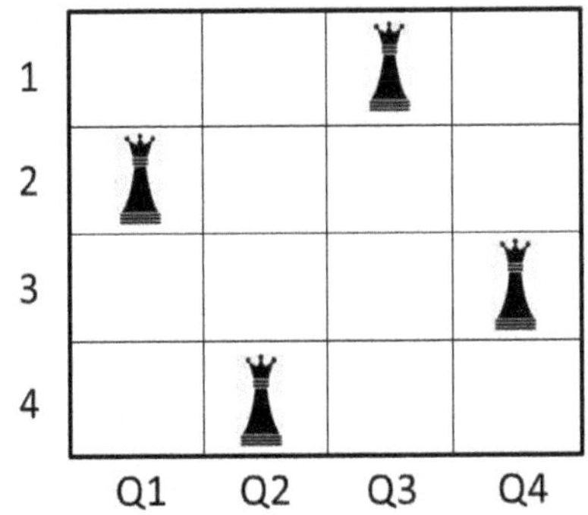

Figure 6.1. An N-Queens problem in 4 × 4 chess board.

attack any piece that lies in the same row, column, or diagonal. A feasible solution in a 4×4 chess board is shown in Figure 6.1, where the four queens are properly placed and no two may attack each other.

To present a CP model for the N-Queens problem on a general $n \times n$ board, define $c_1, c_2, \ldots, c_n$ to be the row positions where a queen is placed for each column $1, 2, \ldots, n$. In the example above, for instance, $c_2 = 4$ as the queen in column 2 is placed in row 4. The domain of each decision variable is $\{1, 2, \ldots, n\}$. Note that defining the decision variables in this way automatically guarantees that no pair of queens are placed in the same column (since each column has exactly the c_i variable associated with it). Then we need three constraints to be satisfied for $i \in \{1, 2, \ldots, n-1\}$ and $j \in \{i+1, i+2, \ldots, n\}$

(i) $c_i \neq c_j$: no two queens are placed in the same row;
(ii) $c_i \neq c_j + j - i$: no two queens are placed in the SW-NE diagonal;
(iii) $c_i \neq c_j + i - j$: no two queens are placed in the NW-SE diagonal.

Example 6.3 (The Magic Series Problem). A magic series is defined as a sequence of n integers $x_0, x_1, \ldots, x_{n-1}$, where x_i equals the number of occurrences of i in the sequence. For example, the sequence of numbers: {2, 1, 2, 0, 0} is a magic series for $n = 5$. To find such series for an arbitrary value of n, we formulate it as a CP model. The following constraint must be satisfied for x_i with $i = 0, 1, \ldots, n-1$:

$$x_i = \sum_{i=0}^{n-1} (x_i \doteq i) \tag{6.1}$$

Note that $x \doteq a$ is treated as a logical constraint that is checked to determine if x equals a. It returns 1 if so, and 0 otherwise. The LHS of the constraint counts the occurrence of x_i equaling i, and ensures that x_i equals the total number of occurrences, i.e., the requirement of magic series.

The constraint employed in this CP model is known as a *high-order constraint*, in that it embeds another constraint inside it. While this way of formulating a constraint is natural in CP, making the model extremely compact, it is not a convention available in mathematical programming.

6.3 CP for Scheduling Problems

Although CP was originally employed mainly for solving CSPs, it proves to be effective and efficient for certain types of optimization problems, especially scheduling problems widely studied in operations research and supply chains. Our coverage in this section will focus on using CP to model some classical scheduling problems.

A fundamental aspect of most scheduling problems is the temporal (time) relationships among activities (or tasks and jobs in certain settings). For example, drilling must precede fabrication: building a wall cannot start until foundation work is done; lab testing must come before clinical trial; debugging can only start at least two weeks after the start of GUI development.

An activity has three main attributes: start time, its duration (processing time) and finish time, all of which can be used to model temporal relationships. We shall focus on the use of a *start-start* approach to model the relationship between the start times of a pair of activities. Let the start time, duration and finish time of activity i be denoted by S_i, p_i and F_i, respectively. Without loss of generality, assume that the minimum time lag between activities i and j is δ_{ij}, i.e., activity j can only start *at least* δ_{ij} time units after i starts. Mathematically, the constraint for satisfying this can be written as:

$$S_j \geq S_i + \delta_{ij}. \tag{6.2}$$

Figure 6.2 shows three cases of using minimum time lag between the start-start of a pair of activities.

Case 1: $\delta_{ij} < p_i$. Activity j may start before j finishes.

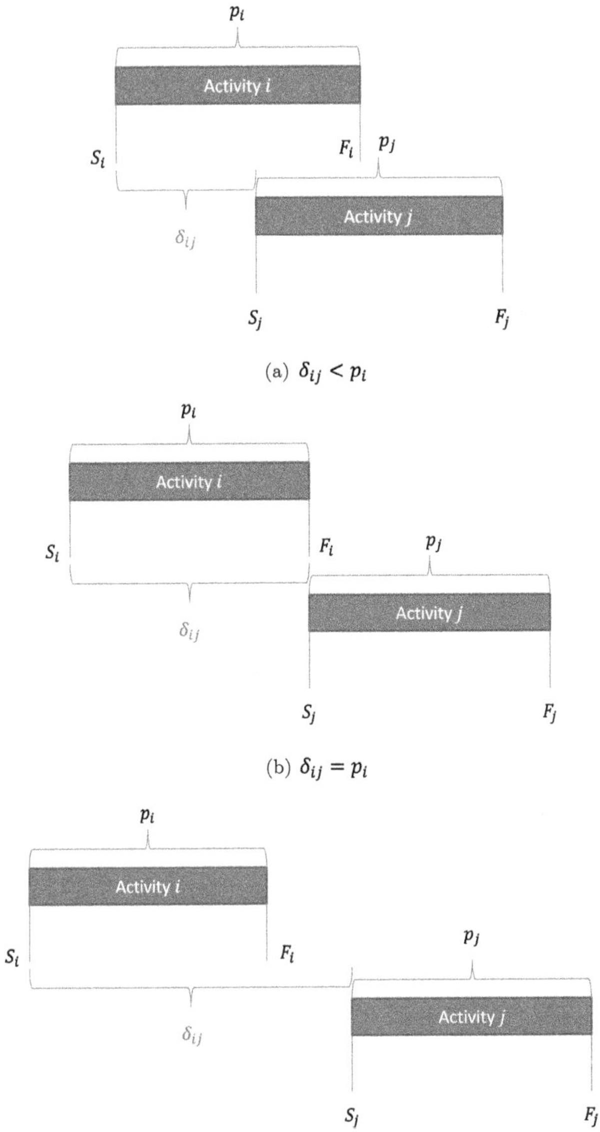

(a) $\delta_{ij} < p_i$

(b) $\delta_{ij} = p_i$

(c) $\delta_{ij} > p_i$

Figure 6.2. Three cases of minimum time lag relationship.

Case 2: $\delta_{ij} = p_i$. The constraint (6.2) becomes:

$$S_j \geq S_i + p_i. \tag{6.3}$$

In this case, the minimum time lag constraint reduces to the special case of precedence constraint, i.e., activity j can only start after i finishes, which may (or may not) be at the finish time F_i of i.

Case 3: $\delta_{ij} > p_i$. Now activity j cannot start before or at the finish time of i.

6.3.1 *Just-In-Time Scheduling*

A set of activities are to be completed. There are temporal/precedence relationships among the activities due to technical requirements that must be satisfied. A just-in-time (JIT) performance metric stipulates that either early completion or tardiness (lateness) will incur a certain penalty cost. The goal is to find a feasible schedule, in terms of activity start times, that minimizes the total penalty cost of completing all activities.

Example 6.4 (Construction Project Scheduling). ABC Construction is working on a house building project. Starting an activity too early will put pressure on the supply of materials, while finishing an activity too late will delay the project makespan, thus both earliness and lateness will be penalized. The company would like to find a feasible schedule for the project to minimize the total earliness-tardiness costs. Detailed information of the 10 tasks is provided in Table 6.1.

An activity-on-node (AON) network for the project is depicted below, where each node represents a task, and each arc denotes a precedence relationship between a pair of nodes.

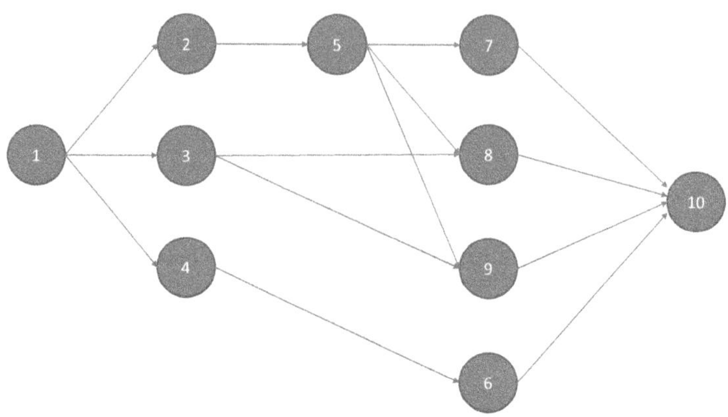

Table 6.1. Project information at ABC Construction.

Index	Task	Duration (in days)	Predecessors	Earliest start	Due date	$/day of earliness	$/day of lateness
1	Foundation	35		25		200	
2	Utility	15	1	75		300	
3	Plumbing	40	1				
4	Ceiling	15	1	75		100	
5	Roofing	5	2				
6	Painting	10	4				
7	Windows	5	5				
8	Garage	10	3, 5				
9	Interior	5	3, 5				
10	Inspection	5	6, 7, 8, 9		100		400

An LP model for this problem can be written as.

Sets and parameters

V: set of activities
E: set of precedence relationships
p_i: duration of activity $i \in V$
a_i: earliest start time of activity $i \in V$
d_i: latest finish time (due date) of activity $i \in V$
e_i: cost per time unit of starting activity $i \in V$ earlier than its earliest start time a_i
l_i: cost per time unit of finishing activity $i \in V$ later than its due date time d_i

Decision variables

$t_i \geq 0$: the start time of activity $i \in V$
$E_i \geq 0$: amount of earliness for starting activity $i \in V$
$L_i \geq 0$: amount of lateness for finishing activity $i \in V$

Objective function

$$\text{Minimize} \sum_{i \in V} (e_i E_i + l_i L_i) \tag{6.4}$$

Constraints

$$t_j \geq t_i + p_i, \ \forall (i,j) \in E, \tag{6.5}$$

$$L_i \geq t_i + p_i - d_i, \ \forall i \in V, \tag{6.6}$$

$$E_i \geq e_i - t_i, \ \forall i \in V, \tag{6.7}$$

$$t_i, E_i, L_i \geq 0 \tag{6.8}$$

The objective function (6.4) minimizes the total earliness-tardiness of all activities. Constraint (6.5) satisfies the precedence relationship between a pair of activities $(i, j) \in E$, i.e., activity j can only start after activity i is finished. Constraint (6.6) computes the tardiness (lateness) of finishing activity i. Note that when $t_i + p_i - d_i < 0$, ativity i is not late, and since $L_i \geq 0$, it will be assured to be zero in the minimization objective function; when $t_i+p_i-d_i \geq 0$, the amount of lateness is $t_i + p_i - d_i$, which L_i will equal due to minimization.

A similar argument applies for Constraint (6.7): when $e_i \leq t_i$, E_i will equal zero; and when $e_i \geq t_i$, E_i will equal $e_i - t_i$.

CP provides a convenient way to compute the earliness-tardiness of an activity using the function $\max\{a, b\}$, which takes the larger of the values a and b. Thus, the earliness of starting activity i is $\max\{e_i - t_i, 0\}$, and lateness of finishing i is $\max\{t_i + p_i - d_i, 0\}$. The resulting CP model can be written as below.

$$\text{Minimize} \sum_{i \in V} (e_i \max\{e_i - t_i, 0\} + l_i \max\{t_i + p_i - d_i, 0\}) \quad (6.9)$$

Subject to:

$$\text{Activity } i \, precedes \text{ Activity } j, \ \forall (i,j) \in E, \quad (6.10)$$

Compared to the LP model, the CP model is clearly more compact due to its expressive and intuitive way of formulating the objective function and constraints.

An optimal solution to Example 6.4 is shown in the following Gantt chart of Figure 6.3 with a minimum total cost of 5,000.

6.3.2 *Job Shop Scheduling*

A job shop is a multi-stage production system where each stage operates one machine. A job may be restricted to being processed on a specified subset of machines in a specific order. One machine can only operate on one job at any time. The objective is to minimize the makespan, i.e., the completion time of all the jobs. Compared to other machine scheduling settings, e.g., parallel machine, flow shop, etc., job shop scheduling has the advantage of flexibility, and thus is suitable for a low volume and high variety production environment. Examples of job shop scheduling include wafer fabrication in

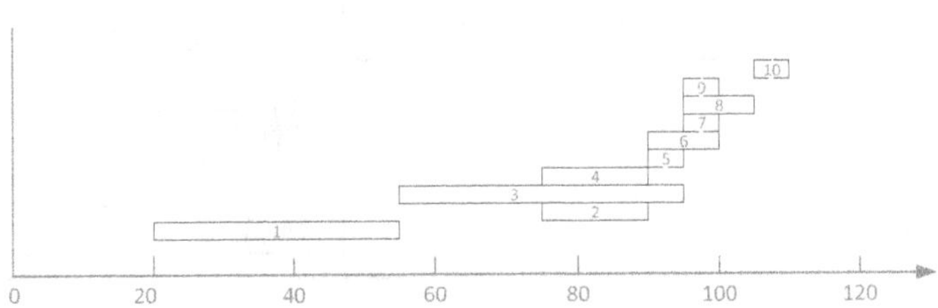

Figure 6.3. Gantt chart of optimal solution to Example 6.4.

the semiconductor industry, patient service at a hospital, and service scheduling in a typical car repair shop. A systematic treatment of machine scheduling problems is provided in Chapter 11.

Example 6.5 (Job Shop Scheduling). Consider a job shop with three jobs and four machines/operations. Each job requires performing some or all of the four operations in a certain order due to technical requirements:

$$Job\,1\colon M1 \to M2 \to M3$$
$$Job\,2\colon M1 \to M2 \to M4$$
$$Job\,3\colon M2 \to M1 \to M4 \to M3$$

Note that a job shop is flexible enough to process jobs with different operations in different orders. Let (i, j) denote job j processed on machine i. A Gantt chart with each row representing the jobs scheduled on a machine is shown below, with operations of the same job shown in the same shaded pattern. A feasible schedule must satisfy two types of constraints: (i) the precedence constraints among operations of one job; and (ii) no jobs can overlap on one machine. As shown in the Gantt chart of Figure 6.4, jobs processed on the same machine must be properly sequenced.

Let J denote a set of jobs and M denote a set of machines. Also let n_j be the number of operations in job $j \in J$, and let the order of operations $m = 1, 2, \ldots, n_j$ performed on job $j \in J$ be denoted by $O(m, j)$, such that $O(m, j) \to O(m+1, j)$ for $m = 1, 2, \ldots, n_j - 1$. Define $O(m, j)$ to be an activity, where *Makespan* is a dummy

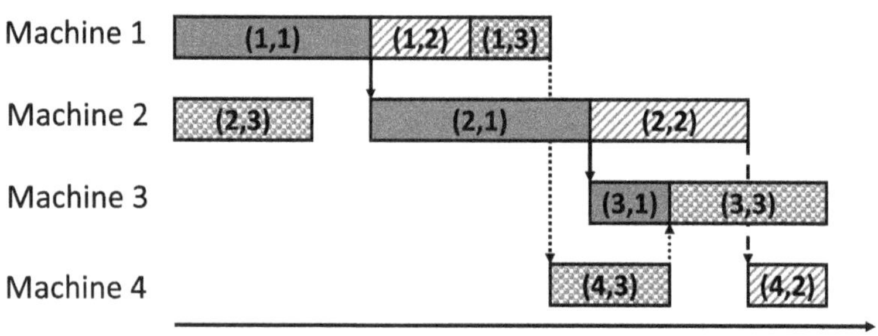

Figure 6.4. Example job shop scheduling problem with three jobs and four machines.

activity. The CP model for the job shop scheduling problem can then be written then:

$$Minimize\ Makespan \tag{6.11}$$

Subject to:

$$\text{Activity } O(m,j) \textit{ precedes } \text{Activity } O(m+1,j),$$
$$\forall j \in J, m = 1, 2, \ldots, n_j - 1 \tag{6.12}$$
$$\text{Activity } O(m,j) \text{ precedes Activity } \textit{Makespan}, \ \forall j \in J, \tag{6.13}$$
$$No\,overlap\,of\,jobs \text{ on Machine } m, \ \forall m \in M, \tag{6.14}$$

Objective function (6.11) minimizes the makespan of completing all jobs. Constraint (6.12) satisfies the precedence constraints over all operations of a job. Constraint (6.13) ensures that the dummy Makespan activity is the last to complete. Constraint (6.14) guarantees that all jobs being processed on the same machine will be properly sequenced, i.e., no overlap of jobs is allowed.

As one can see, the CP model is very expressive and intuitive in accordance with the verbal description of the scheduling problem. As for implementation of the CP formulation, the good news is that there are various modeling languages available for CP. Among them is the OPL Studio introduced in this text. Refer to Appendix 1 for how to use OPL Studio for building and implementing CP models and methods.

6.3.3 *Resource-Constrained Project Scheduling*

A Resource-Constrained Project Scheduling Problem (RCPSP) seeks a time- and resource-feasible schedule of project activities that optimizes certain performance metric, e.g., minimizing project makespan (completion time of all the activities). It is an extension of the classical critical path method (CPM) by explicitly considering limited available resource capacity, in addition to the CPM precedence constraints. The RCPSP includes a rich set of scheduling problems with applications in various industries including manufacturing, construction, professional service and military. A systematic treatment of RCPSPs is provided in Chapter 12 of this text.

A formal description of the single-mode RCPSP follows, where there is only a single execution mode for each activity. Consider a project consisting of a set V of activities and K of *renewable* resources. A resource is *renewable* if its capacity is renewed in every time period of the planning horizon. The processing time of activity j is p_j and preemption is not allowed, i.e., an activity cannot be interrupted once started. Each activity $j \in V$ requires r_{jk} units of resource $k \in K$. Both precedence and resource constraints must be satisfied: (i) activity i must precede activity j for $(i, j) \in E$, where E is the set of all the precedence constraints; and (ii) at each time point of the planning horizon, the total required resource of each type $k \in K$ cannot exceed its available capacity R_k. The goal is to minimize the project makespan.

Example 6.6 (Single-Mode RCPSP). Consider a project consisting of six activities which require one type of renewable resource. Information about the activities including their durations, predecessors and resource requirements is provided in Table 6.2.

Assuming there are 6 units of the resource available, an optimal solution with makespan of 8 is shown in Figure 6.5(a). Note that all the precedence relationships are satisfied, and the total resource requirement in each time period does not exceed 6. When the resource capacity is reduced by 2 to equal 4 as in Figure 6.5(b), the schedule in (a) is no longer feasible, and the new optimal schedule is delayed to yield a makespan of 10.

Now consider two types of resources: 4 units of type — 1 resource and 2 units of type — 2 resource available, with the data in Table 6.3.

Table 6.2. Data for an example of single-mode RCPSP with one resource.

	Duration	Predecessor	Resource requirement
1	2	—	3
2	3	—	1
3	1	—	2
4	4	1, 2	2
5	2	2, 3	3
6	1	4	3

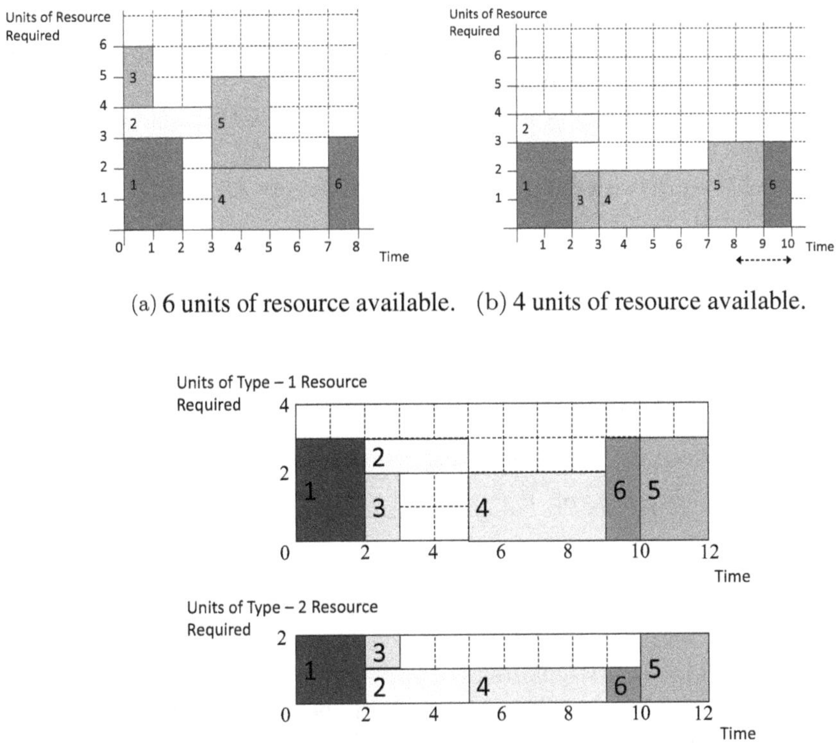

(a) 6 units of resource available. (b) 4 units of resource available.

(c) With two types of resources.

Figure 6.5. Optimal solutions to the single-mode RCPSP examples.

Table 6.3. Data for an example of single-mode RCPSP for two resources.

	Duration	Predecessor	Resource type — 1 requirement	Resource type — 2 requirement
1	2	—	3	2
2	3	—	1	1
3	1	—	2	1
4	4	1, 2	2	1
5	2	2, 3	3	2
6	1	4	3	1

An optimal schedule in this case has a makespan of 12 as shown in Figure 6.5(c). Note how the activity start times change to ensure resource-feasibility for both types of resources.

The main constructs in the CP model for RCPSP ensure: (i) the precedence relationships in the set E; and (ii) the requirement of all types of resources in every time period does not exceed the available resource capacities.

$$Minimize\ Makespan \tag{6.15}$$

Subject to:

$$\text{Activity } i\, \textit{precedes}\, \text{Activity } j,\ \forall (i,j) \in E \tag{6.16}$$

$$\text{Activity } i\, \text{precedes Activity } Makespan,\ \forall i \in V, \tag{6.17}$$

$$\textit{ResourceProfile}\, of\ \text{Resource}\ \leq R_k,\ \forall k \in K, \tag{6.18}$$

Objective function (6.15) minimizes the project makespan. Constraint (6.16) satisfies all precedence constraints. Constraint (6.17) states that all activities must proceed the dummy Makespan activity. Constraint (6.18) ensures that the requirement for each type of resource does not exceed its capacity in each time period. *Resource-Profile* is a CP construct to compute the resource requirement over time for each resource type. Such CP construct is available in the OPL Studio, and is introduced in Appendix 1.

6.4 Additional Notes

The early development of CP in the AI area focused on solving the CSP in the context of logic programming [27, 28]. We refer to [27] for general-purpose constraint propagation techniques and [29, 30] for constraint propagation for scheduling problems. An accessible coverage of various search strategies is available in [31]. More advanced developments in this area address the integration of CP and math programming to take advantage of the complementary strengths of the two [32, 33]. Hybrid MILP-CP algorithms have been successfully applied for scheduling [34–36] and supply chain configuration problems [37].

Exercises

6.1. Use CP in the OPL Studio to solve the following riddle:

```
  D O N A L D
+ G E R A L D
-------------
= R O B E R T
```

6.2. Flow shop scheduling. Consider the following two-machine flow shop with 10 jobs. All jobs have to be processed first on machine 1 and then on machine 2. Let p_{ij} denote the processing time of job j on machine i.

Jobs	**1**	**2**	**3**	**4**	**5**	**6**	**7**	**8**	**9**	**10**	**11**
p_{1j}	3	6	4	3	4	2	7	5	5	6	12
p_{2j}	4	5	5	2	3	3	6	6	4	7	2

Formulate the problem as a CP model to minimize makespan. Use OPL Studio to obtain an optimal solution, and illustrate it via the Gantt chart.

6.3. Job shop scheduling. Consider the following job shop scheduling problem with three jobs and three machines. Here a job may go through the machines in an arbitrary order. For instance, Job 2 starts with Machine 3, then Machine 1 followed by Machine 2. Let p_{ij} denote the processing time of job j on machine i. And the weight, release time (earliest time a job may start), and due date (latest to finish a job) are denoted by w_j, r_j and d_j, respectively.

Jobs	w_j	r_j	d_j	**Machine sequence**	**Processing times**
1	1	3	23	1, 2, 3	$p_{11} = 4$, $p_{21} = 9$, $p_{31} = 5$
2	2	2	17	3, 1, 2	$p_{32} = 4$, $p_{12} = 5$, $p_{22} = 5$
3	2	0	15	3, 2, 1	$p_{33} = 6$, $p_{23} = 4$, $p_{13} = 6$

(a) Formulate a CP model to minimize makespan and use OPL Studio to obtain an optimal solution.
(b) Formulate a CP model to minimize the total weighted lateness and use OPL Studio to find an optimal solution.
(c) Formulate a CP model to minimize the total weighted earliness-tardiness, as in JIT operations, and use OPL Studio to find an optimal solution.
(d) Compare and discuss the differences of the schedules obtained in (a), (b) and (c).

6.4. RCPSP. An AON project network is given below with eight real activities and two dummy activities (Activity 1 and Activity 10).

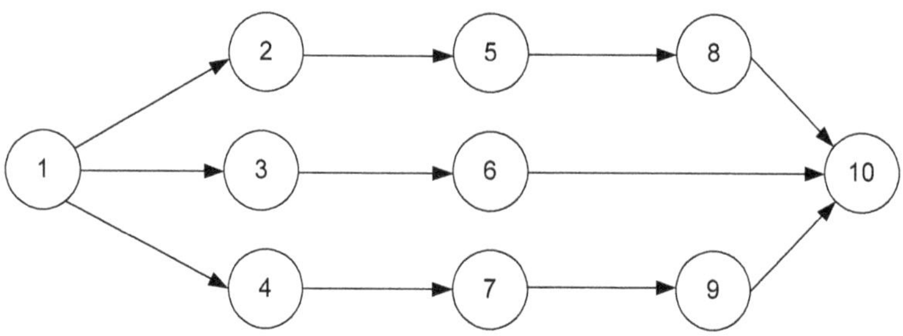

Two types of resource R1 and R2 are needed for conducting the project. R1 has 8 units available, and R2 has 6 units available. The duration and resource requirements of each task are provided below.

Task ID	Duration (days)	Requ. for R1 (units)	Requ. for R2 (units)
1	0	0	0
2	2	2	1
3	4	4	3
4	7	3	2
5	3	4	2
6	6	2	1
7	4	3	2
8	8	3	1
9	2	4	3
10	0	0	0

(a) Formulate a CP model to minimize the project makespan.
(b) What is the optimal schedule for the project (starting times of each activity)? What is the earliest completion time of the project? Show your schedule in a Gantt chart.
(c) What if there is an opportunity to acquire more units of R1 and R2? How do you assess the cost-benefit of such opportunity? Show details of your analysis.

Part II
Supply Chain Applications

Chapter 7

Supply Chain Network Design

7.1 Introduction and Overview

A heavy machine manufacturer sources globally for parts, components and raw materials for its production and sales world-wide. The design of its global supply chain network involves determining the locations for its production plants, warehouses and distribution centers to best support the production and transportation operations.

A retailer is expanding its markets by adding online shopping and e-commerce to its existing brick-and-mortar business. The company needs to determine how many and where to build additional warehouses to efficiently serve its growing population of customers.

A furniture company relies on its inbound logistics network to ship products procured from oversea suppliers to its central warehouse. The company needs to design an efficient logistic network through multiple transportation modes: ocean, barge, train and truck. The design involves the location (selection) of warehouses, ports and transportation modes.

A utility company receives large variety of raw materials, parts and products procured from its suppliers and vendors at its distribution center. It operates a number of warehouses and operating centers to provide customer-centric services: installation, maintenance, repairing and emergency response. An outbound supply service network needs to be properly designed to efficiently distribution/allocate goods to its warehouses and operating centers.

Also, there is opportunity to reduce the number of facilities by consolidating demands at multiple warehouses and operating centers.

A food processor operates a holistic supply chain from farm-gate of fresh grapes to its franchised retailer stores for a variety of grape products: table grapes, raisins and grape juice. Due to perishability nature of fresh grapes, it is crucial to locate processing and packaging facilities close enough to the farm-gate with consideration of potential loss and quality deterioration of fresh grapes.

The above applications share a common theme of decision need for designing a *physical* supply chain network: inbound, outbound or a holistic combination of both. It encompasses a very important strategic-level decision in supply chains that has long-term impact of a company or organization: five to ten years. It typically involves determining the locations of physical facilities for production, packaging, processing, warehousing/storage and distribution, and flow of goods through the network. The objective is often to minimize the total operating cost, which may include, in the most general case, fixed setup/operating cost of facilities, transportation cost of goods, and inventory holding cost of on-hand and safety stock at facilities. The main constraints include: satisfying the exogenous demand at facilities throughout the network, meeting the limited capacities (if any) at certain facilities, and maintaining the flow conservation or flow balancing constraints through the network.

A generic multi-tier supply chain network design problem can be illustrated in Figure 7.1. It consists of four tiers (stages): suppliers, manufacturers, distribution centers and retailers, which are represented by nodes. Possible flow of goods between nodes is indicated by an arc between a pair of nodes. The focal firm can be anywhere in the chain, and is assumed to have a holistic view and control of operations. Nodes with dashed circles indicate those being candidates for which selection decision needs to be determined. For instance, the firm is open to choose from three suppliers S1, S2 and S3 and three distribution centers D1, D2 and D3, but the question is which and how many to select. A node colored in yellow indicates the node has limited capacity (for supply, production or storage) that cannot be exceeded. The triangles at R1 and R2 indicate the need for safety stock to meet the uncertain exogenous demand of goods.

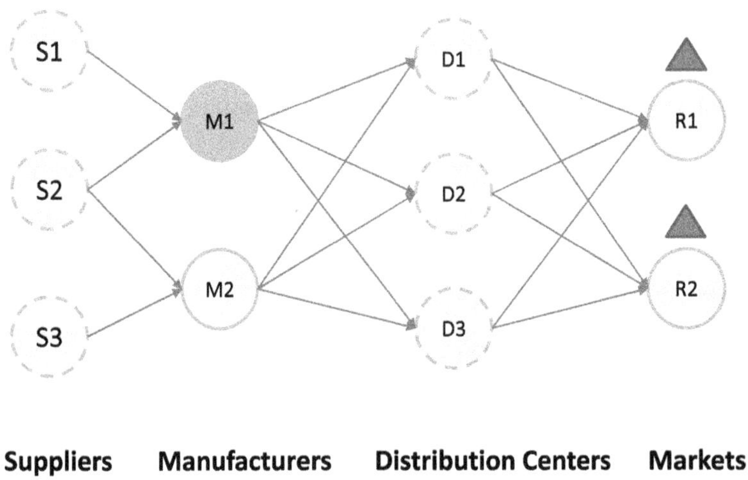

Figure 7.1. A generic multi-tier supply chain network design problem.

One observes that a supply chain network design problem has its underlying feature of a network flow problem as introduced in Chapter 4, with an extension of determining the selection of facilities. The general modeling strategy is to define binary decision variables for the facility location/selection decision, with the big-M formulation to ensure that no flow can be handled at a facility (flowing through the corresponding node) if it is not selected. The flow conservation or flow balancing constraints must also be satisfied as in the NETFORM.

In this chapter, we shall introduce the basic version of supply chain network design problem, with its variants and extensions to address a variety of real life operational settings, e.g., multiple sourcing, multi-product network, multi-modal network, and dynamic network design.

7.2 Facility Location Problems

We start with the simplest version of supply chain design, known as the p-median problem, to lay the foundation for more sophisticated variants.

7.2.1 *p-Median Problem*

In the p-median problem, one places p facilities out of a set I of candidate locations to serve a set J of customers, so that the total distances between facilities and customers weighted by the demand at customer nodes is minimized. Each customer is served by exactly one facility.

Key to Formulation: Binary decision variables are defined for representing the selection of facility locations and assignment of customers to the selected facilities. The objective function minimizes the total cost of serving the customers. A big-M constraint is needed to ensure that a facility cannot serve any customer unless it is selected. A side constraint is added to specify the total number of selected facilities to be p. A BIP formulation for the p-Median problem can be written as below.

Sets and parameters

I: set of candidate facilities
J: set of customers
c_{ij}: distance between facility $i \in I$ and customer $j \in J$
d_j: demand at customer $j \in J$
p: total number of facilities to be placed

Decision variables

$y_i = 1$ if facility is located at site $i \in I$; 0, otherwise
$x_{ij} = 1$ if customer $j \in J$ is served by facility $i \in I$; 0, otherwise

Objective function

$$\text{Minimize} \sum_{i \in I} \sum_{j \in J} d_j c_{ij} x_{ij} \tag{7.1}$$

Subject to:

$$\sum_{i \in I} x_{ij} = 1, \quad \forall j \in J \tag{7.2}$$

$$x_{ij} \leq y_i, \quad \forall i \in I, j \in J \tag{7.3}$$

$$\sum_{i \in I} y_i = p, \tag{7.4}$$

$$x_{ij}, \quad y_i \in \{0, 1\} \tag{7.5}$$

The objective function (7.1) minimizes the total demand-weighted distances for proving services from facilities to customers. Constraint (7.2) assigns a customer to exactly one facility. Constraint (7.3) is the big-M formulation to ensure that a facility can serve a customer only if it is selected. Note that the big-M coefficient of y_i on the right-hand-side of (7.3) is 1, which is the upper bound of x_{ij}. Constraint (7.4) guarantees that a total of p facilities are placed.

7.2.2 *Uncapacitated Facility Location Problem*

While in the p-median problem the number of facilities to locate is exogenously given, many applications require the optimal number of facilities being as part of the network design decision, as in the Uncapacitated Facility Location Problem (UFLP).

One selects among a set I of candidate locations to build facilities to meet the demand at a set J of customers. Each customer $j \in J$ must be served by one facility $i \in I$ (single sourcing). A facility cannot serve any customer if it is not selected. A facility i, if selected, incurs a fixed setup cost of f_i. The cost for facility i to serve customer j is c_{ij}. The objective of UFLP is to minimize the total operational costs, which includes the total fixed cost and the total transportation cost of goods. Note that the main difference between the UFLP and p-median problem is the consideration of fixed setup cost of facility.

Figure 7.2 provides a schematic view of the UFLP with four candidate facility locations (denoted by a square) and fifteen customers (denoted by +) to serve as in Figure 7.2(a). A possible feasible solution is shown in Figure 7.2(b), which selects/opens only three facilities (out of four), with their assigned customers indicated by arrows. Note that with the facility selection decisions fixed, the UFLP reduces to the standard transportation problem (introduced in Section 2.5.3).

Key to Formulation: The model formulation for UFLP is very similar to that of the p-median problem. Here the objective function includes an additional cost term of total fixed setup cost of selected facilities. The constraint requiring a given number of facilities to be selected is no longer needed because the number of facilities can be optimized in the UFLP. A BIP formulation for the UFLP can be written as below.

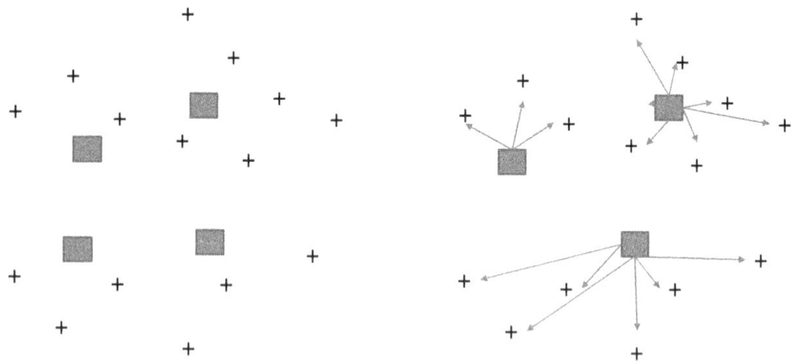

(a) Four candidate locations. (b) Three selected locations.

Figure 7.2. A schematic view of UFLP.

Sets and parameters

I: set of candidate facilities
J: set of customers
f_i: fixed setup cost of facilities $i \in I$
c_{ij}: cost for facility $i \in I$ to serve customer $j \in J$

Decision variables

$y_i = 1$ if facility is located at site $i \in I$; 0, otherwise
$x_{ij} = 1$ if customer $j \in J$ is served by facility $i \in I$; 0, otherwise

Objective function

$$\text{Minimize} \sum_{i \in I} f_i y_i + \sum_{i \in I} \sum_{j \in J} c_{ij} x_{ij} \tag{7.6}$$

Subject to:

$$\sum_{i \in I} x_{ij} = 1, \quad \forall j \in J \tag{7.7}$$

$$x_{ij} \leq y_i, \quad \forall i \in I,\ j \in J \tag{7.8}$$

$$x_{ij}, \quad y_i \in \{0, 1\} \tag{7.9}$$

The objective function (7.6) minimizes the total operational costs consisting of two terms: the total setup cost of all the selected facilities and the total transportation cost of all facility-customer service

Table 7.1. Data for the CFLP example.

Store	New York	Chicago	St. Louis	Atlanta	Memphis
1	20	24	11	26	31
2	27	28	83	84	75
3	73	98	72	97	72
4	5	56	74	70	62
5	47	97	60	84	6
6	43	23	30	68	60
7	4	8	74	60	58
8	12	74	15	45	96
9	94	36	64	86	48
10	48	66	56	72	96

pairs. Constraint (7.7) is an assignment-type constraint that assigns each customer to exactly one facility. Constraint (7.8) ensures that a facility cannot serve any customer unless it is selected.

7.2.3 *Capacitated Facility Location Problem*

A limitation of the UFLP is the assumption that a facility has unlimited capacity. Relaxation of this assumption is achieved by considering the Capacitated Facility Location Problem (CFLP), where each facility $i \in I$ can serve at most k_i customers.

Example 7.1 (CFLP). ABC Inc. is considering constructing new warehouses among the following five candidate cities: New York, Chicago, St. Louis, Atlanta and Memphis. There are ten targeted stores to be served by these warehouses. The fixed setup cost of each warehouse is 30. There is capacity limit for each warehouse: St. Louis can serve 2 store, New York can serve 4, Chicago 3, Memphis 1 and Atlanta 3. The supply cost between a warehouse and a store is provided in Table 7.1.

Key to Formulation: The model formulation for the CFLP is similar to that of the UFLP. A big-M constraint is needed to enforce the capacity of a facility if selected, with the big-M value being the capacity of the corresponding facility. A BIP formulation for the CFLP can be written as below.

Sets and parameters

I: set of candidate facilities
J: set of customers
f_i: fixed setup cost of facilities $i \in I$
c_{ij}: cost for facility $i \in I$ to serve customer $j \in J$
k_i: maximum number of customers that can be served by facility $i \in I$

Decision variables

$y_i = 1$ if facility is located at site $i \in I$; 0, otherwise
$x_{ij} = 1$ if customer $j \in J$ is served by facility $i \in I$; 0, otherwise

Objective function

$$\text{Minimize} \sum_{i \in I} f_i y_i + \sum_{i \in I} \sum_{j \in J} c_{ij} x_{ij} \tag{7.10}$$

Subject to:

$$\sum_{i \in I} x_{ij} = 1, \quad \forall j \in J \tag{7.11}$$

$$x_{ij} \leq y_i, \quad \forall i \in I, j \in J \tag{7.12}$$

$$\sum_{j \in J} x_{ij} \leq k_i y_i, \quad \forall i \in I \tag{7.13}$$

$$x_{ij}, \quad y_i \in \{0, 1\} \tag{7.14}$$

The formulation of CFLP is similar to that of UFLP, with only one additional Constraint (7.13) to guarantee that each selected facility cannot serve more than k_i customers. Constraint (7.13) is a big-M formulation with the large M number taking the value of capacity at a facility. Note that Constraint (7.12) is redundant as it is implied by (7.13). But keeping (7.12) makes the formulation tighter.

7.2.4 *CFLP with Multiple-Sourcing*

Both the introduced UFLP and CFLP assume *single-sourcing*, i.e., a customer/store is served by exactly one facility. While single-sourcing is advantageous to achieve economies of scale, quantity discount and less operational complexity, it does suffer vulnerability of supply risk or disruption due to natural disasters, accidents, among others. A viable strategy in practice for mitigating such risk is to consider multiple-sourcing, which allows the demand d_j at node $j \in J$ to be fulfilled by multiple facilities. Note that in this case, the amount of demand must be explicitly considered.

Key to Formulation: Different from the single-sourcing FLP, the key to formulate the model for the multi-sourcing version is to define a new continuous variable to *allocate* the demand at a customers to multiple suppliers. This leads to an MILP model, which can be written as below.

Sets and parameters

I: set of candidate facilities
J: set of customers
f_i: fixed setup cost of facilities $i \in I$
d_j: units of goods demanded at customer $j \in J$
c_{ij}: cost per unit of goods shipped from facility $i \in I$ to customer $j \in J$
k_i: maximum capacity of units of goods at facility $i \in I$

Decision variables

$y_i = 1$ if facility is located at site $i \in I$; otherwise
$x_{ij} \geq 0$: units of goods shipped from facility $i \in I$ to customer $j \in J$

Objective function

$$\text{Minimize} \sum_{i \in I} f_i y_i + \sum_{i \in I} \sum_{j \in J} c_{ij} x_{ij} \tag{7.15}$$

Subject to:

$$\sum_{i \in I} x_{ij} = d_j, \quad \forall j \in J \tag{7.16}$$

$$\sum_{j \in J} x_{ij} \leq k_i y_i, \quad \forall i \in I \tag{7.17}$$

$$y_i \in \{0, 1\}, \quad x_{ij} \geq 0 \tag{7.18}$$

The objective function (7.15) minimizes the total operational cost consisting of total fixed setup cost and the total shipping cost. Note that c_{ij} represents cost per unit of goods, which is different from its definition in the single-sourcing case. Constraint (7.16) guarantees that the shipping quantity to customer j from all facilities must satisfy the demand d_j. Constraint (7.17) is the big-M formulation to ensure that facility i, if selected, cannot ship more than its capacity k_i to customers.

7.2.5 *Multi-Commodity Facility Location Problem*

Another important variant of the basic FLPs is to address the one with multiple commodities, products or categories of SKUs (stock-keeping-units). This adds another dimension of complexity to the problem to handle the optimal capacity allocation at a facility among multiple commodities. Formally, consider a set I of facilities serving a set J of customers for a set L of commodities. The demand of commodity $l \in L$ at customer $j \in J$ is d_{jl}. The maximum capacity of facility $i \in I$ for all commodities is k_i. The fixed setup cost of facility i is f_i. The shipping cost per unit of commodity l from facility i to customer j is c_{ijl}. Assume multiple-sourcing strategy is used, i.e., each commodity at a customer can be served by multiple facilities.

Key to Formulation: The decision variables need to be expanded with another dimension of products. The assignment-type constraint in the single-sourcing model is replaced by a demand allocation constraint. An MILP formulation for the addressed multi-product FLP can be written as below.

Sets and parameters

I: set of candidate facilities
J: set of customers
L: set of products
f_i: fixed setup cost of facilities $i \in I$
d_{jl}: units of commodity $l \in L$ demanded at customer $j \in J$
c_{ijl}: cost per unit of commodity $l \in L$ shipped from facility $i \in I$ to customer $j \in J$
k_i: maximum capacity of all commodities at facility $i \in I$

Decision variables

$y_i = 1$ if facility is located at site $i \in I$; 0, otherwise
$x_{ijl} \geq 0$: units of commodity $l \in L$ shipped from facility $i \in I$ to customer $j \in J$

Objective function

$$\text{Minimize} \sum_{i\in I} f_i y_i + \sum_{i\in I}\sum_{j\in J}\sum_{l\in L} c_{ijl}x_{ijl} \tag{7.19}$$

Subject to:

$$\sum_{i\in I} x_{ijl} = d_{jl}, \quad \forall j \in J, l \in L \tag{7.20}$$

$$\sum_{j\in J}\sum_{l\in L} x_{ijl} \leq k_i y_i, \quad \forall i \in I \tag{7.21}$$

$$y_i \in \{0,1\}, \quad x_{ijl} \geq 0 \tag{7.22}$$

The objective function (7.19) minimizes the total operational costs consisting of the total fixed setup cost and the total shipping cost of all commodities. Constraint (7.20) satisfies the demand of each commodity at a customer from all the facilities. Constraint (7.21) ensures that the total units of all products shipped out of facility i, if it is selected, does not exceed its capacity k_i.

7.3 Fixed-Charge Network Design

Many planning and optimization applications in transportation, logistics and telecommunication require considering the cost of allowing or setting up flow via an arc, no matter how much the amount of flow through the arc is. This has motivated the study of Fixed-Charge Network Flow Problems (FCNFP). For example, to design a pipeline system between gas fields and delivery locations requires determining optimal pipe diameters by selecting from a discrete set of configurations which varies in their capacity and cost. The design of a switching center network in telecommunication involves determining both the locations of distribution boxes and the selection of arcs (with cost and flow capacity) between the switching centers, distribution boxes and service nodes. A multimodal distribution system design application often involves selecting optimal transportation modes between a pair of facilities, e.g., truck, rail, air or barge, which may incur different setup costs for infrastructure, contract, rent or toll, etc.

Example 7.2 (Pipeline Network Design). A pipeline network is shown in Figure 7.3 with demand locations connected with the gas field. A dashed arc indicates a possible connection between a pair of nodes. Establishing a connection/pipe incurs a fixed setup cost independent from the flow volume on it, which is a function of diameters of the pipe and the depth of water where the pipe is installed. The decision is to find feasible paths of pipelines that connect all the nodes, and flow of gas on the paths to minimize the total setup and distribution costs.

Key to Formulation: The FCNFP is an extension of the network flow problem by considering fixed cost of utilizing an arc, i.e., sending non-zero flow through it. Binary decision variables are defined to indicate whether an arc is utilized. Continuous decision variables are defined to represent the amount of flow through an arc. The flow

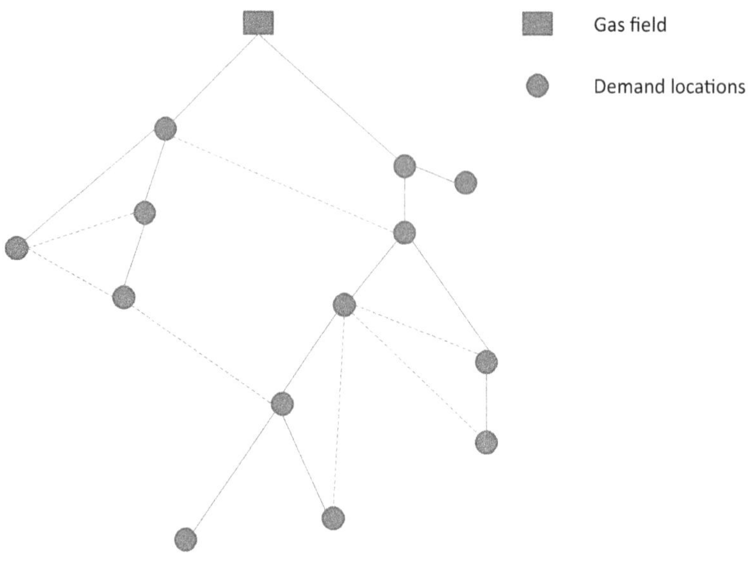

Figure 7.3. An illustrative example of pipeline network.

conservation constraint in a general network flow model also applies. In addition, one needs a big-M constraint to make sure that no flow can be sent through an arc unless the arc is utilized. The resulting MILP formulation for the FCNFP can be written as follows.

Sets and parameters

N: set of nodes
A: set of candidate arcs
d_i: the constant associated node $i \in N$ as in the NETFORM setting.
Specifically, $d_i > 0$ if node i is a supply node, $d_i < 0$ if it is a demand node, and $d_i = 0$ if it is a transshipment node.
u_{ij}: maximum capacity of flow on arc $(i, j) \in A$
s_{ij}: fixed setup cost of arc $(i, j) \in A$
c_{ij}: cost per unit of flow on arc $(i, j) \in A$

Decision variables

$y_{ij} = 1$ if arc $(i, j) \in A$ is selected and 0 o.w.
$x_{ij} \geq 0$: the amount of flow on arc $(i, j) \in A$

Objective function

$$\text{Minimize} \quad \sum_{(i,j)\in A} (s_{ij}y_{ij} + c_{ij}x_{ij}) \tag{7.23}$$

Subject to:

$$\sum_{(i,k)\in A} x_{ik} - \sum_{(k,i)\in A} x_{ki} = d_i, \quad \forall i \in N \tag{7.24}$$

$$x_{ij} \leq u_{ij}y_{ij}, \quad \forall (i, j) \in A \tag{7.25}$$

$$x_{ij} \geq 0, \quad y_{ij} \in \{0, 1\} \tag{7.26}$$

The objective function (7.23) minimizes the total costs consisting of setup cost and transportation cost. Constraint (7.24) is the flow conservation constraint to ensure the total flow out of node i subtracting the total flow into i equals d_i. Constraint (7.25) is the big-M formulation to ensure that no flow can be sent on an arc unless it is selected, with the big-M number being the capacity of the arc.

7.4 Multi-Modal Network Design

A useful extension of the standard network design is to consider multiple transportation modes in a network, e.g., truck, rail, barge, or air. These modes differ in transportation cost, transit time, capacity, and sometimes fixed setup cost. The diagram in Figure 7.4 shows an example of multi-modal network design problem with different colored arcs representing the available modes. For instance, there are three modes available between Node 1 (Supplier) and Node 3 (Manufacturer): barge, rail and truck; whereas there is only truck mode available between Node 4 (Manufacturer) and Node 7 (Distribution Center). The airfreight mode is available between Node 6 (Distribution Center) and Node 9 (Markets), in addition to rail and truck.

Here the network design involves selecting the feasible transportation mode(s) of all the arcs, and determining the amount of flow through them to minimize the total transportation cost. Note that due to limited capacity of a transportation mode, multiple modes can be chosen for an arc.

Key to Formulation: The multi-modal network design problem can be viewed as a generalization of the FCNFP by considering multiple

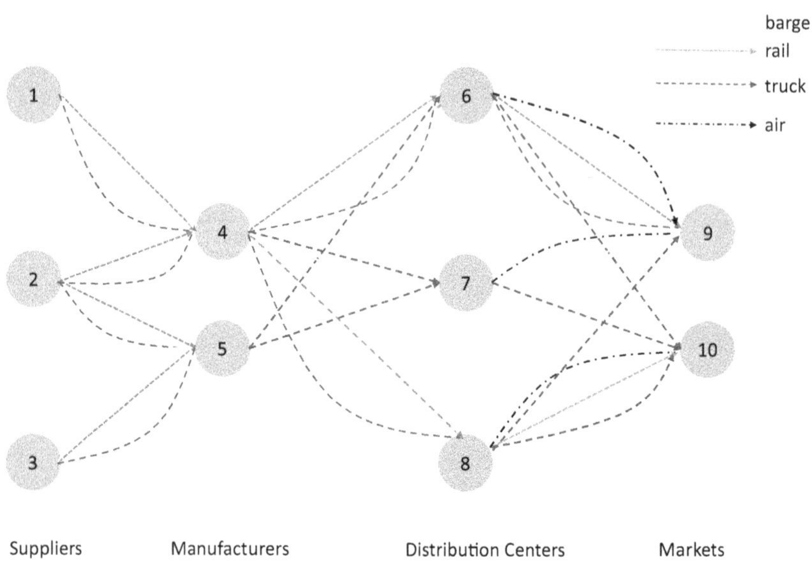

Figure 7.4. An illustrative example of multi-modal network design.

modes (ways) to connect between a pair of nodes. Its formulation is similar to that of FCNFP, except that the decision variables need to be expanded to cover an additional dimension of transportation modes. Its MILP formulation can be written as below.

Sets and parameters

N: set of nodes
A: set of candidate arcs
M_{ij}: set of available modes for arc $(i,j) \in A$
d_i: the constant associated node $i \in N$ as in the NETFORM setting. Specifically, $d_i > 0$ if node i is a supply node, $d_i < 0$ if it is a demand node, and $d_i = 0$ if it is a transshipment node.
s_{ij}^m: fixed setup cost of selecting mode $m \in M_{ij}$ on arc $(i,j) \in A$
c_{ij}^m: cost per unit of flow via mode $m \in M_{ij}$ on arc $(i,j) \in A$
u_{ij}^m: maximum capacity of flow via mode $m \in M_{ij}$ on arc $(i,j) \in A$

Decision variables

$y_{ij}^m = 1$ if mode $m \in M_{ij}$ is selected for arc $(i,j) \in A$, and 0 o.w.
$x_{ij}^m \geq 0$: the amount of flow via mode $m \in M_{ij}$ on arc $(i,j) \in A$

Objective function

$$\text{Minimize} \quad \sum_{(i,j)\in A} \sum_{m \in M_{ij}} (s_{ij}^m y_{ij}^m + c_{ij}^m x_{ij}^m) \tag{7.27}$$

Subject to:

$$\sum_{(i,k)\in A} \sum_{m \in M_{ij}} x_{ik}^m - \sum_{(k,i)\in A} \sum_{m \in M_{ij}} x_{ki}^m = d_i, \quad \forall i \in N \tag{7.28}$$

$$x_{ij}^m \leq u_{ij}^m y_{ij}^m, \quad \forall (i,j) \in A, m \in M_{ij} \tag{7.29}$$

$$x_{ij}^m \geq 0, \quad y_{ij}^m \in \{0, 1\} \tag{7.30}$$

Objective function (7.27) minimizes the total costs consisting of fixed setup cost and transportation cost. Constraint (7.28) satisfies the supply ($d_i > 0$), demand ($d_i < 0$) or flow conservation ($d_i = 0$) of node i. Constraint (7.29) is the big-M formulation to ensure that no flow can be sent via a mode on an arc, if the mode is not selected on the arc. The formulation is similar to that of FCNFP with added complexity of multiple modes on an arc.

7.5 Dynamic Network Design

The network design problems and models we have shown so far are *static*, in the sense that they all address the one-time structure of a network. It applies for most scenarios where network design is a strategic decision that has long-term impact. In the decision environment of more tactical nature, however, firms may opt to operate in a more flexible way by addressing a *dynamic* (multi-period) network design problem, where the structure of supply chain network may evolve over time. For instance, a grain distributor's logistic network may be flexible to cope with the seasonality of yields and market demands. Instead of operating its own facilities, it may rely on renting warehouses and partnering with processors to enable more frequent facility selection decisions for flexible logistic operations. Next consider a furniture retailer who contracts with overseas manufacturers and suppliers, ships the products to its domestic distribution centers, then retail stores. To take advantage of the low cost of barge transportation, it may consolidate shipment during certain periods of a year to save the total logistic costs.

To address the above decision needs calls for a *time-spatial network*, with nodes being associated with both geographical location and time, and arcs between nodes in the same time period or to nodes in a future time period. The time-spatial network has been widely applied in various logistics and scheduling applications, e.g., managing a cash distribution network by a national bank, configuring a two-way street transportation network by a city-planner, fleet and flight scheduling, emergency response in humanitarian logistics, car and truck rental, train routing and scheduling, and convoy movement in military. Below we present two representative applications of time-spatial network with illustrative examples and model formulations.

7.5.1 *FLP with Time-Spatial Network*

Let $N = \{1, 2, \ldots, n\}$ denote a set of spatial locations, and $T = \{1, 2, \ldots, t\}$ denote a set of time periods. A directed network $G(V, A)$ can be defined with V being a set of nodes associated a spatial location and a time period, and A representing a set of arcs between nodes in the same period or different periods. A node is a 2-tuple element

(i, r) in the set $V = \{(i, r) \,|i \in N, r \in T\}$. Thus, an arc is a 4-tuple element in $A = \{(i, r, j, s) \,|i, j \in N : i \neq j \text{ or } r, s \in T : r \neq s\}$. Typically, we assume $s \geq r$, i.e., flow is only allowed in the same time period or to the future periods. However, one may allow $s < r$ in some special circumstance, e.g., to model the backorder operation as shown in Section 4.7. The fixed operating cost at a facility node $(i, r) \in \bar{V} \subset V$ is s_{ir}, where $\bar{V}$ is a subset of V which can be either in operation or not. As in a NETFORM, the supply, demand or constant of zero at node $(i, r) \in V$ is generically denoted by d_{ir}, such that $d_{ir} > 0$ means supply, $d_{ir} < 0$ indicates demand, and $d_{ir} = 0$ implies the corresponding node is a transshipment node where the flow conservation assumption holds. The variable shipping cost per unit of goods on arc $(i, r, j, s) \in A$ is c_{ir}^{js}. The Facility Location Problem in a Time-Spatial Network, which we call FLP-TSN, aims to select a feasible set of facilities and determine the feasible flow of goods through the network that minimizes the total operational costs.

Example 7.3 (Grain Distribution). ABC Grain operates its production and distribution network in North America with two growing regions (P1 and P2), three warehouses (W1, W2 and W3), and four wholesalers (H1, H2, H3 and H4). Because of seasonality of yield (supply) at each grow region, it may need all three warehouses during the production season, but fewer during other times to save the fixed warehouse operating cost. The company maintains good partner relationship with third-party warehousing providers to make its operations and change of grain flows less costly. As conceptually shown in Figure 7.5, dashed circles denote facilities that can be selected to open or not, and arrows colored in brown (to avoid additional complexity, we only show these going out of W1 from time period 1 to 2) indicate inventory carried over time periods. Note that the inventory at W1 can be carried within W1 if W1 is still in operation in the next time period, or transshipped to other warehouses if W1 is not in operation in the next period. The grain production and distribution network design for ABC Grain involves selecting the set of warehouses and determine the grain flow plan to minimize the total operational costs.

Key to Formulation: The FLP-TSN is a generalization of the FLP by considering a multi-stage network with the time dimension, i.e.,

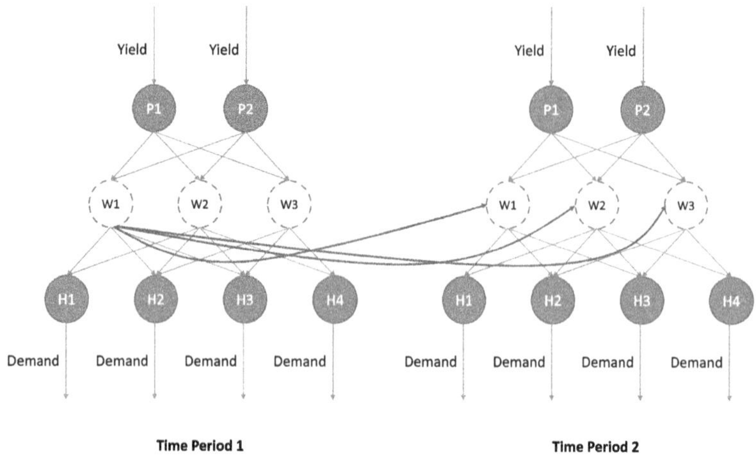

Figure 7.5. ABC Grain's distribution network.

flow and carrying of goods across time periods, in addition to flow of goods among facilities. With the NETFORM framework in place, binary decision variables are defined for the facility selection decision, and continuous decision variables are defined to present the flow on arcs. The flow conservation constraint is constructed to maintain flow conservation among nodes in the network representing facilities in different time periods. An MILP formulation for the FLP-TSN can be written as below.

Sets and parameters

- N: set of geographical locations
- T: set of time periods
- V: set of nodes (i, r) for location $i \in N$ in time period $r \in T$
- $\bar{V}$: set of facilities to be selected/opened or not in a time period, $\bar{V} \subset V$
- A: set of arcs (i, r, j, s) between node (i, r) and node (j, s), where $i, j \in N : i \neq j$ or $r, s \in T : r \neq s$
- s_{ir}: fixed setup cost of facility at location i in time period r, where $(i, r) \in \bar{V}$
- k_{ir}: maximum capacity at location i in time period r, where $(i, r) \in \bar{V}$
- d_{ir}: the supply ($d_{ir} > 0$), demand ($d_{ir} < 0$) or flow reservation ($d_{ir} = 0$) at node $(i, r) \in V$

c_{ir}^{js}: variable shipping cost per unit of goods shipped from node (i, r) to node (j, s) via arc $(i, r, j, s) \in A$

Decision variables

$y_{ir} = 1$: if facility i is selected in time period t, and 0 o.w. for $(i, r) \in \bar{V}$

$x_{ir}^{js} \geq 0$: flow of goods from node (i, r) to node (j, s) via arc $(i, r, j, s) \in A$

Objective function

$$\text{Minimize} \sum_{(i,r)\in\bar{V}} s_{ir}y_{ir} + \sum_{(i,r,j,s)\in A} c_{ir}^{js}x_{ir}^{js} \tag{7.31}$$

Subject to:

$$\sum_{(i,r,j,s)\in A} x_{ir}^{js} - \sum_{(j,s,i,r)\in A} x_{js}^{ir} = d_{ir}, \quad \forall (i,r) \in V, \tag{7.32}$$

$$x_{ir}^{js} \leq k_{ir}y_{ir}, \quad \forall\, (i,r) \in \bar{V},\ (j,s) : (i,r,j,s) \in A \tag{7.33}$$

$$y_{ir} \in \{0,1\}, \quad x_{ir}^{js} \geq 0 \tag{7.34}$$

The objective function (7.31) minimizes the total operational costs consisting of total fixed setup cost and total transportation cost. Constraint (7.32) maintains the flow conservation at each node. Constraint (7.33) is the big-M formulation to ensure no flow can be sent out of a facility unless it is selected.

7.5.2 *FCNFP with Time-Spatial Network*

The sets N, T, V and A, and the parameters d_{ir} and c_{ir}^{js} are defined in the same way as in Section 7.5.1. There is a fixed setup cost s_{ir}^{js} for sending any goods via arc $(i, r, j, s) \in A$, and the maximum capacity of arc (i, r, j, s) is k_{ir}^{js}. The FCNFP in a Time-Spatial Network, which we call FCNFP-TSN, aims to select a feasible set of arcs and determine the feasible flow of goods through the network that minimizes the total operational costs.

Example 7.4 (Furniture Supply Network). ABC Furniture's top priority is to continuously optimize the distribution of furniture sourced from vendors all over the world to its warehouses and retail stores in domestic markets. Historically inbound ocean freight from oversea vendors had been shipped via the West Port. Recent development and improvement made at South Port and its connected river system offers a potential less costly alternative. However, since barge transit takes longer lead time, its use implies less frequency but with more bulky size shipments needed. ABC Furniture's supply network can be schematically depicted by Figure 7.6. It consists of one vendor (S1), two ports for the import operation (P1 and P2) and one warehouse (W1). The dashed arcs indicate alternative shipping routes from the vendor to the warehouse. The shipping from P1(West Port) to W1 via truck is quicker but more expensive than shipping from P2(South Port) to W1 via barge, which takes longer time and has more capacity. Note there is one period lag due to the longer lead time. The arcs colored in brown show the inventory carried from one period to the next. Suppose the supply in time period 1 is bounty and the demand in time period 2 is low. The company may carry inventory at P2 to time period 2, then ship from P2 to W1 via barge which is to satisfy a high demand in period 3. ABC Furniture's network design problem involves determining the plan of shipping paths to meet the demands over time that minimizes the total operational costs.

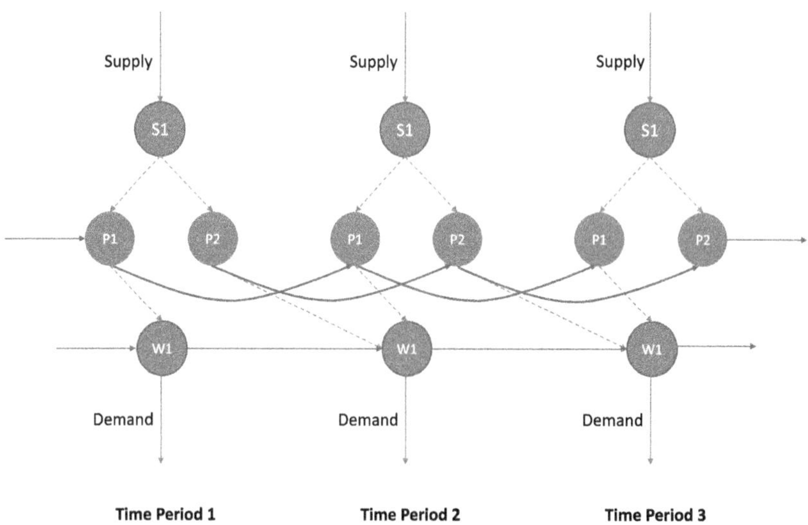

Figure 7.6. ABC Furniture's supply network.

Key to Formulation: The FCNFP-TSN is a generalization of the FCNFP by considering the carrying of goods across time periods, in addition to flow of goods among facilities. Binary decision variables are defined for selection of arcs. Continuous decision variables are defined for flow of goods on arcs. The flow conservation constraint maintains flow conservation among nodes in the network representing facilities in different time periods. An MILP formulation for the FCNFP-TSN can be written as follows.

Sets and parameters

- N: set of geographical locations
- T: set of time periods
- V: set of nodes (i, r) for location $i \in N$ in time period $r \in T$
- A: set of arcs (i, r, j, s) between node (i, r) and node (j, s), where $i, j \in N : i \neq j$ or $r, s \in T : r \neq s$
- d_{ir}: the supply ($d_{ir} > 0$), demand ($d_{ir} < 0$) or flow reservation ($d_{ir} = 0$) at node $(i, r) \in V$
- s_{ir}^{js}: fixed setup cost of shipping from node (i, r) to node (j, s) via arc $(i, r, j, s) \in A$
- c_{ir}^{js}: variable shipping cost per unit of goods shipped from node (i, r) to node (j, s) via arc $(i, r, j, s) \in A$
- u_{ir}^{js}: maximum capacity of flow from node (i, r) to node (j, s) via arc $(i, r, j, s) \in A$

Decision variables

- $y_{ir}^{js} = 1$: if the arc from node (i, r) to node (j, s) is selected, and 0 o.w. for $(i, r, j, s) \in A$
- $x_{ir}^{js} \geq 0$: flow of goods from node (i, r) to node (j, s) via arc $(i, r, j, s) \in A$

Objective function

$$\text{Minimize} \sum_{(i,r,j,s) \in A} (s_{ir}^{js} x_{ir}^{js} + c_{ir}^{js} x_{ir}^{js}) \tag{7.35}$$

Subject to:

$$\sum_{(i,r,j,s)\in A} x_{ir}^{js} - \sum_{(j,s,i,r)\in A} x_{js}^{ir} = d_{ir}, \quad \forall (i,r) \in V, \tag{7.36}$$

$$x_{ir}^{js} \leq u_{ir}^{js} y_{ir}^{js}, \quad \forall (i,r,j,s) \in A \tag{7.37}$$

$$y_{ir}^{js} \in \{0,1\}, \quad x_{ir}^{js} \geq 0 \tag{7.38}$$

The objective function (7.35) minimizes the total operational costs consisting of the total fixed setup cost and the total shipping cost. Constraint (7.36) maintains the flow conservation at each node. Constraint (7.37) is the big-M formulation to ensure no flow can be sent via an arc unless it is selected.

7.6 Hub Location Problems

There is a special category of applications in logistics and transportation where demand incurs at an origin-destination (OD) pair or an arc, as opposed to a node in an FLP and its variants we have shown so far. A central question in this setting is where to locate the hub(s) and how to connect them with non-hub nodes for meeting the demands of all OD pairs with minimum transportation cost. This motivates the study and application of the well-known Hub Location Problems (HLPs).

HLPs have a variety of prominent applications in airline and airport operations for passengers and/or cargos, transportation and logistics operations, packing and delivery services, telecommunication network design and emergency response, etc. For example, an airline needs to design its service network to meet all its OD demands by properly locating hubs so that an OD pair can be connected via one or multiple hubs. A third-party logistics (3PL) provider needs to build hubs as cross-docking or transshipment facilities to consolidate operations of packaging, shipping and handling with economies of scale. A telecommunication firm needs to locate its switches or tower stations to enable the amount of information flow between all its OD pairs.

Figure 7.7 provides illustrative examples of different hub-spoke networks. A fully connected network in Figure 7.7(a) has 5 nodes

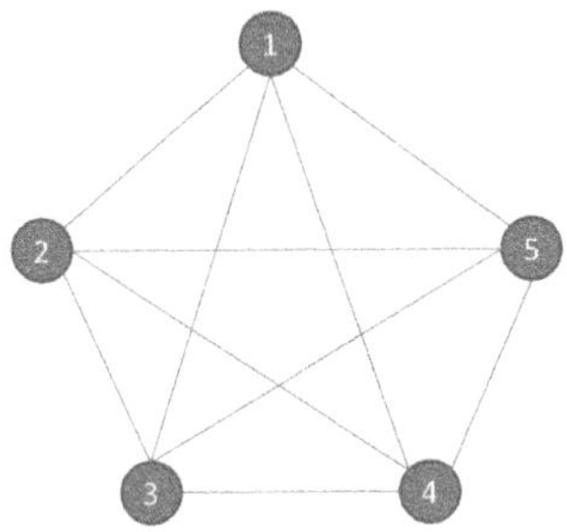

(a) A fully connected network with 5 nodes and 20 OD pairs

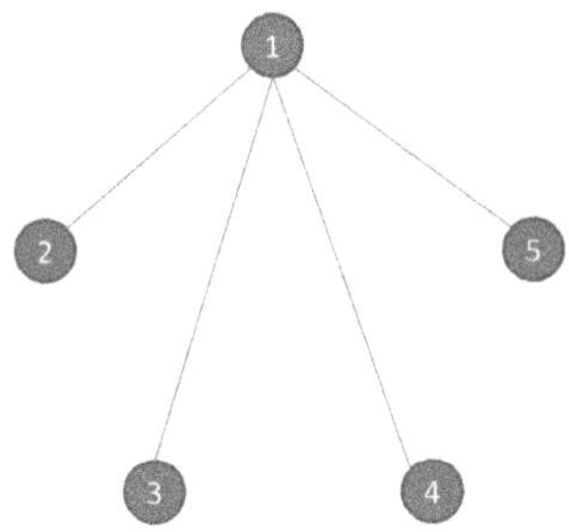

(b) A hub-spoke with 5 nodes and 20 OD pairs

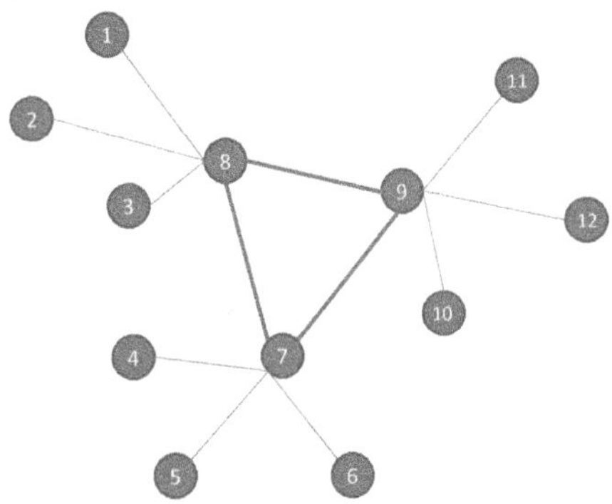

(c) A 3-hub spoke network with 12 nodes and 132 OD pairs

Figure 7.7. Illustrative examples of hub-spoke networks.

with 20 possible OD pairs. Note that the OD pair (i, j) is different from (j, i). In general, there are $n(n-1)$ possible OD pairs for a fully connected network of n nodes. Figure 7.7(b) shows a hub-spoke network with a single hub located at Node 1 with 8 links to serve all the 20 OD pairs. In general, one needs a minimum of $2(n-1)$ links in a single-hub network to serve all the OD pairs. A disadvantage of the single-hub network is that every OD pair between non-hub nodes must travel through two links. In a multi-hub spoke network as shown in Figure 7.7(c), each non-hub node is connected to (at least) one hub node, and all hub nodes (Node 7, 8 and 9) are connected to each other. In this way, the demand at a non-hub nodes is *consolidated* at a hub, which serves as a transshipment/cross-docking facility or transport terminal in real life applications. The advantage of consolidation is to achieve the *economies of scale* with less variable transportation cost per unit of goods transported between hubs. We shall present three well-known HLPs with their model formulations next.

7.6.1 *p-Hub Median Problem*

Consider a transportation network consisting of a set V of nodes and a set of OD pairs $(i, j) \in V \times V$. Each OD pair (i, j) has a load demand of d_{ij}. The transportation cost per unit of goods shipped from node i to j is c_{ij}. A non-hub node must be assigned to exactly one hub (single-allocation). Due to economies of scale, shipping between hub nodes is less costly than shipping between a hub node and a non-hub node. Let $0 \leq \alpha < 1$ denote the discount factor to compute the unit shipping cost between hub nodes. The p-hub median problem seeks to locate p hubs to serve the OD pairs so that the total transportation cost is minimized.

Key to Formulation: Binary decision variables are defined for the selection of hubs and the assignment of OD pairs to pairs of hubs. Big-M constraints ensure that a non-hub node must be connected with a hub node. The BIP formulation for the p-hub median problem can be written as below.

Sets and parameters

V: set of all nodes
d_{ij}: load demand of OD pair $(i, j) \in V \times V$
c_{ij}: shipping cost per unit of goods from node $i \in V$ to node $j \in V$
α: discounting factor for unit shipping cost between hub nodes
C_{ij}^{lm}: shipping cost per unit of goods on OD pair $(i, j) \in V \times V$ routed from $l \in V$ to hub $m \in V$, such that $C_{ij}^{lm} = c_{il} + \alpha c_{lm} + c_{mj}$

Decision variables

$y_k = 1$ if a hub is located at node $k \in V$, and 0 o.w.
$x_{ij}^{lm} = 1$ if the OD pair $(i, j) \in V \times V$ is routed from hub $l \in V$ to $m \in V$, and 0 o.w.

Objective function

$$\text{Minimize} \quad \sum_{(i,j)\in V\times V} \sum_{l\in V} \sum_{m\in V} d_{ij} C_{ij}^{lm} x_{ij}^{lm} \tag{7.39}$$

Subject to:

$$\sum_{l\in V} \sum_{m\in V} x_{ij}^{lm} = 1, \quad \forall (i,j) \in V \times V, \tag{7.40}$$

$$x_{ij}^{lm} \le y_l, \quad \forall\, (i,j) \in V \times V,\, l \in V, m \in V, \tag{7.41}$$

$$x_{ij}^{lm} \le y_m, \quad \forall\, (i,j) \in V \times V,\, l \in V, m \in V, \tag{7.42}$$

$$\sum_{k\in V} y_k = p, \tag{7.43}$$

$$y_k,\, x_{ij}^{lm} \in \{0,\, 1\} \tag{7.44}$$

The objective function (7.39) minimizes the total transportation costs. Constraint (7.40) sends an OD pair via a pair of hub nodes. Constraints (7.41) and (7.42) is the big-M formulation to ensure that only a hub node can be connected to a non-hub node. Constraint (7.43) locates a total of p hubs. It can be shown that without a capacity constraint at a hub, the integral requirement of x_{ij}^{lm} can be relaxed, because an optimal solution should always select the least cost hub pair for each OD pair.

The p-hub median problem is analogous to the p-median problem in Section 7.2.1, in that the demand of an OD pair corresponds to the demand at a node in the p-median problem. It can be shown that the formulation of p-hub median problem is equivalent to a p-median problem with two facilities to be located.

7.6.2 *Multiple-Allocation p-Hub Median Problem*

Now consider the case where an OD pair can be routed via multiple hub pairs. At the same time, there is a maximum handling capacity Γ_k for both inbound and outbound flows at a hub $k \in V$. With other parameters being the same as those in the single-allocation p-hub median problem, we define $x_{ij}^{lm} \ge 0$ as the fraction of demand on OD pair $(i,j) \in V \times V$ routed via the pair of hubs (l,m) for $l \in V, m \in V$.

Key to Formulation: The model formulation is very similar to that of p-hub median problem. An additional constraint is needed to limit the inbound and outbound flow through a hub. An MILP formulation for the multiple-allocation p-median problem can be written as follows.

Objective function

$$\text{Minimize} \quad \sum_{(i,j)\in V\times V} \sum_{l\in V} \sum_{m\in V} d_{ij} C_{ij}^{lm} x_{ij}^{lm} \tag{7.45}$$

Subject to:

$$\sum_{l\in V} \sum_{m\in V} x_{ij}^{lm} = 1, \quad \forall (i,j) \in V \times V, \tag{7.46}$$

$$x_{ij}^{lm} \leq y_l, \quad \forall\, (i,j) \in V \times V, l \in V, m \in V, \tag{7.47}$$

$$x_{ij}^{lm} \leq y_m, \quad \forall\, (i,j) \in V \times V, l \in V, m \in V, \tag{7.48}$$

$$\sum_{k\in V} y_k = p, \tag{7.49}$$

$$\sum_{(i,j)\in V\times V} d_{ij} \left[\sum_{m\in V} \left(x_{ij}^{lm} + x_{ij}^{ml} \right) - x_{ij}^{ll} \right] \leq \Gamma_l y_l, \quad \forall l \in V, \tag{7.50}$$

$$y_k \in \{0,\, 1\}\,,\, x_{ij}^{lm} \geq 0 \tag{7.51}$$

The formulation is the same as that of single-allocation p-hub median problem, except for the new constraint (7.50), which ensures that the total inbound and outbound flow at a hub does not exceed its maximum capacity.

7.6.3 *Uncapacitated Hub Location Problem*

To address the need of determining optimal number of hubs to be placed, we present the Uncapacitated Hub Location Problem (UHLP), as an analogy to the UFLP in Section 7.2.2. It also relaxes the constraint on the number of hubs in the p-Hub median problem. Let F_k denote the fixed setup cost of a hub located at node $k \in V$.

Key to Formulation: The formulation is similar to that of the p-hub median problem, except that the requirement of p hubs is no longer needed. With other parameters and decision variables being the same as those in the p-hub median problem, a BIP formulation for the UHLP can be written as below.

Objective function

$$\text{Minimize} \sum_{k \in V} F_k y_k + \sum_{(i,j) \in V \times V} \sum_{l \in V} \sum_{m \in V} d_{ij} C_{ij}^{lm} x_{ij}^{lm} \tag{7.52}$$

Subject to:

$$\sum_{l \in V} \sum_{m \in V} x_{ij}^{lm} = 1, \quad \forall (i,j) \in V \times V, \tag{7.53}$$

$$x_{ij}^{lm} \leq y_l, \quad \forall\, (i,j) \in V \times V,\, l \in V, m \in V, \tag{7.54}$$

$$x_{ij}^{lm} \leq y_m, \quad \forall\, (i,j) \in V \times V,\, l \in V, m \in V, \tag{7.55}$$

$$y_k,\, x_{ij}^{lm} \in \{0,\, 1\} \tag{7.56}$$

The objective function (7.52) minimizes the total operational cost consisting of total fixed setup cost of hubs and total transportation cost. Constraints (7.53) through (7.55) are the same as Constraints (7.40) through (7.42) in the formulation of the p-hub median problem. Note that without capacity constraints, the integral requirement of x_{ij}^{lm} can be relaxed because a non-hub node will always be connected with least cost hub pair in the optimal solution.

To allow demand to be allocated to multiple hub pairs, one may consider the limited handling capacity at hubs and define $x_{ij}^{lm} \geq 0$ as the fraction of demand on OD pair $(i,j) \in V \times V$ routed via the pair of hubs (l,m) for $l \in V, m \in V$. An MILP formulation for the capacitated hub location problem (CHLP) can be written as.

Objective function

$$\text{Minimize} \sum_{k \in V} F_k y_k + \sum_{(i,j) \in V \times V} \sum_{l \in V} \sum_{m \in V} d_{ij} C_{ij}^{lm} x_{ij}^{lm} \tag{7.57}$$

Subject to:

$$\sum_{l\in V}\sum_{m\in V} x_{ij}^{lm} = 1, \quad \forall (i,j) \in V \times V, \tag{7.58}$$

$$x_{ij}^{lm} \le y_l, \quad \forall\, (i,j) \in V \times V,\, l \in V, m \in V, \tag{7.59}$$

$$x_{ij}^{lm} \le y_m, \quad \forall\, (i,j) \in V \times V,\, l \in V, m \in V, \tag{7.60}$$

$$\sum_{(i,j)\in V\times V} d_{ij}\left[\sum_{m\in V}\left(x_{ij}^{lm} + x_{ij}^{ml}\right) - x_{ij}^{ll}\right] \le \Gamma_l y_l, \quad \forall l \in V, \tag{7.61}$$

$$y_k \in \{0,\, 1\},\, x_{ij}^{lm} \ge 0 \tag{7.62}$$

The formulation is similar to that of the UHLP with a new capacity constraint (7.61) to ensure that the maximum handling capacity of both inbound and outbound loads at a hub cannot be exceeded.

7.7 Additional Notes

We refer to Daskin [38] for a comprehensive treatment of network design including its algorithmic aspect and various applications. Efficient exact and heuristic algorithms for solving the FCNFP are available in [39–41]. The dynamic (multi-period) network design problem, often addressed while considering uncertainty, was studied in [42, 43]. Surveys on the hub location problem and its variants are available in [44–46]. A number of other variants of the network design problem go beyond the scope of this text. For instance, inventory or safety stock can be optimized in the context of network design, giving rise to the so-called inventory location problem [47, 48].

Exercises

7.1. Discuss the connections and differences between the p-median problem and the facility location problem.

7.2. Discuss how the multi-commodity facility location problem can be applied in different scenarios (up to three). *Hint*: for example, in healthcare, food/agriculture, utility/energy and retail.

7.3. Discuss the connections and differences between the facility location problem and the FCNFP.

7.4. Discuss the connections and differences between the facility location problem and the hub location problem.

7.5. Vanuatu is a South Pacific Ocean nation consisting of about 80 islands. The nation's health department is planning for the distribution operations of vaccines to serve its population in need. Due to complex geography and less-developed transportation infrastructure, a combination of transportation modes, e.g., airplane, boat and truck, are needed for vaccine distribution. It is critical to maintain the cold-chain requirement, e.g., the maximum travel time of vaccines cannot exceed 24 hours during transport. In addition to cost and efficiency, the health department would also like to achieve effectiveness and equity of covering the population in different regions. Propose a research project on vaccine distribution network design to provide decision-support for the health department in Vanuatu. Conceptually discuss your model with its decision variables, objective function(s) and constraints. What input data will be needed? How do you plan to obtain these data?

7.6. ABC Inc. is an edible oil processor in New Delhi, India, who produces a variety of high quality cooking oil products to serve the greater New Delhi markets. Fresh crops are sourced from either the local farmers/growers, the mandis, or the regional wholesale markets. Depending on the technical process for different oil products, the crops are then sent to some processors for the crush/mill operation, or directly transported to ABC's processing plants. The final products reach retailers through two channels: the wholesale markets and the carrying/forwarding agents. What decisions, objective function(s) and constraints would be involved in the design of ABC Inc.'s edible oil supply chain network? What are some unique features of ABC Inc.'s supply chain design application? What input data will be needed?

7.7. Virtual diagnostic/clinic and telecare is a transformational technology that helps improve the accessibility and quality of healthcare in the rural and less developed regions. Real world implementation of an effective, efficient and equitable telecare system requires not only the technology, but also proper planning and management tailored to such new healthcare paradigm. Consider the case of the State of Missouri in the US, where such new telecare system is to be deployed to cover its millions of population living in the rural areas. High-tech and high-value virtual diagnostic equipment and sensors need to strategically installed at satellite clinic facilities, as extension of the existing hospitals and healthcare clinics. Proper planning of healthcare providers, including doctors and nurses, must be in place to support the telecare system. Discuss the decision variables, objective function(s) and constraints involved in the optimal design of a new telecare system. What input data will be needed?

7.8. ABC Energy is a Fortune 500 power utility company who provides electricity and natural gas to over 10 million customers in the Midwest Region of US. When a service outage hits due to hurricane, ice storms or high winds, the company's service technicians drive to the outage, assess what is needed to fix the problem, retrieve the tools, supplies and parts, and return to the site to make the repairs, which requires the right amount of materials, parts and equipment to be at the right place and right time. ABC implements a multi-tier network for its outbound supply operations: Tier 1 — Distribution Center, Tier 2 — Warehouse, and Tier 3 — Operating Center. Both Tier 1 and Tier 2 facilities may serve as "stocking location" to keep inventories to meet the demands at operating centers. ABC Energy manages up to millions of SKUs (stock-keeping-units) worth hundreds of millions of dollars. Propose a research project to help ABC Energy optimize its supply operations. Conceptually describe the decision variables, objective function(s) and constraints of your proposed model. What input data will be needed?

7.9. When addressing the new telecare system design in Problem 7.7, the planner also need to consider the transportation needs of patients, especially the elderly people and those with special medical conditions. Ideally, the new healthcare system would be supported by a well-designed transport system, which connects the patients/customers, satellite clinics, and existing hospitals and care centers. Propose a research project for this purpose. Conceptually describe your modeling approach for the design of the patient transport system, and provide sufficient justifications. Elaborate the decision variables, objective function, constraints, and the input data needed in your model.

7.10. The Mississippi River System is the largest among all inland waterways in the US, with about 1,800 navigable miles and a large tributary system. The Upper Mississippi is the major transport channel for grain, corn and soybean exports through the Gulf Coast. However, data shows that a significant part of the Mississippi River and its tributaries have been underutilized. Waterway and barge are generally suitable for transporting bulk commodities such as grain, lumber, coal, fertilizer and chemicals, which complements with and underpins the capability of multiple transportation modes, i.e., trucking and rail, for inland transportation and last-mile-delivery. Significant synergies exist in the triad intermodal system of water-trucking-rail. While waterway/barge is known for its low cost, it also has a significant disadvantage of long lead time. How to properly design a distribution system and plan for its operations to achieve cost efficiency with reasonable lead times? What are the unique features of your modeling approach? Conceptually elaborate the components of your proposed model: decision variables, objective function and constraints.

Chapter 8

Production Planning

8.1 Introduction and Overview

Production planning typically involves determining the production quantity and timing to meet some estimated demand over multiple time periods subject to limited resources. It plays a crucial role in a variety of industries including manufacturing, agriculture and energy, among others. Decisions to be made in production planning address the questions of both *how much* and *when* to produce, so that production is performed at the right quantity, the right time, and the right cost. It is often a tactical-level application (6 months to 2 years), which on one hand takes the strategic-level capacity, product portfolio and supply chain network design decisions as given; and on the other hand, provides information and inputs needed for decisions at the operational level, e.g., scheduling, assignment, routing and dispatching. We show four motivating application settings below.

An electronic device company manufactures a variety of electronic equipment and products for its customers worldwide. Its Marketing Department collects and maintains good sales data for demand forecasting of its most popular lines of products. With the forecasted monthly demand for the next year, the Supply Chain Analytics team carries on to address the following questions regarding its production: (i) what is the optimal monthly production level of each product; (ii) how to best utilize the limited resource capacity: machine hours and workforce; and (iii) any additional resources (outsourcing) and/or overtime working hours required.

A mower manufacturer has several popular models well-received by its customers all over the country. Due to seasonality of market demand, the company faces important decisions on planning its production to: (i) meet the fluctuating demand; (ii) determine the amount and timing of the needed parts and components to be procured from its suppliers; and (iii) carry the proper amount of inventory to meet the seasonal demand and to level resource utilization.

A brewery produces several varieties of crafted beer and sells to its local and national markets. Given its limited resources and capacities, the company must determine: (i) how much of each variety to produce in each time period; (ii) how much ingredients and packaging materials will be needed; and (iii) whether overtime or extra capacity is needed.

An online retail company specializes in festival and holiday costumes through its supply-distribution network of suppliers, vendors, warehouses and customers. Its network is *virtual* in the sense that the company does not own any physical plant or facility, thus "production" works in the way of sourcing/procuring from its suppliers and vendors. Since the demands for costumes are highly seasonal, the company needs to be very careful about the product lines to offer, and be prudent about its utilization of resource, especially workforce needed for order processing, handling and packaging. The following decision needs can be addressed: (i) how much and when to order for each variety of costumes; (ii) how to better plan for its workforce utilization: regular, part-time or overtime; and (iii) what is the right level of inventory and safety stock to carry.

These applications all call for various production planning models to be introduced in this chapter. We shall start with a basic version of production planning to lay the foundation for more sophisticated models for the well-known Master Production Scheduling (MPS), Material Requirement Planning (MRP), Manufacturing Resource Planning (MRP II), and an integrated framework for simultaneously optimizing production and distribution decisions.

Figure 8.1 shows the conceptual relationships between MPS, MRP and MRP II. Exogenous input data is colored in gray. The MPS takes production costs, i.e., fixed setup cost and variable production cist, and demand of end products in each time period during the planning horizon, as inputs, to generate an optimal production plan (lot-sizing, colored in orange) that meets the demand while minimizing the total

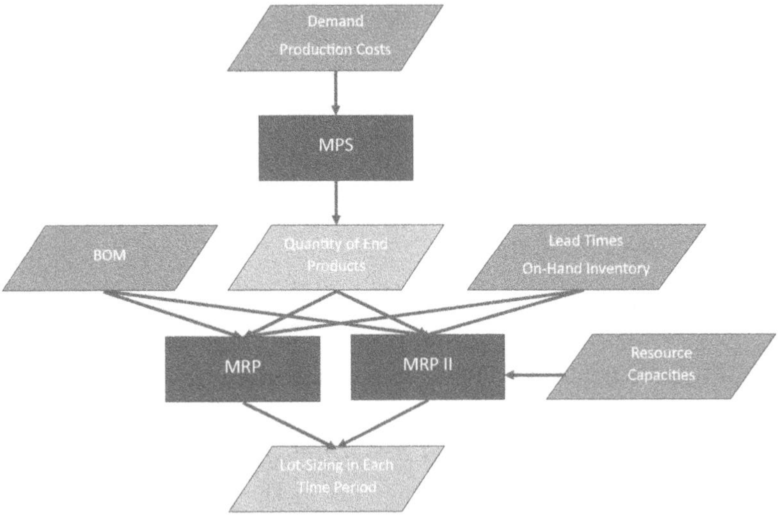

Figure 8.1. Conceptual relationship between MPS, MRP and MRP II.

production costs. The lot-sizing of end products, bill-of-materials (BOM), lead times of production/order, and on-hand inventory, are then taken as inputs to the MRP to obtain lot-sizing plan of raw materials and parts in the BOM. The MRP II improves over MRP by explicitly taking limited resource capacities into consideration.

8.2 The Basic Production Planning Problem

Consider a manufacturer who produces one type of product for $1, 2, \ldots, T$ time periods. Each time period t has a known demand of d_t to be satisfied. Production in each time period t requires a fixed setup cost q_t, with a variable production cost of c_t per unit. Products not sold can be carried as inventory to the next period with an inventory holding cost of h_t per unit per time period. The manufacturer needs to find a feasible production plan that minimizes the total operational costs. This problem is known as the *single-item, single-level uncapacited lot-sizing problem* (LS-U), because it deals with only one type of product at one level/stage of a supply chain assuming unlimited resource capacity.

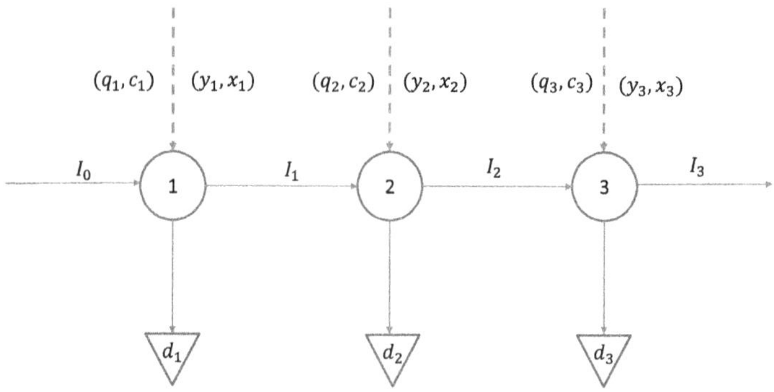

Figure 8.2. A NETFORM representation for the LS-U.

The LS-U can be modeled as a Fixed-Charge Network Flow Problem (FCNFP) presented in Section 7.3 in the following way. Define a node as a time period, and an arc as a production activity or inventory flow as in the NETFORM of Figure 8.2. A dashed arc indicates the decision of whether production is active in the corresponding time period.

Key to Formulation: Production quantity (lot-size) in each time period can be represented by a continuous decision variable. To capture the fixed setup cost, a binary decision variable is needed to determine whether production is on in each time period. Another continuous decision variable is needed to represent the inventory carried from one period to the next. Flow conservation constraint is maintained for each time period. The big-M constraint is employed to ensure that the lot-size in a time period must be zero unless production is on in that time period.

An MILP formulation for the LS-U can be written as follows.

Sets and parameters

T: number of time periods
c_t: unit production cost in period $t = 1, 2, \ldots, T$
q_t: fixed set-up cost in period $t = 1, 2, \ldots, T$
h_t: inventory holding cost per unit in period $t = 0, 1, 2, \ldots, T$
d_t: demand to be satisfied in period $t = 1, 2, \ldots, T$
M: a large positive number

Decision variables

$x_t \geq 0$: production lot size in period $t = 1, 2, \ldots, T$
$y_t = 1$ if production is on in period $t = 1, 2, \ldots, T$; and 0 o.w.
$I_t \geq 0$: ending inventory in period $t = 1, 2, \ldots, T$, with the initial inventory I_0 being zero

Objective function

$$\text{Minimize} \sum_{t=1}^{T} (q_t y_t + c_t x_t + h_t I_t) \tag{8.1}$$

Subject to:

$$I_{t-1} + x_t = I_t + d_t, \quad \forall t = 1, 2, \ldots, T, \tag{8.2}$$

$$x_t \leq M \cdot y_t, \quad \forall t = 1, 2, \ldots, T, \tag{8.3}$$

$$I_0 = 0 \tag{8.4}$$

$$x_t \geq 0, \quad I_t \geq 0, \quad y_t \in \{0, 1\} \tag{8.5}$$

The objective function (8.1) minimizes the total operational costs consisting of three terms: total fixed setup cost, total variable production cost and total inventory holding cost. Constraint (8.2) is the flow conservation constraint ensuring that there is no loss or gain for flow through a node. Constraint (8.3) is the big-M constraint to guarantee that no products can be produced in a time period if the production is not on. Note that the big-M value can be the production capacity in the corresponding time period if the capacity is known. The initial inventory I_0 of zero is enforced in Constraint (8.4). This initial condition for the decision variable I is needed on the LHS of Constraint (8.2) for $t = 1$.

8.3 Master Production Scheduling

The LS-U can be extended with more complexity in various ways. Two immediate considerations of multiple products and limited production capacity can be addressed in the so-called multi-item, single-level capacitated lot-sizing problem, also known as MPS in practice.

In a typical MPS, a manufacturer produces a set N of products, or stock keeping units (SKUs) with known demands d_{it} of product $i \in N$ in period $t \in \{1, 2, \ldots, T\}$. A set K of resources are needed for production, each of which has a capacity of L_t^k available in period t for resource $k \in K$. Producing product i in period t requires a fixed setup cost q_t^i and fixed amount β_{ik} of resource $k \in K$. Then the variable production cost of product i in period t is p_t^i, and the amount of resource $k \in K$ required per unit of product i is α_{ik}. The inventory holding cost per unit of product i in period t is h_t^i. The manufacturer needs to find a feasible production plan that minimizes the total operational costs.

The consideration of multiple products and limited resource capacities in one problem effectively enables the decision-maker to optimally allocate the available capacities to products competing for limited resources, which is an important function in supply chain operations. In practice, the set of products can be finished goods (end products) of different varieties, for which some demand forecasts or projections can be obtained using predictive analytical methods.

Key to Formulation: The MPS problem is an extension of LS-U by considering multiple products. Both the decision variables and constraints in the LS-U model need to be expanded by adding another dimension of products. An MILP formulation for the MPS can be written as below.

Sets and Parameters

- N: set of items to be produced
- K: set of shared resources with limited capacity
- T: set of time periods of the planning horizon
- p_t^i: variable production cost per unit of product $i \in N$ produced in period $t \in T$
- q_t^i: fixed set-up cost of product $i \in N$ in period $t \in T$
- h_t^i: inventory holding cost per unit of product $i \in N$ in period $t \in T$
- d_t^i: demand of $i \in N$ to be satisfied in period $t \in T$
- L_t^k: the available capacity of resource $k \in K$ in period $t \in T$
- α_{ik}: amount of resource $k \in K$ consumed per unit of item $i \in N$
- β_{ik}: amount of resource $k \in K$ required by setting up production of item $i \in N$

Decision variables

$x_t^i \geq 0$: production lot size of item $i \in N$ in period $t \in T$
$y_t^i = 1$ if production is on for item $i \in N$ in period $t \in T$; and 0 o.w.
$I_t^i \geq 0$: inventory of item $i \in N$ to hold at the end of period $t \in T$, with initial inventory I_0^i being zero for $i \in N$

Objective function

$$\text{Minimize} \sum_{i \in M} \sum_{t \in T} (q_t^i y_t^i + p_t^i x_t^i + h_t^i I_t^i) \tag{8.6}$$

Subject to:

$$I_{t-1}^i + x_t^i = d_t^i + I_t^i, \quad \forall i \in N, t \in T, \tag{8.7}$$

$$x_t^i \leq M \cdot y_t^i, \quad \forall i \in N, t \in T, \tag{8.8}$$

$$\sum_{i \in N} \alpha_{ik} x_t^i + \sum_{i \in N} \beta_{ik} y_t^i \leq L_t^k, \quad \forall k \in K, t \in T, \tag{8.9}$$

$$I_0^i = 0, \quad \forall i \in N \tag{8.10}$$

$$x_t^i \geq 0, \quad I_t^i \geq 0, \quad y_t^i \in \{0, 1\} \tag{8.11}$$

The objective function (8.6) minimizes the total operational costs consisting of the total setup cost, total variable production cost and total inventory holding cost. Constraint (8.7) is the flow conservation constraint maintained for each product and time period. Constraint (8.8) is the big-M formulation to ensure that no product can be produced if the production is not on. Constraint (8.9) ensures that total consumption of each resource, incurred by setup and production, does not exceed its capacity in every time period. Constraint (8.10) sets the boundary conditions for the initial amount of inventories.

Note that Constraints (8.7) and (8.8) in the formulation resemble Constraints (8.2) and (8.3) in the formulation of LS-U with an additional product dimension. The reason why they cannot be treated as N separate LS-U models is due to Constraint (8.9), which restricts the combined resource consumption of all products.

Part Number	Lead Time	Required Parts	Min Lot Size	Initial Inventory
PQ-001	2	PQ-031 (2) PQ-022 (1)	100	25
PQ-032	3	PQ-008 (1) PQ-006 (1)	400	90
PQ-022	4	-	70	50
PQ-008	1	-	20	0
PQ-006	12	-	500	600

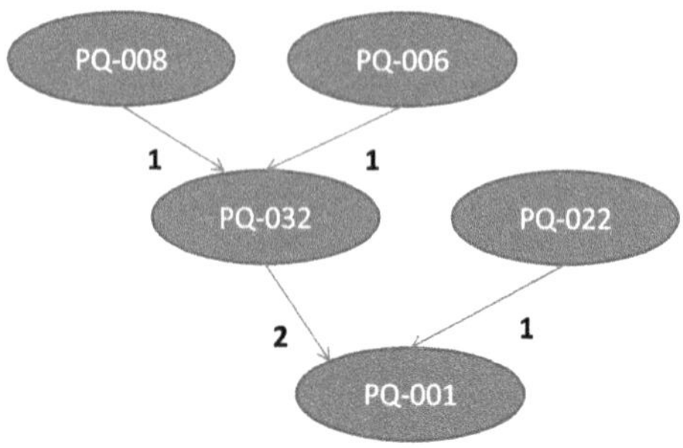

Figure 8.3. An example of BOM with one end product and four parts.

8.4 Material Requirement Planning

Both the LS-U and MPS models deal with the *single-level* decision in that they address products at one level of a supply chain, often the finished goods or end products at the last level/stage. Real life production requires planning decisions not only for the end products, but also for all inputs: raw materials, ingredients, parts and components at multiple supply chain levels/stages. In practice, there is a well-known term for describing a complete list of all items and their quantities required to manufacture a product, i.e., bill-of-materials (BOM).

Example 8.1 (BOM). An example of BOM in Figure 8.3 shows one end product requiring four parts for it to be manufactured. For example, 1 unit of end product PQ-001 at the root requires 2 units of PQ-031 and 1 unit of PQ-022, with a lead time of 2 days, minimum lot size of 100 and initial inventory of 25 (at the start of the current time period). The part PQ-006 requires 12 days to be ready as it has to be ordered from a supplier with a minimum order quantity of 500 units. The "lot size" in general may also mean "order size" when an item needs to be sourced or procured from an external supplier/vendor. Note that the information of lead time is crucial to achieve the essence of production, i.e., to optimize both the *quantity* and *timing* of production or ordering.

The BOM describes the demand dependencies of a product, and in some way, the "supply chain structure" for the product. Note that differing from the physical supply chain network of facilities, the supply chain network based on BOM consists of the items required to manufacture a product. Both approaches are viable ways to describe a supply chain, but from different perspectives.

Figure 8.4 shows various possible BOM structures in real life applications. Figure 8.4(a) shows the simplest serial (linear) structur[illegible]ere each node has at most one predecessor and successor. F[illegible]) shows the *convergent* structure where the chain starts [illegible]s and ends with fewer, which is often encountered in [illegible] The divergent structure is show in Figure 8.4(c), [illegible]erges to more at the end, which is often found in [illegible] commonality shared by Figures 8.4(a)–8.4(c) [illegible] the *spanning tree* structure, which is a connected [illegible]e.[a] A real world BOM or supply chain can be com[illegible]be a general network as shown in Figure 8.4(d). Note [illegible]de A is required by multiple nodes including the two en[illegible]ts.

Planning for the quantity and timing of production and/or procurement for all the items in a BOM is known as material requirement planning (MRP). One could also address the supply chain configuration problem in the context of BOM, which is the topic of Chapter 10.

In a typical MRP, one seeks to optimize the quantity and timing to procure, source or produce all the raw materials, parts and components needed to produce certain end products. Compared to the LS-U and MPS that only deal with the planning for end products, MRP addresses the more detailed planning decision at the operational level ranging from weekly to monthly. Its fundamental logic works in the following way. Given some forecasted demand of end products and their lead times, an MRP process iterates *backwardly*

[a]In graph theory, it can be proved that a spanning tree with n vertices must have exactly $n-1$ edges.

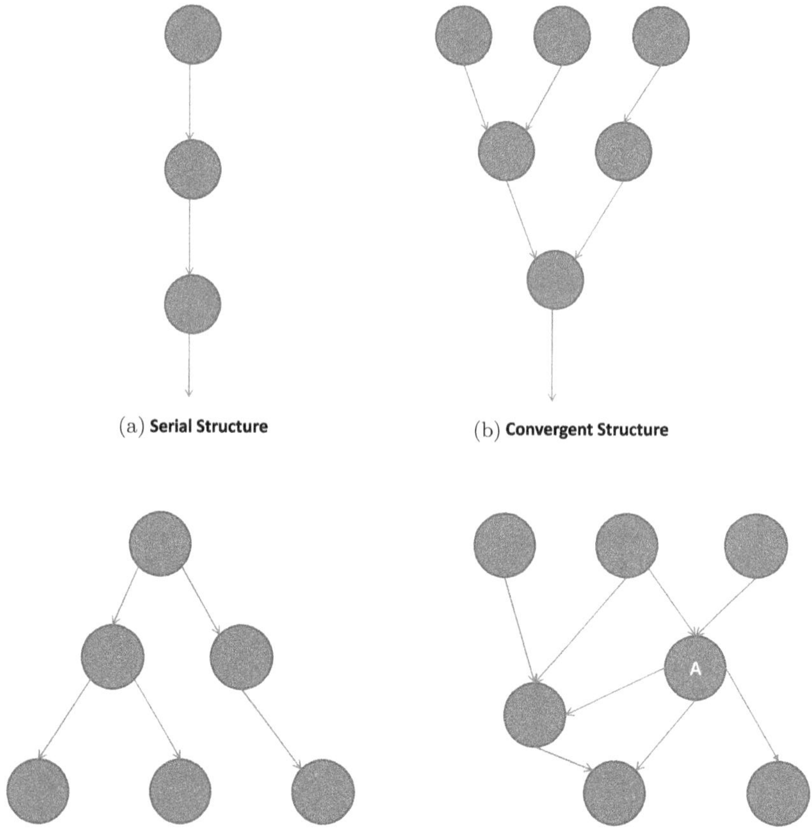

(a) **Serial Structure** (b) **Convergent Structure**

(c) **Divergent Structure** (d) **General Structure**

Figure 8.4. Different BOM structures in real life applications.

to compute the quantity and timing needed for each part, component or raw material based on their demand dependencies and lead times. The MRP logic implements the concept and practice of just-in-time (JIT), i.e., items arrive at the time when needed, not earlier nor later. There is clearly a close connection between MPS and MRP: the outputs of MPS in terms of the lot sizing for end products in different time periods serve as inputs to MRP.

Formally in an MRP, a manufacturer plans for the production and/or procurement a set V of SKUs over the next T time periods.

Let d_{it} denote the exogenous demand of SKU $i \in V$ to be met in time period $t = 1, 2, \ldots, T$. The set of all demand dependencies in a BOM is denoted by A, with r_{ij} being the units of SKU i required to make one unit of SKU j for $(i, j) \in A$. The lead time, minimum lot size and initial inventory of SKU i is l_i, K_i and I_{i0}, respectively. The goal is to find a JIT-type plan so that the right amount of SKUs are produced or procured exactly at the time when needed. The MRP optimization problem is also known as the multi-item, multi-level lot sizing problem.

Example 8.2 (MRP Logic). A partial MRP solution to Example 8.1 is provided in Table 8.1 (without considering the minimum lot size). Suppose the exogenous demand of the end product PQ-001 is 100 units in Week 8 and 100 units in Week 5. With 25 units on-hand inventory, receipts of $100 - 25 = 75$ units are needed in Week 8 and Week 5. Since the lead time of PQ-001 is 2 weeks, the order of 75 units needs to be released 2 weeks earlier, i.e., in Week 6 and Week 3, respectively. Then since one unit of PQ-001 requires two units of PQ-032, $75 \times 2 = 150$ units of PQ-032 is needed in Week 6 and Week 3. Subtracting the on-hand inventory of 90, 60 units of PQ-032 are needed in Week 6 and Week 3, the order of which needs to be released in Week 3 (to meet the demand in Week 6).

Table 8.1. A partial solution to Example 8.1.

PQ-001	**1**	**2**	**3**	**4**	**5**	**6**	**7**	**8**
Demand					100			100
Inventory(25)					25			25
Receipts					75			75
Releases			75			75		
PQ-032	**1**	**2**	**3**	**4**	**5**	**6**	**7**	**8**
Demand			150			150		
Inventory(90)			90			90		
Receipts			60			60		
Releases			60					
PQ-022	**1**	**2**	**3**	**4**	**5**	**6**	**7**	**8**
Demand			75			75		
Inventory(50)			50			50		
Receipts			25			25		
Releases		25						

Key to Formulation: Continuous decision variables are defined to represent the quantities to order/produce in all time periods during the planning horizon. The most complex part of the formulation is the constraint to guarantee that the cumulative production or purchase quantity in each time period satisfies the total demand of each item (SKU), both internal and external, in that time period. Note that the use of cumulative quantity avoids the need for explicitly considering the inventory carrying decision. A binary decision variable is needed to model the minimum lot size in a time period. Big-M constraints can be used in two ways: (i) to specify the logical relationship between the continuous lot-sizing and the binary production/order setup decision variables; and (ii) to specify the minimum lot-size in each time period. An MILP formulation is presented below to emulate the MRP logic and process.

Sets and parameters

V: set of SKUs
A: set of demand dependencies, such that $(i, j) \in A$ means that SKU j requires SKU i
T: number of time periods
l_i: lead time of SKU i
r_{ij}: units of SKU i required to make one unit of SKU j
d_{it}: external demand for SKU $i \in V$ in period $t = 1, 2, \ldots, T$
I_{i0}: beginning inventory of SKU i
K_i: minimum lot size for SKU i
M: a large positive number

Decision variables

$x_{it} \geq 0$: units of SKU $i \in V$ to order/produce in period $t = 1, 2, \ldots, T$
$y_{it} = 1$ if any of SKU i will be ordered/produced in period $t = 1, 2, \ldots, T$; and 0 o.w.

Objective function

$$\text{Minimize} \sum_{i \in V} \sum_{t=1}^{T} (T - t) \cdot x_{it} \tag{8.12}$$

Subject to:

$$\sum_{\tau=1}^{\max\{0,t-l_i\}} x_{i\tau} + I_{i0} - \sum_{\tau=1}^{t} (d_{i\tau} + \sum_{j\in V:(i,j)\in A} r_{ij} x_{j\tau}) \geq 0,$$

$$\forall i \in V, \quad t = 1, 2, \ldots, T \tag{8.13}$$

$$x_{it} \geq K_i \cdot y_{it}, \quad \forall i \in V, \quad t = 1, 2, \ldots, T \tag{8.14}$$

$$x_{it} \leq M \cdot y_{it}, \quad \forall i \in V, \quad t = 1, 2, \ldots, T \tag{8.15}$$

$$y_{it} \in \{0, 1\}, \, x_{it} \geq 0 \tag{8.16}$$

The objective function (8.12) minimizes the total weighted production/order quantity to achieve the goal of JIT. To see how it works, note that the weight of the quantity in time period t is $T - t$, so that the earlier the quantity incurs, i.e., with smaller t, the larger penalty of $T - t$ for it. In this way, an optimal solution will defer the production or ordering of SKUs as late as possible (while satisfying the exogenous demands). Constraint (8.13) ensures that the cumulative units of SKU i received in time period t, plus the initial on-hand inventory, must meet the cumulative demand of SKU i in period t. The first term on the LHS of (8.13) computes the cumulative receipt of SKU i in time period t as the summation of production/order quantity of i from time period 1 up to l_i periods prior to t (any quantity released afterwards will not arrive due to the lead time l_i). Note that when $t - l_i$ is negative, the upper bound of the summation on the LHS is zero, meaning that no prior production is able to meet the demand at t. The third term computes the cumulative demand of SKU i up to time period t as the summation of the exogenous demand of i and the internal demand derived from the demands of i's successors j in the BOM. Constraint (8.14) is the big-M formulation to satisfy the minimum lot size requirement. Constraint (8.15) is again the big-M formulation to ensure that production/order quantity is zero if no production or order is made in each time period.

8.5 Manufacturing Resource Planning (MRP II)

The traditional MRP approach is also known as *backward infinite loading* in industry, which has a clear weakness in that the capacity of production or supply is assumed to be unlimited. This often leads to infeasible production plans with the need for an iterative trial-and-error approach to come up a feasible plan. For this reason, it is necessary to introduce an improved version of MRP called Manufacturing Resource Planning or MRP II. With the problem setting being the same as that in the MRP, we now consider the resource consumption of SKUs. Let K denote a set of resources needed for the production and procurement operations, and u_{ik} be the fraction of resource $k \in K$ required by one unit of SKU $i \in V$.

Key to Formulation: The model formulation for MRP II is similar to that of MRP with an additional constraint to impose the maximal available capacities of resources. An MILP formulation for the MRP II can be written as below.

Decision variables

$x_{it} \geq 0$: units of SKU $i \in V$ to order/produce in period $t = 1, 2, \ldots, T$

$y_{it} = 1$ if any of SKU i will be ordered/produced in period $t = 1, 2, \ldots, T$; and 0 o.w.

Objective function

$$\text{Minimize} \sum_{i \in V} \sum_{t=1}^{T} (T - t) \cdot x_{it} \tag{8.17}$$

Subject to:

$$\sum_{\tau=1}^{\max\{0, t-l_i\}} x_{i\tau} + I_{i0} - \sum_{\tau=1}^{t} (d_{i\tau} + \sum_{j \in V:(i,j) \in A} r_{ij} x_{j\tau}) \geq 0,$$

$$\forall i \in V, \quad t = 1, 2, \ldots, T \tag{8.18}$$

$$x_{it} \geq K_i \cdot y_{it}, \quad \forall i \in V, \quad t = 1, 2, \ldots, T \tag{8.19}$$

$$x_{it} \leq M \cdot y_{it}, \quad \forall i \in V, \quad t = 1, 2, \ldots, T \tag{8.20}$$

$$\sum_{i \in V} u_{ik} x_{it} \leq 1, \quad \forall k \in K, \ t = 1, 2, \ldots, T \tag{8.21}$$

$$y_{it} \in \{0, 1\}, \ x_{it} \geq 0 \tag{8.22}$$

The formulation is similar to that of the MRP, with one new Constraint (8.21) to ensure that the consumed resources in any time period does not exceed the available capacity.

The basic MRP and MRP II models can be extended to include a variety of other features in real life applications. For example, the fixed setup cost for production or ordering can be conveniently incorporated in the model with the existing binary decision variable y_{it}. One could also consider a more complex setting where there is sequence-dependent setup cost between the changeover of SKU productions.

8.6 Additional Notes

A focused treatment of the mathematical programming approach for various production planning applications is available in [49, 50]. Production planning can often be addressed in the context of logistics and transportation, which leads to more complex optimization problems, e.g., the integrated production and distribution problem [51–54], and the integrated production and transportation scheduling problem (PTSP [55, 56]), among others.

Exercises

8.1. Discuss the input data needed for production planning problems, and how it is related to Demand Management, Accounting and other business functions.

8.2. Discuss possible variants and extensions of the basic production planning problem, in terms of decision variables, objective functions and/or constraints.

8.3. Discuss the connections and differences between MPS and MRP, and their positioning in the general framework of production planning. Show one application example of MPS and MRP, e.g., in the context of manufacturing, healthcare, food/agriculture, energy/utility, etc.

8.4. Explain the role of BOM in MRP. Show up to three real world examples of BOM in different settings: manufacturing, food/agriculture, construction, etc.

8.5. Discuss possible variants and extensions of the basic MPS, MRP and MRP II models, in terms of decision variables, objective functions and/or constraints.

8.6. ABC Inc. is a small-size manufacturer for portable music boxes and sound systems. Based on historical demand data, the demand for both line of products experience clear seasonality. Since some parts and components are sourced from suppliers and vendors thousands of miles away, the company needs to properly plan for its production and procurement to achieve profitability and efficiency. Propose a data-driven decision-support approach to assist ABC Inc. for its production and procurement planning. Describe the decision needs at different levels: strategic, tactical, operational, and their connections. Elaborate the decision variables, objective functions, constraints, and the input data needed in your proposed approach.

8.7. ABC Health is a large hospital system with more than 20 hospitals and clinics in the Midwest region serving over a million population. It manages a myriad of medical supplies, equipment and devices to support smooth operations and effective healthcare delivery. The Purchasing Department of ABC Health aims to ensure the right supplies with the right quantity be available at the right time with the right cost. Production quality and reliability of a supplier are often important factors to consider. Quantity discount is a common industry practice. Sometimes doctors' preference of suppliers/vendors must also be taken into consideration. Propose a data-driven decision-support approach to assist the Purchasing Department to achieve its goal. Explain and elaborate the decision variables, objective function(s), constraints and the input data needed in your proposed model(s). How will this approach impact other business functions at ABC Health, e.g., Accounting, Finance, IT and Operations?

8.8. ABC Brewery is a micro-brewery specialized in Irish-style crafted beer in the Midwest. To meet the increasing market demand, the company needs to improve its production planning process with data-driven solutions. The company has been sourcing some of the ingredients from suppliers in California at relatively lower price than local suppliers, but with much longer lead time. While sourcing from one supplier may achieve lower purchasing price, the company is interested in exploring the benefit of multiple-sourcing to mitigate potential supply disruption risk. Propose a data-driven decision-support approach to assist ABC Brewery for making these decisions. Explain and elaborate the decision variables, objective function(s), constraints and the input data needed in your proposed approach.

Chapter 9

Resource Planning

9.1 Introduction and Overview

The production planning models presented in Chapter 8 have their main applications in the manufacturing setting. In this chapter, we introduce a parallel topic on Resource Planning (RP) with a focus of applications in the service sector. While production planning and RP share a common theme of optimizing the utilization of limited resources, the RP aims to deal with, in particular, human resource or workforce, which is the most important resource a service firm or organization can own.

The main goal of RP is to properly plan for the acquisition, retention and utilization of workforce resources, so that services can be delivered by the right people, at the right time, and with the right cost. We may address decision needs from the strategic level in the long-run to the operational level in the short-term. Figure 9.1 shows a hierarchy of strategic, tactical, operational and executional decision needs that can be addressed in a typical service firm.

At the *strategic level*, an executive council or chief finance officer is interested to know whether the firm, in the long run (two to three years), has the workforce with the right capacity and capability (skill-mix) to support its business strategies and target revenues. This can be addressed by the Labor Strategy Optimization (LSO), which helps senior executives to identify gaps in the capacity and capability of workforce to be coped with under limited budgets in a proactive way.

Then at the *tactical level* (six months to one year), a portfolio manager of the firm may address a Project Portfolio Optimization

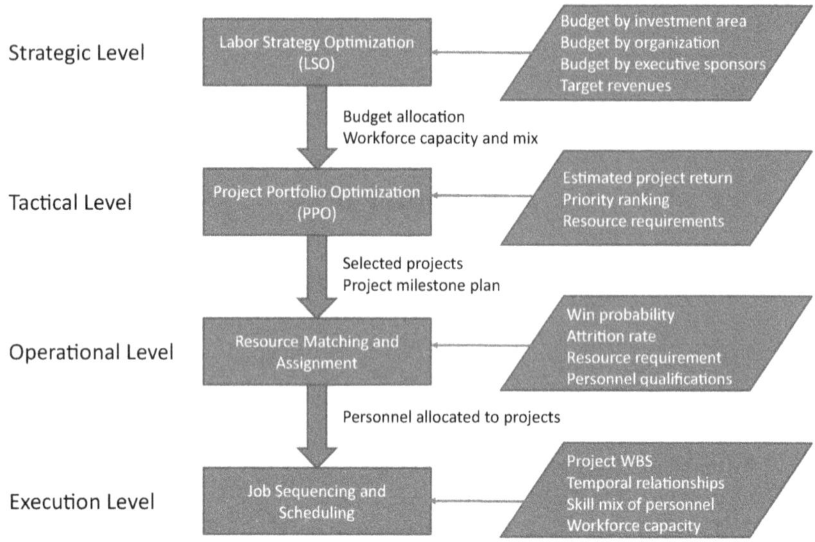

Figure 9.1. A hierarchical decision framework for RP.

(PPO) problem to select a set of projects that best align with the firm's business strategy and limited resources. The main inputs of PPO, i.e., budget allocation and the available capacity and capability of workforce, can be provided by the outputs of LSO. Additional input data may include the expected return, priority ranking, temporal relationship and resource requirements of the project opportunities. A PPO simultaneously determines both project selection and planning (for project milestones) decisions that maximizes the total expected portfolio return.

Next, a resource manager of the firm may address an *operational level* decision to match its available multi-skilled personnel with projects and/or tasks, with the objective to minimize the total staffing cost. Additional complexity arises when attrition of resources from the supply side and uncertain availability of tasks from the demand side are considered.

Finally at the *execution level*, given the allocated personnel and their workload capacities, a project manager often needs to properly schedule/sequence project tasks and assign multi-skilled personnel to ensure timely project completion and delivery. This problem and its model formulation are introduced in Chapter 12 as a variant of the Resource-Constrained Project Scheduling Problem (RCPSP).

9.2 Labor Strategy Optimization

The LSO problem aims to prescribe an optimal staffing plan of internal workforce, contingent/contractor workforce, training and re-skilling to meet the target revenues of a professional service firm. Consider a service firm engaged in a set M of market offerings. At the beginning of each fiscal cycle, the firm specifies a target revenue R_m for each market offering $m \in M$ based on target market share levels and confirmed, anticipated or forecasted orders.

The firm's service delivery process can be described by a bill-of-labor (BOL), similar to BOM in the manufacturing setting. A BOL translates the target market offering revenue (demand) into a hierarchy of labor requirements. Let the BOL be described by a directed graph $G(V, E)$, with V being the set of resource/labor items (nodes) with certain attributes, and E representing the set of dependent-demand relationships (arcs). Each arc $(i, j) \in E$ means that some amount of resource item j is required for delivering i. Compared to BOM, BOL captures the unique characteristics in service operations: (1) Resource/labor items need to be differentiated with different nature and the corresponding cost structure; (2) The demand-dependencies in BOL are more diverse than those in BOM, requiring more than just a scalar type of weights to describe; (3) Some resource/labor items in BOL can be transformed to other items through training; and (4) The weight describing demand-dependency can be uncertain.

We classify the node set V into subsets of nodes with different nature: set V^{I} of internal workforce owned by the company, set V^{O} of resources outsourced to contractors or third-party partner (3PP) who are not owned by the company, and set V^{M} of market offering or demand nodes. (We use V^{M} to replace the earlier notation of M to emphasize that M is a subset of V.) Assuming that none of the subsets overlap, we have $V = V^{\mathrm{O}} \cup V^{\mathrm{I}} \cup V^{\mathrm{M}}$. For non-enterprise-owned resource $i \in V^{\mathrm{O}}$, we define δ_i as the ratio between the payment to i and the revenue generated by i. For enterprise-owned resource $i \in V^{\mathrm{I}}$, the cost per unit of resource per day is denoted by c_i. We assume that the only nodes that generate revenue are the set V^{M} of market offering nodes.

We let the demand-dependency in BOL be described by a weight function $h_{ij}(\cdot)$ associated with a pair of arc $(i, j) \in E$. $h_{ij}(\cdot)$ serves the role of multiplier as in a generalized network in the NETFORM.

That is, the outflow of node i is multiplied by $h_{ij}(\cdot)$ before entering into node j. Then the following demand-dependency holds:

$$x_j = \sum_{i:(i,j)\in E} h_{ij}(\cdot)x_i \tag{9.1}$$

Given the richness of service operations, $h_{ij}(\cdot)$ may have different interpretations when modeling different (i,j) pairs as shown in Figure 9.2. When modeling allocation decisions as in Figure 9.2(a) or headcount as in Figure 9.2(b), $h_{ij}(\cdot)$ simply equals 1. When converting one measurement to another, $h_{ij}(\cdot)$ should be a scalar appropriate for the conversion. For instance, when converting from FTE headcount to revenue as in Figure 9.2(c), $h_{ij}(\cdot)$ is the FTE's productivity, i.e., the revenue generated by one FTE over the planning horizon. When modeling supply risk or inefficiency, $h_{ij}(\cdot)$ may be a function of some risk or efficiency factor. For instance, the productivity of offshore workforce can be discounted by a risk factor λ, i.e., the ratio between average delay of projects and project durations as in Figure 9.2(d), due to the difficulty of coordinating a virtual team. As in Figure 9.2(e), the headcount of regular and contingent workforce (CTW) FTEs needs to be discounted by μ, i.e., the ratio between average number of hours billed and the total number of hours worked,

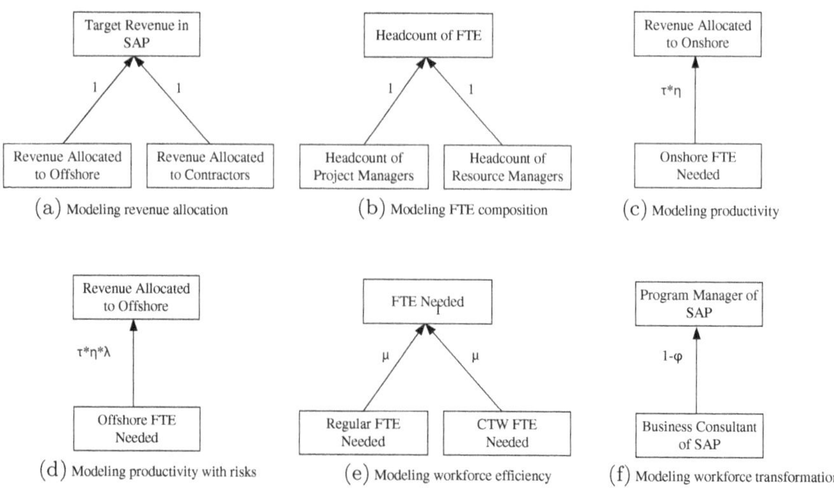

Figure 9.2. Modeling various dependent-demand of labor in BOL.

due to less-than-100% commitment and/or learning. Of course, the value of μ for regular and CTW FTE is not necessarily the same. When modeling workforce transformation as in Figure 9.2(f), the input role/skill is discounted by $1 - \varphi$, where φ represents the effort of training as a percentage of the number of working days.

One way to achieve operational flexibility is through workforce transformation or training. We let φ_{ij} denote the percentage of effort (lead time) needed to train one FTE with attribute i to j.

The LSO problem seeks to find the best staffing plan, i.e., capacity and capability of workforce, outsourcing and cross-training, to meet the target revenues.

Key to Formulation: The main decision variable is the amount of resource items of different types in the BOL. It can be modeled as the flow in a *generalized* NETFORM with multipliers being the demand dependence coefficient in the BOL. The flow balancing constraint is needed to ensure proper relationships between amount of resource needed, cross-training and excessive or idled resources. An MILP formulation for the LSO can be written as below.

Sets and parameters

- V^{M}: set of marketing offerings
- V^{I}: set of internally-owned resource/labor
- V^{O}: set of outsourced resource/labor
- V: set of all nodes in a BOL, i.e., $V = V^{\mathrm{O}} \cup V^{\mathrm{I}} \cup V^{\mathrm{M}}$
- E: set of arcs in a BOL, representing the demand-dependency of resource/labor
- T: set of arcs in a BOL that are eligible for training
- R_i: target revenue of market offering $i \in V^{\mathrm{M}}$
- ρ_i: cost ratio of outsourcing to external source $i \in V^{\mathrm{O}}$. It is the ratio between the payment to i and the revenue generated by i.
- c_i: cost per day per internally-owned resource $i \in V^{\mathrm{I}}$. For a regular FTE, it is the salary; for a CTW FTE, it refers to the payment to the CTW.
- η: number of working days over the planning horizon.
- τ: discounted internal rate of an employee, i.e., revenue generated by an internal FTE per day.
- I_i: available inventory of internally-owned resource $i \in V^{\mathrm{I}}$.

φ_{ij}: percentage of effort (lead time) needed to cross-train one FTE from resource item i to j.

α_i: cost of idled internally-owned resource $i \in V^{\mathrm{I}}$

M: a big positive number

μ_i: commitment rate of a resource $i \in V^{\mathrm{I}}$ (often an FTE), i.e., percentage of time of an FTE that generates revenue. It can be calculated as the average number of hours billed divided by the total number of hours worked.

λ_i: risk of a resource $i \in V^{\mathrm{I}}$ (often offshore), i.e., percentage of deliverable time that is not billable due to project disruption. It can be estimated as the ratio between average delay of projects and project duration.

$h_{ij}(\cdot)$: multiplier on arc $(i,j) \in E$. $h_{ij}(\cdot)$ should take the appropriate functional form of other parameters for modeling different pair of (i,j) as discussed in Figure 9.2

Decision variables

$x_i \geq 0$: amount of resource item $i \in V$

$y_{ij} \geq 0$: amount of resource item i trained to j for an eligible training pair $(i,j) \in T$

$\chi_i \geq 0$: excess internally-owned resource $i \in V^{\mathrm{I}}$

$\varepsilon_i \in \{0,1\}$: $\varepsilon_i = 1$ if the idled internally-owned resource $i \in V^{\mathrm{I}}$ can be positive ($\chi_i > 0$); and $\varepsilon_i = 0$ o.w.

$\delta_{ij} \in \{0,1\}$: $\delta_{ij} = 1$ if the training from i to j can be positive for $(i,j) \in T$ ($y_{ij} > 0$); and $\delta_{ij} = 0$ o.w.

Objective function

$$\text{Maximize} \quad \sum_{i:(i,j)\in E, j\in V^{\mathrm{M}}} x_i - \sum_{i\in V^{\mathrm{O}}} \rho_i x_i - \sum_{i\in V^{\mathrm{I}}} c_i x_i - \sum_{(i,j)\in T} c_i \varphi_{ij} y_{ij} - \sum_{i\in V^{\mathrm{I}}} \alpha_i \chi_i \tag{9.2}$$

Subject to:

$$\sum_{j:(j,i)\in E} x_j \leq R_i, \quad \forall i \in V^{\mathrm{M}}, \tag{9.3}$$

$$x_j = \sum_{i:(i,j)\in E} h_{ij}(\cdot)x_i, \quad \forall j \in V\backslash V^{\mathrm{M}}, \tag{9.4}$$

$$x_i = I_i - \sum_{j:(i,j)\in T} y_{ij} + \sum_{j:(j,i)\in T} (1-\varphi_{ij})y_{ji} - \chi_i, \quad \forall i \in V^{\mathrm{I}}, \tag{9.5}$$

$$\chi_i \leq M \cdot \varepsilon_i, \quad \forall i \in V^{\mathrm{I}}, \tag{9.6}$$

$$y_{ij} \leq M \cdot \delta_{ij}, \quad \forall (i,j) \in T, \tag{9.7}$$

$$\varepsilon_i + \delta_{ij} \leq 1, \quad \forall (i,j) \in T, \tag{9.8}$$

$$x_i \geq 0, \quad y_{ij} \geq 0, \quad \chi_i \geq 0, \quad \varepsilon_i \in \{0,1\}, \quad \delta_{ij} \in \{0,1\}. \tag{9.9}$$

The objective function (9.2) maximizes the total gross margin, which consists of five terms. The first is the total allocated market offering revenue to various sources, which are immediate predecessors of the market offering nodes. The remaining four terms represent four cost components. Specifically, the second term in (9.2) denotes the total cost of outsourced services. The third term represents the total internally-owned staffing cost. The fourth term is the total cross-training cost. The fifth term penalizes the idled internally-owned workforce. Constraint (9.3) allocates target revenue R_i of market offering i to its set of immediate predecessors. Since R_i itself may not be optimal, it specifies an upper bound of revenue for market offering i, with the possibility that an optimal staffing plan may deliver less than R_i. Constraint (9.4) follows (9.1) to calculate the dependent-demand for nodes other than market offering. Constraint (9.5) balances the demand for internally-owned resource i with the available inventory of i, capacity lost due to training i to other item j, capacity gained due to training other item j to i, and excess of i to be idled. Constraints (9.6) and (9.7) are the big-M constraints to define binary variables ε and δ, respectively. Constraint (9.8) prevents training idled workforce.

9.3 Project Portfolio Optimization

Taking the resource allocations obtained from LSO as inputs, a service firm or organization may address the project selection decision in Project Portfolio Optimization (PPO). A PPO problem seeks to select a feasible set of projects given limited resources, i.e., budgets, workforce, and threshold of different market offerings, which maximizes the total expected return of the portfolio. It is an extension of two prominent optimization problems: the portfolio optimization in finance and the knapsack problem in combinatorial optimization.

In the well-known Markowitz model, also known as the mean-variance model, for the portfolio optimization problem in finance, a set of investments: stocks, bonds, etc. is selected to minimize the portfolio risk (total variance of return) subject to some threshold of total expected return. In the knapsack problem as shown in Section 3.2.1, a set of items is selected to maximize the total utility without exceeding the maximum capacity of the knapsack. The PPO problem shares the common theme of optimally allocating limited resources to candidate items, i.e., project opportunities in this case, to maximize the total utility. It differs by simultaneously addressing an important dimension in the project portfolio setting, i.e., the timing and dynamics of resource requirement and capacity.

We now formally describe the basic PPO problem. Consider a set I of project opportunities to be selected for the next set T of time periods. Each project $i \in I$ has an estimated return π_i with a success probability of p_i. The project opportunities can be classified into a set M of market offerings (each opportunity belongs to exactly one market offering), with the set of opportunities in market offering $m \in M$ denoted by I^m, such that $I = I^1 \cup I^2 \cdots \cup I^{|M|}$. Each marketing offering $m \in M$ must have a minimum threshold θ_m of percentage of the total expected portfolio return, which reflects the firm's business strategy for the planning horizon. A set R of resources are required for executing the project opportunities. Each resource $r \in R$ has a maximum capacity of k_{rt} available in time period $t \in T$. Assume the time window $[a_i, b_i]$ of a project $i \in I$ is known, i.e., it starts in period a_i and ends in period b_i with a duration of $b_i - a_i + 1$ time periods. A project opportunity $i \in I$, once selected and started, cannot be interrupted and requires ρ_{irt} of resource $r \in R$ during its duration $t \in [a_i, b_i]$. One selects a set of feasible project opportunities to maximize the total expected return of the portfolio.

Key to Formulation: The basic PPO can be viewed as a multi-knapsack problem as an extension of the basic knapsack problem, where there are multiple resource constraints associated with each resource type and every time period. The key is a binary decision variable for the selection decision of each project opportunity. And the main constraint is to ensure the total requirement of each type of resource does not exceed its maximum capacity in each time period. Note that an important assumption here is that the time window of each project is known, which simplifies the formulation of the resource constraints. A BIP formulation for the basic PPO can be written as below.

Sets and parameters

- I: set of project opportunities
- R: set of resources
- T: set of time periods in the planning horizon
- M: set of market offerings
- I^m: set of projects in market offering $m \in M$
- θ_m: minimum threshold of percentage of the total expected portfolio return for market offering $m \in M$
- π_i: estimated return of project $i \in I$
- p_i: probability of success of project $i \in I$
- k_{rt}: maximum capacity of resource $r \in R$ available in time period $t \in T$
- a_i: starting period of project $i \in I$
- b_i: ending period of project $i \in I$
- ρ_{irt}: amount of resource $r \in R$ required by project $i \in I$ in time period $t \in [a_i, b_i]$; for $t \notin [a_i, b_i]$, $\rho_{irt} = 0$

Decision variables

$x_i = 1$ if project opportunity $i \in I$ is selected, and 0 o.w.

Objective function

$$\text{Maximize} \sum_{i \in I} p_i \pi_i x_i \tag{9.10}$$

Subject to:

$$\sum_{i \in I} \rho_{irt} x_i \leq k_{rt}, \quad \forall r \in R, t \in T, \tag{9.11}$$

$$\sum_{i \in I^m} p_i \pi_i x_i \geq \theta_m \sum_{i \in I} p_i \pi_i x_i, \quad \forall m \in M, \tag{9.12}$$

$$x_i \in \{0, 1\} \tag{9.13}$$

The objective function (9.10) maximizes the total expected return of the project portfolio. Constraint (9.11) guarantees that for each type of resource and time period, the total required amount of the resource cannot exceed its available capacity in the corresponding period. Constraint (9.12) satisfies the minimum percentage threshold of each market offering in the total expected portfolio return. Note that this constraint in its original form: $\sum_{i \in I^m} p_i \pi_i x_i / \sum_{i \in I} p_i \pi_i x_i \geq \theta_m$ is nonlinear and computationally inconvenient. With denominator on the LHS being positive, it can be easily transformed to its linear form in (9.12).

9.4 Resource Matching and Assignment

After project opportunities are selected, the next phase of RP concerns matching/assigning multi-skilled personnel to heterogeneous projects and tasks. A task can be defined in a general way as a project milestone or subproject based on the project's work-breakdown structure (WBS). Consider a set R of resources (personnel) to be assigned to a set J of tasks. The cost of utilizing resource $r \in R$ during the planning horizon is c_r^{U}. The matching score of assigning resource $r \in R$ to task $j \in J$ is $0 \leq \delta_{rj} \leq 1$, with 1 being perfect match and 0 being complete mismatch. Then the adjusted cost assigning resource r to task j considering quality of the matching is $c_r^{\mathrm{U}}/\delta_{rj}$. Without loss of generality, we assume that a task requires exactly one resource, and a resource can be assigned to at most one task. If a task requires multiple resources, dummy tasks can be created corresponding with the task. Similarly, if a resource can be assigned to multiple tasks, dummy resources can be created corresponding with the resource. In situation where there are more tasks than the available resources, an unassigned task $j \in J$ incurs a loss cost of c_j^{L}. Conversely, when there are more resources than tasks to be assigned, an unutilized resource $r \in R$ incurs an idle cost c_r^{I}. The objective is to find a resource-task matching that minimizes the total assignment costs.

Figure 9.3 elaborates the concept of matching in this context. The link and matching between a resource and task is established through a set of *attributes* relevant to the service operation. Skill Group specifies the technology or skill category, e.g., ASP, Python, Blockchain, Analytics etc. Job Level indicates the rank or experience level, which often has to do with the level of expertise required by a task and the pay grade/rate of a resource. Examples of Workforce Type include regular, part-time or contingent workforce, often with different pay rates. Location refers the geographical location, which often impacts the easiness of communication and collaboration for service delivery. Business Domain indicates the market offering or application area of the service, e.g., manufacturing, telecommunication, transportation, and agriculture, etc.

The use of matching score is an important feature in this problem. It allows for *flexible matching*, i.e., matching a resource with a task without having 100% the required attributes. Such less than perfect matching is important in practice, as a 100% perfect matching often

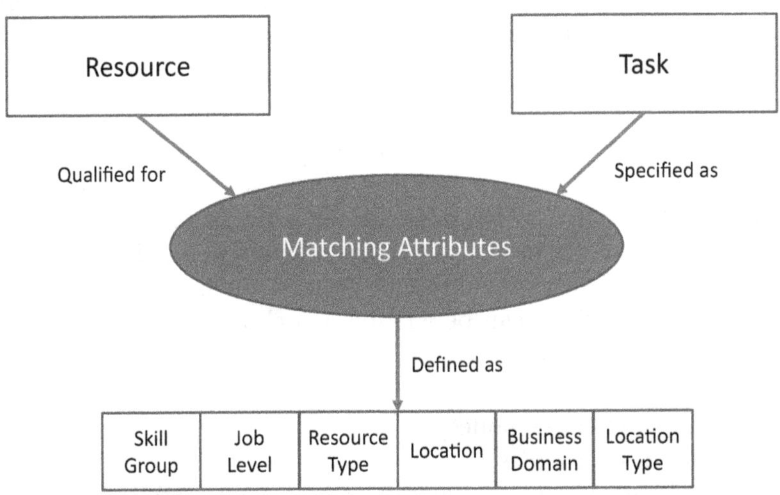

Figure 9.3. Resource-task matching based on matching attributes.

results in poor resource utilization, although it is straightforward to implement.

The addressed resource-task matching problem can be modeled as an *unbalanced transportation problem*, where the total supply does not necessarily equal the total demand. Its NETFORM can be built in the following way. Create nodes of the following types: resource nodes, task nodes, one dummy task node to indicate resource idleness, and one dummy resource node to indicate task loss. The demand of each task node is 1; the supply of each resource node is 1. The demand of the resource idleness node is bounded by the number of resources $|R|$; the supply of the task loss note is bounded by the number of tasks $|J|$. Assignment arcs are created between all pairs of resource and task nodes with assignment cost $c_r^{\mathrm{U}}/\delta_{rj}$. Arcs between the task loss node and all the task nodes are created to indicate job loss with cost c_j^{L}. Arcs between all the resource nodes and the resource idleness node are created to indicate resource idleness with cost c_r^{I}. A concrete example is provided below.

Example 9.1 (NETFORM for Resource Matching). Consider four tasks to be staffed with three available resources. Its NETFORM in Figure 9.4 consists of three resource nodes, four task nodes, one task loss node and one resource idleness node. Each task node has a demand of 1 and each resource node has a supply of 1. Note that the resource idleness node has a demand bounded by 3 (number of resources), and the task loss node has a supply bounded by 4 (number of tasks).

Key to Formulation: Built upon the NETFORM for the resource matching problem, the assignment decision variables can be viewed as representing the flow through the network. Due to the pure network structure of the model, the integral (binary) requirement of the assignment decision variable can be relaxed, such that the resulting model is an LP, which can be written as below.

Sets and parameters

R: set of resource nodes
J: set of task nodes
g: dummy resource node indicating loss of a job
i: dummy task node indicating idleness of a resource

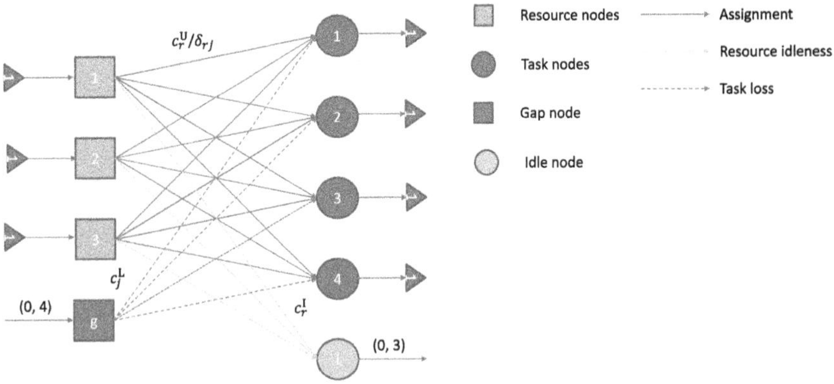

Figure 9.4. Example of NETFORM for the resource matching problem.

c_r^{U}: cost of utilizing (assigning) resource $r \in R$ in the planning horizon
δ_{rj}: matching score (between 0 and 1) of assigning resource $r \in R$ to task $j \in J$
c_j^{L}: cost of loss, i.e., not assigning any resource, for task $j \in J$
c_r^{I}: cost of idleness, i.e., not assigning task, for task $j \in J$

Decision variables

$x_{rj} = 1$ if resource $r \in R$ is assigned to task $j \in J$, and 0 o.w.

Objective function

$$\text{Minimize} \sum_{r \in R \backslash \{g\}} \sum_{j \in J \backslash \{i\}} c_r^{\mathrm{U}} \backslash \delta_{rj} \cdot x_{rj} + \sum_{j \in J \backslash \{i\}} c_j^{\mathrm{L}} x_{gj} + \sum_{r \in R \backslash \{g\}} c_r^{\mathrm{I}} x_{ri} \tag{9.14}$$

Subject to:

$$\sum_{r \in R} x_{rj} = 1, \quad \forall j \in J : j \neq i, \tag{9.15}$$

$$\sum_{j \in J} x_{rj} = 1, \quad \forall r \in R : j \neq i, \tag{9.16}$$

$$\sum_{r \in R: r \neq g} x_{ri} \leq |R|, \tag{9.17}$$

$$\sum_{j \in J: j \neq i} x_{gj} \leq |J|, \tag{9.18}$$

$$x_{rj} \geq 0. \tag{9.19}$$

The objective function (9.14) minimizes the total costs consisting of total assignment cost, total task loss cost and total resource idleness cost. Constraint (9.15) satisfies the 1 unit of demand of each task node. Constraint (9.16) ensures that each resource node sends exactly 1 unit of supply. Constraint (9.17) restricts the total inflow into the dummy task node does not exceed the number of resources $|R|$. Constraint (9.18) limits the total inflow out of the dummy resource node does not exceed the number of tasks $|J|$. Note that Constraint (9.19) only requires non-negativity but not integer for the assignment variables, due to the unimodularity property of the underlying pure network structure.

9.5 Multi-Period Resource Assignment

Real life resource matching and assignment applications are almost always implemented in dynamic fashion over multiple time periods. In this section, we present a more complex and flexible multi-period assignment/matching problem and its model formulation. The multi-period framework also allows us to consider other interesting ways to staff project tasks, e.g., through hiring and cross-training.

Consider a set J of tasks to be staffed by a set R of internal resources over the next T time periods. Each task $j \in J$ has a known time window $[s_j, e_j]$, where s_j and e_j denote the starting and ending times of job j, respectively. A task j must be assigned with a resource during its time window, i.e., for every time periods $t \in [s_j, e_j - 1]$. A task can be assigned in three ways: (i) being directly assigned to an internal resource; (ii) being assigned to an internal resource via training; and (iii) being assigned to an external resource via hiring. Assume no change can be made for a resource-task assignment through duration of the task, and a resource can be assigned to at most one task in a time period. Let c_{rj} be the cost of assigning resource $r \in R$ to job $j \in J$. The training cost of assigning resource $r \in X_j$ to job j is c^{T}_{rj}, and the cost of hiring for job j is c^{H}_j. A task j with no resource assigned is identified as a loss with a cost of c^{L}_j. Hiring for task j has a lead time ρ_j, meaning that only those hired ρ_j periods earlier can be assigned to j. The total number of new hires cannot exceed H_t in period t during the planning horizon. Some business rule of an organization can be factored into these costs. For instance, a service firm may opt to increase its workforce utilization, such that $c_{rj} < c^{\mathrm{T}}_{rj} < c^{\mathrm{H}}_j < c^{\mathrm{L}}_j$. The decision maker seeks to determine plan for assignment, cross-training and hiring that minimizes the total staffing costs.

Key to Formulation: Binary decision variables can be defined to directly assign a resource to a task, to make assignment via cross-training, to assign through hiring, or to identify a loss of task if needed. Constraints are needed to maintain continuity of assignment, i.e., once an assignment is made between a resource and a task, the resource must be assigned to the task during the entire course of the task. A BIP formulation for the multi-period resource matching problem can be written as below.

Sets and parameters

- J: set of tasks to be staffed
- R: set of internal resources available
- T: number of time periods in the planning horizon
- s_j: starting time of task $j \in J$
- e_j: ending times of task $j \in J$
- c_{rj}: cost of assigning resource $r \in R$ to task $j \in J$
- c^{T}_{rj}: the training cost of assigning resource $r \in R$ to task $j \in J$
- c^{H}_j: cost of hiring for task $j \in J$
- c^{L}_j: cost of loss for task $j \in J$, i.e., cost of not assigning any resource to task j
- ρ_j: lead time of hiring for task $j \in J$
- H_t: maximum number of hiring in time period $t \in \{1, 2, \ldots, T\}$

Decision variables

$x_{rjt} = 1$ if an internal resource $r \in R$ is assigned to task $j \in J$ in period $t \in [s_j, e_j - 1]$, and 0 o.w.

$x_{rj}^{\text{U}} = 1$ if an internal resource $r \in R$ is assigned to task $j \in J$, and 0 o.w.

$y_{rjt} = 1$ if an internal resource $r \in R$ is assigned to task $j \in J$ in period $t \in [s_j e_j - 1]$ through training, and 0 o.w.

$y_{rj}^{\text{U}} = 1$ if an internal resource $r \in R$ is assigned to task $j \in J$ through training, and 0 o.w.

$h_{jt} = 1$ if task $j \in J$ is assigned with an external resource hired in period $t \in [s_j e_j - 1]$, and 0 o.w.

$h_j^{\text{U}} = 1$ if task $j \in J$ is assigned with an external resource through hiring, and 0 o.w.

$z_{jt} = 1$ if task $j \in J$ has a loss in period $t \in [s_j e_j - 1]$, and 0 o.w.

$z_j^{\text{U}} = 1$ if task $j \in J$ is identified as a loss during the planning horizon, and 0 o.w.

Objective function

$$\text{Minimize} \sum_{j \in J} \sum_{r \in Q_j} c_{rj}^{\text{Q}} x_{rj}^{\text{U}} + \sum_{j \in J} \sum_{r \in X_j} c_{rj}^{\text{T}} y_{rj}^{\text{U}} + \sum_{j \in J} c_j^{\text{H}} h_j^{\text{U}} + \sum_{j \in J} c_j^{\text{G}} z_j^{\text{U}} \tag{9.20}$$

Subject to:

$$\sum_{r \in Q_j} x_{rj}^{\text{U}} + \sum_{r \in X_j} y_{rj}^{\text{U}} + h_j^{\text{U}} + z_j^{\text{U}} = 1, \quad \forall j \in J, \tag{9.21}$$

$$\sum_{r \in Q_j} x_{rjt} + \sum_{r \in X_j} y_{rjt} + h_{j,t-\rho_j} + z_{jt} = 1, \quad \forall j \in J, t \in [s_j e_j - 1], \tag{9.22}$$

$$\sum_{j \in J : r \in Q_j} x_{rjt} + \sum_{j \in J : r \in X_j} y_{rjt} \leq 1, \quad \forall r \in R, t \in \{0, 1, \ldots, T, \tag{9.23}$$

$$x_{rjt} = x_{rj}^{\text{U}}, \quad \forall j \in J,\ r \in Q_j, t \in [s_j, e_j - 1], \tag{9.24}$$

$$y_{rjt} = y_{rj}^{\text{U}}, \quad \forall j \in J,\ r \in X_j, t \in [s_j, e_j - 1], \tag{9.25}$$

$$h_{jt} = h_j^{\mathrm{U}}, \quad \forall j \in J, t \in [s_j - \rho_j, e_j - \rho_j - 1], \tag{9.26}$$

$$\sum_{j \in J} h_j^{\mathrm{U}} \leq H_t, \quad \forall t = 0, 1, \ldots, T, \tag{9.27}$$

$$x_{rjt}, \, y_{rjt}, \, h_{jt}, \, z_{jt}, x_{rj}^{\mathrm{U}}, y_{rj}^{\mathrm{U}}, h_j^{\mathrm{U}}, z_j^{\mathrm{U}} \in \{0, \, 1\} \tag{9.28}$$

The objective function (9.20) minimizes the total staffing costs, which consists of four terms: (i) cost of assigning internal resources; (ii) cost of assigning internal resources through training; (iii) cost of hiring; and (iv) cost of task loss. Constraint (9.21) ensures that a task is assigned with an internal resource (directly or through training), or fulfilled via hiring, or identified as a loss. Constraint (9.22) ensures that a task is assigned with an internal resource (directly or through training), or fulfilled via hiring, or identified as gap, in every period of its duration. Note that the third term on the left-hand-side employs the hiring occurred ρ_j periods prior to the period in need. Constraint (9.23) states that an internal resource cannot be assigned to a task and be trained in any time period. Constraint (9.24) requires that if an internal qualified resource is assigned to a task, the resource must be assigned to the task's entire duration. Constraints (9.25) and (9.26) require the continuity of assignment of an internal resource via training and hiring, respectively. Constraint (9.27) limits the number of new hires in every time period during the planning horizon. Constraint (9.28) specifies the domain of all the decision variables.

9.6 Additional Notes

A formal study of LSO is available in [57], which optimizes a professional service firm's source, mix and transformation strategy of labor. The history of PPO can be traced back to the study of Capital Budgeting problem in finance in the 1960s [58]. It is also known as Capital Rationing for allocating limited resources to multiple risky investment project opportunities [59, 60]. Various industry applications of PPO are available in [61–64]. The resource matching model in Section 9.4 is based on that of [65]. The resource-job matching score, a key input to the model, can computed using the analytical hierarchy process (AHP) as in [66]. A dynamic and adaptive solution to a multi-period RP problem under uncertainty is presented in [67].

Exercises

9.1. Discuss the connections among LSO, PPO and Resource Matching/Assignment, and their positioning in the hierarchy of RP.

9.2. Discuss the concept of bill-of-labor, its role in the LSO, and how it is related to BOM. Explain how the NETFORM framework can be applied to model the LSO.

9.3. What alternative metrics can be optimized in an LSO? What other constraints can be considered?

9.4. Discuss possible variants and extensions of the basic PPO, in terms of decision variables, objective functions and constraints.

9.5. Discuss possible variants and extensions of the Resource Matching/Assignment problem, in terms of decision variables, objective functions and constraints.

9.6. ABC Inc. is a Fortune 500 financial investment and consulting firm, who provides financial consultation and management service for its clients: both corporate and personal. To achieve customer satisfaction and efficiency, ABC Inc. would like to better plan for its staffing needs on an annual basis. The range of domain expertise and skills are classified to four categories: Corporate Finance, Investment, Trading and Personal Finance. In each category, three levels are differentiated based on experience: Entry, Medium and Senior. The firm would like to properly plan for its workforce to ensure the right people with the right skills and capacities be available for the right projects/jobs at the right time. Propose a data-driven decision-support approach to address ABC's RP needs. Elaborate the decision variables, objective function(s), constraints, and the input data needed in your approach.

9.7. ABC Inc. is an IT and software company dedicated in developing customized business solutions in logistics and supply chains. In addition to the contracted projects, ABC Inc. puts in a budget pool for R&D every year. It has its Project and Financial Planning Committee (the Committee) in place who oversees the project review and selection process. In addition to multiple project attributes: NPV, annualized cost, workforce requirement, skill set requirement, timeline (major milestones), etc., the Committee requires project managers to assess the risk of project outcomes (e.g., High Success,

Success, Low Success, Failure). Sometimes, the Committee would also like to balance investment in different application domains: Manufacturing, Construction, Healthcare, Food/Agriculture, Professional Service and Military/Defense. Propose a data-driven decision-support approach to help ABC better plan for its R&D projects. Elaborate the decision variables, objective function(s), constraints, and the input data needed in your approach.

Chapter 10

Supply Chain Configuration

10.1 Introduction and Overview

While the topic of supply chain network design covered in Chapter 7 addresses the strategic location of facilities and flow of goods through a *physical* supply chain network, in this chapter we introduce a tactical-level supply chain design topic on supply chain configuration. Consider the following motivating examples.

An electronic manufacturer produces several models of music players and sells to its domestic and international markets. The company sources most of the parts and components from its suppliers, and assembles them in-house for the finished products (assembly-to-stock or ATS). A crucial decision in the company's operations is to determine the right amount of safety stock of parts and components to meet its forecasted markets demands of different player models. At the same time, purchasing and sourcing decisions come into play regarding the selection of suppliers, vendors and transportation modes: container/ocean, air, truck or rail.

A grape food processor produces a variety of grape products: table grape, raisins, and grape juice. It sources fresh grapes and packing materials from its network of suppliers and sometimes directly from farms. The company operates in a make-to-stock (MTS) process, with finished products inventory to meet the demands in several of its markets nationwide. Given the significant seasonality of demand, proper configuration of its supply chain is needed to determine the right level of safety stock throughout the network. Additional complexity faced by the food processor is the issue of food perishability, which directly impacts the product quality and market value.

A tooling company manufactures custom tools and parts and serve as supplier for several large manufacturing companies in the automobile and aerospace industry. Its business model is make-to-order (MTO) in that purchasing and production activities do not start until an order is received. To achieve operational effectiveness and efficiency, the company opts to properly determine the mode/option for each operation in its supply chain. For instance, which parts/components should be made-in-house or purchased; and if purchased, from which suppliers/vendors. When multiple contracts and orders are active, making these decisions requires limited resources to be explicitly taken account for, e.g., equipment, machines, workforce and budget.

A pharmaceutical company frequently launches innovative drugs through research & development (R&D), and needs to design and configure its supply chains to ensure timely and costly-effective production, logistics and sales. While facing similar decision needs as above, a new challenge here is the lack of historical information or data about demand of the new drugs, thus the demand cannot be treated exogenously as given. This requires the configuration decision to be made in conjunction with the launching, production, sales decisions, and the *demand diffusion* process of new products.

The above decision settings share a common theme of a Supply Chain Configuration Problem (SCCP), where the key decisions involve: (i) determining the level and location of safety stock throughout a supply chain; and (ii) selection of modes/options for each stage or operation through the supply chain. Note that both (i) and (ii) must be addressed simultaneously as the mode selection decision directly impacts direct cost and lead time (among other metrics) of a stage, which in turn influences the amount of safety stock in the entire supply chain system.

To understand the important role of SCCP in supply chain design and optimization, we start with some fundamental concept in supply chain management: push system versus pull system. As shown in Figure 10.1, in a pure push system, production is completely driven by the forecasted demand, so that physical goods are produced and "pushed" *forwardly* through a supply chain, where most safety stock is kept at the end of the chain (although there could be

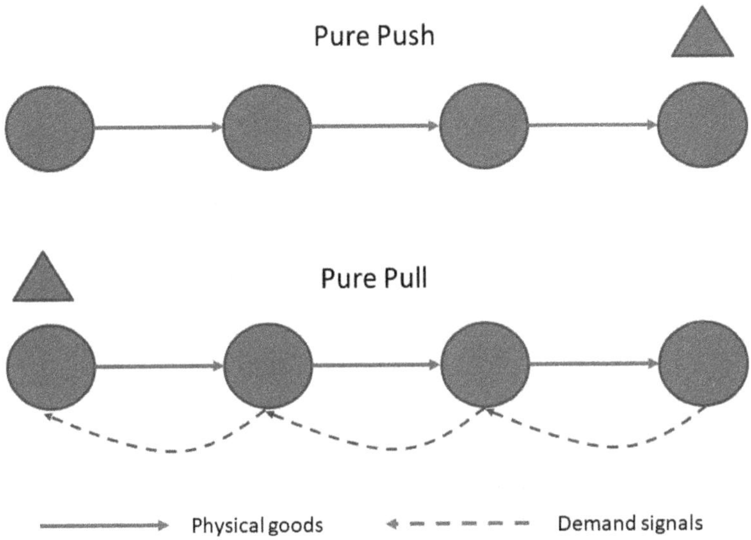

Figure 10.1. Illustration of push and pull systems.

significant work-in-process or WIP inventory due to "bottlenecks" in an unbalanced process). In a pure pull system, in contrast, production is completely driven by the actual order, such that the demand (order) signal is passed *backwardly* through a supply chain, where most inventory is kept at the start of the chain.

Push and pull systems have complementary strengths and are suitable for different supply chain paradigms. A push system facilitates production in large lot size, thus can be efficient from the economies of scale perspective. It is suitable for assembly line or flow shop type of operations, where products are more generic with less variety. A pull system, on the other hand, enables production in small lot size with more variety, thus is more lean and flexible in a just-in-time (JIT) fashion. It fits well for job shop type of operations, where orders arrive in small batches but with more variety.

Given the complementary strengths of the push and pull systems, there is an incentive to integrate the two. While the pure push and pull systems exist as two extreme cases, where most safety stock is kept at either the end or start of a supply, respectively, one may conjecture that an optimal safety stock positioning exists in between which delineates stock-keeping versus non-stock-keeping.

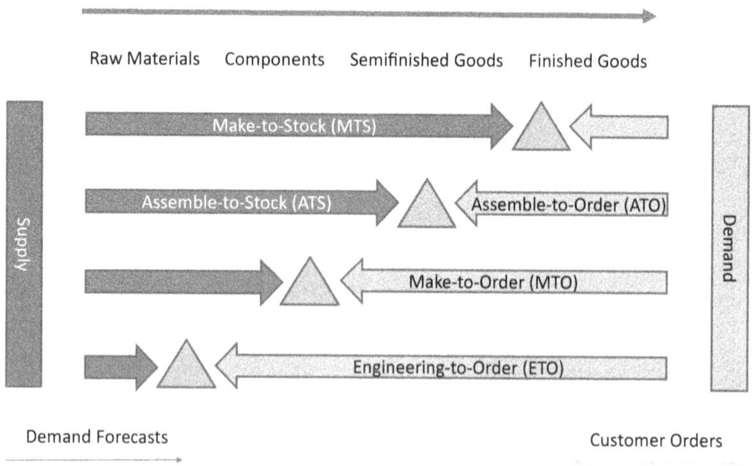

Figure 10.2. Safety stock placement in a hybrid push-pull system with decoupling point.

This point/stage is known as the *decoupling point* (DP) of push-pull boundary.

Figure 10.2 shows how DP (denoted by green triangle) can be used in practice for describing *safety stock placement* in a hybrid push-pull system. Safety stock is kept from the supply side of supply chain all the way down to the DP, i.e., to the left-hand-side of the DP. Different positioning of the DP leads to different supply chain paradigms. For example, having DP most close to the finished goods stage (demand side) is a typical MTS supply chain, where safety stock exists throughout the supply chain (including the finished goods), and flow of goods is mainly driven by demand forecasts. It is suitable for commodity goods with large volume but little variety. Moving the DP upward to the semi-finished good stage leads to either an assemble-to-order (ATO) or assembly-to-stock (ATS) supply chain, where little safety stock is kept for finished goods. It is driven by both demand forecasts and customer orders, and is suitable for products with both large value and some variety. Moving the DP further up to the components stage represents a typical MTO supply chain, where safety stock is limited to raw materials and components, and the production is driven mainly by customer orders. The engineering-to-order (ETO) paradigm at the bottom has its DP most close to the

Table 10.1. Summary of supply chain paradigms based on DP positions.

Paradigm	DP position	Volume	Variety	Examples
MTS	Finished goods	High	Low	Diapers, toilet paper
ATS	Semi-finished goods	Medium-high	Medium	Canned food, mowers
ATO	Semi-finished goods	Medium	Medium-high	Computers, digital cameras,
MTO	Components	Medium-low	High	Small tooling, special equipment
ETO	Raw materials	Low	High	Aircraft, ambulance

raw materials stage (supply side), which incurs least amount of safety stock, and often requires the engineering design of product to be customized according to the unique requirements of customer order. Both MTO and ETO often require managing tasks and operations a *project*, which is covered in Chapter 12.

Table 10.1 summarizes the characteristics of different DP positions and the corresponding supply chain paradigms with their representative application examples.

10.2 Safety Stock Placement Problem

Consider a general supply chain network $G(V, A)$ consisting of a set V of nodes and a set A of arcs. A node $i \in V$ represents a supply chain function in general, which can be a part, component, semi-finished goods in a bill-of-materials (BOM), or some process or operation such as production, storage and transportation. An arc $(i, j) \in A$ specifies the demand dependency between functions i and j. Without loss of generality, it is assumed that one unit of j requires one unit of i for $(i, j) \in A$. In addition, according to the service guarantee requirement, the *inbound service time* of j cannot be less than the *outbound service time* of i for $(i, j) \in A$. That is, node j must receive

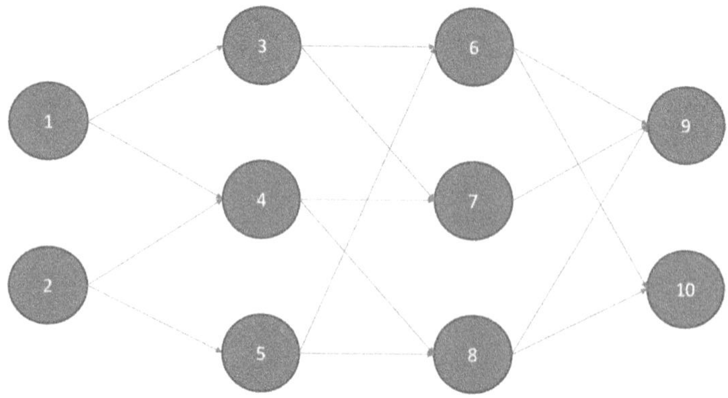

Figure 10.3. A 10-node supply chain network.

the service from its predecessor i before it can start its own inbound service time. Each node $i \in V$ has a constant lead time of T_i, and maximum limit of C_i time periods of safety stock. The amount of safety stock to keep at a node i is a function of the net replenishment time of i, computed as the difference between completion time of i (inbound service time plus lead time) and its outbound service time. Assuming the exogenous demand follows normal distribution $N(\mu, \sigma^2)$ with mean μ and variance σ^2, the amount of safety stock of a node is proportional to $\sigma\sqrt{\tau}$, where τ is the net replenishment time of the node. A typical safety stock placement problem seeks to find feasible inbound and outbound service times of all nodes that minimize the total safety stock cost (SSC).

Example 10.1 (Safety Stock Placement Problem). Consider the supply chain network of ten nodes and two end product nodes with their dependencies shown in Figure 10.3. It has a general structure that is more complex than a serial or a spanning tree structure.

The data of lead time, maximum customer-quoted service time, maximum capacity of safety stock, mean and standard deviation of each node is provided in Table 10.2. We assume the inventory holding cost rate is 0.1 per unit per time period, and use 90% service level with z-value of 1.645.

Table 10.2. Additional data of each node.

Node index	Successors	Lead time	Max service time	Max capacity	Mean demand	Std demand
1	{3,4}	30	5	50	480	44.72
2	{4,5}	15	-	50	480	44.72
3	{6,7}	20	-	50	240	31.62
4	{7,8}	30	-	50	240	31.62
5	{8}	40	-	50	240	31.62
6	{9}	10	-	50	120	22.36
7	{9}	5	-	50	120	22.36
8	{9}	10	-	50	120	22.36
9	-	7	0	50	100	0
10	-	9	0	50	20	10

Table 10.3. Optimal solutions of the safety stock placement problem example.

Node index	Inbound time	Lead time	Outbound time	Net replenish. time
1	0	30	30	0
2	0	15	15	0
3	30	20	50	0
4	30	30	60	0
5	15	40	55	0
6	55	10	41	24
7	60	5	41	24
8	60	10	41	29
9	41	7	0	48
10	41	9	0	50

An optimal solution to the example has a minimum total SSC of 90.27, with optimal inbound service times, outbound service times and net replenishment time shown in Table 10.3.

Key to Formulation: Integer decision variables are defined to represent the inbound and outbound service times. The net replenishment time of each node is computed by obeying the service guarantee requirement. An integer nonlinear programming formulation for the safety stock placement problem can be written as below.

Sets and parameters

V: set of supply chain nodes
A: set of arcs such that $(i, j) \in A$ indicates node i immediately precedes node j
D: set of nodes representing the finished nodes, $D \subset V$
T_i: lead time of node $i \in V$
C_i: maximum number of periods of safety stock at node $i \in V$
k_i: safety stock cost of node $i \in V$ per time period
ρ_i: maximum customer-quoted service time of end node $i \in D$. The smaller its value, the more urgent is the customer demand.

As explained earlier, k_i can be obtained as the product of the standard deviation σ_i of node i, inventory holding cost h_i per unit of i per period, and the z-value associated with certain service level. And σ_i can be computed as a function of the demand variance of i's successors, assuming there is no correlation between the random demand of each node. That is:

$$\sigma_i = \sqrt{\sum_{j:(i,j)\in A} \sigma_j^2}. \tag{10.1}$$

Given the variance of the exogenous demand of finished goods, the standard deviation of each supply chain node can be recursively computed using (10.1).

Decision variables

$SO_i \geq 0$ and integer: outbound service time of node $i \in V$
$SI_i \geq 0$ and integer: inbound service time of node $i \in V$
$\tau_i \geq 0$ and integer: net replenishment time of node $i \in V$

Objective function

$$\text{Minimize} \sum_{i \in V} k_i \sqrt{\tau_i} \tag{10.2}$$

Subject to:

$$SI_j \geq SO_i, \quad \forall (i, j) \in A \tag{10.3}$$

$$\tau_i = SI_i + T_i - SO_i, \quad \forall i \in V \tag{10.4}$$

$$SO_i \leq \rho_i, \quad \forall i \in V \tag{10.5}$$

$$\tau_i \leq C_i, \quad \forall i \in V \tag{10.6}$$

$$SI_i, \ SO_i, \tau_i \in Z^+ \tag{10.7}$$

The objective function (10.2) minimizes the total SSC. Constraint (10.3) satisfies the service guarantee requirement, i.e., the inbound service time of node i must be no less than the outbound service time of node j for every pair of arc $(i, j) \in A$. Constraint (10.4) computes the net replenishment time based on its definition. Constraint (10.5) ensures that the inbound service time of an end node is no later than its maximum allowed service time. The inventory capacity constraint is satisfied by Constraint (10.6). Note that the formulation (10.2)–(10.7) is nonlinear due to the nonlinear objective function (10.2).

Below we show that the safety stock placement problem can be modeled as a project scheduling problem, and present its constraint programming (CP) formulation. The Gantt chart in Figure 10.4 shows the temporal relationship between the inbound and outbound service times of a pair of connected nodes: Node-1 preceding Node-2. A supply chain node is represented by a horizontal bar with inbound service time SI, lead time T, and outbound service time SO (indicated by triangle). The amount of safety stock of a node is a function of its net replenishment time, colored in gray. For instance, the gray

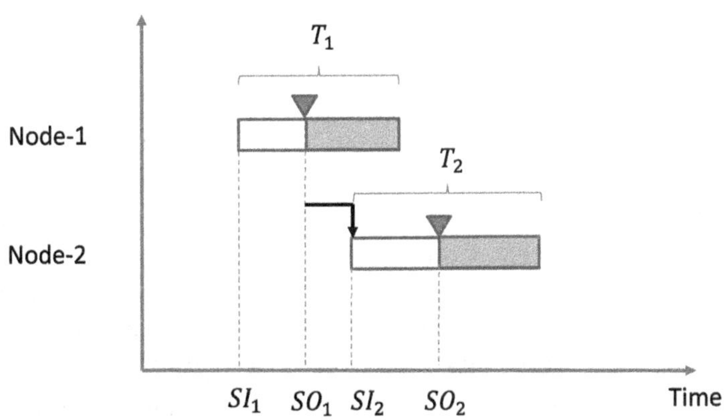

Figure 10.4. Temporal relationship between a pair of supply chain nodes.

portion of Node-1 equals $SI_i + T_i - SO_i$. The temporal relationship between Node-1 and Node-2 is highlighted by the solid arrow, which means that the outbound service time SO_1 of Node-1 must be no greater than the inbound service time SI_2 of Node-2.

Built upon the above modeling framework, we define a real activity for a supply chain node (horizontal bar), and a dummy activity for an outbound service time (triangle) with zero lead time. All other sets and parameters remain the same as those in the nonlinear program. Using the constructs and keywords (in italic font) in OPL Studio, we express the CP model below.

Activity **a**[i *in* V] with lead time **T**[i]
Activity **b**[i *in* V] with lead time zero

The above statements define an array **a** of real activities for the set V of supply chain nodes with their corresponding lead times T, and an array **b** of dummy activities for the supply chain nodes with zero lead time. The objective function is the same as (10.2). The set of CP constraints can be written as:

$$\mathbf{a}[\mathrm{j}]\mathit{startsAfterStart}(\mathbf{b}[\mathrm{i}]), \quad \forall(\mathrm{i},\mathrm{j}) \in \mathrm{A}, \tag{10.8}$$

$$\tau_{\mathrm{i}} = \mathbf{a}\,[\mathrm{i}]\,.\,\mathit{start} + \mathrm{T}\,[\mathrm{i}] - \mathbf{b}\,[\mathrm{i}]\,.\,\mathit{start}, \quad \forall \mathrm{i} \in \mathrm{V}, \tag{10.9}$$

$$\mathbf{b}[\mathrm{i}]\mathit{startsBefore}\rho[\mathrm{i}], \quad \forall \mathrm{i} \in \mathrm{D}, \tag{10.10}$$

$$\mathbf{b}[\mathrm{i}]\mathit{startsAfterStart}(\mathbf{a}[\mathrm{i}], \mathrm{T}\,[\mathrm{i}] - \mathrm{C}[\mathrm{i}]), \quad \forall \mathrm{i} \in \mathrm{V} \tag{10.11}$$

Constraint (10.8) is equivalent to (10.3) to specify the precedence relationship between dummy activity $\mathbf{b}[i]$ and real activity $\mathbf{a}[j]$ for a pair of arcs $(i, j) \in \mathrm{A}$. Constraint (10.9) follows (10.4) to compute the net replenishment time of each node, using the *start* time attribute of an activity. Constraint (10.10) serves the same role of (10.5) to ensure that dummy activity $\mathbf{b}[i]$ starts no later than the maximum service time quoted by customer. Constraint (10.11) states that dummy activity $\mathbf{b}[i]$ must start at least $\mathrm{T}\,[i]-\mathrm{C}[i]$ after the start of real activity $\mathbf{a}[i]$, where $\mathrm{T}\,[i]-\mathrm{C}[i]$ is the minimum time lag between the start of $\mathbf{a}[i]$ and $\mathbf{b}[i]$.

10.3 The Basic Supply Chain Configuration Problem

One limitation of the safety stock placement problem is the assumption that the lead time of each supply chain node is given as constant. It does not explicitly consider the cost of each node either. In reality, lead time and direct cost added of a supply chain function (part, component, semi-finished goods, or purchasing, production, and transportation) often depend on the way (mode) to execute the function. Different transportation modes, e.g., truck versus airfreight, differ in their lead time and cost. Purchasing from an overseas supplier has a long lead time, but can be less costly. Working in multiple shifts shortens the production lead time, but is more costly. Thus, the choice of modes/options to execute a supply chain function can be a decision to be optimized. This has motivated the study and application of the Supply Chain Configuration Problem (SCCP).

The basic version of SCCP can be formally described below. Consider a general supply chain network $G(V, A)$ consisting of a set V of nodes and a set A of arcs. Similar to the safety stock placement problem, a node $i \in V$ represents a supply chain function in general. An arc $(i, j) \in A$ specifies the demand dependency between functions i and j in the BOM. Without loss of generality, it is assumed that one unit of j requires one unit of i for $(i, j) \in A$. Each node $i \in V$ has a set O_i of modes/options available, and must be assigned with exactly one mode. The lead time and direct cost added of node $i \in V$ in mode $k \in O_i$ is T_{ik} and C_{ik}, respectively.

Assume that the demand of each node $i \in V$ follows normal distribution $N(\mu_i, \sigma_i^2)$ with mean μ_i and variance σ_i^2. Given the mean and variance of the *external* demand of the end nodes (products), the mean and variance of the *internal* demand of non-end nodes can be recursively computed following the demand-dependencies in the BOM in the following way, assuming there is no correlation of random demand between the supply chain nodes.

$$\mu_i = \sum_{j:(i,j)\in A} \mu_j$$

$$\sigma_i = \sqrt{\sum_{j:(i,j)\in A} \sigma_j^2}.$$

The maximum customer-quoted service time at end node $i \in E$, where E is a set of end nodes representing customer demand. Assume that the service guarantee is required, such that the *inbound service time* of j cannot be less than the *outbound service time* of i for $(i, j) \in A$. One seeks to find feasible assignment of modes to all the nodes, and inbound/outbound service times of all the nodes, which minimizes the total supply chain costs (TSC), consisting of three terms: (i) the cost of goods sold (COGS); (ii) the pipeline stock cost (PSC); and (iii) the safety stock cost (SSC).

Key to Formulation: The SCCP is an extension of the safety stock placement problem by treating lead time and direct cost added of each node as an *endogenous* decision dependent upon the mode selected for the node. It also considers the more comprehensive TSC including the SSC as one cost component. Binary decision variables are defined for mode selection. Continuous decision variables are defined to obtain the lead time, direct cost added and cumulative cost added of each node.

The SCC in the objective function is computed in a similar way as in the safety stock placement problem. The COGS is a function of the cumulative cost added and mean demand of each node. The PSC can be computed using the Little's Law. The system of constraints consists of two parts. The first part takes care of the mode assignment and computes the lead time, direct cost added and cumulative cost added as functions of the mode selection decision variables. The second part is similar to the constraints in the safety stock placement problem. A mixed-integer nonlinear programming (MINLP) formulation for the basic SCCP can be written as below.

Sets and parameters

- V: set of supply chain nodes
- A: set of arcs
- E: set of end demand nodes
- O_i: set of available modes/options for node $i \in V$
- C_{ik}: direct cost added of option $k \in O_i$ for node $i \in V$
- T_{ik}: lead time of option $k \in O_i$ for node $i \in V$
- μ_i: mean demand rate at node $i \in V$
- σ_i: standard deviation of demand at node $i \in V$

S_i: maximum allowed outbound service time at demand node $i \in E$

α: inventory holding cost rate per unit per time period

β: scaler converting the model's time interval to the planning horizon of interest

Decision variables

$x_{ik} = 1$ if option $k \in O_i$ is chosen for node $i \in V$; and 0 o.w.

$t_i \geq 0$: lead time of node $i \in V$

$c_i \geq 0$: direct cost added for node $i \in V$

$\bar{c}_i \geq 0$: cumulative cost of node $i \in V$

$s_i^{in} \geq 0$ and integer: inbound service time of node $i \in V$

$s_i^{out} \geq 0$ and integer: outbound service time of node $i \in V$

Objective function

$$\text{Minimize} \sum_{i \in V} [\beta c_i \mu_i + \alpha \left(\bar{c}_i - \frac{c_i}{2}\right) t_i \mu_i + \alpha c_i z \sigma_i \sqrt{s_i^{in} + t_i - s_i^{out}}] \tag{10.12}$$

Subject to:

$$\sum_{k \in O_i} x_{ik} = 1, \quad \forall i \in V, \tag{10.13}$$

$$t_i = \sum_{k \in O_i} T_{ik} x_{ik}, \quad \forall i \in V, \tag{10.14}$$

$$c_i = \sum_{k \in O_i} C_{ik} x_{ik}, \quad \forall i \in V, \tag{10.15}$$

$$\bar{c}_i = c_i + \sum_{j:(j,i) \in A} \bar{c}_j, \quad \forall i \in V, \tag{10.16}$$

$$s_j^{in} \geq s_i^{out}, \quad \forall (i,j) \in A, \tag{10.17}$$

$$s_i^{in} + t_i - s_i^{out} \geq 0, \quad \forall i \in V, \tag{10.18}$$

$$s_i^{out} \leq S_i, \quad \forall i \in E, \tag{10.19}$$

$$x_{ik} \in \{0,1\}, \quad t_i, c_i, \bar{c}_i \geq 0, \quad s_i^{in}, s_i^{out} \in Z^+. \tag{10.20}$$

The objective function (10.12) minimizes the TSC with three terms: the first term is COGS as the summation of the direct cost added of

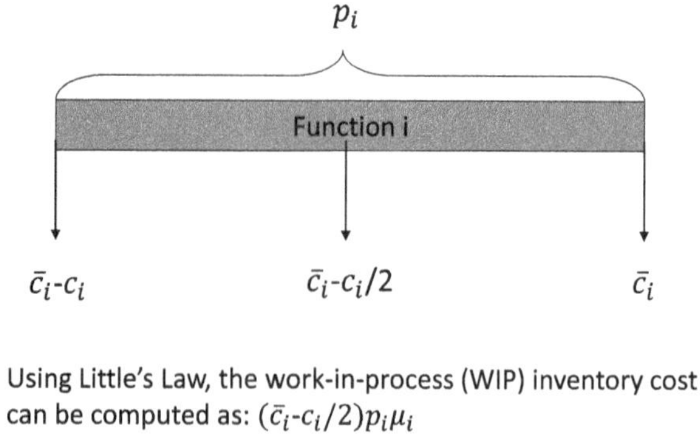

Figure 10.5. Illustration on how to compute the PSC.

all the nodes scaled by β; the second term is the PSC; and the third term is the SSC similar to that in objective function (10.2) of the safety stock placement model. Figure 10.5 shows how to compute the PSC of one node using the Little's Law.

Constraint (10.13) assigns exactly one mode to a node. Constraints (10.14) and (10.15) compute the lead time and direct cost added of each node, respectively. Constraint (10.16) obtains the cumulative cost of each node i as the summation of i's direct cost added and the cumulative costs of all of i's predecessors. Constraint (10.17) requires that for arc $(i, j) \in A$, the inbound service time of i must be no less than the outbound service time of j, which serves the same role as Constraint (10.3). Constraint (10.18) ensures that the net replenishment time of a node must be non-negative, so that the square root of it in the objective function is valid. Constraint (10.19) satisfies the customer-quoted maximum service time for each end node. Constraint (10.20) specifies the domain of all the decision variables.

The safety stock placement problem is clearly a special case of the SCCP with the mode selection variables x_{ik} being fixed. The additional assignment decision in the SCCP makes it more complex and harder to solve than the safety stock placement problem. However, the added complexity makes it widely applicable for real life supply chain design in various settings: MTS, ATS, ATO, MTO and ETO. We will present next several extensions of the basic SCCP for different applications next.

10.4 Food Supply Chain Configuration

In this section, we present an application of SCCP for food supply chains. Consider a food supply chain described by the BOM of multiple end products in a graph $G(V, A)$, where the node set V denotes the *entities* (materials, ingredients, by-products) and *functions* (processing, production, transportation) in the supply chain, and the arc set A represents the dependent demand between pairs of nodes. Specifically, a coefficient λ_{ij} on arc $(i, j) \in A$ indicates the amount of i needed for one unit output of j. λ_{ij} may take different meaning and measurement depending on nature of the relationship between i and j. For instance, transporting goods from one location to another without loss is simply handled by a λ value of 1. But it can be customized to indicate the ratios of ingredients to be mixed for food processing, or for conversion between measurements, e.g., pounds to boxes, etc.

Let F denote the set of end products, with each $f \in F \subset V$ having an external mean demand of μ_f per time period, standard deviation of demand of σ_f, and unit market price of p_f. The maximum service time allowed for end product $f \in F$ is Γ_f. Some nodes in the set $B \subset V$ produce by-products. The amount of by-product generated by one unit of $b \in B$ is η_b with a unit market price of p_b. Each node $i \in V$ has a set O_i of available modes to be fulfilled. We assume single-sourcing for each node, i.e., one and exact one mode is selected for each node. Each mode may differ in their direct cost added and lead time during transportation, production and processing. A node has a quality score q_i affected by its lead time and maximum shelf time. We use the parameters l_{ik}, c_{ik}, δ_{ik} and ε_{ik} to denote the lead time, direct cost added, loss rate and maximum shelf time, respectively, for node i to be fulfilled in mode $k \in O_i$.

10.4.1 *Food Loss*

There is a unique need for modeling food loss during harvesting, packing, processing, storage and transit of a food supply chain, especially for perishable food items. Let the demand of a non-finished good node $i \in V \backslash F$ be denoted by μ_i. Assuming node i has a loss rate of Δ_i, the nominal demand of $\mu_i^{'}$ equals $\mu_i/(1-\Delta_j)$, i.e.,

$$\mu_i^{'} = 1/(1-\Delta_i) \cdot \sum_{j:(i,j)\in A} \mu_j \lambda_{ij} \tag{10.21}$$

Equation (10.21) is obtained via the flow computation in a generalized network with a multiplier on the arc $(i^{'}, i)$ being $1 - \Delta_i$.

10.4.2 *Food Quality*

While the rate of loss quantifies the effect of perishability on the *quantity* of food items, an alternative measure is needed to capture the change of *quality* through the supply chain. Let the quality score of a node i be represented by a ratio $0 \leq q_i \leq 1$, with 1 meaning the highest quality with respect to the benchmark; and 0 meaning the lowest quality with complete loss of value. Assume that the quality score is a function $g(\cdot)$ of the lead time L_i and the maximum shelf time E_i of node i:

$$q_i = g\left(E_i, L_i\right). \tag{10.22}$$

Depending on the dynamics of quality deterioration, $g(\cdot)$ may take a simple linear form or a nonlinear form, e.g., the exponential decaying function. A linear quality function can be written as:

$$q_i = q_i^0 (1 - \omega \cdot L_i/E_i), \tag{10.23}$$

where q_i^0 is the initial (input) quality score of node i, ω is a constant deterioration coefficient, such that the quality degradation is proportional to L_i/E_i. A nonlinear quality function may take the following form:

$$q_i = q_i^0 \cdot e^{-\tau \cdot L_i/E_i}, \tag{10.24}$$

where τ is the decaying factor.

We now show how to compute the system-wide quality score depending on the structure of the food supply chain. Assume that each node i in Figure 10.6 has a quality score of q_i. The overall quality of the pure parallel structure in (a) is the lowest quality score of the three unrelated entities in (a), i.e., $Q_a = \min\{q_1, q_2, q_3\}$. The overall quality score of the pure serial structure in (b) can be computed by multiplying the scores of all three nodes, i.e., $Q_b = q_1 \cdot q_2 \cdot q_3$, because

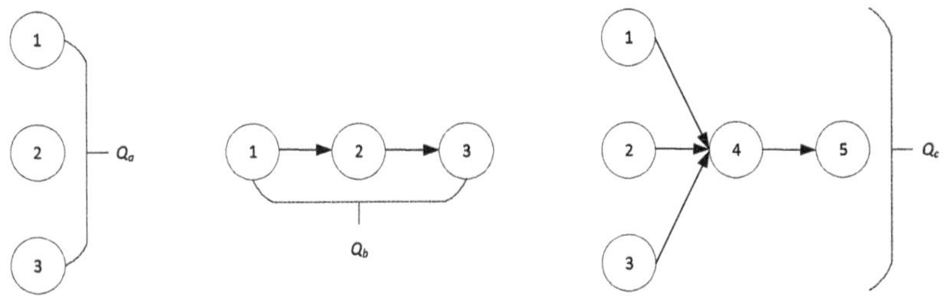

(a) Parallel structure (b) Serial structure (c) Hybrid serial-parallel structure

Figure 10.6. Computation of system-wide quality in a food supply chain.

of the sequential dependency between pairs of nodes. In the general structure in (c) with both serial and parallel sub-structures, the computation of the overall quality requires a mixture of min(·) and multiplicative operations. For instance, $Q_c = \min\{q_1, q_2, q_3\} \cdot q_4 \cdot q_5$.

Example 10.2 (Optimizing Food Supply Chain Configuration). Consider an example of grape supply chain as shown in Figure 10.7. It consists of 18 nodes including 12 entities (ingredients, parts), five processes and one byproduct.[a] The demand dependency is represented by an arc; a dashed arc indicates possible loss between a pair of nodes. The ratio on an arc is the multiplier to describe the corresponding demand dependency. For instance, the multiplier between Box and Packing is 1, meaning that one unit of packed fresh grape requires one box; the multiplier between Fresh Grape and Packing is 10, indicating that 10 kg of fresh grape is packed into one box; the multiplier between Wine Producing and Bottled Wine is 1/300, reflecting the fact that a barrel of wine can be packaged into 300 bottles. 1 kg of grape is crushed to generate 300 g of grape skin and seeds as by-product, i.e., at the ratio of 10/3.

To illustrate the benefit of optimizing food supply chain configuration, we compare the optimal solution with two heuristics: MinCost and MaxQuality. The MinCost heuristic chooses the modes/options with minimum directed cost added, aiming to reduce the unit manufacturing cost (UMC), but sacrificing in lead time, food loss and quality; The MaxQuality heuristic chooses the modes/options with

[a]The aging process of wine requires a special environment and procedure, which is not considered in this case study.

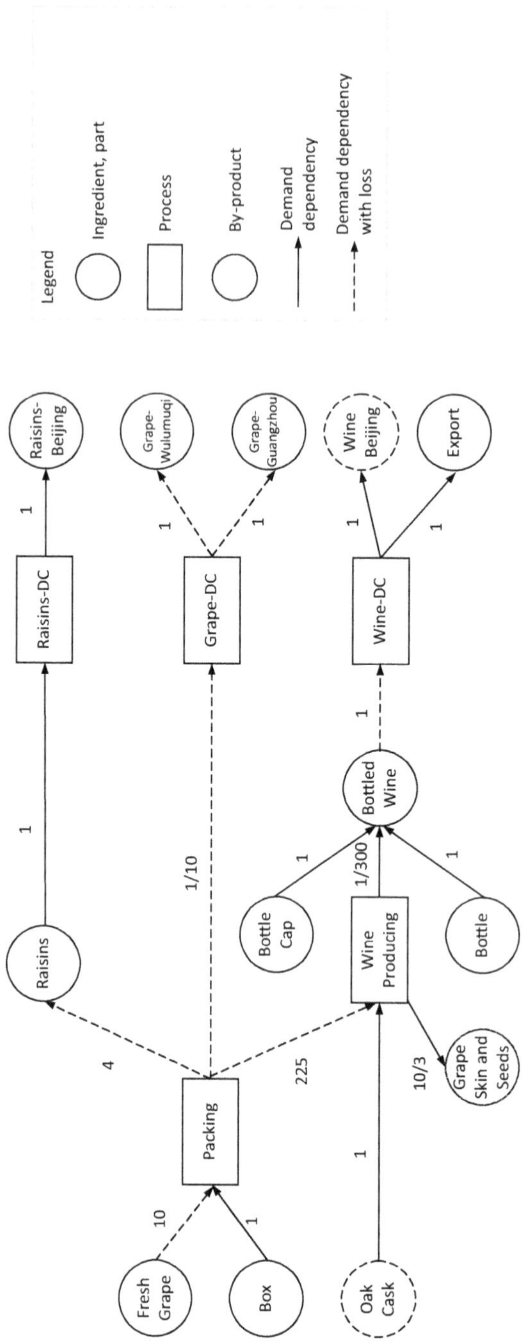

Figure 10.7. An example of grape supply chain network.

maximum quality score, aiming to reduce food loss and deterioration, but incurring more direct cost added.

As shown in Figure 10.8, the MinCost configuration in Figure 10.8(a) stores large amount of stock at the Raisins-DC and Wine-Producing nodes, suggesting more of a MTS paradigm for these two nodes. In comparison, the MaxQuality configuration in Figure 10.8(b) suggests a more *lean*, or close to MTO type paradigm, which cuts the amount of stock at Raisins-DC and Wine-Producing by half, and keeps low level of stock for the end products. The optimal configuration in Figure 10.8(c) prescribes a balance between the two to achieve a hybrid MTS-MTO configuration for different end products. Notably, the stages required for wine are recommended to employ a MTS-like process due to its bulk-production nature. For the highly perishable end product of fresh grapes, the configuration opts to adopt an MTO-like process with low (not zero) level of inventory. More stock level is recommended for the less perishable end product of raisins.

Key to Formulation: The Food Supply Chain Configuration Problem (FSCCP) is an extension of the standard SCCP by considering the more complex BOM structure with by-products and general demand dependencies, plus food loss and food quality deterioration through the supply chain. Its model formulation builds upon that of the SCCP with additional decision variables defined for loss rate and quality score. The constraints are also expanded accordingly to properly compute the loss rate and quality score using the constructs presented earlier for FSCCP. An MINLP formulation for the FSCCP can be written as below.

<u>Sets and parameters</u>

- V: set of all the nodes representing the entities and functions in the supply chain
- F: set of finished food products, and $F \subset V$
- I: set of initial nodes in the supply chain with no predecessor
- B: set of by-products, and $B \subset V$
- A: set of arcs describing the demand dependency in the BOM associated with the supply chain
- O_i: set of modes available for fulfilling node $i \in V$
- λ_{ij}: a multiplier for the amount of entity i needed for one unit output of entity j for $(i,j) \in A$

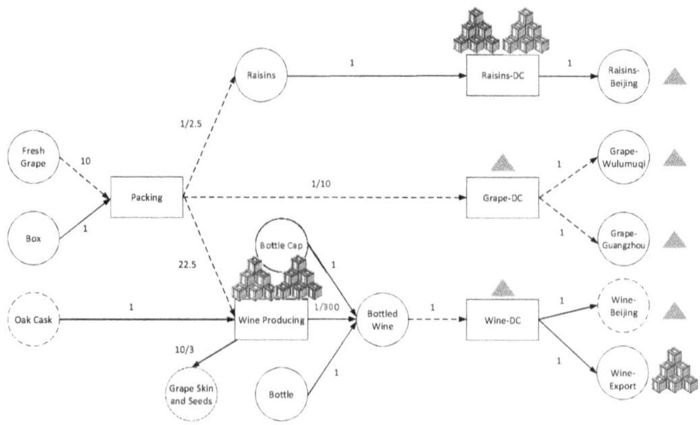

(a) MinCost configuration.

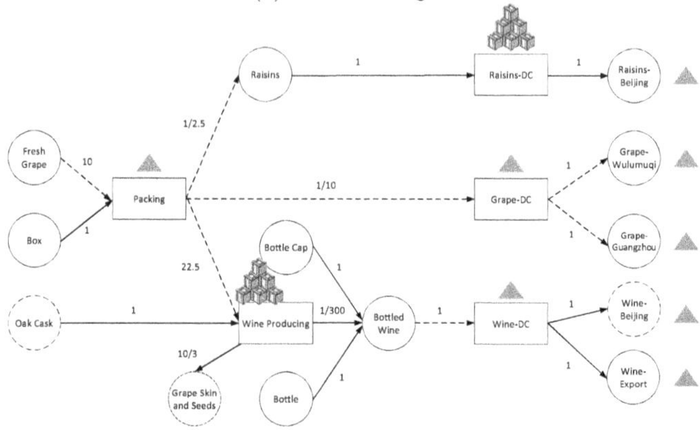

(b) MaxQuality configuration.

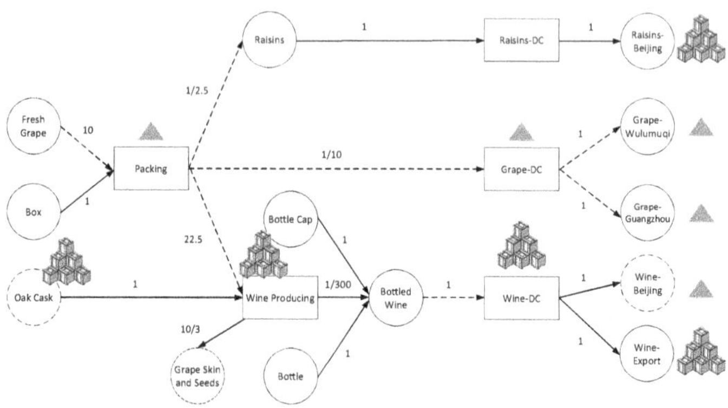

(c) Optimal configuration.

Figure 10.8. Comparison of optimal and heuristic configurations of the grape supply chain.

μ_f: mean external demand of end product $f \in F$
σ_f: standard deviation of the external demand of end product $f \in F$
σ_i: standard deviation of the internal demand of entity $i \in V \backslash F$, which can be computed as $\sigma_i = \sqrt{\sum_{j:(i,j)\in A} \lambda_{ij}^2 \sigma_j^2}$
Γ_f: the latest service time of end product $f \in F$
p_f: selling price per unit of end product $f \in F$
p_b: selling price per unit of by-product $b \in B$
η_b: amount of by-product generated by one unit of $b \in B$
l_{ik}: lead time for node i to be fulfilled by mode $k \in O_i$
c_{ik}: direct cost added for node i to be fulfilled by mode $k \in O_i$
δ_{ik}: loss rate for node i to be fulfilled by mode $k \in O_i$
ε_{ik}: maximum shelf time for node i to be fulfilled by mode $k \in O_i$
h: inventory holding cost per unit of entity per time period
β: a scalar converting the model's underlying time unit into the firm's time interval of interest

Decision variables

X_{ik}: binary decision variable for mode selection, $X_{ik} = 1$ if and only if node $i \in V$ is assigned with mode $k \in \{1, 2, \ldots, R_i\}$, which R_i is the number of modes of node i
$S_i^{\text{in}} \geq 0$ and integer: the in-bound service time of node $i \in V$
$S_i^{\text{out}} \geq 0$ and integer: the out-bound service time of node $i \in V$
$L_i \geq 0$ and integer: lead time of node $i \in V$
$C_i \geq 0$: direct cost added per unit of node $i \in V$
$\bar{C}_i \geq 0$: cumulative cost per unit of node $i \in V$
$\Delta_i \geq 0$: rate of loss of node $i \in V$
$E_i \geq 0$ and integer: maximum shelf time of node $i \in V$
$Q_i \geq 0$: quality score of node $i \in V$
$\bar{Q}_i \geq 0$: inbound quality score into node $i \in V \backslash \mathrm{I}$
$U_i \geq 0$: adjusted mean demand of node $i \in V$

Objective function

$$\text{Maximize} \sum_{f\in F} p_f Q_f U_f + \sum_{b\in B} p_b Q_b \eta_b U_b - \sum_{i\in V}$$
$$\left[\beta C_i U_i + h\bar{C}_i \sigma_i \sqrt{S_i^{\text{in}} + L_i - S_i^{\text{out}}} + h\left(\bar{C}_i - \frac{C_i}{2}\right) L_i U_i\right] \quad (10.25)$$

Subject to:

$$\sum_{k\in O_i} X_{ik} = 1, \quad \forall i \in V \tag{10.26}$$

$$L_i = \sum_{k\in O_i} l_{ik}X_{ik}, \quad \forall i \in V \tag{10.27}$$

$$C_i = \sum_{k\in O_i} c_{ik}X_{ik}, \quad \forall i \in V \tag{10.28}$$

$$\Delta_i = \sum_{k\in O_i} \delta_{ik}X_{ik}, \quad \forall i \in V \tag{10.29}$$

$$E_i = \sum_{k\in O_i} \varepsilon_{ik}X_{ik}, \quad \forall i \in V \tag{10.30}$$

$$\bar{C}_j = C_j + \sum_{i:(i,j)\in A} \lambda_{ij}\bar{C}_i, \quad \forall j \in V \tag{10.31}$$

$$U_i = \frac{\mu_i}{1-\Delta_i} \quad \forall i \in F \tag{10.32}$$

$$U_i = \frac{1}{1-\Delta_i}\sum_{j:(i,j)\in A} \lambda_{ij}U_j \quad \forall i \in VF \tag{10.33}$$

$$Q_i = 100\% \cdot g(E_i,\, L_i), \quad \forall i \in \mathrm{I} \tag{10.34}$$

$$\bar{Q}_j \le Q_i, \quad \forall j \in V\backslash \mathrm{I},\, i:(i,j)\in A \tag{10.35}$$

$$Q_i = \bar{Q}_i \cdot g(E_i,\, L_i), \quad \forall i \in V\backslash \mathrm{I} \tag{10.36}$$

$$S_j^{\text{in}} \ge S_i^{\text{out}}, \quad \forall (i,j) \in A \tag{10.37}$$

$$S_i^{\text{in}} + L_i - S_i^{\text{out}} \ge 0, \quad \forall i \in V \tag{10.38}$$

$$S_f^{\text{out}} \le \Gamma_f, \quad \forall f \in F \tag{10.39}$$

$$X_{ik} \in \{0,\, 1\}, \quad S_i^{\text{in}}, \quad S_i^{\text{out}}, \quad L_i, \quad E_i \ge 0 \text{ and integer} \tag{10.40}$$

$$C_i, \quad \bar{C}_i, \quad \Delta_i, \quad Q_i, \quad \bar{Q}_i \ge 0. \tag{10.41}$$

The objective function (10.25) maximizes the total net profit (TNF) as the difference between the total revenue (TR) and the TSC. The TR is the sum of the revenue of all the end products and all the by-products, assuming a linear relationship between the revenue and the quality score of the corresponding product. The TSC is computed as the sum of three components, namely, COGS, SSC and PSC.

Constraint (10.26) assigns exactly one mode to a node from all the available modes. Constraints (10.27)–(10.30) compute the lead time, direct cost added, loss rate and maximum shelf time of each node depending upon the mode selected for the node, respectively. Constraint (10.31) defines the cumulative cost of each node j as the summation of the direct cost added of j, and the direct cost added of all of j's predecessor i multiplied by the demand dependency λ_{ij} between i and j. Constraint (10.32) adjusts the external demand of an end product with its loss rate. Constraint (10.33) computes the internal demand of a non-end product node. Constraints (10.34)–(10.36) calculate the quality score of each node in a generalized supply chain network that has both the serial and parallel structures as shown in Figure 10.6. Specifically, the quality score of an initial node with no predecessor in (10.34) is provided by the function $g(\cdot)$ of (10.23) or (10.24). The quality score of other nodes j is computed in two steps in (10.35) and (10.36): (i) To get the in-bound quality score $\bar{Q}_j$ into node j as the minimum quality score of j's predecessor nodes in a parallel structure as shown in Figure 10.6(a). Constraint (10.35) is a way to linearize the $\min(\cdot)$ function for getting the minimum quality score of j's predecessor nodes; (ii) to multiply $\bar{Q}_j$ with the function $g(\cdot)$ in Constraint (10.36) as in a serial structure of Figure 10.6(b). Constraint (10.37) requires that the in-bound service time of a successor node j cannot be early than the out-bound service time of j's predecessor i for $(i, j) \in A$. Constraint (10.38) ensures that the net replenishment time of node i must be non-negative. Constraint (10.39) makes sure that the out-bound service time of an end product must not exceed its latest service time. Finally, Constraints (10.40) and (10.41) specify the domains of all the decision variables.

10.5 SCCP with Resource Constraints

Note that the determination of inbound and outbound service times in the safety stock placement problem and the SCCP is only constrained by temporal constraints, i.e., the precedence relationship between the outbound service time of a predecessor and the inbound service time of a successor, the maximum customer-quoted service for end product nodes, and the non-negativity of net replenishment time. An optimal solution can behave such that multiple supply chain functions (the real activities in Figure 10.4) overlap in their execution, without considering whether there would be sufficient resources to sustain the operation. Indeed, an assumption implicitly made in the basic SCCP is that there are ample resources available in the scheduling of the inbound and outbound service times of all supply chain functions.

Consider two types of resources, renewable and non-renewable, that would directly impact the determination of inbound and outbound service times and the amount of safety stock. A *renewable* resource is one with its availability and full capacity renewed and required in every time period of the planning horizon. Examples include machines, equipment and personnel. A *non-renewable* resource is one with its capacity defined and consumed for the entire planning horizon, e.g., budget, raw materials and supplies.

Figure 10.9 shows conceptually how the non-renewable and renewable resources would impact supply chain configuration, in terms of both mode selection and inbound/outbound service times. Each horizontal bar represents a supply chain function with its starting time (inbound service time SI), lead time (T) and outbound service time SO (indicate by the blue triangle). The difference between $SI+t$ and SO, colored in gray, indicates the length of net replenishment time of a function, which positively relates to the amount of safety stock in the system. The inbound service time of a function must be no less than the outbound service time of its predecessor, as indicated by the solid arrows in (a). Suppose Function-1 is a predecessor to Function-2, then the inbound service time of Function-2, SI_2, must be greater than or equal to the outbound service of Function-1, SO_1.

Consider the case in (b) when the non-renewable resource (e.g., budget) is tight, then supply chain functions will be configured with modes/options requiring less cost, which may take longer to complete, i.e., longer durations of T_1 and T_2. With the inbound and outbound service times being the same as in (a), more net replenishment time is needed, which incurs more SSC.

Next consider the case in (c) when the renewable resource is low enough that there is not sufficient capacity to allow simultaneous execution of Function-1 and Function-2. That is, Function-2 can no longer overlap with Function-1 as in (a), but needs to be pushed

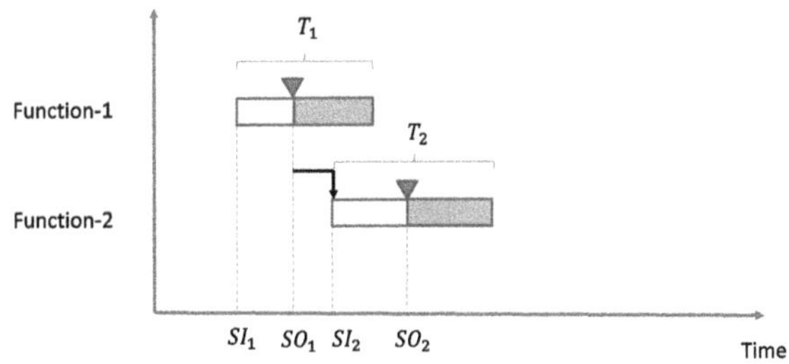

(a) The base case.

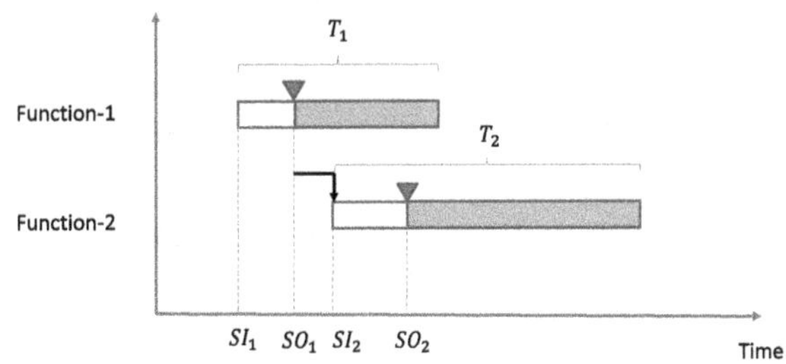

(b) The case of less non-renewable resource.

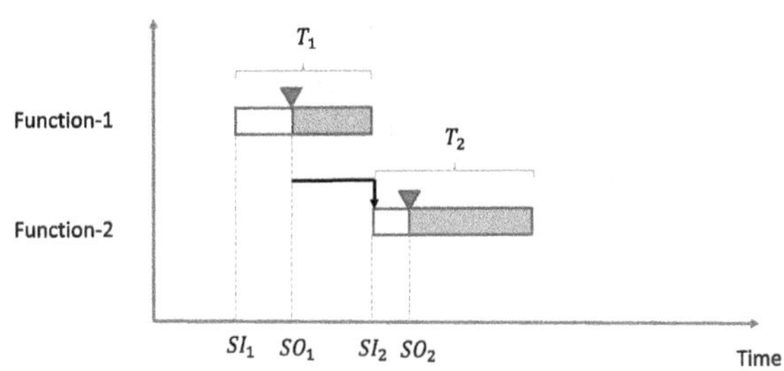

(c) The case of less renewable resource.

Figure 10.9. The impact of limited resources on supply chain configuration.

back after Function-1 is completed. This immediately increases the amount of safety stock needed for Function-2 compared to that in (a).

The above observations have motivated the study and development of SCCP with Resource Constraints, which we call SCCP-RC in the sequel. It can also be applied for configuring a food supply chain, where the growing, picking, packing and processing stages all require significant amount of labor (renewable resources) and capital investment (non-renewable resources).

The SCCP-RC shares the same problem setting of the basic SCCP. On top of that, one considers a set R of renewable resources, each of which has a capacity of ω_r available in every time period for $r \in R$. The execution of function $i \in V$ requires a_{ikr} units of renewable resource $r \in R$ in mode $k \in O_i$. There is also a set Γ of non-renewable resources, with $\gamma \in \Gamma$ having a capacity of φ_γ available for the entire planning horizon. Function $i \in V$ consumes $b_{ik\gamma}$ units of non-renewable resource $\gamma \in \Gamma$ in mode $k \in O_i$.

Key to Formulation: The SCCP-RC is an extension of the standard SCCP by explicitly considering two types of resource constraints: renewable and non-renewable. The non-renewable resource constraint restricts the mode assignment decision, while the renewable resource constraint limits the inbound and outbound service time decision. It is also a variant of the Multi-Mode Resource-Constrained Project Scheduling to be introduced in Chapter 12.

To model the renewable resource constraints, we employ the time-indexed decision variables to compute the inbound and outbound service times, which facilitates the expression of renewable resource constraint. We refer the reader to Chapter 12 for the use of time-indexed decision variables to model complex scheduling applications.

Sets and parameters

- V: set of supply chain nodes
- A: set of arcs
- E: set of end demand nodes
- R: set of renewable resources
- Γ: set of non-renewable resources
- T: set of time periods in the planning horizon
- O_i: set of available modes/options for node $i \in V$
- ω_{ik}: direct cost added of option $k \in O_i$ for node $i \in V$
- T_{ik}: lead time of option $k \in O_i$ for node $i \in V$
- λ_{ij}: a multiplier for the amount of entity i needed for one unit output of entity j for $(i,j) \in A$
- μ_f: mean external demand of end product $f \in F$
- σ_f: standard deviation of the external demand of end product $f \in F$

σ_i: standard deviation of the internal demand of entity $i \in V \backslash F$, which can be computed as $\sigma_i = \sqrt{\sum_{j:(i,j) \in A} \lambda_{ij}^2 \sigma_j^2}$

a_{ikr}: amount of renewable resource $r \in R$ required by node $i \in V$ in mode $k \in O_i$

b_{ikr}: amount of non-renewable resource $\gamma \in \Gamma$ required by node $i \in V$ in mode $k \in O_i$

ω_r: maximum capacity of renewable resource $r \in R$ in every time period of the planning horizon

φ_γ: maximum capacity non-renewable resource $\gamma \in \Gamma$ available for the entire planning horizon

μ_i: mean demand rate at node $i \in V$

σ_i: standard deviation of demand at node $i \in V$

S_f: maximum customer-quoted service time at end product node $f \in E$

α: inventory holding cost rate per unit per time period

β: scaler converting the model's time interval to the planning horizon of interest.

Decision variables

X_{ikt}: binary decision variable for mode selection, $X_{ikt} = 1$ if and only if node $i \in V$ is assigned with mode $k \in \{1, 2, \ldots, R_i\}$ and starts in time period $t \in T$ (inbound service time)

$S_i^{\text{out}} \geq 0$ and integer: the outbound service time of node $i \in V$

$S_i^{\text{in}} \geq 0$ and integer: the inbound service time of node $i \in V$, which can be computed as a function of X_{ikt}

$L_i \geq 0$ and integer: lead time of node $i \in V$

$C_i \geq 0$: direct cost added per unit of node $i \in V$

$\bar{C}_i \geq 0$: cumulative cost per unit of node $i \in V$

$A_{ir} \geq 0$: requirement of renewable resource $r \in R$ by node $i \in V$

$B_{i\gamma} \geq 0$: consumption of non-renewable resource $\gamma \in \Gamma$ by node $i \in V$.

Objective function

$$\text{Minimize} \sum_{i \in V} \left[\beta C_i \mu_i + h \bar{C}_i \sigma_i \sqrt{S_i^{\text{in}} + L_i - S_i^{\text{out}}} + h \left(\bar{C}_i - \frac{C_i}{2} \right) L_i \mu_i \right] \tag{10.42}$$

Subject to:

$$\sum_{k\in O_i}\sum_{t=ES_i}^{LS_i} X_{ikt} = 1, \quad \forall i \in V \tag{10.43}$$

$$L_i = \sum_{k\in O_i}\sum_{t=ES_i}^{LS_i} T_{ik}X_{ikt}, \quad \forall i \in V \tag{10.44}$$

$$C_i = \sum_{k\in O_i}\sum_{t=ES_i}^{LS_i} \omega_{ik}X_{ikt}, \quad \forall i \in V \tag{10.45}$$

$$A_{ir} = \sum_{k\in O_i}\sum_{t=ES_i}^{LS_i} a_{ikr}X_{ikt}, \quad \forall i \in V, r \in R \tag{10.46}$$

$$B_{i\gamma} = \sum_{k\in O_i}\sum_{t=ES_i}^{LS_i} b_{ik\gamma}X_{ikt}, \quad \forall i \in V, \gamma \in \Gamma \tag{10.47}$$

$$\bar{C}_j = C_j + \sum_{i:(i,j)\in A} \lambda_{ij}\bar{C}_i, \quad \forall j \in V \tag{10.48}$$

$$S_i^{\text{in}} = \sum_{k\in O_i}\sum_{t=ES_i}^{LS_i} t \cdot X_{ikt}, \quad \forall i \in V \tag{10.49}$$

$$S_j^{\text{in}} \geq S_i^{\text{out}}, \quad \forall (i,j) \in A \tag{10.50}$$

$$S_i^{\text{in}} + L_i - S_i^{\text{out}} \geq 0, \quad \forall i \in V \tag{10.51}$$

$$S_f^{\text{out}} \leq \Gamma_f, \quad \forall f \in F \tag{10.52}$$

$$\beta \sum_{i\in V} B_{i\gamma} \leq \varphi_\gamma, \quad \forall \gamma \in \Gamma \tag{10.53}$$

$$\sum_{i\in V}\sum_{k\in O_i} r_{ik} \cdot \sum_{\tau=\max\{t-l_{ik},\, ES_i\}}^{\min\{t-1,\, LS_i\}} X_{ik\tau} \leq \omega_r, \quad \forall r \in R, t \in T \tag{10.54}$$

$$X_{ikt} \in \{0,\, 1\}, \quad S_i^{\text{in}}, \quad S_i^{\text{out}}, L_i \geq 0 \text{ and integer} \tag{10.55}$$

$$C_i, \quad \bar{C}_i, \quad A_{ir}, \quad B_{i\gamma} \geq 0. \tag{10.56}$$

The objective function (10.42) minimizes supply chain costs, similar to the (10.12) in basic SCCP model. Constraint (10.43) ensures that each supply chain function is assigned with exactly one model and starts only once, i.e., there is no preemption (interruption and restart). ES_i and LS_i are the earliest start time and latest time of function $i \in V$, respectively. They can be obtained through the critical path method (CPM) type of approach without considering resource constraint. Constraints (10.44)–(10.47) computes the lead time, direct cost added, renewable resource requirement and non-renewable resource consumption of a function, respectively. Constraint (10.48) computes the cumulative cost of a function. Constraint (10.49) computes the inbound service time of a function using the binary time-indexed decision variable. Constraint (10.50) satisfies the precedence relationship between the outbound service time of function i and the inbound service time of function j for a pair of arcs $(i, j) \in A$ as in (10.18). Constraint (10.51) ensures that the net replenishment time of a function must be non-negative. Constraint (10.52) guarantees that the outbound service time of an end product node must be not exceed the maximum customer-quoted service time as in (10.19). Constraint (10.53) enforces that the maximum available capacity of each non-renewable resource is not exceeded. Constraint (10.54) ensures that for each renewable resource and time period, the total required capacity of the resource does not exceed its available capacity. Constraints (10.55) and (10.56) specify the domains of the decision variables.

10.6 Integrated SCCP with New Product Diffusion

The SCCP models introduced so far all assume that the exogenous demand of end products can be properly estimated or forecasted through historical sales/demand data. While this works most of the time when quality historical demand data is available using various predictive analytical methods: regression, time series, neural networks and machine learning; in situations where historical demand data is not available, e.g., for a new product that has not been launched, treating demand as an exogenous input may not work. This calls for a new modeling framework that endogenously predicts the demand of new product for supply chain configuration.

A viable approach in the marketing literature to predict demand dynamics of new products is through the well-known *Bass diffusion model*. It assumes that the market demand of new product is driven by two factors: the level of innovation and the degree of imitation among customers. Figure 10.10 depicts the concept of the Bass diffusion model.

As shown in Figure 10.10(a), at time zero, innovators adopt early and gradually diminish over time. Influenced by word-of-mouth and observation of the innovation in use, the number of imitators starts to increase. As more people adopt, there is more chance for imitators to become adopters, thus the number of adopters increases at an increasing rate until reaching the peak.

Figure 10.10(b) shows the dynamics of new adopters, including both innovators and imitators, and cumulative adopters. Note that the number of cumulative adopters follows an S-shape trend, i.e., the increase of adopters is slow initially, then the rate of increase goes up before it decreases.

In each time period t, a manufacturer produces r_t units of products and sells y_t units. The cumulative sales up to t is denoted by Y_t. Let d_t and D_t represent the instantaneous and cumulative demand, respectively. The demand dynamics described by a variant of the Bass diffusion model can be expressed as:

$$d_t = p\,(m - D_t) + \frac{q}{m} Y_t (m - D_t), \qquad (10.57)$$

where p is the coefficient of innovation, q is the coefficient of imitation, and m represents the fixed market potential. The demand d_t at time t is expressed as a fraction of the remaining potential adopters

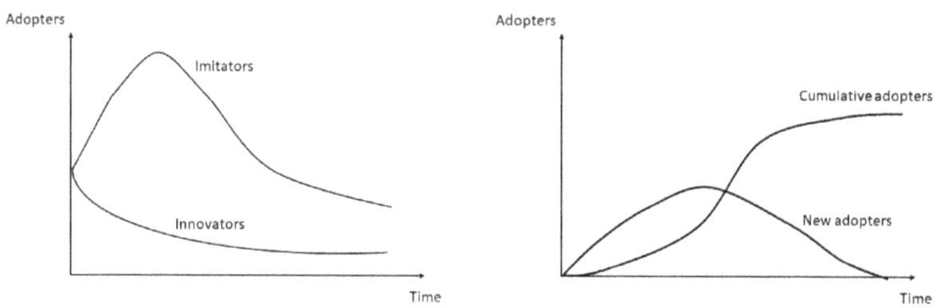

(a) Innovators and imitators (b) New and cumulative adopters

Figure 10.10. Conceptual illustration of the Bass diffusion model.

$m - D_t$ consisting of two components: one due to the impact of mass-media or coefficient of innovation p, and the other proportional to the cumulative sales Y_t due to positive word-of-mouth or coefficient of imitation q. The unmet demand up to t can be represented as $D_t - Y_t$, which can be completely lost or backlogged at a percentage of ξ.

Under limited production and supply capacity, the manufacturer might be overwhelmed by potentially rapid growth of demand for the new product due to marketing promotion activities and positive word-of-mouth. Real world examples of this phenomenon include Nitendo's Wii and Apple's prominent iPhones. Both were hit by the rapid growth of demand of these innovative products, which caused insufficient capacity to satisfy the demand after launching. Thus, there is incentive to study the optimal timing and level of production and sales to avoid loss of sales due to sufficient capacity, and to maximize the total profit during the product's lifecycle. This can be achieved by a New Production Diffusion (NPD) model.

The NPD and SCCP models are related in the following two ways: (i) The NPD model endogenously determines the demand/sales pattern for the entire planning horizon, by finding the mean, μ, and standard deviation, δ, of the demand for the new product; and (ii) The SCCP model provides the UMC as the cumulative cost of end product for the NPD model.

Key to Formulation: In the integrated SCCP-NPD model, the modeling constructs of NPD and SCCP are each maintained. Linking decision variables are defined to represent the mean and standard deviation of endogenous demand. The production cost in the NPD sub-model is replaced by the UMC obtained from the SCCP sub-model. The following sets and parameters are needed for the integrated SCCP-NPD model.

Sets and parameters

m: initial size of potential adopter population of product
T: number of time periods of the planning horizon
V: set of functions in the supply chain
N: number of functions in the supply chain, i.e., $N = |V|$
E: set of arcs in the supply chain
ξ: fraction of unmet demand that is backlogged

p: coefficient of innovation
q: coefficient of imitation
K: production capacity per time period
π: sales price ratio over the UMC, which is the cumulative direct cost added of the end product
w: waiting cost rate per unit backlogged per unit time
h: inventory holding cost rate per time period
O_i: set of available options for supply chain function $i \in V$
T_{ik}: lead time of the k-th option for function $i \in V$
ω_{ik}: direct cost added of the k-th option for function $i \in V$
Γ: maximum customer-quoted service time of the end product
z: z-value determined by user-specified service level

<u>Decision variables</u>

Decision variables related to SCCP

$x_{ik} = 1$ if option $k \in O_i$ is chosen for supply chain node $i \in V$; and 0 o.w.
$t_i \geq 0$: lead time of node $i \in V$
$c_i \geq 0$: direct cost added for node $i \in V$
$\bar{c}_i \geq 0$: cumulative cost of node $i \in V$
$s_i^{in} \geq 0$ and integer: inbound service time of node $i \in V$
$s_i^{out} \geq 0$ and integer: outbound service time of node $i \in V$

Decision variables related to NPD

$y_t \geq 0$: sales of product at time $t \in T$
$Y_t \geq 0$: cumulative sales of product at time $t \in T$
$d_t \geq 0$: demand at time $t \in T$
$D_t \geq 0$: cumulative demand at time $t \in T$
$L_t \geq 0$: cumulative units of backlogged products at time $t \in T$
$I_t \geq 0$: inventory at time $t \in T$
$r_t \geq 0$: production level at time $t \in T$
$R_t \geq 0$: cumulative production level at time $t \in T$

Decision variables connecting SCCP and NPD

$\mu_N \geq 0$: mean supply of the end product (supply chain function N) over the planning horizon
$\sigma_N \geq 0$: standard deviation of supply of the end product over the planning horizon

Objective function

$$\text{Maximize} \sum_{t=0}^{T} \bar{c}_N \left[\pi y_t - r_t - wL_t - hI_t\right] - \sum_{i=1}^{N} h\left(\bar{c}_i - \frac{c_i}{2}\right) p_i \mu_i$$

$$-\sum_{i=1}^{N} h\bar{c}_i \kappa \sigma_i \sqrt{s_i^{in} + p_i - s_i^{out}} \tag{10.58}$$

Subject to:

Constraints on NPD

$$R_{t+1} = R_t + r_t, \quad \forall t = 0, 1 \ldots, T-1, \tag{10.59}$$

$$D_{t+1} = D_t + d_t, \quad \forall t = 0, 1 \ldots, T-1, \tag{10.60}$$

$$Y_{t+1} = Y_t + y_t, \quad \forall t = 0, 1 \ldots, T-1, \tag{10.61}$$

$$d_t = p\,(m - D_t) + \frac{q}{m} Y_t (m - D_t), \forall t = 0, 1 \ldots, T, \tag{10.62}$$

$$I_t = R_t - Y_t, \quad \forall t = 0, 1 \ldots, T, \tag{10.63}$$

$$L_{t+1} = \xi(L_t + d_t - y_t), \quad \forall t = 0, 1 \ldots, T, \tag{10.64}$$

$$L_t \geq 0 \,\text{and}\, L_0 = 0, \tag{10.65}$$

$$I_t \geq 0 \,\text{and}\, I_0 = 0, \tag{10.66}$$

$$r_t \leq K \,\text{and}\, R_0 = 0. \tag{10.67}$$

Constraints on SCCP

$$\sum_{k \in O_i} x_{ik} = 1, \quad \forall i = 1, \ldots, N, \tag{10.68}$$

$$t_i = \sum_{k \in O_i} T_{ik} x_{ik}, \quad \forall i = 1, \ldots, N, \tag{10.69}$$

$$c_i = \sum_{k \in O_i} C_{ik} x_{ik}, \quad \forall i = 1, \ldots, N, \tag{10.70}$$

$$\bar{c}_i - \sum_{j:(j,i) \in A} \bar{c}_j - c_i = 0, \quad \forall i = 1, \ldots, N, \tag{10.71}$$

$$s_i^{in} \geq s_j^{out}, \quad \forall i = 1, \ldots, N, \quad j : (j, i) \in E, \tag{10.72}$$

$$s_i^{in} + p_i - s_i^{out} \geq 0, \quad \forall i = 1, \ldots, N, \tag{10.73}$$

$$s_N^{out} \leq \Gamma, \tag{10.74}$$

$$\mu_i = \sum_{j:(i,j)\in E} \mu_j, \quad \forall i = 1, \ldots, N, \tag{10.75}$$

$$s_i^{in}, \quad s_i^{out} \geq 0 \, \text{and integer}, \, \forall i = 1, \ldots, N, \tag{10.76}$$

$$x_{ik} \in \{0, 1\}, \quad \forall i = 1, \ldots, N, \quad k \in O_i \tag{10.77}$$

Linking Constraints

$$\mu_N = Y_T/(T + 1) \tag{10.78}$$

$$\sigma_N = \sqrt{\sum_{t=0}^{T} (y_t - \mu_N)^2 / T} \tag{10.79}$$

The objective function (10.58) maximizes the total net profit over the new product's lifetime as the difference between the total life-cycle revenue and TSC. The total life-cycle revenue is calculated as the total sales revenue minus three items: the cost of goods produced, waiting cost of backlogged demand and inventory holding cost of finished goods. Notice that the per-unit product cost is represented by the cumulative cost of the end product $\bar{c}_N$, which is endogenously determined through configuring the corresponding supply chain. This reflects the second link in the hybrid model. The supply chain configuration cost is defined as the sum of PSC and SSC as in the basic SCCP model.

Constraints (10.59) through (10.61) compute the cumulative production, demand and sales of the product in each time period of the new product diffusion process, respectively. Constraint (10.62) follows (10.57) as explained earlier. Constraint (10.63) calculates the inventory of finished product in each time period as the difference between cumulative production and cumulative sales. Constraint (10.64) states that a fraction ξ of the unmet demand is instantaneously backlogged. By adjusting ξ, the model is able to capture various scenarios ranging from complete loss of sales ($\xi = 0$) to complete backlog ($\xi = 1$). Constraints (10.65) through (10.67) specify the bounds of the decision variables in the NPD sub-problem.

Constraints (10.68) through (10.77) are similar to those in the SCCP model. Constraint (10.68) assigns exactly one mode/option to a supply chain function. Constraints (10.69) and (10.70) compute the lead time and direct cost added of each function, respectively. Constraint (10.71) calculates the cumulative cost added for each function. Constraint (10.72) states that the inbound service time of a function must be no less than the outbound service time of its immediate predecessors. Constraint (10.73) ensures that the net replenishment time of a function is non-negative. Constraint (10.74) guarantees than the deadline of the new product (end product N) be satisfied. Constraint (10.75) computes the internal demand of each function assuming the multipliers of demand dependency all equal 1. Constraints (10.76) and (10.77) specify the domains of decision variables in the SCCP sub-problem.

Constraints (10.78) and (10.79) calculate the mean and standard deviation of sales of the new product over its entire life cycle, respectively. Note that the demand pattern is now endogenously determined by the production and sales plan during the new product diffusion process. They establish the first link between the product diffusion and supply chain configuration.

10.7 Additional Notes

The SCCP has its roots in the guaranteed service model (GSM [68, 69]) for the safety stock placement or inventory positioning problem [70–73]. It was coined by the seminal work of [74, 75]. The full study of SCCP model for food supply chains in Section 10.4 is available in [76]. While the original SCCP mainly deals with the MTS and/or assemble-to-stock supply chains, the model in Section 10.5 handles the MTO SCCP with explicit resource constraints of machines and workforce [37, 77]. This situation becomes more relevant during the COVID-19 pandemic, which caused significant shortage of workforce and supply chain disruptions in multiple industries. The stream of research addressing the SCCP for new products with an endogenous demand diffusion process is available in [78–80]. An application of SCCP with low carbon emission consideration is available in [81].

Exercises

10.1. How is BOM of a product related to the supply chain of the product? How is it related to and differs from the physical supply chain (e.g., facilities, distribution centers, warehouses) of the product?

10.2. Explain how the safety stock placement problem can be applied to prescribe data-driven optimal supply chain paradigms, e.g., MTS, ATS, ATO, MTO and ETO.

10.3. Show and discuss application examples of the safety stock problem.

10.4. Discuss the connections and differences between the SCCP and Supply Chain Network Design.

10.5. Discuss the relationships between the SCCP and the safety stock placement problem, and explain why SCCP is a comprehensive and flexible modeling approach for supply chain planning?

10.6. Show and discuss application examples of the SCCP.

10.7. Discuss possible variants and extensions of the basic SCCP with real world examples.

10.8. ABC Inc. manufactures and sells portable computer tablets with various models and configurations. In addition to standard sales channels through wholesalers and contracted retailers, it also adopts the Dell-type business paradigm to allow customers to choose and configure their preferred portable pads online in terms of CPU speed, memory, storage space, display size, cover color, and a number of other optional features. The company sources most of its parts and components from suppliers in East Asia, but also has options to source from suppliers in North America. In the past, ABC Inc. has been relying on a sole supplier for its CPU chips and other core components, but the COVID-19 pandemic has caused significant disruption with shortage of supply and prolonged lead time. Realizing this issue and the potential future supply risk and disruption, ABC Inc. would like reconfigure its supply chain to achieve better efficiency and resilience. Explain and discuss ABC's supply chain configuration needs. Propose an optimization model to address these needs. Explain how your model is able to improve the supply chain resilience. Elaborate the decision variables, objective function(s), constraints and the input data needed for your model.

10.9. ABC Protein is a food manufacturer for novel protein products, serving both of its domestic and international markets. A sketch of the novel protein supply chain is provided below. Food loss (or deterioration of quality) may occur during the supply chain due to perishability of food items and/or improper handling, storage and transit. Valuable by-products of water and starch can be generated, while refuse and hulls are generally treated as disposable wastes. Explain and discuss ABC Protein's needs for optimally configuring its supply chains. Propose an optimization model to address these needs. Explain how your model is able to address the food loss and quality issue. Elaborate the decision variables, objective function(s), constraints and the input data needed for your model.

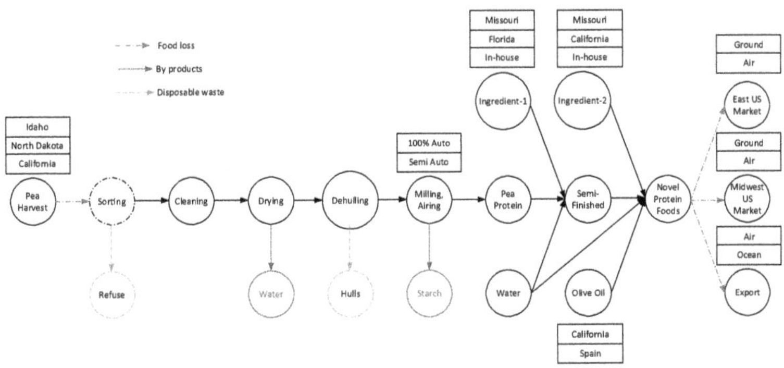

10.10. ABC VR is a start-up manufacture for its innovative and high-tech virtual reality device and equipment. With proper customization and configuration, these device can be used for gaming, training and education. The company would like to optimize the configuration of its supply chain in terms of sourcing/transportation options and safety stock placement decisions. Since most of ABC VR's products are new in the market, it had a hard time collecting the demand data. The supply chain analyst also realizes that the demand pattern of the product may vary during its lifecycle. Propose a data-driven optimization approach to address ABC VR's supply chain configuration needs. What is unique about your approach? Elaborate the decision variables, objective function(s), constraints and the input data needed.

Chapter 11

Machine Scheduling

11.1 Introduction and Overview

Machine scheduling studies a prominent class of combinatorial optimization problems with *sequencing/permutation* decisions. Its applications are found not only in manufacturing, but also in various service settings where jobs are assigned to and processed by limited resources: machines, equipment, personnel, among others.

A classification scheme is in place to delineate the rich family of scheduling problems. A triplet $\alpha|\beta|\gamma$ can be used to identify a scheduling problem at high level, where the α field represents the machine environment, the β field describes processing characteristics and constraints, and the γ field specifies the objective function. Table 11.1 shows examples of different types of scheduling problems introduced in this chapter.

11.2 Single-Machine Scheduling

In the single-machine scheduling problem minimizing total tardiness, denoted by $1||\sum T_j$, a set J of jobs are processed on one machine. Each job $j \in J$ has a constant processing time p_j and a due date d_j. The tardiness of job $j \in J$ is the amount of its delay $\max\{0, C_j - d_j\}$, where C_j is the completion time of j. The goal is to find a feasible schedule that minimizes the total tardiness. Below we present three different integer programming formulations for this problem. The following sets and parameters are needed for all the formulations.

Table 11.1. Examples of classification of scheduling problems.

Fields	Notation	Meaning	Problem setting
α	1	Single machine	All jobs are sequenced on one machine
	Pm	m identical parallel machine	Each job requires a single operation and can be processed on any of the m machines
	F_m	Flow shop with m machines in series	Each job must be processed on each of the m machines in the same order
	FF_c	Flexible flow shop	Generalization over Pm and F_m: c stages in series, each stage has multiple machines in parallel
	J_m	Job shop with m machines	Generalization over F_m to allow each job has its own route to be processed
	O_m	Open shop with m machines	Each job must be processed on each of the m machines, but can be in any order
β	r_j	Release date	A job j cannot start before its release date r_j
	s_{ij}	Sequence-dependent setup times	Sequence-dependent setup time between the processing of job i and job j
	nwt	No-wait	Jobs are not allowed to wait between two consecutive machines
γ	C_{max}	Makespan	The completion time of the last job to leave the system
	$\sum T_j$	Total tardiness	Sum of tardiness of all the jobs
	$\sum w_j T_j$	Total weighted tardiness	Sum of weighted lateness of all the jobs

Sets and parameters

J: set of jobs
p_j: processing time of job $j \in J$
d_j: due date of job $j \in J$

11.2.1 *The Disjunctive Formulation*

This is the most widely applied modeling approach for scheduling problems of all kinds.

Key to Formulation: It focuses on the *disjunctive* nature of a sequencing problem: a pair of jobs (i, j) cannot overlap on one machine, i.e., either i is processed before j or vice versa. It can be modeled using the big-M formulation.

Decision variables

$y_{ij} = 1$ if job i is processed before job j, and 0 if j is processed before i
$s_j \geq 0$: start time of job $j \in J$
$T_j \geq 0$: tardiness of job $j \in J$

Objective function

$$\text{Minimize} \sum_{j \in J} T_j \tag{11.1}$$

Subject to:

$$s_i + p_i \leq s_j + M(1 - y_{ij}), \quad \forall i \in J, j \in J : i < j \tag{11.2}$$

$$s_j + p_j \leq s_i + My_{ij}, \quad \forall i \in J, j \in J : i < j \tag{11.3}$$

$$T_j \geq s_i + p_i - d_j, \quad \forall i \in J, j \in J : i < j \tag{11.4}$$

$$y_{ij} \in \{0, 1\}, \quad s_j, T_j \geq 0 \tag{11.5}$$

The objective function (11.1) minimizes the total tardiness of all the jobs. Constraints (11.2) and (11.3) are the disjunctive constraints (big-M formulation) to ensure that no jobs overlap on the machine, and the starting times of jobs are consistent with the sequencing decisions. Specifically, when $y_{ij} = 1$, i.e., job i precedes job j, Constraint (11.2) ensures that the start time of j must be no less than the completion time of i $(s_i + p_i)$, and Constraint (11.3) is always satisfied with the big-M on the RHS; when $y_{ij} = 0$, i.e., job j precedes i, Constraint (11.2) is ineffective, and Constraint (11.3) guarantees that the start time of i must be no less than the completion time of j $(s_j + p_j)$. Constraint (11.3) linearizes the original $\max\{\cdot\}$ function in the definition of tardiness. It is equivalent to $T_j = \max\{0, C_j - d_j\}$, because:

(i) $T_j \geq 0$; and (ii) the objective function minimizes the total tardiness, such that equality in (11.4) will hold. Constraint (11.5) specifies the domain of all the decision variables.

11.2.2 *Position Based Formulation*

The second approach works differently, which is based on the observation that there should be no idleness in an optimal schedule for $1||\sum T_j$. As shown in Figure 11.1, each job starts right after its preceding job with no lag (machine idleness). Thus, the completion time of the j-th job in a sequence is the summation of the processing times of the j-th job and all its preceding jobs. For instance, the completion of the third job in Figure 11.1 equals the summation of the processing times of the third, second and first jobs, i.e., $p_1 + p_5 + p_2$.

Key to Formulation: Define position-based decision variables $x_{jk} = 1$ if job j is scheduled at the k-th position in the sequence, and 0 o.w. Then the processing time of the k-th job equals $\sum_{j \in J} p_j x_{jk}$. Therefore, the completion time of the k-th job is $\sum_{i=1}^{k} \sum_{j \in J} p_j x_{ji}$. The position-based formulation can be written as below.

Decision variables

$x_{jk} = 1$ if job j is scheduled at the k-th position in the sequence, and 0 o.w.
$T_j \geq 0$: tardiness of job $j \in J$

Objective function

$$\text{Minimize} \sum_{j \in J} T_j \tag{11.6}$$

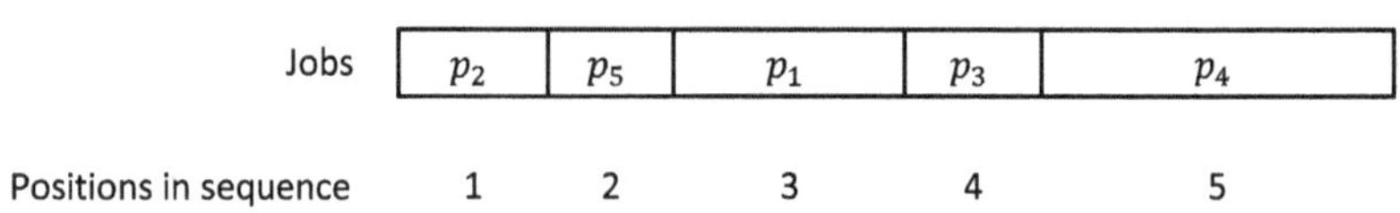

Figure 11.1. Example solution of a five-job instance.

Subject to:

$$\sum_{j\in J} x_{jk} = 1, \quad \forall k \in J \tag{11.7}$$

$$\sum_{k\in J} x_{jk} = 1, \quad \forall j \in J \tag{11.8}$$

$$T_k \geq \sum_{i=1}^{k}\sum_{j\in J} p_j x_{ji} - \sum_{j\in J} d_j x_{jk}, \quad \forall k \in K \tag{11.9}$$

$$x_{jk} \in \{0,1\}, \quad T_j \geq 0 \tag{11.10}$$

The objective function remains the same as (11.1). Constraint (11.7) assigns exactly one job at each position. Constraint (11.8) ensures that each job is assigned with exactly one position. Constraint (11.9) computes the tardiness of the k-th job in the sequence, where $\sum_{j\in J} d_j x_{jk}$ is the due date of the k-th job.

11.2.3 *Linear Ordering Formulation*

Key to Formulation: The third formulation exploits the logical relationships among the linear ordering decision. That is, if job i precedes j, and j precedes k, then k cannot precede i. Then the job tardiness can be expressed as a function of the linear ordering decision variable.

Decision variables

$x_{ij} = 1$ if job i is processed before job j, and 0 if j is processed before i

$T_j \geq 0$: tardiness of job $j \in J$

Objective function

$$\text{Minimize} \sum_{j\in J} T_j \tag{11.11}$$

Subject to:

$$x_{ij} + x_{ji} = 1, \quad \forall i \in J, j \in J : i \neq j, \tag{11.12}$$

$$x_{ij} + x_{jk} + x_{ki} \leq 2, \quad \forall i \in J, j \in J, k \in J : i \neq j \neq k, \tag{11.13}$$

$$T_j \geq \sum_{i \in J} p_i x_{ij} + p_j - d_j, \quad \forall j \in J, \tag{11.14}$$

$$x_{ij} \in \{0, 1\}, \quad T_j \geq 0 \tag{11.15}$$

The objective function (11.11) minimizes the total tardiness. Constraint (11.12) states that either job i precedes job j or vice versa for two different jobs i and j. Constraint (11.13) enforces the sequencing relationships among three different jobs: the transitivity property. That is, if job i precedes job j, and j precedes k, then k cannot precede i. Constraint (11.14) computes the tardiness of each job. And Constraint (11.15) specifies the domain of all the decision variables.

11.3 Parallel Machine Scheduling

In the parallel identical machine scheduling problem minimizing makespan, denoted by $Pm||C_{max}$, each job $j \in J$ is processed on any of a set M of machines. Each job $j \in J$ has a constant processing time p_{jm} on machine $m \in M$. The goal is to find a feasible schedule that minimizes the makespan. Below we present four different integer programming formulations for this problem. The following sets and parameters are needed for all the formulations.

Sets and parameters

J: set of jobs
M: set of machines
p_{jm}: processing time of job $j \in J$ on machine $m \in M$

11.3.1 *Position-Based Formulation*

The first approach extends the position-based formulation for $1||\sum T_j$ in the parallel machine setting.

Key to Formulation: The main idea is to define decision variables to determine the positioning of each job on each machine, then model the ordering/sequencing relationships among jobs on each machine.

<u>Decision variables</u>

$x_{jk}^m = 1$: if job $j \in J$ is assigned to the k-th position on machine $m \in M$

$u_k^m \geq 0$: completion time of the job at position $k \in J$ on machine $m \in M$

$C_j \geq 0$: completion time of job $j \in J$

$C_{\max} \geq 0$: makespan of all the jobs

<u>Objective function</u>

$$\text{Minimize } C_{\max} \tag{11.16}$$

Subject to:

$$\sum_{m \in M} \sum_{k \in J} x_{jk}^m = 1, \quad \forall j \in J, \tag{11.17}$$

$$\sum_{j \in J} x_{jk}^m \leq 1, \quad \forall k \in J, m \in M, \tag{11.18}$$

$$u_1^m \geq \sum_{j \in J} p_{jm} x_{j1}^m, \quad \forall m \in M, \tag{11.19}$$

$$u_k^m \geq u_{k-1}^m + \sum_{j \in J} p_{jm} x_{jk}^m, \quad \forall m \in M,\ k \in J : k \geq 2, \tag{11.20}$$

$$C_j \geq u_k^m - M(1 - x_{jk}^m), \quad \forall j \in J, k \in J, m \in M, \tag{11.21}$$

$$C_{\max} \geq C_j, \quad \forall j \in J, \tag{11.22}$$

$$x_{jk}^m \in \{0, 1\}, \quad u_k^m, \quad C_j, \quad C_{\max} \geq 0 \tag{11.23}$$

The objective function (11.16) minimizes the makespan of completing all the jobs. Constraint (11.17) assigns a job to exactly one position on a machine. Constraint (11.18) ensures that each position on a machine is assigned with no more than one job. Constraints (11.19) and (11.20) together determine completion time of the job at each position on a machine. Specifically, the completion time of the first job must be no less than the processing of the first job as in (11.19). For other jobs (after the first job) on a machine as in (11.20), its completion time must be no less than its processing time plus the completion time of the job at the previous position. Constraint (11.21) is the big-M formulation to determine the completion time of job j as being no less than that of the job at position k on machine m, if job j is assigned at position k on machine m. Constraint (11.22) guarantees that the makespan must be no less than the completion times of all the jobs. Domains of all the decision variables are specified in Constraint (11.23).

11.3.2 *Linear Ordering Formulation*

Key to Formulation: This formulation extends that in Section 11.2.3 for the single-machine scheduling problem, such that the ordering of jobs is determined in conjunction with the job-machine assignment decision.

Decision variables

$x_{ij} = 1$: if job $i \in J$ is processed before job $j \in J$; and 0 o.w.
$y_{ij} = 1$: if job $i \in J$ and job $j \in J$ are *not* processed on the same machine; and 0 o.w.
$z_{jm} = 1$: if job $j \in J$ is assigned on machine $m \in M$
$C_j \geq 0$: completion time of job $j \in J$
$C_{\max} \geq 0$: makespan of all the jobs

Objective function

$$\text{Minimize} \quad C_{\max} \tag{11.24}$$

Subject to:

$$\sum_{m \in M} z_{jm} = 1, \quad \forall j \in J, \tag{11.25}$$

$$x_{ij} + x_{ji} + y_{ij} = 1, \quad \forall i \in J, j \in J : i < j, \tag{11.26}$$

$$x_{ij} + x_{jk} + x_{ki} \leq 2, \quad \forall i \in J, j \in J, k \in J : i < j < k, \tag{11.27}$$

$$z_{im} + z_{jm} + y_{ij} \leq 2, \quad \forall i \in J, j \in J, m \in M, \tag{11.28}$$

$$C_j \geq p_{jm} z_{jm}, \quad \forall j \in J, m \in M, \tag{11.29}$$

$$C_j \geq C_i + p_{jm}\left(x_{ij} + z_{im} + z_{jm} - 2\right) - M(1 - x_{ij}),$$
$$\forall i \in J, j \in J, m \in M, \tag{11.30}$$

$$C_{\max} \geq C_j, \quad \forall j \in J, \tag{11.31}$$

$$x_{ij}, y_{ij}, z_{jm} \in \{0, 1\}, \quad C_j, C_{max} \geq 0, \tag{11.32}$$

The objective function (11.24) minimizes the makespan. Constraint (11.25) assigns a job to exactly one machine. Constraint (11.26) ensures that if two jobs are processed on the same machine, then one job must precede the other. Constraint (11.27) guarantees the transitivity property, similar to Constraint (11.13). Constraint (11.28) properly determines if two jobs are assigned to the same machine. Constraint (11.29) states that the completion time of a job can be no less than its process time on a machine. Constraint (11.30) is the big-M formulation to ensure proper completion times for a pair of jobs (i, j) based on their sequencing decisions. Specifically, when jobs i and j are assigned on the same machine and i precedes j, i.e., $z_{im} = z_{jm} = x_{ij} = 1$, the completion time of j must be no less than the completion time of i plus i's processing time on machine m. Constraint (11.31) requires that the makespan must be no less than the completion times of all the jobs. Constraint (11.32) specifies the domains of all the decision variables.

11.3.3 *Time-Indexed Formulation*

We now present a widely applied formulation approach for scheduling problems using time-indexed decision variables.

Key to Formulation: The key is to determine the time point at which a job is scheduled to start using binary decision variables. Then constraints are constructed to ensure no jobs overlap on each machine. Let T be the upper bound on the makespan. A straightforward value for T is $\max\{\sum_{j\in J} p_{j1}, \sum_{j\in J} p_{j2}, \ldots, \sum_{j\in J} p_{j|M|}\}$.

<u>Decision variables</u>

$x_{jmt} = 1$: if job $i \in J$ starts at time $t \in \{0, 1, \ldots, T\}$ on machine $m \in M$

$C_j \geq 0$: completion time of job $j \in J$
$C_{\max} \geq 0$: makespan of all the jobs

Objective function

$$\text{Minimize } C_{\max} \tag{11.33}$$

Subject to:

$$\sum_{m \in M} \sum_{t=0}^{T-1} x_{jmt} = 1, \quad \forall j \in J, \tag{11.34}$$

$$\sum_{j \in J} \sum_{\tau=\max\{0, t-p_{jm}-1\}}^{t} x_{jmt} \leq 1, \quad \forall m \in M,$$
$$t \in \{0, 1, \ldots, T\}, \tag{11.35}$$

$$C_j = \sum_{m \in M} \sum_{t=0}^{T-1} (t + p_{jm}) x_{jmt}, \quad \forall j \in J, \tag{11.36}$$

$$C_{\max} \geq C_j, \quad \forall j \in J, \tag{11.37}$$

$$x_{jmt} \in \{0, 1\}, \quad C_j, C_{max} \geq 0 \tag{11.38}$$

The objective function (11.33) minimizes the makespan. Constraint (11.34) states that a job is assigned to exactly one machine and starts only once, i.e., no preemption is allowed. Constraint (11.35) is the resource constraint to ensure that the number of machine m required at any time point t must not exceed 1 (since there is one machine of type m available). The inner summation of the LHS of (11.35) is a bit intricate: it sums up all time periods during which job j can be active at time t. In order to be active at t, job j cannot start earlier than $t - p_{jm} - 1$ (or 0 if $t - p_{jm} - 1 < 0$), and cannot start later than t. Constraint (11.36) computes the completion time of each job, and Constraint (11.37) ensures that makespan is no less than the completion time of each job. Constraint (11.38) specifies the domains of all the decision variables.

11.3.4 *Routing-Based Formulation*[a]

This formulation approach is motivated by that of a Capacitated Vehicle Routing problem (CVRP) to be introduced in Section 14.2. We first identify the relevance between $Pm||C_{max}$ and CVRP in Table 11.2. They share the intrinsic feature of sequencing or permutation as the key decision to optimize. Machines in $Pm||C_{max}$ are equivalent to vehicles in CVRP, by which jobs or nodes are processed or visited. Both also have the feature of assignment decision to determine which jobs are to be processed on a machine as in $Pm||C_{max}$, and which nodes to be visited by a vehicle as in CVRP.

Figure 11.2 illustrates other relevant characteristics between the two problems. The solution of *schedule* to $Pm||C_{max}$ is in the form of multiple paths on the machines, with a dummy finish node C_m at the end of the path associated with machine $m \in M$. The solution of *route* to CVRP has the configuration of multiple tours (or Hamiltonian tour to be precise), each of which is associated with a vehicle. While each vehicle has a maximum load capacity to serve all the nodes with their demands, each machine m can be viewed to

Table 11.2. Relevance between $\mathbf{Pm||C_{max}}$ and CVRP.

Features	$Pm\|\|C_{max}$	CVRP
Sequencing	Order of jobs to be processed	Sequence of nodes to be visited
Assignment	Assigning jobs to machines	Assignment nodes to vehicles
Resources	Machines	Vehicles
Solution configuration	A path of jobs for each machine	A Hamiltonian tour for each vehicle
Capacity	Completion time of the last job on a machine	Capacity of loads for a vehicle
Objective	Minimizing completion time of all the jobs	Minimizing the total travel cost

[a]This subsection is better to be covered after Section 14.2 on the vehicle routing problem (VRP).

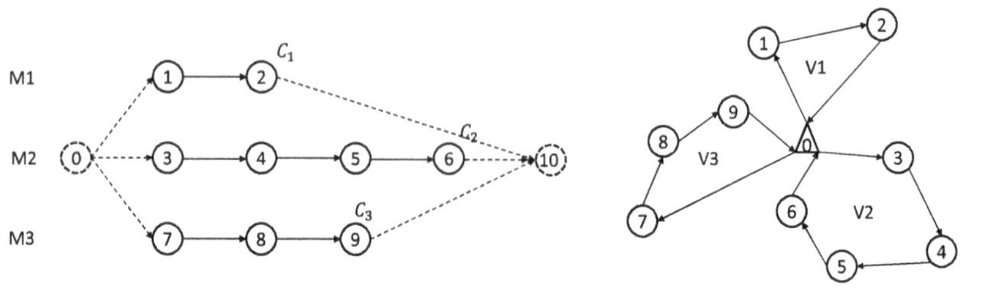

a. Schedule solution to a 9-job 3-machine $Pm \mid\mid C_{max}$.

b. Schedule solution to a 9-node 3-vehicle CVRP.

Figure 11.2. Illustration of the equivalence between $Pm||C_{max}$ and CVRP.

have a "capacity" of its makespan C_m for completing all the jobs on the machine, which is itself a decision variable. In addition, a typical objective in vehicle routing is to minimize the total travel cost or time of all the vehicles; while in $Pm||C_{max}$ one minimizes the makespan of completing all the jobs.

Key to Formulation: In order to model the $Pm||C_{max}$ as a CVRP, we create dummy jobs 0 and $n+1$, with zero processing time, to represent the start and finish of all the jobs, where $n = |J|$. Define binary rout sequencing decision variables to assign and sequence nodes on each machine. Completion time on each machine can be modeled as the cumulative time of job processing, or the cumulative load of the vehicle in the CVRP analogy.

Decision variables

$x_{ij}^m = 1$: if job $i \in J \cup \{0, n+1\}$ is processed immediately before job $j \in J \cup \{0, n+1\}$ on machine $m \in M$, and 0 o.w.

$C_j \geq 0$: completion time of job $j \in J$

$C_{\max} \geq 0$: makespan of all the jobs

Objective function

$$\text{Minimize} \quad C_{\max} \tag{11.39}$$

Subject to:

$$\sum_{m \in M} \sum_{i \in J \cup \{0\}} x_{ij}^m = 1, \quad \forall j \in J, \tag{11.40}$$

$$\sum_{m \in M} \sum_{j \in J \cup \{n+1\}} x_{ij}^m = 1, \quad \forall i \in J, \tag{11.41}$$

$$\sum_{i \in J : i \neq j} x_{ij}^m = \sum_{i \in J : i \neq j} x_{ji}^m, \quad \forall j \in J,\ m \in M, \tag{11.42}$$

$$C_j \geq C_i + p_{jm} - M(1 - x_{ij}^m), \ \ \forall j \in J,\ m \in M, \tag{11.43}$$

$$\sum_{i \in J} x_{i,n+1}^m \leq 1, \quad \forall m \in M, \tag{11.44}$$

$$\sum_{j \in J} x_{0,j}^m \leq 1, \quad \forall m \in M, \tag{11.45}$$

$$C_{\max} \geq C_j, \quad \forall j \in J, \tag{11.46}$$

$$x_{ij}^m \in \{0,\ 1\}, \quad C_j,\ C_{\max} \geq 0. \tag{11.47}$$

The objective function (11.39) minimizes the makespan. Constraints (11.40) and (11.41) ensure that each real job has exactly one predecessor and exactly one successor on a machine, respectively. Constraint (11.42) states that a job can only have a predecessor on a machine if it also has a successor on the same machine. Constraint (11.43) is the big-M formulation to ensure the completion time of job j on machine m is no less than the completion time of i plus the processing time of j on machine m, if job i immediately precedes job j on machine m. Constraints (11.44) and (11.45) guarantee that the dummy finish has at most one predecessor and the dummy start has at most one successor on a machine, respectively. Constraint (11.46) ensures that makespan is no less than the completion time of each job. Constraint (11.47) specifies the domains of all the decision variables.

11.4 Shop Scheduling

Shop scheduling consists of a rich set of problems with more complex machine structure and environment, which deal with a variety of technical requirements in a manufacturing and production process.

11.4.1 *Flow Shop Scheduling Problem*

In a flow shop scheduling problem, all jobs must be processed through a set of machines in the same order. It is suitable for a *product-focused process* such as an assembly line with high throughput but low product variety as in an MTS environment. Formally, a set of $n = |J|$ jobs must be processed by a set of $m = |M|$ machines in the order of $1, 2, \ldots, m$. The processing time of job $j \in J$ on machine k is p_{jk}. A machine can process at most one job at any time. A job cannot be processed on machine k before it is finished on machine $k-1$. The objective of $Fm||C_{max}$ is to minimize the makespan of completing all the jobs.

11.4.1.1 *Disjunctive Formulation*

Key to Formulation: The disjunctive formulation for flow shop scheduling exploits the relationship between job sequencing and start time decisions. The starting time of a job is defined and determined on each machine it is processed.

Decision variables

$x_{ij} = 1$: if job $i \in J$ precedes job $j \in J$ in the schedule (not necessarily immediately precedes it); and 0 if otherwise.

$S_{jk} \geq 0$: starting time of job j on machine $k \in M$

$C_{\max} \geq 0$: makespan of all the jobs

Objective function

$$\text{Minimize} \quad C_{\max} \tag{11.48}$$

Subject to:

$$S_{jk} \geq S_{j,k-1} + p_{j,k-1}, \quad \forall k = 2, 3, \ldots, m,\ j \in J, \tag{11.49}$$

$$S_{jk} \geq S_{ik} + p_{ik} - M(1 - x_{ij}), \quad \forall i, j \in J : i < j,\ k \in M, \tag{11.50}$$

$$S_{ik} \geq S_{jk} - Mx_{ij}, \quad \forall i, j \in J : i < j,\ k \in M, \tag{11.51}$$

$$C_{\max} \geq S_{jm} + p_{jm}, \quad \forall j \in J \tag{11.52}$$

$$x_{ij} \in \{0, 1\}, \quad S_{jk}, C_{\max} \geq 0 \tag{11.53}$$

The objective function (11.48) minimizes the makespan. Constraint (11.49) specifies the precedence relationships between jobs being processed on adjacent machines. The big-M formulation in (11.50) and (11.51) establishes the relationship between the sequencing and starting time decision variables. Constraint (11.52) ensures that the makespan is the time to complete all the jobs on the last machine.

11.4.1.2 *Position-Based Formulation*

Key to Formulation: This formulation extends that of the single-machine scheduling problem by exploiting the relationship between the positioning of jobs on a machine and the job starting times.

Decision variables

$x_{ij} = 1$: if job $i \in J$ is in the j-th position of the sequence; 0 o.w.
$S_{jk} \geq 0$: start time of the j-th job on machine $k = 1, 2, \ldots, m$
$C_{\max} \geq 0$: makespan of completing all the jobs

Objective function

$$\text{Minimize } C_{\max} \tag{11.54}$$

$$\sum_{i \in J} x_{ij} = 1, \quad \forall j \in J, \tag{11.55}$$

$$\sum_{j \in J} x_{ij} = 1, \quad \forall i \in J, \tag{11.56}$$

$$S_{j+1,k} \geq S_{jk} + \sum_{i \in J} p_{ik} x_{ij},$$

$$\forall j \in \{1, 2, \ldots, n-1\}, \; k \in K \tag{11.57}$$

$$S_{j,k+1} \geq S_{jk} + \sum_{i \in J} p_{ik} x_{ij},$$

$$\forall k = \{1, 2, \ldots, m-1\}, \; j \in J, \tag{11.58}$$

$$C_{\max} \geq S_{nm} + \sum_{i \in J} p_{im} x_{in}, \tag{11.59}$$

$$x_{ij} \in \{0, 1\}, \quad S_{jk}, \; C_{\max} \geq 0 \tag{11.60}$$

The objective function (11.54) minimizes the makespan. Constraints (11.55) and (11.56) is the assignment constraint to ensure that a job is assigned to exactly one position and a position is assigned with exactly one job. Constraint (11.58) properly sequences the jobs on a machine, i.e., the job at position j must proceed the job at position $j-1$ on the machine. Constraint (11.58) properly sequences the operations of a job, i.e., the job must be finished on machine k before it can be processed on machine $k+1$. Constraint (11.59) requires that the makespan to be no less than the completion times of all the operations.

11.4.2 *Job Shop Scheduling Problem*

In a job shop scheduling problem, jobs are processed on a set of machines in an arbitrary order specified by some technical requirements. Each job can be processed on its own set of machines in certain orders. Compared to the flow shop scheduling problem, the job shop scheduling problem is more general and flexible in that it allows for arbitrary set of machines in different orders for each jobs, reflecting heterogeneous and highly customized technical requirement as in a make-to-order (MTO) environment. It is suitable for the *process-focused processes* such as repair shops, medical clinics, etc.

Formally, a set J of n jobs are to be processed on a set M of m machines. For each job $j \in J$, let an ordered set $O_j = (O_j^1, O_j^2, \ldots, O_j^k, \ldots, O_j^{m_j})$ of machines represent the order of m_j operations of job j to be processed, where O_j^m denotes the k-th operation of job j, and m_j is the number of operations (machines) required by job j. The processing time of job j on machine k is p_{jk}. Each machine can process at most one job at any time. A job, once started, cannot be interrupted. The $J_m||C_{max}$ minimizes the makespan, i.e., completion time of all the jobs.

11.4.2.1 *Disjunctive Formulation*

Key to Formulation: The disjunction formulation for the job shop scheduling problem is similar to that of the flow shop scheduling problem. The difference is that the optimal job sequence on each machine can be different, thus the sequencing decision variable needs to be defined corresponding to each machine.

<u>Decision variables</u>

$x_{ij}^k = 1$: if job $i \in J$ precedes job $j \in J$ on machine $k \in M$ (not necessarily immediately precedes it); and 0 if vice versa

$S_{jk} \geq 0$: starting time of job j on machine $k \in M$
$C_{\max} \geq 0$: makespan of all the jobs

Objective function

$$\text{Minimize} \quad C_{\max} \tag{11.61}$$

Subject to:

$$S_{j,O_j^k} \geq S_{j,O_j^{k-1}} + p_{j,O_j^{k-1}}, \quad \forall j \in J, k \in \{2, 3, \ldots, m_j\}, \tag{11.62}$$

$$S_{jk} \geq S_{ik} + p_{ik} - M(1 - x_{ij}^k), \quad \forall i, j \in J : i < j,\ k \in M, \tag{11.63}$$

$$S_{ik} \geq S_{jk} + p_{jk} - Mx_{ij}^k, \quad \forall i, j \in J : i < j,\ k \in M, \tag{11.64}$$

$$C_{\max} \geq S_{j,m_j} + p_{j,m_j}, \quad \forall j \in J, \tag{11.65}$$

$$x_{ij}^k \in \{0,\ 1\}, S_{jk},\ C_{\max} \geq 0 \tag{11.66}$$

The objective function (11.61) minimizes the makespan. Constraint (11.62) satisfies the precedence relationship between consecutive operations of a job. Specifically, for each job j and its k-th operation, the start time of j on machine O_j^k must be no less than the completion time of j on machine O_j^{k-1}. Constraints (11.63) and (11.64) are the big-M formulation to guarantee proper relationship between the sequencing and starting time decisions of jobs on each machine. Constraint (11.65) states that the makespan must be no less than the completion time of all the jobs on their last machine.

11.4.2.2 *Time-Indexed Formulation*

Key to Formulation: This formulation extends that of the single-machine scheduling problem by defining time-indexed decision variables and maintaining the precedence relationships for each machine.

Let T be the upper bound on the makespan of the job shop scheduling problem. Similarly, to that in the flow shop scheduling problem, a straightforward value for T is $\max\{\sum_{j\in J} p_{j1}, \sum_{j\in J} p_{j2}, \ldots, \sum_{j\in J} p_{j|M|}\}$.

Decision variables

$x_{ikt} = 1$ if job $i \in J$ starts at time $t = 0, 1, 2, \ldots, T-1$ on machine $k \in M$; and 0 o.w.

$C_{\max} \geq 0$: makespan of completing all the jobs

Objective function

$$\text{Minimize} \quad C_{\max} \tag{11.67}$$

Subject to:

$$\sum_{t=0}^{T-1} x_{ikt} = 1, \quad \forall i \in J, k \in M \tag{11.68}$$

$$\sum_{t=0}^{T-1} t \cdot x_{ikt} \geq \sum_{t=0}^{T-1} t \cdot x_{i,k-1,t} + p_{i,O_i^{k-1}},$$
$$\forall i \in J, k \in \{2, 3, \ldots, m_j\}, \tag{11.69}$$

$$\sum_{i \in J} \sum_{\tau=t-p_{ik}+1}^{t} x_{ikt} \leq 1, \quad \forall k \in M, t = \{0, \ldots, T-1\} \tag{11.70}$$

$$C_{\max} \geq \sum_{t=0}^{T-1} t \cdot x_{ikt} + p_{ik}, \quad \forall i \in J, k \in M \tag{11.71}$$

$$x_{ikt} \in \{0,\ 1\}, \quad C_{\max} \geq 0 \tag{11.72}$$

The objective function (11.67) minimizes the makespan. Constraint (11.68) ensures that each job is started only once on a machine. Constraint (11.69) satisfies the precedence relationship of consecutive operations of each job. Constraint (11.70) limits no more than one job to be processed at any time on a machine. Constraint (11.71) computes the makespan as the time to complete all the jobs.

11.4.3 *Flexible Flow Shop Scheduling Problem*

A flexible flow scheduling shop problem generalizes a flow shop scheduling problem by having multiple machines available at each operation of the process. Apparently, it includes the flow shop scheduling problem as a special case. In addition to all the input parameters in a flow shop scheduling problem, we define R_k to denote the number of machines available for operation $k \in M$.

Key to Formulation: The time-indexed formulation makes it convenient to track the active jobs at each time point on a machine, and to ensure the number of active jobs processed at any time on machine does not exceed the number of available machines.

Decision variables

$x_{ikt} = 1$ if job $i \in J$ starts at time $t = 0, 1, 2, \ldots, T$ on machine $k \in M$

$C_{\max} \geq 0$: makespan of completing all the jobs

Objective function

$$\text{Minimize } C_{\max} \tag{11.73}$$

Subject to:

$$\sum_{t \in T} x_{ikt} = 1, \qquad \forall i \in J, k \in K \tag{11.74}$$

$$\sum_{t \in T} t \cdot x_{i,k+1,t} - \sum_{t \in T} t \cdot x_{ikt} \geq p_{ik},$$
$$\forall i \in J, k \in \{1, 2, \ldots, |K| - 1\} \tag{11.75}$$

$$\sum_{i \in J} \sum_{s=t-p_i+1}^{t} x_{iks} \leq R_k, \quad \forall k \in K, t \in T \tag{11.76}$$

$$\sum_{t \in T} t \cdot x_{ikt} \leq C_{\max}, \quad \forall i \in J, k \in K \tag{11.77}$$

$$x_{ikt} \in \{0,\ 1\}, \quad C_{\max} \geq 0 \tag{11.78}$$

Constraint (11.73) minimizes the makespan. Constraint (11.74) ensures that each job is started only once on a machine. Constraint (11.75) satisfies the precedence relationship of consecutive operations of each job. Constraint (11.76) limits the number of jobs being processed at any time on a machine to be no more than the number of available machines. The makespan decision variable is enforced to be no less than the completion times of all the jobs in Constraint (11.77).

11.4.4 *Flexible Job Shop Scheduling Problem*

A flexible job shop scheduling problem generalizes a job shop scheduling problem by having multiple machines available at each operation of the process. It includes the job shop scheduling problem as a special case. In addition to all the input parameters in a job shop scheduling problem, we define R_k to denote the number of machines available at operation $k \in M$.

Key to Formulation: The time-indexed formulation for the job shop scheduling problem can be immediately extended to model the flexible job shop scheduling problem by revising the right-hand-side of Constraint (11.70) to be the corresponding number of machines.

Decision variables

$x_{ikt} = 1$ if job $i \in J$ starts at time $t = 0, 1, 2, \ldots, T-1$ on machine $k \in M$; and 0 o.w.

$C_{\max} \geq 0$: makespan of completing all the jobs

Objective function

$$\text{Minimize} \quad C_{\max} \tag{11.79}$$

Subject to:

$$\sum_{t=0}^{T-1} x_{ikt} = 1, \quad \forall i \in J, k \in M \tag{11.80}$$

$$\sum_{t=0}^{T-1} t \cdot x_{ikt} \geq \sum_{t=0}^{T-1} t \cdot x_{i,k-1,t} + p_{i,O_i^{k-1}}, \quad \forall i \in J, k \in \{2, 3, \ldots, m_j\}, \tag{11.81}$$

$$\sum_{i \in J} \sum_{\tau = t - p_{ik} + 1}^{t} x_{ikt} \leq R_k, \quad \forall k \in M, t = \{0, \ldots, T-1\} \tag{11.82}$$

$$C_{\max} \geq \sum_{t=0}^{T-1} t \cdot x_{ikt} + p_{ik}, \quad \forall i \in J, k \in M \tag{11.83}$$

$$x_{ikt} \in \{0,\ 1\}, \quad C_{\max} \geq 0 \tag{11.84}$$

Constraint (11.80) assigns exactly one starting time for each job on a machine. Constraint (11.81) maintains the precedence requirement for a job to be processed on two consecutive machines. Constraint

(11.82) ensures that the number of each type of machine required at any time does not exceed the maximum available. The makespan decision variable is enforced to be no less than the completion times of all the jobs in Constraint (11.83).

11.5 Additional Notes

Machine scheduling is an extensively studied area in optimization and operations research. We refer to [82, 83] for a systematic treatment of the theories, model formulations and applications of machine scheduling. A comprehensive coverage on the broader topics in the scheduling field is available in [84].

Exercises

11.1. Explain the three-field classification of scheduling problems, and show three examples for different types of scheduling problems.

11.2. Show and discuss variants and extensions of the basic single-machine scheduling problem, in terms of scheduling setting/requirement, objective functions and constraints.

11.3. Show and discuss application examples of the class of single-machine scheduling problems.

11.4. Show and discuss variants and extensions of the basic parallel-machine scheduling problem, in terms of scheduling setting/requirement, objective functions and constraints.

11.5. Show and discuss application examples of the class of flow-shop scheduling problems.

11.6. Show and discuss variants and extensions of the basic flow-shop scheduling problem, in terms of scheduling setting/requirement, objective functions and constraints.

11.7. Show and discuss application examples of the class of job-shop scheduling problems.

11.8. Show and discuss variants and extensions of the basic job-shop scheduling problem, in terms of scheduling setting/requirement, objective functions and constraints.

11.9. Discuss the connections and differences among the flow-shop, job-shop and flexible shop scheduling problems.

11.10. ABC Fabrication is a medium-size tooling company who manufactures both standard and custom tools. It recently installed a state-of-the-art multi-purpose numerical control machine that is capable of performing different fabrication operations. However, it soon becomes a scarce resource and bottleneck of many orders/jobs. Propose a data-driven approach to help ABC Fabrication optimize the utilization of the multi-purpose numerical control machine. Conceptually describe your model with its key components. Discuss at least three objective functions and explain their application scenarios. The company would like to install more such machines in the upcoming years. How would you modify your optimization approach accordingly?

11.11. Emergency room operations often require proper scheduling of medical activities with limited resources of nurses, physicians and medical equipment. A patient usually goes through the following process at an emergency room: Arrival, Initial Exam (by nurse), Order Test (by physician), Tests (blood, urine, X-ray or CT), Diagnosis and Consultation (by physician). The type of tests needed and their order are patient-dependent and subject to discretion of the physician. Propose a data-driven optimization model to improve the efficiency and effectiveness of emergency room operations. What performance metrics can be relevant, and why? Elaborate the decision variables, objective function(s), constraints and the input data needed in your model.

11.12. Driven by fast growth of technologies such as sensors, drones and internet of things (IoT), Precision Agriculture has evolved from a concept to reality. A typical planting process includes Data Collecting (via drone), Land Preparation (via tractor), Sowing (via planter), Cultivating (water and fertilizer management via drone). Each operation requires sensor-equipped machinery and vehicles with limited availability and capacity for a farmer. Conceptually describe the scheduling problem faced by a farmer for the crop planting/growing operations. Elaborate the decision variables, objective function(s), constraints and the input data needed.

Chapter 12

Resource-Constrained Project Scheduling

12.1 Introduction and Overview

As shown in Chapter 10, project or program management is widely applied for MTO or ETO supply chain operations in various industries, including construction, manufacturing, and professional service. Project management typically involves three phases: Planning, Scheduling, and Controlling. Project planning encompasses identifying tasks and their time-dependencies to form the work-breakdown-structure (WBS). It also identifies the resource requirement of each task and the available resources for executing the project. With the input data prepared in the planning phase, project scheduling is the phase that determines project schedule, i.e., start times of tasks, to optimize certain performance metric, e.g., minimizing makespan, maximizing net present value (NPV), or minimizing total project costs. Well-known techniques in project scheduling include the critical-path-method (CPM) to minimize makespan.[a] Because CPM does not consider limited resources, a project control phase is often needed to make sure that resource requirement does not exceed the available resource capacity. In case resource capacity violation occurs, the *a priori* project schedule is infeasible, and

[a]Another popular approach is the program evaluation and review technique (PERT) to handle uncertain task processing times. The optimization approach to deal with uncertainty is beyond the scope of this text.

feasibility can be restored by either delaying the start of some tasks or increasing resource capacity.

Such limitation of CPM has motivated the study of the Resource-Constrained Project Scheduling Problem (RCPSP) to explicitly account for limited resources prior to project execution. Consider a project consisting of activities with known durations and precedence relationships. Execution of the project requires a set of resources, each of which has a maximum capacity available in every time period of the planning horizon. Each activity requires a constant amount of resources during its entire duration. Assume no preemption is allowed, i.e., an activity, once started, cannot be interrupted. The basic RCPSP seeks to find a time- and resource-feasible schedule that minimizes the makespan. By assuring resource-feasibility in addition to time-feasibility (as addressed in the CPM), RCPSP offers project scheduling solutions less prone to infeasibility in practice. It has a wide range of applications in various industries as shown in Table 12.1.

The primary use of RCPSP in Project Management is to optimize task scheduling and resource utilization decisions, with the objective of minimizing makespan, maximizing NPV, or minimizing total project costs. In the construction industry, projects consist of tasks, operations and milestones for buildings, roads and bridges, with resources being construction workers, machines and equipment. In manufacturing, RCPSP can be applied for managing MTO or R&D projects/programs, where resources can be machines, equipment, labs, technicians and budget, often with the objective of maximizing the NPV. In the professional service industry, RCPSP can be applied for resource planning in conjunction with scheduling to ensure timely and cost-effective project delivery. It can also be applied for the tactical-level project portfolio optimization to determine project selection and planning decisions, while maximizing NPV. In healthcare, operating room scheduling can be modeled as an RCPSP, with resources being operating rooms, nurses and equipment.

Recall that in Chapter 10, we have shown that the temporal relationship between the inbound and outbound time in the safety stock placement problem can be modeled as the precedence relationship in project scheduling. Thus, an RCPSP can also be adapted for the Supply Chain Configuration Problem with resource constraints. This

Table 12.1. Industry applications of RCPSPs.

Industry	Function	Decision	Objective metric
Construction	Project management	Scheduling, resource utilization	Makespan, NPV, project costs
Manufacturing	Supply chain configuration	Safety stock placement, mode selection	Total supply chain costs
	R&D	Scheduling, resource utilization	Makespan, NPV, project costs
Professional Service	Resource planning	Scheduling, resource assignment	Makespan, project costs
	Project portfolio planning	Project selection, planning	NPV
Agriculture	Supply chain configuration	Safety stock placement, mode selection	
	Food pick-up and delivery	Scheduling, routing	Makespan, operating costs
Healthcare	Supply chain configuration	Safety stock placement, mode selection	Total supply chain costs
	Operating room scheduling	Scheduling, resource utilization	Makespan, operating costs
	Vaccine delivery	Scheduling, routing	Makespan, operating costs
Energy and Utility	Technician dispatching and scheduling	Scheduling, routing	Makespan, operating costs

can be applied for configuring an MTO supply chain in manufacturing, or a food supply chain in agriculture.

Given the intrinsic permutation nature of both RCPSP and a routing problem (TSP or VRP), extensions of the basic RCPSP can be applied for various routing decisions, e.g., pickup and delivery in the food industry, vaccine delivery in healthcare, and technician dispatching in the energy and utility industry. For instance, an integrated routing and scheduling is covered in Chapter 14.

12.2 The Family of RCPSPs

The family of RCPSPs contains a rich set of problems, which can be classified based on ways to execute an activity, the nature of resources, and different objective functions.

Single-mode and Multi-mode: The single-mode RCPSP assumes each activity has only one way to be executed, whereas the multi-mode RCPSP considers multiple ways to execute an activity, which often have tradeoffs in duration, cost, or resource requirement.

Renewable and Non-renewable Resource: A renewable resource has its capacity available (renewed) in every time period of the planning horizon. Examples of renewable resource include machines, equipment and personnel. A non-renewable resource, on the other hand, has its capacity defined over the entire planning horizon, and cannot be renewed once consumed. Examples include budget, cash, supply of materials, etc.

Different Objective Functions: Various project performance metrics can be optimized, including task-based, resource-based, financial-based and customer-based metrics. Table 12.2 summarizes different objective functions and their application examples that can be addressed in an RCPSP.

Table 12.2. Objective functions in RCPSPs.

Objective function	Nature	Application examples
Minimizing makespan	Task-based	Construction projects
Minimizing total tardiness	Customer-based	Production scheduling
Maximizing total NPV	Financial-based	R&D planning
Minimizing total cost	Resource-based	Resource planning
Minimizing resource capacity	Resource-based	Fleet sizing

12.3 Time-Cost Tradeoff Problems

A Time-Cost Tradeoff Problem (TCTP) is also known as *project crashing* in project management. It is based on the general premise that there is an intrinsic tradeoff between activity duration and cost. That is, dedicating more resource, thus cost, to an activity, would shorten its duration. Depending on the type of time-cost relationship, the TCTPs can be classified to linear TCTP and discrete TCTP.

Figure 12.1 shows three types of time-cost tradeoff relationships: linear, nonlinear or concave, and discrete. In the linear time-cost tradeoff in Figure 12.1(a), the activity's duration decreases at a constant rate as its cost increases. The two end points are (d_{max}, c_{min}) and (d_{min}, c_{max}), where d_{max} and d_{min} are the maximum duration and minimum duration, respectively; and c_{min} and c_{max} are the minimum cost and maximum cost, respectively. The nonlinear concave relationship in Figure 12.1(b) has a diminishing return of increasing cost on duration, which is typically the case in practice. It implies that the effectiveness of increasing cost on duration reduction goes down as more resources/cost is devoted to an activity. Modeling such nonlinear time-cost tradeoff relationship makes the model formulation to be nonlinear. An effective way to maintain linearity for the model is to discretize the nonlinear relationship as in Figure 12.1(c). With five discrete (time, cost) points, the discrete time-cost tradeoff effectively approximate the concave relationship in Figure 12.1(b).

12.3.1 *Linear TCTP*

Consider a project consisting of a set V of activities and a set A of arcs describing the precedence relationships. For each $(i, j) \in A$, activity j cannot start until activity i is finished. With minimum resource/cost of c_i^{min} for activity $i \in V$, the normal (maximum) duration of i is d_i^{max}. For every unit of more resource/cost dedicated to activity i, its duration can be reduced by a constant of k time units. The total available budget for all the activities is B, which serves the role of non-renewable resource. The linear TCTP seeks to find feasible cost and the corresponding duration of all the tasks, and

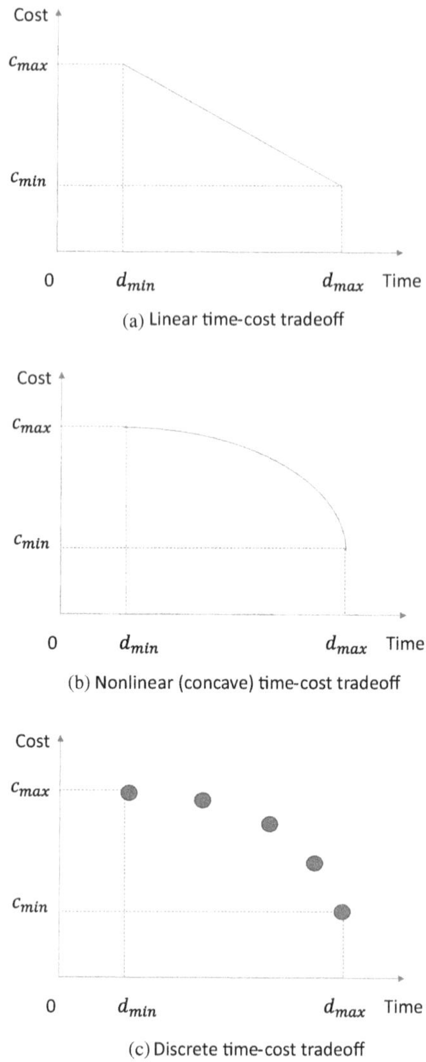

Figure 12.1. Different time-cost tradeoff relationships.

their starting times, that minimize the makespan. The linear TCTP can be formulated as a linear programming model.

Key to Formulation: Define continuous decision variables for the duration and cost of each activity. Then the duration of an activity can be computed as a function of its cost through the linear time-cost relationship. Define another continuous decision variable for the starting time of each activity. Precedence constraints for pairs of activities can be established through inequalities that involve the starting time decision variables and duration decision variables.

Sets and parameters

V: set of activities in the project
A: set of precedence relationships, i.e., for each $(i, j) \in A$, activity j cannot start until activity i is finished
d_i^{min}: minimum duration of activity $i \in V$
d_i^{max}: maximum duration of activity $i \in V$
c_i^{min}: minimum cost of activity $i \in V$
c_i^{max}: maximum cost of activity $i \in V$
k_i: reduction of the duration of activity $i \in V$ per unit of increase of its cost
B: total budget available for the project

Decision variables

$d_i \geq 0$: duration of activity $i \in V$
$c_i \geq 0$: cost of activity $i \in V$
$t_i \geq 0$: starting time of activity $i \in V$
L: project makespan

Objective function

$$\text{Minimize} \quad L \tag{12.1}$$

Subject to:

$$d_i = d_i^{\max} - k \cdot (c_i - c_i^{\min}), \quad \forall i \in V, \tag{12.2}$$

$$t_j \geq t_i + d_i, \quad \forall (i, j) \in A, \tag{12.3}$$

$$\sum_{i \in V} c_i \leq B, \tag{12.4}$$

$$L \geq t_i + d_i, \quad \forall i \in V, \tag{12.5}$$

$$d_i, c_i, t_i, L \geq 0 \tag{12.6}$$

The objective function (12.1) minimizes the project makespan. Constraint (12.2) computes the duration of an activity based on how much resource (cost) is devoted in the activity. The precedence relationship between pairs of jobs is satisfied by Constraint (12.3). Constraint (12.4) limits that the total project cost does not exceed the maximum available budget. Constraint (12.5) computes the project makespan to be no less the completion times of all the activities.

12.3.2 *Discrete TCTP*

The discrete TCTP has a similar problem setting with that of the linear TCTP, except that the time-cost tradeoff is described by a set of *discrete* time-cost pairs for each activity. Specifically, let K^i denote a set of options for activity $i \in V$, where option k has a cost of c_{ik} and duration of d_{ik} for activity i. The discrete TCTP can be modeled as an MILP.

Key to Formulation: Define binary decision variables for the option selection of each activity, which can be used to compute the activities' durations and costs. Additional constraints involving the starting time decision variables and activity durations are imposed to satisfy the precedence relationships.

Sets and parameters

V: set of activities in the project
A: set of precedence relationships, i.e., for each $(i, j) \in A$, activity j cannot start until activity i] is finished
K^i: set of options of activity $i \in V$
d_{ik}: duration of activity $i \in V$ in option $k \in K^i$
c_{ik}: cost of activity $i \in V$ in option $k \in K^i$
B: total budget available for the project
L: project makespan

Decision variables

$x_{ik} = 1$ if activity $i \in V$ selects option $k \in K^i$
$d_i \geq 0$: duration of activity $i \in V$
$c_i \geq 0$: cost of activity $i \in V$
$t_i \geq 0$: starting time of activity $i \in V$

Objective function

$$\text{Minimize} \quad L \tag{12.7}$$

Subject to:

$$\sum_{k \in K^i} x_{ik} = 1, \quad \forall i \in V, \tag{12.8}$$

$$d_i = \sum_{k \in K^i} d_{ik} x_{ik}, \quad \forall i \in V, \tag{12.9}$$

$$c_i = \sum_{k \in K^i} c_{ik} x_{ik}, \quad \forall i \in V, \tag{12.10}$$

$$t_j \geq t_i + d_i, \quad \forall (i, j) \in A, \tag{12.11}$$

$$\sum_{i \in V} c_i \leq B, \tag{12.12}$$

$$L \geq t_i + d_i, \quad \forall i \in V, \tag{12.13}$$

$$x_{ik} \in \{0, 1\}, d_i, c_i, t_i \geq 0 \tag{12.14}$$

Constraint (12.8) assigns exactly one mode (option) to each activity. Constraints (12.9) and (12.10) compute the duration and cost of each activity based on selected mode for the activity, respectively. Constraint (12.11) satisfies the precedence relationship between pairs of activities. The maximum available budget cannot be exceeded as in Constraint (12.12). Constraint (12.13) computes the project makespan.

12.4 Single-Mode RCPSP

Consider a project consisting of a set V of activities and a set A of arcs. For $(i, j) \in A$, activity j cannot start until activity i is finished. Each activity $i \in V$ has a constant duration p_i, and requires r_{ik} units of renewable resource $k \in K$ during its execution, where K is a set of renewable resources, with R_k units available in every period of the planning horizon. The single-mode RCPSP seeks to find both time and resource-feasible schedule, i.e., starting times of all the activities, to minimize the makespan.

Figure 12.2 shows a small example of single-mode RCPSP with six activities and one renewable resource. An activity-on-node diagram in Figure 12.2(a) describes the precedence relationships among activities. The numbers in the parenthesis on top of each node are

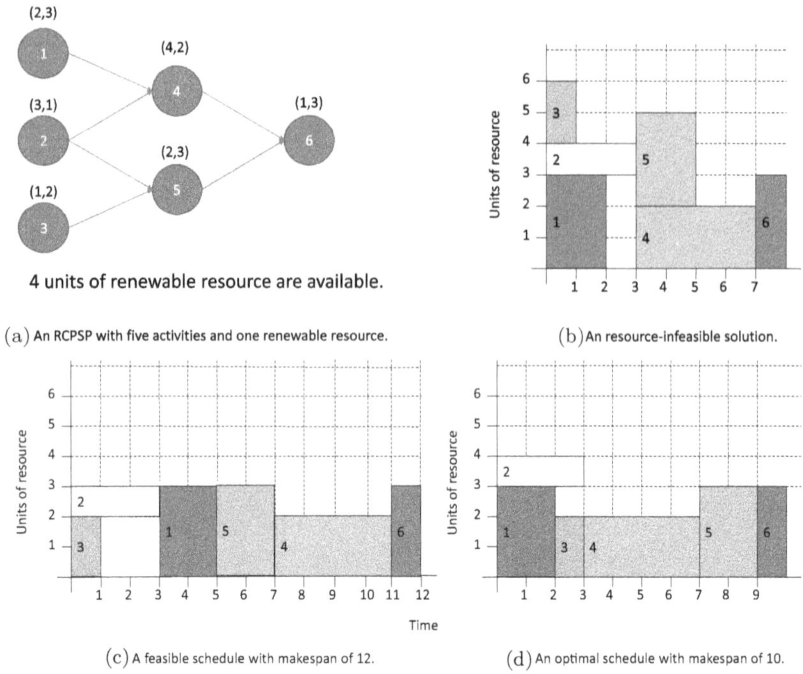

(a) An RCPSP with five activities and one renewable resource.

(b) An resource-infeasible solution.

(c) A feasible schedule with makespan of 12.

(d) An optimal schedule with makespan of 10.

Figure 12.2. An example of single-mode RCPSP with five activities and one renewable resource.

(duration, resource requirement) of the corresponding activity. For instance, Activity 1 has duration of 2 time units and requires 3 units of resource during its execution. The schedule in Figure 12.2(b) is time-feasible, i.e., it satisfies all the precedence relationships, but not resource-feasible because it exceeds the maximum 6 units of the renewable resource. A feasible solution, obtained by the shortest processing time (SPT) heuristic, is shown in Figure 12.2(c) with a makespan of 12. The minimum makespan of this problem is 10, with an optimal schedule shown in Figure 12.2(d). One can verify that it satisfies both the precedence and resource constraints.

12.4.1 *Time-Indexed Formulation*

The single-mode RCPSP can be modelled using a time-indexed formulation with polynomial number of decision variables and constraints.

Key to Formulation: Time-indexed decision variables can be used to conveniently compute the starting time of each activity and express the precedence constraints. The most complex constraints are those for the resource constraint in each time period and for each type of resource. The intricate expression at the LHS of a constraint computes the amount of resource required in the corresponding time period. The key is to identify the activities that are active in the time period based on in which period they are started, i.e., the time-indexed decision variables.

Sets and parameters

- V: set of $n+1$ activities in the project, i.e., $V = \{1, 2, \ldots, n+1\}$, where activity $n+1$ is the dummy finish activity (makespan) of the project
- A: set of precedence relationships, i.e., for each $(i, j) \in A$, activity j cannot start until activity i is finished
- K: set of renewable resources
- p_i: duration of activity $i \in V$
- R_k: maximum available capacity of resource $k \in K$
- r_{ik}: units of resource $k \in K$ required by activity $i \in V$

For the convenience of expressing the formulation, some additional parameters can be derived from the above input data. An upper bound T of makespan can be obtained using a heuristic. Let ES_i and LS_i denote the earliest starting time and latest starting time of activity $i \in V$, respectively.

Decision variables

$x_{it} = 1$ if activity $i \in V$ starts at time period $t \in \{ES_i, ES_i + 1, \ldots, LS_i\}$, and 0 o.w. With this definition, the starting time of activity i equals $\sum_{t=ES_i}^{LS_i} t \cdot x_{it}$.

Objective function

$$\text{Minimize} \sum_{t=ES_{n+1}}^{LS_{n+1}} t \cdot x_{n+1,t} \tag{12.15}$$

Subject to:

$$\sum_{t=ES_i}^{LS_i} x_{it} = 1, \quad \forall i \in V, \tag{12.16}$$

$$\sum_{t=ES_j}^{LS_j} t \cdot x_{jt} - \sum_{t=ES_i}^{LS_i} t \cdot x_{it} \geq p_i, \quad \forall (i,j) \in A, \tag{12.17}$$

$$\sum_{i \in V} \left(r_{ik} \cdot \sum_{\tau=\max\{ES_i, t-p_i+1\}}^{\min\{t, LS_i\}} x_{it} \right) \leq R_k, \quad \forall t \in, T, k \in K, \tag{12.18}$$

$$x_{it} \in \{0, 1\}. \tag{12.19}$$

The objective function (12.15) minimizes the starting time of the dummy finish activity, i.e., project makespan. Constraint (12.16) states that each activity starts exactly once and cannot be interrupted, i.e., no preemption is allowed. Constraint (12.17) satisfies the precedence relationship between a pair of activities $(i, j) \in A$. Resource constraint is guaranteed by (12.18), such that the resources required in every time period do not exceed the available capacities. One advantage of the time-indexed formulation for RCPSP is that it is polynomial in size, i.e., $n \cdot (|T| + 1)$ binary decision variables and $|A| + |T| \cdot |K| + n + 1$ constraints, which is amenable for implementing the model using various optimization solvers.

12.4.2 *Disjunctive Formulation*

We present an alternative MILP formulation for the single-mode RCPSP, using the classical disjunctive constraints for scheduling problems. Define F as a *minimal forbidden set* of activities that satisfies two conditions: (i) all the activities in F cannot be simultaneously executed; and (ii) imposing one precedence relationship is sufficient to avoid resource-infeasibility of F. Let $\mathcal{F}$ denote the set of all minimal forbidden sets. For the small example in Figure 12.2, the set $\mathcal{F}$ of all minimal forbidden sets is: $\{\{1,3\}, \{1,4\}, \{1,5\}, \{1,6\}, \{3,5\}, \{3,6\}, \{4,5\}, \{4,6\}, \{5,6\}\}$.

Key to Formulation: Define a binary decision variable to indicate whether an activity is finished before the other is started, and a continuous decision variable to represent the starting time of an activity.

Decision variables

$x_{ij} = 1$ if activity $i \in V$ is finished before activity j is started, for every pair of i and j, i.e., $(i,j) \in V \times V$

$S_i \geq 0$: the starting time of activity $i \in V$

Objective function

$$\text{Minimize} \quad S_{n+1} \tag{12.20}$$

Subject to:

$$x_{ij} + x_{ji} \leq 1, \quad \forall (i,j) \in V \times V : i \neq j, \tag{12.21}$$

$$x_{ij} + x_{jk} - x_{ik} \leq 1, \quad \forall (i,j,k) \in V \times V \times V : i \neq j,\ j \neq k, i \neq k \tag{12.22}$$

$$x_{ij} = 1, \quad \forall (i,j) \in A, \tag{12.23}$$

$$\sum_{i,j \in F : i \neq j} x_{ij} \geq 1, \quad \forall F \in \mathcal{F}, \tag{12.24}$$

$$S_j - S_i + M(1 - x_{ij}) \geq p_i, \quad \forall\, (i,j) \in V \times V : i \neq j, \tag{12.25}$$

$$x_{ij} \in \{0,1\},\ S_i \geq 0, \tag{12.26}$$

The objective function (12.20) minimizes the project makespan. Constraint (12.21) states that only one of the following three may occur between a pair of distinctive activities i and j: (i) i precedes j; (ii) j precedes i; or (iii) i overlaps with j. To see why Constraint (12.22) must be satisfied, consider its negation inequality: $x_{ij}+x_{jk}-x_{ik} \geq 2$. It only holds when $x_{ij} = x_{jk} = 1$ and $x_{ik} = 0$, i.e., i precedes j, j precedes k, but i does not precede k, which cannot be true. Constraint (12.23) fixes precedence relationship specified by the set A of arcs. Constraint (12.24) requires the precedence relationship of at least one pair of activities in a minimal forbidden set is determined. Constraint (12.25) is a big-M formulation to ensure proper relationship between the sequencing decision variable x_{ij} for activity i and j, and their starting times. Since there are a total of $2^{|V|}$ possible constraints, the size of this formulation grows exponentially with the number of activities in the project.

12.4.3 *Special cases of single-mode RCPSP*

The single-mode RCPSP is general enough to include a number of classical machine scheduling problems, including those introduced in Chapter 11, as special cases.

Single-Machine Scheduling Problem: It is equivalent to a single-mode RCPSP with one resource, i.e., $|K| = 1$. Its capacity is 1 ($R_1 = 1$), and each activity i requires 1 unit of the resource ($r_{ik} = 1$).

m−Parallel-Machine Scheduling Problem: It is equivalent to a single-mode RCPSP with one resource, i.e., $|K| = 1$. Its capacity is m ($R_1 = m$), and each activity i requires 1 unit of the resource ($r_{ik} = 1$).

Flow Shop Scheduling Problem: A flow shop scheduling problem with n jobs and m machines are equivalent to a single-mode RCPSP with $n \cdot m$ activities and m resources, i.e., $|K| = m$. Each resource has a capacity of 1 ($R_k = 1$ for $k \in K$), and each activity i requires 1 unit of a particular resource, and 0 unit of other resources. Precedence constraints must hold for the activities corresponding to the operations of a job processed on different machines in the same order.

Job Shop Scheduling Problem: A job shop scheduling problem with n jobs and m machines are equivalent to a single-mode RCPSP with $n \cdot m$ activities and m resources, i.e., $|K| = m$. Each resource has a capacity of 1 ($R_k = 1$ for $k \in K$), and each activity i requires 1 unit of a particular resource, and 0 unit of other resources. Precedence constraints must hold for the activities corresponding to the operations of a job processed on different machines in certain order.

Open Shop Scheduling Problem: An open shop scheduling problem with n jobs and m machines are equivalent to a single-mode RCPSP with $n \cdot m$ activities and m resources, i.e., $|K| = m$. Each resource has a capacity of 1 ($R_k = 1$ for $k \in K$), and each activity i requires 1 unit of a particular resource, and 0 unit of other resources. No precedence constraint exists in this case.

Flexible Flow Shop Scheduling Problem: A flexible flow shop scheduling problem with n jobs, m operations, each operation $k \in \{1, 2, \ldots, m\}$ having R_k machines available, is equivalent to a single-mode RCPSP with $n \cdot m$ activities and m resources, i.e., $|K| = m$. Each resource $k \in K$ has a capacity of R_k, and each activity i requires 1 unit of a particular resource, and 0 unit of other resources.

Table 12.3. Reduction of RCPSP to machine scheduling problems.

Machine scheduling problem	$\|V\|$	$\|K\|$	R_k	r_{ik}	Precedence relationship
Single-machine	n	1	1	1	No
Parallel-machine	n	1	m	1	No
Flow shop	n	m	1	1 and 0s	Yes
Job shop	n	m	1	1 and 0s	Yes
Open shop	n	m	1	1 and 0s	No
Flexible flow shop	n	m	R_k	1 and 0s	Yes
Flexible job shop	n	m	R_k	1 and 0s	Yes

Precedence constraints must hold for the activities corresponding to the operations of a job processed on different machines in the same order.

Flexible Job Shop Scheduling Problem: A flexible job shop scheduling problem with n jobs, m operations, each operation $k \in \{1, 2, \ldots, m\}$ having R_k machines available, is equivalent to a single-mode RCPSP with $n \cdot m$ activities and m resources, i.e., $|K| = m$. Each resource $k \in K$ has a capacity of R_k, and each activity i requires 1 unit of a particular resource, and 0 unit of other resources. Precedence constraints must hold for the activities corresponding to the operations of a job processed on different machines in certain order.

Table 12.3 summarizes the above results.

12.5 Multi-Mode RCPSP

While the single-mode RCPSP models the role and effect of renewable resources in project scheduling, it does not consider multiple ways to execute project activities or non-renewable resources. A multi-mode RCPSP generalizes the single-mode version by explicitly handling both non-renewable and renewable resources. It can be viewed as one that combines the single-mode RCPSP and the discrete TCTP.

With the problem setting remaining the same as in the single-mode RCPSP, now consider a set M_i of modes to execute an activity $i \in V$. The duration of activity i in mode $m \in M_i$ is p_{im}. Let Γ denote a set of non-renewable resources, with the maximum capacity of resource $l \in \Gamma$ being R_l over the entire planning horizon. The requirements of non-renewable and renewable resources of activity i in mode m are r_{im} and r_{il}, respectively.

Decision variables

$x_{imt} = 1$ if activity $i \in V$ is assigned with mode $m \in M_i$ starting at time $t \in \{ES_i,\ ES_i+1,\ldots,LS_i\}$, and 0 o.w.

Objective function

$$\text{Minimize} \quad \sum_{t=ES_{n+1}}^{LS_{n+1}} t \cdot x_{n+1,t} \tag{12.27}$$

Subject to:

$$\sum_{m\in M_i} \sum_{t=ES_i}^{LS_i} x_{imt} = 1, \quad \forall i \in V, \tag{12.28}$$

$$\sum_{m\in M_j} \sum_{t=ES_j}^{LS_j} t \cdot x_{jmt} - \sum_{m\in M_i} \sum_{t=ES_i}^{LS_i} t \cdot x_{imt} \geq \sum_{m\in M_i} \sum_{t=ES_i}^{LS_i} p_{im} \cdot x_{imt},$$

$$\forall (i,j) \in A, \tag{12.29}$$

$$\sum_{i\in V} \sum_{m\in M_i} r_{ik} \cdot \sum_{\tau=max\{ES_i,t-p_i+1\}}^{\min\{t,LS_i\}} x_{imt} \leq R_k, \quad \forall t \in T,\ k \in K, \tag{12.30}$$

$$\sum_{i\in V} \sum_{m\in M_i} r_{il} \cdot \sum_{t=ES_i}^{LS_i} x_{imt} \leq R_l, \quad \forall l \in \Gamma, \tag{12.31}$$

$$x_{imt} \in \{0,1\} \tag{12.32}$$

The objective function (12.27) minimizes the project makespan. Constraint (12.28) assigns exactly one mode and one starting time to each activity, i.e., no preemption is allowed. Constraint (12.29) satisfies the precedence relationship between a pair of activities $(i,j) \in A$. Constraint (12.30) guarantees that the available capacity of each renewable resource is not exceeded in every time period of the planning horizon. Constraint (12.31) ensures that the available capacity of each non-renewable resource is not exceeded.

12.6 RCPSP for MTO Supply Chain Configuration

As explained in Chapter 10, an MTO or ETO supply chain can often be managed as a project. It turns out that the RCPSP modeling framework can be extended to model the MTO SCCP under explicit renewable resource constraints. Compared to an MTS or ATO supply chain, an MTO supply chain has several distinctive features: (i) demand is often specified in the customer order/contract rather than based on forecast; (ii) products are highly customized with flexible and complex manufacturing process; some may even require a new design as in ETO; and (iii) limited availability of resources must be explicitly considered to ensure feasible supply chain operations.

Consider an MTO manufacturer managing a set O of new orders. Each order requires delivering Q_o units of end product $o \in O$ before a specified due date d_o. Let V_o denote the set of supply chain functions associated with order o. Again, a function may represent a component, a part or a task/activity (e.g., procurement, fabrication, assembly, transporting, etc.) in the product's bill-of-materials (BOM). We assume that the engineering design of products have been determined, such that the BOM of an end product $o \in O$ is known. Then the supply chain network $G(V, E)$ for O can be described by the set V of all entities with $V = V_1 \cup V_2 \ldots \cup V_{|O|}$, and a set of demand-dependencies E. Each arc $(i, j) \in E$ with a weight of ρ_{ij} describes the demand-dependency between i and its successor j, i.e., production of one unit of j requires ρ_{ij} units of i. Thus, the demand μ_i of $i \in V$ can be derived by the following backward recursion:

$$\mu_i = \sum_{j:(i,j)\in E} \rho_{ij}\mu_j, \tag{12.33}$$

where the demand of end product $o \in O$ is given as Q_o.

12.6.1 *Sourcing and Purchasing*

Management often makes decisions about how to source supply chain operations. That is, the manufacturer can either produce in-house or outsource an entity. If outsourcing is chosen, it must decide which supplier or vendor to choose; if in-house production is preferred, it must make sure that the available internal resource capacity is not exceeded.

Sourcing is defined as the way to provide or execute a supply chain entity $i \in V$. Based on how an entity can be sourced, the set V of all entities can be classified into three subgroups, i.e., $V = V^{in} \cup V^{out} \cup V^{io}$, where V^{in} refers to the set of *in-house only* entities, V^{out} the set of *outsourcing only* entities, and V^{io} the set of *undetermined* entities which can be either outsourced or produced in-house.

As each end product can be distinct and highly-customized in the MTO setting, a frequent decision made for entity $\in V^{io}$ is the make-or-buy decision, which may differ in fixed setup cost F, direct cost added c, lead time l, and resource requirement r included in T_{im}. In-house production usually incurs significant setup cost, sometimes purchasing or renting of new equipment, to facilitate distinct operations in customized orders; whereas outsourcing may incur less setup cost for placing an order. In-house production often requires certain internal resources such as machines, equipment and skilled workforce; whereas outsourcing usually does not require any internal resource.

For entity $i \in V^{out}$, only outsourcing is possible due to the manufacturer's lack of resources, expertise or efficiency. Several suppliers or vendors may be available for an entity, which may differ in F, c and l, reflecting the time-cost tradeoff. For instance, an overseas supplier may supply an item at a lower cost than a domestic supplier, but the transportation lead time may be significantly longer, which may lead to higher pipeline stock cost. The next-day delivery of finished goods is much faster than the ground shipping mode, but is also much more expensive.

12.6.2 *Production Modes*

For entity $i \in V^{in}$, only in-house production is considered. The manufacturer has the option of "crashing" a task by choosing the production mode which utilizes more resources, reflecting the time-resource tradeoff. For instance, a fabrication task may take one machine and one skilled worker 20 days to complete, but only take two machines and two skilled workers 7 days to complete. The available crashing options M_i of task i differ in l and r in the tuple T_{im}.

12.6.3 *Resource Constraints*

There is a set K of internal renewable resources involved. Each resource $k \in K$ has a constant capacity of R_k available in any time period during the planning horizon. Also consider a set Γ of non-renewable resources, with resource $\kappa \in \Gamma$ having maximum R_κ capacity available for the entire planning horizon. For function $i \in V_o$, there is a set M_i of modes (options) available. Each mode $m \in M_i$ is characterized by a tuple: $T_{im} = \{l_{im}, c_{im}, F_{im}, r_{imk} \forall k \in K, r_{im\kappa} \forall \kappa \in \Gamma\}$, where l_{im} denotes the lead time of i executed in mode m, c_{im} is the direct cost added of i executed in mode m, F_{im} is the fixed setup cost of i executed in mode m, r_{imk} represents units of renewable resource k required by i executed in mode m, and $r_{im\kappa}$ denotes the units of non-renewable resource κ consumed by i executed in mode m.

An MINLP model for the MTO supply configuration problem under resource constraints can be written as below.

Sets and parameters

- O: set of orders/contracts
- V_o: set of nodes (supply chain functions) associated with order $o \in O$
- V: set of node associated with all orders, such that $V = V_1 \cup V_2 \ldots \cup V_{|O|}$
- V^{in}: set of in-house entities
- V^{out}: set of outsourced entities
- V^{io}: set of entities which can be either produced in-house or outsourced
- E: set of arcs in the network representing the demand and time dependencies
- K: set of internal resources
- T: number of time periods in the planning horizon
- ρ_{ij}: demand-dependency between i and its successor j
- M_i: set of options (modes) available for entity $i \in V$
- μ_i: demand of entity $i \in V$
- l_{im}: lead time of entity i executed in mode $m \in M_i$
- c_{im}: direct cost added of entity i executed in mode $m \in M_i$
- F_{im}: fixed setup cost of entity i executed in mode $m \in M_i$

R_k: units of resource $k \in K$ in every time period
r_{imk}: units of renewable resource k required by entity i executed in mode m
d_o: customer-specified due date of order $o \in O$
h: inventory holding cost rate per time period

Decision variables

$x_{imt} = 1$ if entity $i \in V$ is assigned with mode $m \in M_i$ and starts at time $t = 1, 2 \ldots, T$; and 0, o.w.
$p_i \in Z^+$: lead time of $i \in V$
$\omega_i \geq 0$: direct cost added of $i \in V$
$\bar{\omega}_i \geq 0$: cumulative direct cost added of $i \in V$

When entity i refers to a supply chain task/activity, x is the start time of this task/activity; when i refers to a part/component, x is the start time of procuring or fabricating the part/component as an aggregated batch.

Objective function

$$\text{Minimize} \sum_{i \in V} \left[\sum_{m \in M_i} \sum_{t=ES_i}^{LS_i} F_{im} x_{imt} + \mu_i \omega_i + h\mu_i(\bar{\omega}_i - \omega_i/2)p_i \right] \tag{12.34}$$

Constraints

$$\sum_{m \in M_i} \sum_{t=ES_i}^{LS_i} x_{imt} = 1, \quad \forall i \in V, \tag{12.35}$$

$$p_i = \sum_{m \in M_i} \sum_{t=ES_i}^{LS_i} l_{im} x_{imt}, \quad \forall i \in V, \tag{12.36}$$

$$\omega_i = \sum_{m \in M_i} \sum_{t=ES_i}^{LS_i} c_{im} x_{imt}, \quad \forall i \in V, \tag{12.37}$$

$$\bar{\omega}_i = \omega_i + \sum_{j:(j,i)\in E} \bar{\omega}_j, \quad \forall i \in V, \tag{12.38}$$

$$\sum_{m\in M_j}\sum_{t=ES_j}^{LS_j} tx_{jmt} - \sum_{m\in M_i}\sum_{t=ES_i}^{LS_i} tx_{imt} \geq p_i, \quad \forall (i,j) \in E, \tag{12.39}$$

$$\sum_{m\in M_i}\sum_{t=ES_i}^{LS_i} tx_{imt} + p_i \leq d_o, \quad \forall o \in O,\ i \in V_o, \tag{12.40}$$

$$\sum_{i\in V^{in}\cup V^{io}}\sum_{m\in M_i}\left(r_{imk} \sum_{\tau=\max\{t-l_{im}+1,ES_i\}}^{\min\{t,LS_i\}} x_{im\tau}\right) \leq R_k, \quad \forall k \in K,\ t \in \{1,\ldots,T\} \tag{12.41}$$

$$x_{imt} \in \{0,1\}, \quad p_i \in Z^+, \quad \omega_i \geq 0, \quad \bar{\omega}_i \geq 0 \tag{12.42}$$

The objective function (12.34) minimizes the total supply chain costs consisting of three elements: total fixed setup cost, COGS, and inventory holding cost of the pipeline stock based on the Little's Law, similar to that shown in Figure 10.5. ES_i and LS_i represent the earliest and latest starting time of i, respectively. They can be obtained by the classical temporal analysis in project scheduling. Since processing times or durations are dependent upon options chosen, we use the least duration (most expensive) option for computing ES, and longest duration (least expensive) option for computing LS.

Constraint (12.35) assigns exactly one mode and starting time for an entity. Constraints (12.36) and (12.37) calculate the lead time and direct cost added of an entity, respectively, based on the option assigned. Constraint (12.38) calculates the cumulative direct cost of an entity as the sum of its predecessors' cumulative direct costs plus its own direct cost added. Constraints (12.39) and (12.40) enforce the precedence constraint and due date constraint, respectively. Constraint (12.41) guarantees that resource requirement of in-house production does not exceed the available resource capacity in every time period. The length of planning horizon T is set to be an upper bound on the completion time (makespan) of all contracts obtained in the temporal analysis.

12.7 Project Scheduling with Multi-Purpose Resources

For RCPSPs involving human resources, it is often necessary to consider the skills required to execute project tasks. Due to specialization and cross-training, a task may require multiple skills and a resource (individual) may possess multiple skills. This is the case in various project management setting of construction, manufacturing, professional service and military. It has motivated the study of Project Scheduling with Multi-Purpose Resources (PSMPR).

Consider a project consisting of a task set J, a skill set K, and a set S of personnel. Each task $j \in J$ has a constant processing time p_j. No preemption is allowed, i.e., a task cannot be interrupted once it has been started. A minimum time lag δ_{ij} must be satisfied between the starting times of task i and j, which is known as *generalized temporal relationship*, and reduces to a precedence relationship when δ_{ij} equals the processing time p_i of task i. There is a deadline $\bar{T}$ on the project makespan. Each task j requires a set of skills $K^j \subseteq K$ to be present simultaneously for the activity to progress. Each skill $k \in K$ requires one individual $s \in S^k$ to perform, where S^k is the set of personnel who possess skill k. An individual can perform only one skill at one time point, but may possess multiple skills, i.e., for each $s \in S$ there is a skill set K^s representing the set of skills that can be performed by s. Each individual s has a workload limit w_s that cannot be exceeded during the scheduling horizon. The cost of utilizing individual s is c_s. The PSMPR seeks to find a feasible schedule of starting times of all the tasks and assignment of personnel to tasks/skills to minimize the total staffing costs.

A distinctive feature of PSMPR is the presence of two layers of resources, with the first layer being the skill set K and the second one being the personnel set S. Technical requirements exist in two ways: one is the generalized temporal constraint, which stipulates the time relation between a pair of tasks in the project; the other is the skill requirement constraint, which states the requirement of skills by each task. Note that each task interacts only with the first layer resources (skills) directly. One needs to choose and assign the second layer resources (personnel) to perform the appropriate tasks/skills. This two-layer-resource structure is depicted in Figure 12.3. The rectangles represent tasks, and δ_{ij} denotes the minimum time lag between tasks i and j. The requirement of the first layer resources is represented by solid arrows between task set J and skill set K. For instance, task $J2$ requires both skill $K1$ and $K3$ simultaneously. The dashed arrows show the skill-mix of the second layer resources, with the actual assignments yet to be determined. For example, $S3$ is the most versatile individual as he/she is able to perform all the three skills, but the actual assignment of $S3$ to tasks/skills is unknown and must be determined.

The PSMPR is a variant of the multi-mode RCPSP in that there are multiple ways to perform each task. The difference is that the multiple modes here come from the flexibility of utilizing multi-skilled personnel, as opposed to the time-cost (resource) tradeoff in a typical multi-mode RCPSP. Thus, the number of modes in PSMPR is combinatorial in nature, i.e., for each task j there are $\prod_{k \in K^j} |S^k|$ modes to be considered. Clearly, if each individual is identical to each other, i.e., $|k| = 1$ and $\left|S^k\right| = 1$ for $s \in S$, the PSMPR reduces to a single-mode RCPSP.

An MILP formulation for the PSMPR can be written as below.

Sets and parameters

- J: set of tasks including the dummy finish task
- A: set of arcs that have minimum time lag relationships
- K: set of skills
- S: set of personnel
- K^j: set of skills required by task $j \in J$

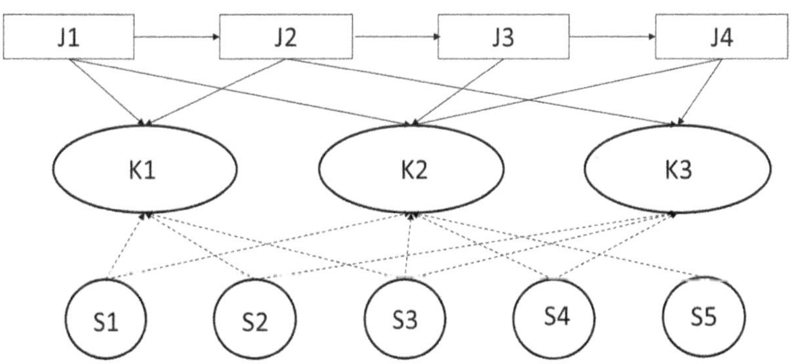

Figure 12.3. The two-layer-resource modeling framework of the PSMPR.

S^k: set of personnel who possess skill $k \in K$; symmetrically, one may obtain K^s as the set of skills possessed by individual $s \in S$

δ_{ij}: the minimum time lag between task i and j for $(i, j) \in A$, i.e., the start time of task j must be at least δ_{ij} time units after the start of task i

p_j: processing time of task $j \in J$

w_s: maximum workload of individual $s \in S$

$\bar{T}$: deadline on project makespan

Decision variables

$z_s = 1$ if individual $s \in S$ is selected to perform the project; and 0 o.w.

$x_{jks} = 1$ if individual $s \in S$ is assigned to task $j \in J$ to perform skill $k \in K^j$

$t_j \geq 0$: the starting time of task $j \in J$

$y_{jj'} = 1$ if task j is finished before the start of task j' for $(j, j') \in A$

Objective function

$$\text{Minimize} \quad \sum_{s \in S} c_s z_s \tag{12.43}$$

Constraints

$$\sum_{s \in S^k} x_{jks} = 1, \quad \forall j \in J,\ k \in K^j, \tag{12.44}$$

$$\sum_{k \in K^j} x_{jks} \leq 1, \quad \forall j \in J,\ s \in S, \tag{12.45}$$

$$\sum_{j \in J} \sum_{k \in K^j} p_j x_{jks} \leq w_s, \quad \forall s \in S, \tag{12.46}$$

$$t_{j'} - t_j \geq \delta_{jj'}, \quad \forall (j, j') \in A, \tag{12.47}$$

$$t_j + p_j \leq \bar{T}, \quad \forall j \in J, \tag{12.48}$$

$$y_{jj'} + y_{j'j} \geq x_{jks} + x_{j'k's}, \quad \forall \text{ordered}(jk, j'k'), s \in S \tag{12.49}$$

$$t_{j'} \geq t_j + p_j - M(1 - y_{jj'}), \quad \forall (j, j') \in J \times J: \quad j \neq j' \tag{12.50}$$

$$z_s, x_{jks} \in \{0, 1\}, \quad t_j \geq 0 \tag{12.51}$$

The objective function (12.43) minimizes the total staffing costs. Constraint (12.44) states that each skill in a task requires one individual who possesses that skill. Constraint (12.45) enforces that no individual is assigned to more than one skill in the same task, since one may perform only one task at a time point. Constraint (12.46) ensures that the total assigned workload of each individual cannot exceed his/her workload capacity. Constraint (12.47) satisfies the minimum time lag between task j and j'. Constraint (12.48) ensures that the project makespan does not exceed the deadline. Constraint (12.49) states the logic relationship between sequencing and assignment variables, i.e., if two tasks are assigned with the same person then these two tasks cannot overlap (one sequencing relation must be determined). Constraint (12.50) is the classical big-M formulation to define the sequencing variables.

12.8 Additional Notes

The RCPSP and its variants is a versatile class of optimization problems that have been extensively studied. We refer to [85, 86] for a comprehensive treatment of the models, algorithms and applications of variants of RCPSPs. Various MILP formulations of the single-mode RCPSP are available in [87]. The RCPSP model for MTO supply chain configuration in Section 12.6 is based on the work of [37]. The multi-mode RCPSP for multi-purpose resources in Section 12.7 and its application for manpower planning and scheduling on a military ship are available in [35, 36, 88].

Exercises

12.1. Discuss three variants and extension of the single-mode RCPSP. Show real world settings where they can be applied.

12.2. Show and discuss three real world settings where the TCTP, linear or discrete, can be applied.

12.3. What alternative decision variables, objective functions and constraints can be considered in the TCTP.

12.4. Discuss and explain the connections and differences between the RCPSP and machine scheduling problems.

12.5. Explain how an MTO supply chain configuration problem can be modeled as a variant of the RCPSP. Show one real world example.

12.6. Explain how to build the two-layer-resource modeling framework for the PSMPR. Show one real world example.

12.7. ABC Building is a construction company specialized in single-residence and small-size commercial buildings. With its limited workforce and construction equipment, the company must properly schedule tasks and activities of multiple projects. Building activities and steps must be performed by the right crew in the right sequence and at the right time for on-time and on-budget completion. A project manager also applies the project crashing techniques to devote more resources, if necessary, to shorten activity duration. Propose a data-driven optimization model to help ABC Building address its project management needs. Elaborate the decision variables, objective function(s), constraints and the input data needed in your model.

12.8. Consider the setting of Problem 11.11. Some emergency room operations at large hospital systems can be so diverse that the technical precedence relationships among medical activities are more flexible and arbitrary. How would you revise your modeling approach to handle this?

12.9. ABC Inc. is a software development firm known for its data-driven information and decision-support solutions. Using historical data, the firm has a systematic WBS approach to estimate and plan the project milestones, tasks and subtasks, with their durations and required resources. Each project task must be performed by a team of professionals with different skills and roles, e.g., software architect, database, GUI/web design and project management. Propose a data-driven optimization model to help ABC Inc. better manage its projects and resource utilization. Elaborate the decision variables, objective function(s), constraints and the input data needed in your model.

12.10. ABC Medical Equipment is a manufacturer specialized in custom designed ambulances. The company implements an ETO-MTO business model to work with its customer for the design of ambulance to meet the customer's unique needs, before initiating an MTO manufacturing and production process. Depending on the model and sophistication of features, the production cycle of an ambulance may last up to 12 months, thus it is crucial for the company to plan for the procurement and supply of parts, components and subassemblies ahead of time to avoid delay. Propose a data-driven approach to help ABC Medical Equipment better manage its operations to achieve on-time and cost-effective order fulfillment. Elaborate the decision variables, objective function(s), constraints and the input data needed in your model.

12.11. ABC Plant Center is a bioscience research institute with over a hundred scientists, technicians, data analysts, and 25 research labs. Managing a large number of research projects with a myriad of tasks and activities to meet the milestone due dates, subject to limited resources: skilled personnel (scientists, technicians and analysts), lab space and equipment, is not a trivial task. Propose a data-driven approach to help ABC Plant Center manage its research projects. Elaborate the decision variables, objective function(s), constraints and the input data needed in your model.

12.12. Project Management plays an important role in disaster relief and emergency logistics. Local plans and operations must be connected and coordinated with those of a central planner at the regional and/or national levels. Scheduling of all activities in the right order, at the right time, and with the right resources, is very critical. The utmost objective is to mitigate human suffering, through protection of life (i.e., rescue, food and shelter), re-establishing telecommunications, air and sea transport facilities and also maintaining adequate security. Considering that there may be insufficient manpower available to undertake the priority tasks in the shortest possible time, additional manpower from external sources can be utilized to shorten task durations. Propose a data-driven decision-support approach to help the central planner better manage disaster relief operations.

Chapter 13

Traveling Salesman Problem and Its Variants

13.1 Introduction and Overview

Starting from an origin city, a traveling salesman seeks a route to visit a set of cities exactly once and returns to the origin, so that the total travel distance is minimized. This is the well-known Traveling Salesman Problem (TSP), perhaps the most famous combinatorial optimization problem in history. Formally, given a set $N = \{1, 2, \ldots, n\}$ of n nodes, and the distance of c_{ij} between node i and node j for a pair of nodes $(i, j) \in N \times N$, a TSP aims to find a Hamiltonian tour with the minimum distance, i.e., to visit a node exactly once and return to the origin node.

Figure 13.1 illustrates an instance of TSP with five nodes and the distances between all pairs of nodes. Supposing node 1 is the origin, an optimal tour is 1-5-2-3-4-1 with the minimum travel distance of 11, which can be obtained by enumerating a total of 24 possible tours.

In general, the number of possible tours for a TSP with n nodes equals $(n-1)!$, which grows rapidly with n. For $n = 6$, there are a total of $5! = 120$ tours; for $m = 41$, the number of possible tours equals 8.16×10^{47}. Such astronomical number of solutions cannot be enumerated in reasonable time, even by the world's fastest computers. Thus, finding optimal solutions to TSPs calls for optimization modeling and methods.

TSP and its variants have numerous applications in logistics and transportation, e.g., mail/freight delivery, food pickup and delivery,

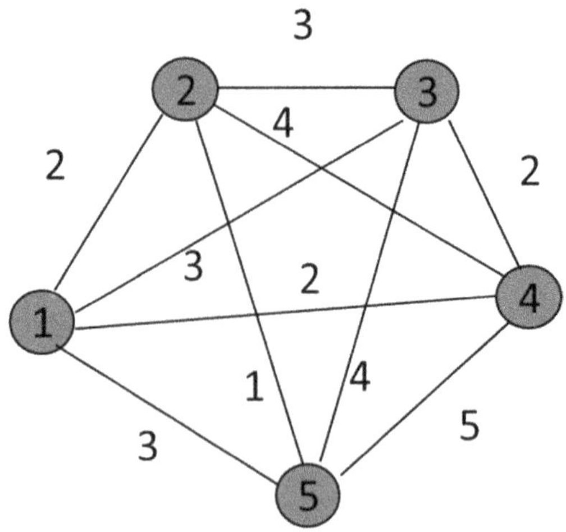

Figure 13.1. An instance of TSP with five nodes.

school bus routing, home care service, technician service, etc. Other notable applications include design of router and switch network in telecommunication, and manufacturing of printed circuit board, etc. The importance of TSP is also due to the fact that it often serves as the foundation and sub-problem for more general and complex routing applications such as the vehicle routing problems to be introduced in Chapter 14.

13.2 Model Formulations of the TSP

We introduce three most prominent formulations for the standard TSP. The first is the subtour elimination formulation due to Dantzig, Fulkerson and Johnson [89], which is the very first mathematical programming formulation proposed for the TSP. It exploits the geometrical configuration of a feasible TSP solution, which prevents the existence of *subtour* in the solution to an assignment sub-problem, a relaxation of the original problem. The idea of *subtour elimination* is the pillar of other formulations for the TSP. The second one is the Miller-Tucker-Zemlin (MTZ) formulation by Miller, Tucker and Zemlin [90]. It employs big-M constraints on top of the formulation of the assignment sub-problem to avoid subtour. The third is the network-flow based formulation, proposed by Gavish and Graves

[91], that prevents subtour by maintaining flow conservation in a Hamiltonian tour.

13.2.1 *Subtour Elimination Formulation*

A *necessary* condition to form a Hamiltonian tour is that: each node in the tour must have a node to traverse *from* and traverse *to*. This entails to the assignment-type constraints, which requires that: (i) every node is assigned with a node to traverse from; and (ii) every node is assigned with a node to traverse to. The assignment sub-problem (ASP) of a TSP can be formulated below. For convenience, we call it ASP-TSP formulation.

Sets and parameters

N: set of nodes to be visited
n: number of nodes in N, and $n = |N|$
c_{ij}: cost of traveling from node i to node j

Decision variables

$x_{ij} = 1$: if the salesman travels from node i to node j, and $i \neq j$; and 0 o.w.

Objective function

$$\text{Minimize} \sum_{i \in N} \sum_{j \in N} c_{ij} x_{ij} \tag{13.1}$$

Constraints

$$\sum_{j \in N: j \neq i} x_{ij} = 1, \quad \forall i \in N \tag{13.2}$$

$$\sum_{i \in N: i \neq j} x_{ij} = 1, \quad \forall j \in N \tag{13.3}$$

$$x_{ij} \in \{0, 1\} \tag{13.4}$$

The objective function (13.1) minimizes the total travel distance. Constraints (13.2) and (13.3) are the assignment constraints. Specifically, Constraint (13.2) assigns exactly one node for every node to traverse *to* (traversing to the same node is not allowed); Constraint (13.3) assigns exactly one node for every node to traverse *from* (traversing from the same node is not allowed).

The ASP-TSP formulation (13.1)–(13.4) models the *necessary* condition for Hamiltonian tour, but not the *sufficient* condition. This means that an optimal solution to (13.1)–(13.4) may not guarantee a Hamiltonian tour. To see this, apply it to the example in Figure 13.1. The initial optimal solution with objective value of 9 is shown in Figure 13.2(a), which is clearly infeasible since it has two subtours: 1-3-4-1 and 2-5. To fix such faulty configuration, we may add a constraint to eliminate the subtour. For instance, to eliminate 1-3-4-1, one may require that no more than two arcs among the node set {1,3,4} be selected. This entails to adding the following *subtour elimination constraint* to the ASP-TSP: $x_{13}+x_{14}+x_{31}+x_{34}+x_{41}+x_{43} \leq 2$. It is important to note that the objective value of 9 is a *lower bound* to the original problem, meaning that the true optimal objective value of the original must be no less than 9. This is because ASP-TSP is a *relaxation* to the original TSP without the restriction needed to eliminate subtours.

Figure 13.2(b) shows an optimal solution with objective value of 10 in the second iteration. Note that the subtour 1-3-4-1 no longer exists, thanks to the subtour elimination constraint added earlier. However, the solution contains two new subtours: 1-2-5-1 and 3-4. Another subtour elimination constraint can be created accordingly and incrementally added to the formulation: $x_{12} + x_{15} + x_{21} + x_{25} + x_{51} + x_{53} \leq 2$. Also note that now the lower bound improves, i.e., increases from 9 to 10.

Solving the ASP-TSP formulation with the two subtour elimination constraints yields a feasible solution in Figure 13.2(c): 1-4-3-5-2-1 with an objective value of 11, which is a better lower bound. Since

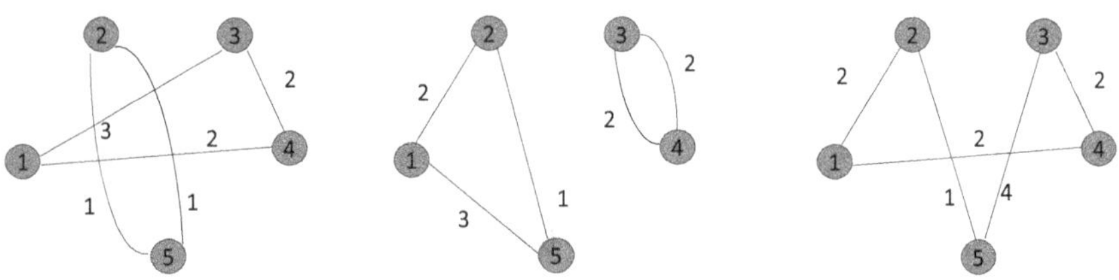

(a) Iteration 1 (b) Iteration 2 (c) Iteration 3

Figure 13.2. Adding subtour elimination constraints to ASP-TSP.

the solution is feasible, it is also an upper bound. Thus, this solution is optimal.

In general, to eliminate a subtour of nodes denoted by the set S, we need: $\sum_{i \in S} \sum_{j \in S: j \neq i} x_{ij} \leq |S| - 1$.

The following constraints satisfy all the subtour elimination constraints for all proper subsets $S \subset N$:

$$\sum_{i \in S} \sum_{j \in S: j \neq i} x_{ij} \leq |S| - 1, \quad \forall S \subset N, \, S \neq \emptyset \tag{13.5}$$

The subtour elimination formulation of TSP includes (13.1)–(13.5), which has $n(n-1)$ binary decision variables, and exponential number of constraints, i.e., $2^n + 2n - 2$ constraints. It is clearly not practical to include all the constraints described by (13.5) *a priori*, but only those violated constraints are needed, which can be added as "cuts" incrementally as demonstrated in Figure 13.2.

13.2.2 *MTZ Formulation*

The MTZ formulation employs a different approach to prevent subtours. In addition to the binary routing decision variables x_{ij}, it defines a continuous decision variable representing the *order of a node to be visited* in the Hamiltonian tour.

Key to Formulation: Subtours are prevented by maintaining a proper order (sequence) of nodes in the route via the big-M type of constraint.

Decision variables

$x_{ij} = 1$: if the salesman travels from node i to node j, and $i \neq j$; and 0 o.w.

$u_i \geq 0$: order of node $i \neq 1$ in the sequence of nodes visited.

Objective function

$$\text{Minimize} \sum_{i \in N} \sum_{j \in N} c_{ij} x_{ij} \tag{13.6}$$

Constraints

Subject to:

$$\sum_{j\in N:j\neq i} x_{ij} = 1, \ \forall i \in N \tag{13.7}$$

$$\sum_{i\in N:i\neq j} x_{ij} = 1, \ \forall j \in N \tag{13.8}$$

$$u_i - u_j + nx_{ij} \leq n-1, \quad \forall (i,j) \in N \times N, i \neq 1, j \neq 1, i \neq j \tag{13.9}$$

$$x_{ij} \in \{0,1\}, \quad u_i \geq 0 \tag{13.10}$$

Constraints (13.7) and (13.8) are the same assignment constraints as in the subtour elimination formulation. Constraint (13.9) is a big-M constraint to enforce the proper order to visit a pair of nodes based on the routing decision variable x_{ij}. To see how it works, consider: (i) when $x_{ij} = 1$, i.e., one travels from node i to node j, (13.9) becomes $u_i + 1 \leq u_j$; and (ii) when $x_{ij} = 0$, $u_i - u_j \leq n-1$, which always holds.

One advantage of the MTZ formulation is that it is polynomial in size: $n(n-1)$ binary decision variables, $n-1$ continuous decision variables, and $n^2 - n + 2$ constraints. However, the big-M type Constraint (13.9) is known to have a loose bound.

13.2.3 *Network Flow Based Formulation*

In the network flow based formulation, subtour is eliminated by maintaining flow conservation through the nodes in the Hamiltonian tour. This approach can be illustrated by Figure 13.3. Send $n-1$ (3) units of flow into the origin node (node 1), and satisfy 1 unit of demand for each of the other nodes. Flow is only allowed through nodes on the Hamiltonian tour.

Key to Formulation: Use the flow conservation constraint to satisfy 1 unit of demand for each node (other than the origin). Then the big-M constraint is needed to ensure that no flow can be sent on an arc that is not in the tour.

Decision variables

$x_{ij} = 1$: if the salesman travels from node i to node j, and $i \neq j$; and 0 o.w.

$y_{ij} \geq 0$: flow on arc $(i,j) : i \neq j$

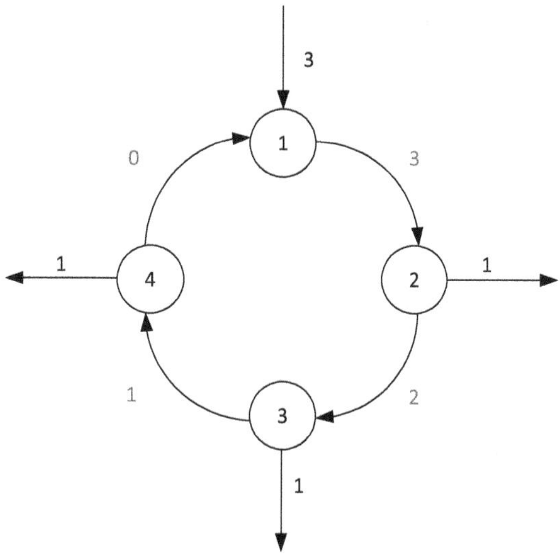

Figure 13.3. Network flow based formulation for TSP.

Objective function

$$\text{Minimize} \sum_{i \in N} \sum_{j \in N} c_{ij} x_{ij} \tag{13.11}$$

Constraints

$$\sum_{j \in N: j \neq i} x_{ij} = 1, \quad \forall i \in N \tag{13.12}$$

$$\sum_{i \in N: i \neq j} x_{ij} = 1, \quad \forall j \in N \tag{13.13}$$

$$\sum_{j \in N: j \neq 1} y_{1j} = n - 1 \tag{13.14}$$

$$\sum_{i \in N: i \neq j} y_{ij} - \sum_{k \in N: k \neq j} y_{jk} = 1, \quad \forall j \in N \backslash \{1\} \tag{13.15}$$

$$y_{ij} \leq (n-1) x_{ij}, \quad \forall (i,j) \in N \times N, i \neq j \tag{13.16}$$

$$x_{ij} \in \{0,1\}, \quad y_{ij} \geq 0 \tag{13.17}$$

Constraints (13.12) and (13.13) are the same assignment constraints as in the previous two formulation. Constraint (13.14) sends

$n - 1$ units of flow into the origin node (node 1). Constraint (13.15) maintains the flow conservation to satisfy the demand at each non-origin node: the total inflow into a node subtracting the total outflow from the node equals 1. Constraint (13.16) is the big-M constraint to ensure that flow only exists on the nodes in the Hamiltonian tour.

This formulation is also polynomial in size with $n(n-1)$ binary decision variables, $n(n-1)$ continuous decision variables, and $n(n+2)$ constraints.

13.3 TSP with Time Windows

While a routing application mostly addresses spatial decision, it often also involves timing requirements to be met, e.g., the earliest or latest time to visit a node. This calls for embedding scheduling components: decision variables, objective function and/or constraints, in a routing optimization model.

An extension of the basic TSP is to consider a time window, i.e., the earliest and latest time, to visit a node, which is known as the TSP with Time Windows (TSPTW). Formally, let $G = (N, A)$ be a directed graph where each node $i \in N$ has a time window $[R_i, D_i]$, where R_i and D_i are the release time (earliest time) and deadline (latest time) to visit node i. Each arc $(i, j) \in A$ has a traveling cost c_{ij} and traveling time θ_{ij}.

Key to Formulation: The TSPTW can be modeled using the MTZ formulation, where the order decision variables u_i can be naturally replaced by scheduling decision variables, representing the time to visit a node.

Sets and parameters

N: set of nodes to be visited
A: set of arcs
n: number of nodes in N, and $n = |N|$
c_{ij}: cost of traveling from node i to node j
θ_{ij}: time of traveling from node i to node j
R_i: release time of node i, i.e., the earliest time to visit node i
D_i: deadline of node i, i.e., the latest time to visit node i
M_{ij}: a large positive number associated with arc $(i, j) \in A$

Decision variables

$x_{ij} = 1$: if the salesman travels from node i to node j, and $i \neq j$; and 0 o.w.

$s_i \geq 0$: time to visit node i

Objective function

$$\text{Minimize} \sum_{i \in N} \sum_{j \in N} c_{ij} x_{ij} \tag{13.18}$$

Constraints

$$\sum_{j \in N: j \neq i} x_{ij} = 1, \quad \forall i \in N \tag{13.19}$$

$$\sum_{i \in N: i \neq j} x_{ij} = 1, \quad \forall j \in N \tag{13.20}$$

$$s_1 = 0, \tag{13.21}$$

$$s_i + \theta_{ij} - (1 - x_{ij}) M_{ij} \leq s_j, \quad \forall (i, j) \in N \times N j \neq 1, i \neq j \tag{13.22}$$

$$R_i \leq s_i \leq D_i, \quad \forall i \in N \tag{13.23}$$

$$x_{ij} \in \{0, 1\}, \quad s_i \geq 0 \tag{13.24}$$

The objective function (13.18) minimizes the total travel cost. Constraints (12.19) and (13.20) are the typical assignment constraints. Constraint (13.21) sets the time to visit the origin node 1 to be zero. Constraint (13.22) is similar to Constraint (13.9) in the MTZ formulation, which ensures proper time to visit a node based on the routing decision variable. Specifically, when $x_{ij} = 1$, i.e., one travels from node i to j, $s_i + \theta_{ij} \leq s_j$ meaning that the time to visit node j can be no less than the time to visit node i plus the travel time θ_{ij} between i and j; when $x_{ij} = 0$, $s_i + \theta_{ij} - M_{ij} \leq s_j$, which always satisfied as long as M_{ij} is large enough. The time window requirements are satisfied by Constraint (13.23), so that the time to visit node i is between its time window of R_i and D_i.

13.4 The Black-and-White TSP

In this section, we introduce a more involving extension of the basic TSP to consider limits and restrictions of the salesman's ability to travel. In short-haul airline operations, an airplane can serve limited number of stops or distance before having maintenance. Design of the Synchronous Optical Network (SONET) in telecommunication requires that the number of hubs and the distance between two consecutive ring offices cannot exceed some upper limit. In food pickup and delivery operations, a vehicle often needs to be replenished after certain number of deliveries and distances traveled. Vaccines such as those for the COVID-19 often require maintaining extremely cold temperature for their storage and transportation, which can be achieved by limiting length of the cold-chain during transit.

The above applications share some common features. First, there are two types of nodes in question: one type is *service* (white) node where service is provided by the salesman or vehicle; the other is *replenishment* (black) node where the salesman or vehicle gets replenished. Second, there is a maximum limit of number of service nodes or travel distance between a pair of replenishment nodes. This problem is called the Black-and-White TSP (BWTSP).

Formally, given a graph $G = (NA)$ where N is a set of nodes consisting of two subsets of black nodes B and white nodes W with $|B| > 2$, and A is a set of arcs. A distance matrix (c_{ij}) is associated with the arc set A. That is, the distance between node i and j, or the length of edge $(i, j) \in A$ is $c_{ij} \geq 0$. The BWTSP aims to find a shortest Hamiltonian tour subject to: (i) *cardinality constraint*: the number of white nodes between any two consecutive black nodes may not exceed a positive value Q; and (ii) *length constraint*: the distance between any two consecutive black nodes may not exceed a positive value L. When $Q = L = \infty$, the BWTSP reduces to the basic TSP.

A small example of BWTSP is shown in Figure 13.4, with a total of six nodes: two black and four white. Specifically, $B = \{1, 4\}$, $W = \{2, 3, 5, 6\}$. Assume $Q = 2$ and $L = 7.5$. The solution in (a) violates the cardinality constraint because there are $3 > Q = 2$ white nodes between the two consecutive black nodes 1 and 4. The solution in (b) violates the length constraint because the travel distance between two consecutive black nodes 1 and 4 is $7.9 > L = 7.5$. The solution in (c) is feasible and optimal, which satisfies both the cardinality constraint and the length constraint.

	1	**2**	**3**	**4**	**5**	**6**
1		2.5	3.1	4.4	1.7	4.5
2	2.5		3.3	2.3	2.6	1.5
3	3.1	3.3		2.1	2.7	1.4
4	4.4	2.3	2.1		5.7	3.4
5	1.7	2.6	2.7	5.7		1.6
6	4.5	1.5	1.4	3.4	1.6	

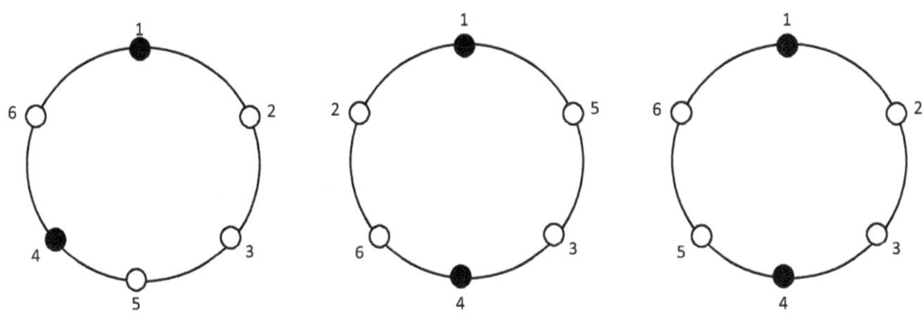

Figure 13.4. A small example of BWTSP.

Key to Formulation: The BWTSP can be modeled using the MTZ modeling approach. The continuous decision variable in the MTZ formulation naturally provides a way to keep track of the cumulative number of white nodes and distance traveled between two consecutive black nodes, which is needed for the cardinality and length constraints.

Sets and parameters

N: set of all nodes, $N = W \cup B$
W: set of white nodes
B: set of black nodes
n: total number of nodes, i.e., $n = |N|$
A: set of arcs
Q: maximum number of consecutive white nodes between two consecutive black nodes allowed
L: maximum distance between two consecutive black nodes allowed

$c_{ij}^* = \min\{c_{i,j} : (i,j) \in A, i \in W, j \in B\}$: minimum distance from any white node to any black node

$c_{ij}^{**} = \min\{c_{ij} : (i,j) \in A, i \in B, j \in W\}$: minimum distance from any black node to any white node

$c_{ij}^{***} = \min\{c_{ij} : (i,j) \in A, i,j \in W\}$: minimum distance between any two white nodes

M: large positive number, i.e., $M = L - c_{ij}^* - c_{ij}^{**} + c_{ij}^{***}$

Decision variables

$x_{ij} = 1$: if one traverses from node i to node j in the tour; and 0 o.w.

$u_i \geq 0$: decision variables used in the MTZ formulation to eliminate sub-tours

$t_i \geq 0$: cumulative number of consecutive white nodes visited after the white node i since the previous black node visited

$l_i \geq 0$: cumulative distance of node i to the previous black node visited

Objective function

$$\text{Minimize} \sum_{(i,j)\in A} c_{ij} x_{ij} \tag{13.25}$$

Constraints

$$\sum_{j\in N:(i,j)\in A} x_{ij} = 1, \quad \forall i \in N \tag{13.26}$$

$$\sum_{i\in N:(i,j)\in A} x_{ij} = 1, \quad \forall j \in N \tag{13.27}$$

$$u_i - u_j + (n-1)\,x_{ij} + (n-3)\,x_{ji} \leq n-2, \quad \forall\,(i,j) \in A, i,j \neq 1 \tag{13.28}$$

$$1 \leq u_i \leq n-1, \quad \forall i \in N, i \neq 1 \tag{13.29}$$

$$t_i - t_j + Qx_{ij} + (Q-2)\,x_{ji} \leq Q-1, \ \forall i,j \in W, (i,j) \in A \tag{13.30}$$

$$1 \leq t_i \leq Q, \quad \forall i \in W \tag{13.31}$$

$$l_i - l_j + Mx_{ij} + (M - c_{ij} - c_{ji})\,x_{ji} \leq M - c_{ij}, \quad \forall i,j \in W, (i,j) \in A \tag{13.32}$$

$$\sum_{j\in B:(j,i)\in A} c_{ij}x_{ji} \le l_i, \quad \forall i \in W \tag{13.33}$$

$$l_i + \sum_{j\in B:(i,j)\in A} c_{ij}x_{ij} \le L, \quad \forall i \in W \tag{13.34}$$

$$x_{ij} \in \{0,1\}, \quad u_i,\, t_i,\, l_i \ge 0 \tag{13.35}$$

The objective function (13.25) minimizes the total travel distance. Constraints (13.26) and (13.27) are the typical assignment constraints for TSP. Constraints (13.28) and (13.29) is an improved version of the subtour elimination constraints in the MTZ formulation. Constraint (13.30) establishes the relationship between t_i and t_j for a pair of white nodes i and j. Specifically, when $x_{ij} = 1$, i.e., node j is traversed after node i, $t_j \ge t_i + 1$; when $x_{ji} = 1$, i.e., node i is traversed after node j, $t_i \le t_j + 1$. Constraint (13.31) limits the number of white nodes visited between two consecutive black nodes is no greater than Q. Constraint (13.32) ensures the proper relationship between l_i and l_j for a pair of white nodes i and j. Specifically, when $x_{ij} = 1$, i.e., node j is traversed after node i, $l_j \ge l_i + c_{ij}$; when $x_{ji} = 1$, i.e., node i is traversed after node j, $l_i \le l_j + c_{ij}$. Constraint (13.33) enforces the lower bound of l_i as the distance from the previous black node visited (if any) to node i. Constraint (13.34) satisfies the length constraint, i.e., the distance between node i and the next black node visited (if any) plus l_i cannot exceed L.

The above formulation for the BWTSP is polynomial in size, with n^2 binary decision variables, $3n$ continuous decision variables, and at most $3n^2 + 6n$ constraints.

13.5 Additional Notes

The TSP is one of the most studied problems in combinatorial optimization. Various MILP formulations for the asymmetric TSP are available in [92]. A technical treatment of the highly successful cutting plane methods for solving TSP is available in [93]. Various MILP formulations for the TSPTW in Section 13.3 and the branch-and-cut algorithms are available in [94]. The MILP formulation of BWTSP in Section 13.4 is based on that of [95], which also provides an efficient tabu search metaheuristic for solving the BWTSP.

Exercises

13.1. Explain the need for the subtour elimination constraint in the TSP and different ways to model it.

13.2. Discuss the connections of TSPTW with a scheduling problem, and show real world examples where it can be applied.

13.3. What could be alternative objective functions and constraints in the standard TSPTW? Show examples for these variants.

13.4. Show and discuss three real world applications for the BWTSP.

13.5. ABC Logistics Inc. is a 3PL service provider who pioneers in using drones for last-mile delivery. While drones are known for its speed, cost effectiveness and low carbon footprint, they are also limited in flying range and payload. Thus, the company employs a combination of truck and drone for last-mile-delivery. A drone is launched from the base station to serve a selected set of customers, which does not exceed its payload and range. The unselected customers are served by trucks or additional drone trips. A customer may specify the preferred time window for delivery. Propose a data-driven decision-support approach to manage ABC Logistics Inc.'s last-mile delivery operations. Elaborate the decision variables, objective function(s), constraints and the input data needed in your approach.

13.6. Coping with the pandemic of an infectious disease often requires efficient and reliable vaccine delivery. A unique and important consideration in vaccine transport is the cold-chain requirement, e.g., extreme low temperature for storage and limited transport distance or time in each trip. In order to serve geographically dispersed locations in a region, a refrigerated vehicle needs to visit certain healthcare facilities to replenish its refrigeration capability as needed. For safety and reliability reasons, a vehicle cannot serve more than five locations, or travel more than 8 hours (without replenishing refrigeration). Propose a data-driven decision-support approach to optimize the vaccine delivery operation. Elaborate the decision variables, objective function(s), constraints, and the input data needed in your approach.

13.7. ABC Foodbank is a non-profit organization who has the mission of coping with food desert and hunger in the region. Its Backpack

School program collaborates with a total of 20 local public schools to provide nutritious foods for the school children with low family income. ABC Foodbank uses one refrigerated truck for its weekly food delivery to these schools. Each school has a preferred delivery time window, and must be served twice a week (on any weekdays). Propose an optimization model to help ABC Foodbank manage its weekly food delivery operations. Elaborate the decision variables, objective function(s), constraints and the input data needed in your approach.

Chapter 14

Vehicle Routing Problem and Its Variants

14.1 Introduction and Overview

Many real life routing applications involve using multiple vehicles to serve customers, which leads to an important extension to the TSP: the Vehicle Routing Problem (VRP). Optimizing multiple routes in a VRP requires an additional dimension of decision to be made, i.e., *assignment* of a node to a vehicle. For instance, a third-party logistics carrier has a fleet of trucks with different size and capacity to dispatch for serving customers in a certain region on a daily basis. Each truck is assigned with a set of customers and the corresponding route. A health organization operates a fleet of unmanned aerial vehicles (UAVs) or drones to deliver vaccines to remote villages on an island. Each drone can serve only a limited number of villages with a maximum range. A foodbank determines the assignment and route for each of its truck fleet to pickup donated foods and deliver to the people in need.

Figure 14.1 illustrates an example of the basic VRP with three vehicles and 17 customers. A feasible solution consists of the assignment of customers to each vehicle and the corresponding route (in different colors).

Due to rich applications of vehicle routing, there are a number of extensions and variants of the basic VRP, which can be classified from different perspectives: types of transportation requests, fleet

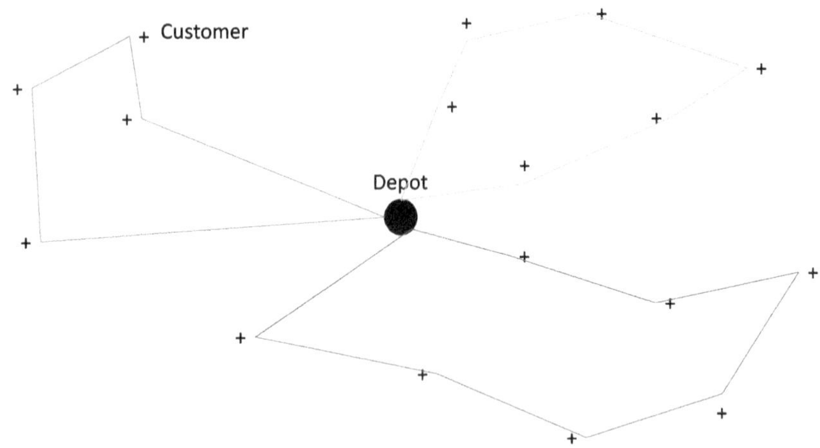

Figure 14.1. An illustration of the basic VRP.

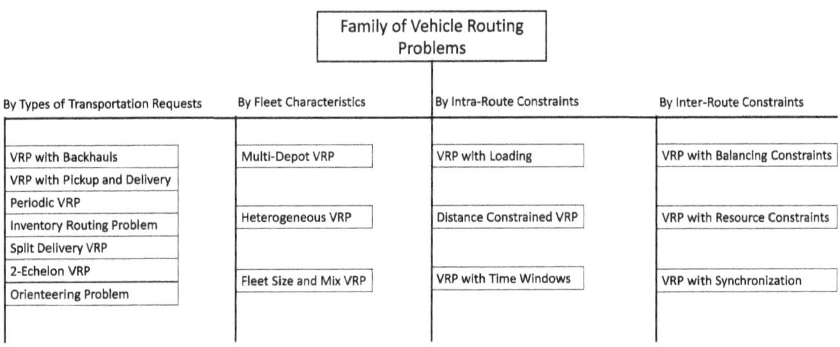

Figure 14.2. Classification of the family of VRPs.

characteristics, intra-route constraints and inter-route constraints. Figure 14.2 shows such a classification scheme.

Certain type of transportation request directly specifies how demands are satisfied thus the configuration of a feasible route. For instance, whether customers are served all at once or over multiple time periods; whether the demand at a customer can be served by multiple vehicles or not. Variants of VRP from this perspective are elaborated below.

VRP with Backhaul (VRPB): A set of customers can be partitioned into two subsets: *linehaul* customers who have certain quantities of products to be delivered, and *backhaul* customers where certain quantities are to be picked up. Backhaul customers can only be served after all linehaul customers are served. A route cannot contain only backhaul customers. The problem is also known as the Linehaul-Backhaul Problem.

VRP with Pickup and Delivery (VRPPD): Each customer request consists of an *origin* location for pickup and a *destination* location for delivery. The origin-destination (OD) pair of a request must be served by the same vehicle, and the origin must precede the destination. The maximum capacity of a vehicle cannot be exceeded.

Periodic VRP (PVRP): A set of customers is to be served by a fleet of vehicles over multiple time periods. Each vehicle can perform at most one trip per day, and its maximum capacity cannot be exceeded. Each customer must be served certain number of times over the planning horizon, often following certain predefined visit patterns, e.g., Monday-Wed-Friday, Tue-Thursday, etc. A solution to the PVRP consists of assignment of a visit pattern to each customer, scheduling of vehicles to employ each day, and their corresponding routes.

Inventory Routing Problem (IRP): A fleet of vehicles repeatedly serve a set of customers over a planning horizon. A customer has some known demand to satisfy, and is able to keep inventory up to a maximum level in every time period. A feasible solution seeks to determine when to serve a customer, how much to deliver to a customer in each service, and which route to use, that minimizes the total travel and inventory carrying cost, while making sure no customer has stock-out in each time period.

Split Delivery VRP (SDVRP): While most VRP applications assume a service is fulfilled by a single vehicle, splitting services is allowed when: (i) demand exceeds the capacity of a single vehicle; and (ii) there is enough cost saving incentive to break a service into smaller pieces to be served by multiple vehicles.

14.2 Formulations of the Capacitated VRP

Formally, a Capacited VRP (CVRP) can be described as follows. A fleet $K = \{1, 2, \ldots, |K|\}$ of homogeneous vehicles deliver goods to meet the demands at a set N of n customers, i.e., $N = \{1, 2, \ldots, n\}$. All the vehicles have the same capacity Q, and must depart from and return to a single depot denoted by 0. The demand at customer $i \in N$ is d_i. The travel cost from customer i to customer j is c_{ij}. The CVRP seeks to find $|K|$ feasible Hamiltonian tours to serve each of the n customers once and only once, such that the total travel cost is minimized.

In parallel with the TSP, three formulations are introduced for the CVRP: the compact formulation, the MTZ formulation, and the flow-based formulation. They serve as recipes for modeling other variants of VRP.

14.2.1 *The Compact Formulation*

The compact formulation for the CVRP directly extends that of the TSP to model multiple routes. Since the vehicles are homogeneous, there is no need to differentiate an individual vehicle in the decision variable. The multi-route configuration can be achieved by enforcing the number of outgoing arcs from the depot to be equal to the number of vehicles.

Key to Formulation: The compact formulation directly extends the subtour elimination formulation of the TSP by maintaining $|K|$ tours. The subtour elimination constraint is needed to prevent subtours.

Sets and parameters

N: set of nodes (customers), with 0 representing the depot
A: set of arcs in the network
K: set of vehicles
q_i: demand at customer i
Q: capacity limit of a vehicle
$\delta^+(S)$: the set of out-arcs out of the set S, i.e., $\delta^+(S) = \{(i, j) \in A : i \in S, j \notin S\}$
$\delta^-(i)$: the set of nodes on the in-arcs into node i, i.e., $\delta^-(i) = \{j : (j, i) \in A\}$
$\delta^+(i)$: the set of nodes on the out-arcs out of node i, i.e., $\delta^+(i) = \{j : (i, j) \in A\}$
c_{ij}: travel cost between node i and node j for $(i, j) \in A$

$r(S)$: the minimum number of vehicle routes needed to serve $S \subseteq N$. In CVRP, $r(S)$ can be computed by solving a bin-packing problem with $|N|$ customers, each of weight q_i, and bins of size Q. One may also use a lower bound instead of $r(S)$, which can be computed by $\lceil q(S)/Q \rceil$, where $q(S)$ is the total demand of the set S of customers, and $\lceil \cdot \rceil$ is the ceiling function.

Decision variables

$x_{ij} = 1$: if a vehicle travels from node i to node j for $(i, j) \in A$; and 0 o.w.

Objective function

$$\text{Minimize} \quad \sum_{(i,j)\in A} c_{ij} x_{ij} \tag{14.1}$$

Constraints

$$\sum_{j\in\delta^+(i)} x_{ij} = 1, \quad \forall i \in N \tag{14.2}$$

$$\sum_{i\in\delta^-(j)} x_{ij} = 1, \quad \forall j \in N \tag{14.3}$$

$$\sum_{j\in\delta^+(0)} x_{0j} = |K|, \quad \forall i \in N \tag{14.4}$$

$$\sum_{(i,j)\in\delta^+(S)} x_{ij} \geq r(S), \quad \forall S \subseteq N, S \neq \emptyset \tag{14.5}$$

$$x_{ij} \in \{0, 1\}, \quad \forall (i, j) \in A \tag{14.6}$$

The objective function (14.1) minimizes the total travel cost. Constraints (14.2) and (14.3) are the assignment constraints to ensure each node has exactly one outgoing node and exactly one incoming node, respectively. Constraint (14.4) guarantees $|K|$ routes are formed. Constraint (14.5) is the subtour elimination constraint to prevent subtours in the solution. Similar to that of the TSP, this formulation is also exponential in size with a large number of subtour elimination constraints. Thus, it is often impractical to include the entire set of constraints (14.5) upfront. They are often generated and included as needed in a dynamic way.

14.2.2 *The MTZ Formulation*

The MTZ formulation of CVRP directly extends that of the TSP.

Key to Formulation: The key is to exploit the capacity constraint. Rather than directly restricting the assigned capacity for each vehicle to be less than or equal to the maximum capacity, we enforce the capacity *incrementally* for each node along the route to serve the role of subtour elimination constraint in the MTZ formulation. Specifically, we define a decision variable to represent the cumulative demand delivered at a node, which replaces the ordering decision variable in the MTZ formulation for the TSP.

Decision variables

$x_{ij} = 1$: if a vehicle travels from node i to node j for $(i,j) \in A$; and 0 o.w.

$u_i \geq 0$: cumulative demand delivered by the vehicle when arriving at customer $i \in N$

Objective function

$$\text{Minimize} \sum_{(i,j)\in A} c_{ij}x_{ij} \tag{14.7}$$

Constraints
Subject to:

$$\sum_{j\in\delta^+(i)} x_{ij} = 1, \quad \forall i \in N \tag{14.8}$$

$$\sum_{i\in\delta^-(j)} x_{ij} = 1, \quad \forall i \in N \tag{14.9}$$

$$\sum_{j\in\delta^+(0)} x_{0j} = |K|, \quad \forall i \in N \tag{14.10}$$

$$u_i - u_j + Qx_{ij} \leq Q - q_j, \quad \forall (i,j) \in A \tag{14.11}$$

$$q_i \leq u_i \leq Q, \quad \forall i \in N \tag{14.12}$$

$$x_{ij} \in \{0,1\}, \quad u_i \geq 0 \tag{14.13}$$

Constraints (14.8)–(14.10) are the same as Constraints (14.2)–(14.4). Constraint (14.11) is a big-M constraint that serves the role of (14.5).

Specifically, it enforces that: (i) if $x_{ij} = 1$, i.e., a vehicle travels from node i to node j, the cumulative demand u_j delivered at node j must be no less than $u_i + q_j$; and (ii) if $x_{ij} = 0$, $u_i - (u_j - q_j) \leq Q$ always holds due to the upper and lower bounds of u_i specified in (14.12). One advantage of the MTZ formulation, compared to the compact formulation, is that it is polynomial in size, which can be implemented in its complete form.

14.2.3 *The Network Flow Based Formulation*

The network flow based formulation for the CVRP directly extends that of the TSP by formulating multiple network flows, each of which is associated with a vehicle.

Key to Formulation: Define a new three-index decision variable, representing the flow along a single vehicle. The three-index decision variable also makes it convenient to consider heterogeneous vehicles with different capacities and operating (travel) costs. Let Q_k denote the maximum capacity of vehicle $k \in K$, and c_{kij} be the travel cost of k from node i to node j.

Sets and parameters

N: set of customers, $N = \{1, 2, \ldots, n\}$
0: the start from the depot
$n + 1$: the return to the depot
V: set of all nodes, i.e., $V = N \cup \{0, n + 1\}$
A: set of arcs in the network
K: set of vehicles
q_i: demand at customer i
Q_k: capacity limit of a vehicle
c_{kij}: travel cost of vehicle k between node i and node j

Decision variables

$x_{kij} = 1$: if vehicle k travels from node i to node j for $k \in K$, $(i, j) \in A$; and 0 o.w.
$u_{ik} \geq 0$: cumulative demand delivered by vehicle $k \in K$ when arriving at customer $i \in N$

Objective function

$$\text{Minimize} \sum_{k \in K} \sum\nolimits_{(i,j) \in A} c_{kij} x_{kij} \tag{14.14}$$

Constraints

$$\sum_{k \in K} \sum_{j \in V : j \neq i} x_{ijk} = 1, \quad \forall i \in N \tag{14.15}$$

$$\sum_{j \in V : j \neq 0, n+1} x_{0jk} = 1, \quad \forall k \in K \tag{14.16}$$

$$\sum_{i \in V : i \neq h} x_{ihk} - \sum_{j \in V : j \neq h} x_{hjk} = 0, \quad \forall k \in K, h \in N \tag{14.17}$$

$$\sum_{i \in V : i \neq n+1} x_{i,n+1,k} = 1, \quad \forall k \in K \tag{14.18}$$

$$u_{ik} - u_{jk} + Q_k x_{kij} \leq Q_k - q_j, \ \forall (i,j) \in V \times V : i \neq j, k \in K \tag{14.19}$$

$$q_i \leq u_{ik} \leq Q_k, \quad \forall i \in N, k \in K \tag{14.20}$$

$$x_{kij} \in \{0,1\}, \quad u_{ik} \geq 0 \tag{14.21}$$

The objective function (14.14) minimizes the total travel cost of all the vehicles. Constraint (14.15) ensures that each customer is served by traversing to another node (possibly the depot) from the customer. Note that traveling from and to the same node is not allowed. Constraint (14.16) guarantees that each vehicle departs from the depot to serve a customer, which constructs $|K|$ tours. Constraint (14.17) is the flow conservation constraint defined for each vehicle and each customer (not including the depot), such that the vehicle traveling *into* a customer must travel *out of* the same customer. Constraint (14.18) states that each vehicle must return to the depot. The big-M constraint is constructed in (14.19) to prevent subtours in each route of a vehicle. It generalizes Constraint (14.11) to incrementally compute the cumulative demand delivered at a node by a heterogeneous vehicle. Constraint (14.20) specifies the upper and lower bounds of u_{ik}.

Compared to the previous formulations for the CVRP, one advantage of the three-index flow-based formulation is that it is able to handle heterogeneous vehicles with different capacities and operating costs. It also offers recipes for building model formulations for more complex variants of VRPs.

14.3 VRP with Time Windows

Considering timing requirements in a VRP is of significant interest in real world applications. As an extension to the TSPTW, the VRP with Time Windows (VRPTW) is introduced in this section to explicitly handle the time window constraint, i.e., the earliest and latest time, to serve a customer.

Formally, consider a fleet $K = \{1, 2, \ldots, |K|\}$ of heterogeneous vehicles to serve a set N of n customers, i.e., $N = \{1, 2, \ldots, n\}$. Each customer $i \in N$ has a demand of d_i, and must be served within the time window $[a_i, b_i]$, where a_i and b_i is the earliest and latest to arrive at customer i, respectively. The maximum capacity of vehicle $k \in K$ is Q_k. The travel cost and time from customer i to customer j via vehicle $k \in K$ is denoted by c_{kij} and τ_{ij}, respectively. The VRPTW seeks to find $|K|$ feasible Hamiltonian tours to serve each of the n customers once and only once within their time windows, such that the total travel cost is minimized.

Example 14.1 (VRPTW). Consider 12 customers to be served by three vehicles. Each customer has a demand of one. Each vehicle has a maximum capacity of 10, and must depart from and return to the same depot. The time windows of customers are provided below.

	1	**2**	**3**	**4**	**5**	**6**	**7**	**8**	**9**	**10**	**11**	**12**
a	7	10	16	10	0	5	0	5	0	10	10	0
b	12	15	18	13	5	10	4	10	3	16	15	5

Assuming the operating costs of all the vehicles are the same, the travel cost matrix is provided below. It is a 14 by 14 matrix, with the first and last row/column representing the depot. For instance, the travel cost from the depot to node 1 is 6; the cost from node 2 to node 1 is 8. Assume the travel time is the same as the travel cost.

```
[
[0, 6, 9, 8, 7, 3, 6, 2, 3, 2, 6, 6, 4, 0],
[6, 0, 8, 3, 2, 6, 8, 4, 8, 8, 13, 7, 5, 6],
[9, 8, 0, 11, 10, 6, 3, 9, 5, 8, 4, 15, 14, 9],
[8, 3, 11, 0, 1, 7, 10, 6, 10, 10, 14, 6, 7, 8],
[7, 2, 10, 1, 0, 6, 9, 4, 8, 9, 13, 4, 6, 7],
[3, 6, 6, 7, 6, 0, 2, 3, 2, 2, 7, 9, 7, 3],
[6, 8, 3, 10, 9, 2, 0, 6, 2, 5, 4, 12, 10, 6],
[2, 4, 9, 6, 4, 3, 6, 0, 4, 4, 8, 5, 4, 2],
[3, 8, 5, 10, 8, 2, 2, 4, 0, 3, 4, 9, 8, 3],
[2, 8, 8, 10, 9, 2, 5, 4, 3, 0, 4, 6, 5, 2],
[6, 13, 4, 14, 13, 7, 4, 8, 4, 4, 0, 10, 9, 6],
[6, 7, 15, 6, 4, 9, 12, 5, 9, 6, 10, 0, 1, 6],
[4, 5, 14, 7, 6, 7, 10, 4, 8, 5, 9, 1, 0, 4],
[0, 6, 9, 8, 7, 3, 6, 2, 3, 2, 6, 6, 4, 0]
];
```

Without the time window constraints, the VRPTW reduces to the CVRP. An optimal solution in this case has the minimum total travel cost of 42, with its configuration shown in Figure 14.3(a). The optimal solution recommends heavily utilizing two vehicles (within their capacity), with one vehicle serving only one customer.

With the time window constraints enforced, an optimal solution to the VRPTW is shown in Figure 14.3(b). The minimum total travel cost increases to 49, with a very different route configuration. To satisfy the earliest and latest service times of customers, the optimal solution has not only shuffled the assignment of customers to vehicles, but also significantly altered the order of customers to visit.

While the graphs in Figures 14.3(a) and 14.3(b) show nicely the spatial characteristics of the routes, they do not reveal any temporal aspect of the routes, which is an essential part of VRPTW. Thus,

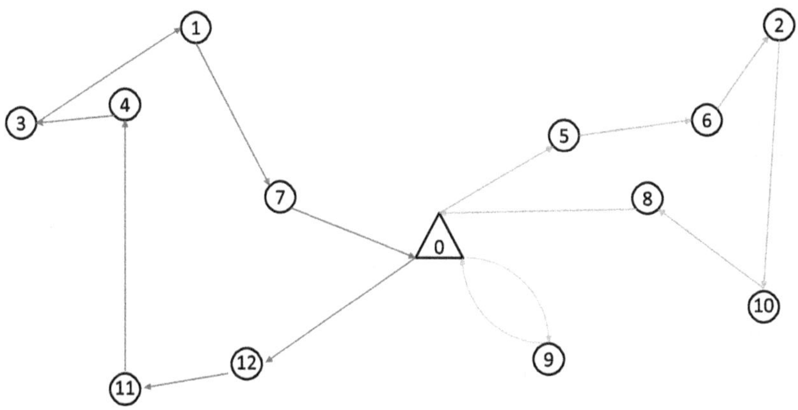

(a) Optimal solution without the time window constraints.

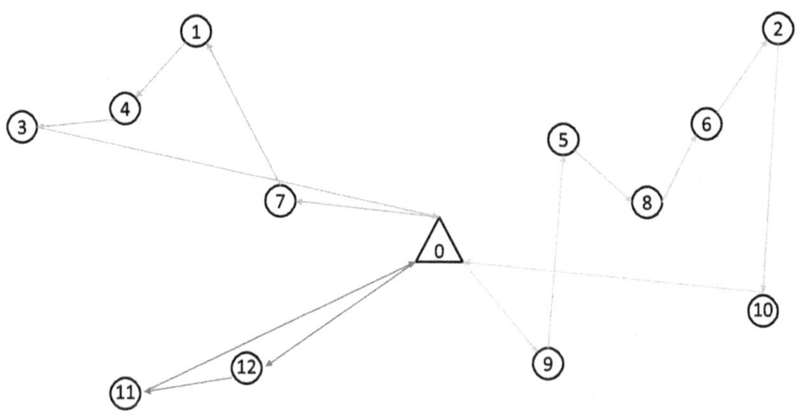

(b) Optimal solution with the time window constraints enforced.

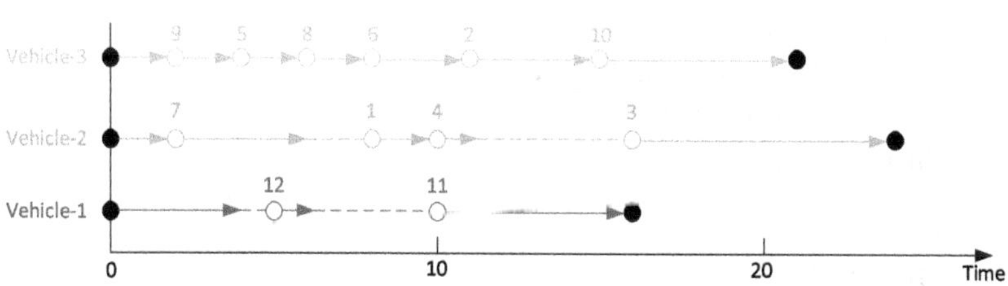

(c) Gantt chart of the optimal solution with time windows.

Figure 14.3. Illustration of optimal solution to Example 14.1.

we may employ the Gantt chart in Figure 14.3(c) to complement the spatial illustration. The solid black circle represents the single depot. Each vehicle and its assigned customers with the corresponding route are identified with a unique color. Each route starts and ends with the same single depot, corresponding with the start and end dummy depot nodes in the formulation. Solid arrows represent the travel of a vehicle, with dashed lines indicating the idle time. The Gantt chart makes it straightforward to examine the scheduling feature of the VRPTW solution and to verify whether the time windows are satisfied.

Key to Formulation: We shall employ the three-index flow-based formulation for the VRPTW. The key is to maintain proper timing of visiting each customer in concert with the order of visits in a route. This can be achieved by using the big-M constraint to ensure that the time to visit a node j must be no less than the time to visit its immediate proceeding node i plus the travel time between i and j. This formulation is a direct extension of the MTZ formulation for the TSPTW presented in Section 13.3 by modeling multiple vehicle routes.

Sets and parameters

N: set of customers, $N = \{1, 2, \ldots, n\}$
0: the start from the depot
$n + 1$: the return to the depot
V: set of all nodes, i.e., $V = N \cup \{0, n + 1\}$
A: set of arcs in the network
K: set of vehicles
q_i: demand at customer i
Q_k: capacity limit of a vehicle
c_{kij}: travel cost of vehicle k between node i and node j
τ_{ij}: travel time from node i to node j
a_i: earliest time to visit customer $i \in N$
b_i: latest time to visit customer $i \in N$
M: large positive number

Decision variables

$x_{ijk} = 1$: if vehicle k travels from node $i \in V$ to node $j \in V$ for $k \in K$, $(i, j) \in A$; and 0 o.w.
$s_{ik} \geq 0$: the time of vehicle $k \in K$ to visit customer $i \in N$

Objective function

$$\text{Minimize} \sum_{k\in K}\sum_{(i,j)\in A} c_{kij}x_{kij} \tag{14.22}$$

Constraints

$$\sum_{k\in K}\sum_{j\in V:j\neq i} x_{ijk} = 1, \quad \forall i \in N \tag{14.23}$$

$$\sum_{j\in V:j\neq 0,n+1} x_{0jk} = 1, \quad \forall k \in K \tag{14.24}$$

$$\sum_{i\in V:i\neq h} x_{ihk} - \sum_{j\in V:j\neq h} x_{hjk} = 0, \quad \forall k \in K, h \in N \tag{14.25}$$

$$\sum_{i\in V:i\neq n+1} x_{i,n+1,k} = 1, \quad \forall k \in K \tag{14.26}$$

$$\sum_{i\in N}\left(q_i \cdot \sum_{j\in V} x_{ijk}\right) \leq Q, \quad \forall k \in K \tag{14.27}$$

$$s_{ik} + \tau_{ij} - M(1 - x_{ijk}) \leq s_{jk}, \quad \forall (i,j) \in V \times V : i \neq j, k \in K \tag{14.28}$$

$$a_i \leq s_{ik} \leq b_i, \quad \forall i \in N, k \in K \tag{14.29}$$

$$s_{0k} = 0, \quad \forall k \in K \tag{14.30}$$

$$x_{ijk} \in \{0,1\}, \quad s_{ik} \geq 0 \tag{14.31}$$

The objective function (14.22) minimizes the total travel cost of all the vehicles. Constraint (14.23) ensures that every customer is served by making sure that the vehicle assigned to a customer travels out of the customer to exactly one node (possibly the depot). Constraint (14.24) guarantees that every vehicle departs from the depot to exactly one node (cannot be the depot), forming $|K|$ routes. Constraint (14.25) is the flow conservation constraint to a vehicle entering *into* a customer (cannot be the depot) must leave *out of* the same customer. Constraint (14.26) requires that all vehicles return to the depot. The vehicle capacity constraint is enforced by Constraint (14.27), where the total assigned load of a vehicle on the left-hand-side cannot exceed the maximum capacity of the vehicle. Constraint (14.28) is the big-M constraint ensuring proper timing of the route based on the binary sequencing decision variables. Specifically, when $x_{ijk} = 1$, i.e., vehicle k travels from node i to node j, the time to visit j must be no less than the time to visit i plus the travel time from i to j; when $x_{ijk} = 0$, (14.28) is always satisfied due to subtracting a large positive number on the left-hand-side. The time window of a customer is satisfied in Constraint (14.29). Constraint (14.30) states that each vehicle departs from the depot at time zero.

It is important to note that the big-M constraint (14.28) serves two roles: (i) maintaining proper timing of the route; and (ii) eliminating subtours as (14.11) in the MTZ formulation. In this way, there is no need to express the capacity constraint incrementally for each node in a route as in (14.19), although it is viable to do so.

14.4 VRP with Pickup-Delivery and Time Windows

In logistics and transportation, a customer request is often associated with an OD pair, requiring picking up goods at an origin *before* delivering at a destination. Both pickup and delivery of a customer must be performed by the same vehicle. Modeling such pickup-delivery operation in the context of VRPTW calls for the VRP with Pickup-Delivery and Time Windows (VRPPDTW).

Formally, there are n customer requests to satisfy. Let $G = (N, A)$ be a directed graph with a node set $N = \{0, 1, \dots, 2n + 1\}$ and an arc set A. Nodes and $2n + 1$ represent the start from and return to the depot, respectively. N can be partitioned to two subsets of pickup nodes $P = \{1, 2, \dots, n\}$ and delivery nodes $D = \{n + 1, n + 2, \dots, 2n\}$. Each request $i = 1, 2, \dots, n$ needs to pickup a load of $q_i > 0$ at node $i \in P$ *before* delivering the load at node $i + n \in D$ with $q_{i+n} = -q_i$ by the same vehicle. Each node $i \in P \cup D$ has a service duration time d_i and a time window $[a_i, b_i]$ to be met, where a_i and b_i are the earliest and latest time to start the service at node i. A fleet of heterogeneous vehicles K are available, which must depart from and return to the depot. Each vehicle $k \in K$ has a capacity Q_i. Let c_{kij} and τ_{kij} represent the travel cost and time of vehicle k from node i to node j. The VRPPDTW seeks to find a feasible route and schedule that minimizes the total travel cost.

Example 14.2 (VRPPDTW). Consider six customer requests in 12 locations. Their loads, service times and time windows are provided below.

	1	2	3	4	5	6	7	8	9	10	11	12
q	2	2	2	2	2	2	−2	−2	−2	−2	−2	−2
d	1	1	1	1	1	1	1	1	1	1	1	1
a	7	0	6	10	0	5	12	6	17	24	10	16
b	20	20	20	20	20	20	20	20	25	30	20	25

There are three homogeneous vehicles available. All the vehicles have the same capacity of 10. The travel cost matrix between all pairs of nodes (including the depot) is below. Assuming the travel cost equals the travel time.

$$
\begin{array}{l}
[\\
[0,6,9,8,7,3,6,2,3,2,6,6,4,0],\\
[6,0,8,3,2,6,8,4,8,8,13,7,5,6],\\
[9,8,0,11,10,6,3,9,5,8,4,15,14,9],\\
[8,3,11,0,1,7,10,6,10,10,14,6,7,8],\\
[7,2,10,1,0,6,9,4,8,9,13,4,6,7],\\
[3,6,6,7,6,0,2,3,2,2,7,9,7,3],\\
[6,8,3,10,9,2,0,6,2,5,4,12,10,6],\\
[2,4,9,6,4,3,6,0,4,4,8,5,4,2],\\
[3,8,5,10,8,2,2,4,0,3,4,9,8,3],\\
[2,8,8,10,9,2,5,4,3,0,4,6,5,2],\\
[6,13,4,14,13,7,4,8,4,4,0,10,9,6],\\
[6,7,15,6,4,9,12,5,9,6,10,0,1,6],\\
[4,5,14,7,6,7,10,4,8,5,9,1,0,4],\\
[0,6,9,8,7,3,6,2,3,2,6,6,4,0]\\
];
\end{array}
$$

Without the time window constraint, an optimal solution has the minimum total travel cost of 68, with its configuration shown in Figure 14.4(a). A dashed arrow shows the OD pair of a customer request, and a solid arrow shows an arc in the route. The optimal solution recommends heavily utilizing one vehicle for meeting

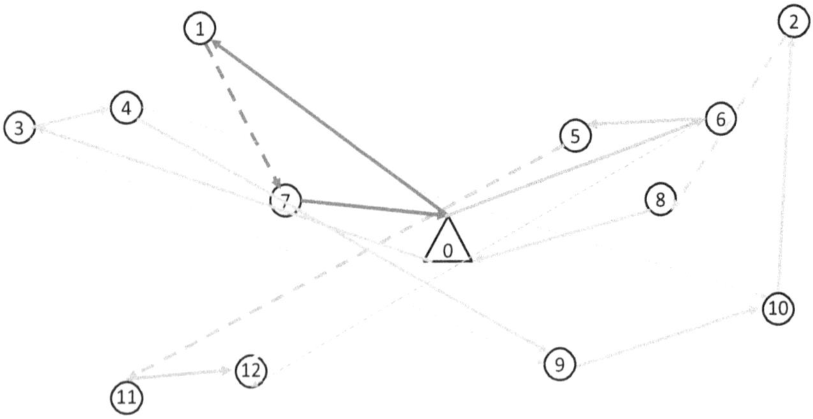

(a) Optimal solution without the time window constraints.

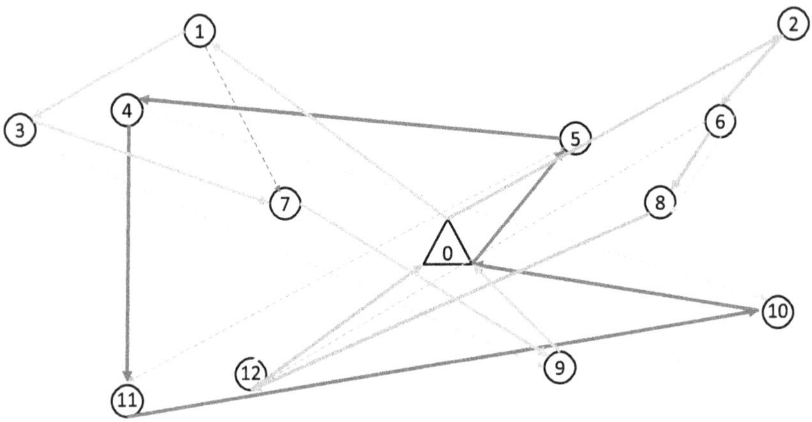

(b) Optimal solution with the time window constraints enforced.

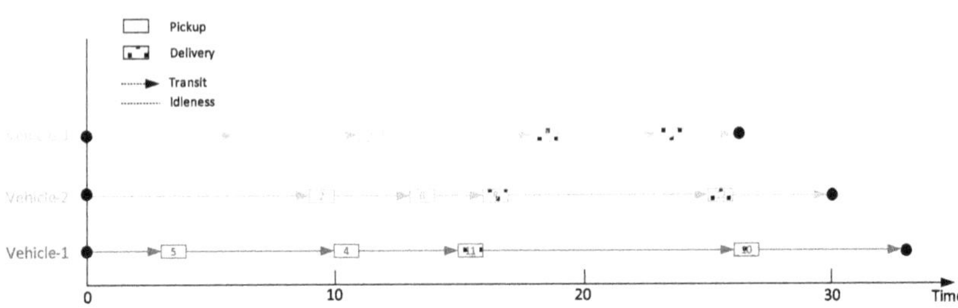

(c) Gantt chart of the optimal solution with time windows.

Figure 14.4. Illustration of optimal solution to Example 14.2.

three customer requests: 2-8, 3-9, 4-10, via the route $0 \to 3 \to 4 \to 9 \to 10 \to 2 \to 8 \to 13$ with alternating pickup and delivery nodes sequenced in the best way, while pickup always occurs before delivery for each request. One least utilized vehicle serves only one request: 1-7, and the other one serves two requests: 5-11, 6-12.

With the time window constraints enforced, an optimal solution to the VRPPDTW is shown in Figure 14.4(b). The minimum total travel cost increases to 79, with a very different route configuration. Vehicle utilization becomes more balanced with each serving two customer requests. One observes some unconventional configuration in the optimal route, e.g., $0 \to 5 \to 4 \to 11 \to 10 \to 13$, due to the need for satisfying the time window constraints.

The Gantt chart for the optimal solution with time windows is shown in Figure 14.4(c). Complementary to the spatial illustration, it provides a nice visualization for the temporal characteristics of the route solution. Here, the service operation at each node is represented by a horizontal bar (instead of a dot as in Example 14.1) to show the duration of service. Note that there is an interval of idleness (with duration of one time unit) for Vehicle-1. This is because the earliest time to serve node 1 is 7, which is longer than the travel time of 6 from the depot to node 1. Such idleness is often needed in the solution of VRPPDTW in order to satisfy the arbitrary time windows specified by customers.

Key to Formulation: It extends the formulation for the VRPTW by adding new constraints to ensure that: (i) the pickup and delivery of a customer request must be performed by the same vehicle; and (ii) pickup must occur before delivery for the same customer request. The flow-based formulation provides a convenient platform to model: (i) Specifically, one may enforce a flow conservation constraint for each vehicle, such that the total outflow from the pickup node of a request must equal the total outflow from the delivery node of the same request. To achieve (ii), one may require that the service at the delivery node of a request can only start after the pickup of the same request is finished. A three-index flow based formulation for the VRPPDTW can be written as below.

Sets and parameters

n: number of requests
N: set of all nodes, $N = \{0, 1, 2, \ldots, 2n + 1\}$

A: set of arcs
P: set of pickup nodes, $P = \{1, 2, \ldots, n\}$
D: set of delivery nodes, $D = \{n+1, n+2, \ldots, 2n\}$
K: set of vehicles
q_i: load of request $i \in P \cup D$, $q_i > 0$ for $i \in P$ and $q_i = -q_{i+n}$
d_i: duration of service for node $i \in N$
a_i: earliest time to start service at node $i \in P \cup D$
b_i: latest time to start service at node $i \in P \cup D$
c_{kij}: travel cost of vehicle k between node i and node j
τ_{kij}: travel time of vehicle k from node i to node j
Q: capacity of a vehicle
M: a large positive number

Decision variables

$x_{ijk} = 1$: if vehicle $k \in K$ travels from node $i \in N$ to node $j \in N$; and 0 o.w.
$s_{ik} \geq 0$: time for vehicle $k \in K$ to visit node $i \in N$
$Q_{ik} \geq 0$: cumulative load of vehicle $k \in K$ at node $i \in N$

Objective function

$$\text{Minimize} \sum_{k \in K} \sum_{(i,j) \in A} c_{kij} x_{kij} \tag{14.32}$$

Constraints

$$\sum_{k \in K} \sum_{j \in N: j \neq i} x_{ijk} = 1, \quad \forall i \in P \tag{14.33}$$

$$\sum_{j \in N: j \neq i} x_{ijk} - \sum_{j \in N: j \neq n+i} x_{n+i,jk} = 0, \quad \forall i \in P, k \in K \tag{14.34}$$

$$\sum_{j \in N: j \neq 0} x_{0jk} = 1, \quad \forall k \in K \tag{14.35}$$

$$\sum_{j \in N: j \neq i} x_{jik} - \sum_{j \in N: j \neq i} x_{ijk} = 0, \quad \forall k \in K, i \in P \cup D \tag{14.36}$$

$$\sum_{i \in N: i \neq 2n+1} x_{i,2n+1,k} = 1, \quad \forall k \in K \tag{14.37}$$

$$s_{ik} + \tau_{ij} + d_i - M(1 - x_{ijk}) \le s_{jk}, \quad \forall i \in N,\, j \in N,\, k \in K \tag{14.38}$$

$$Q_{ik} + q_j - M(1 - x_{ijk}) \le Q_{jk}, \quad \forall i \in N,\, j \in N,\, k \in K \tag{14.39}$$

$$s_{ik} + d_i + \tau_{i,i+n} \le s_{i+n,k}, \quad \forall i \in P,\, k \in K \tag{14.40}$$

$$a_i \le s_{ik} \le b_i, \quad \forall i \in N,\, k \in K \tag{14.41}$$

$$s_{0k} = 0, \quad \forall k \in K \tag{14.42}$$

$$\max\{0,\, q_i\} \le Q_{ik} \le \min\{Q,\, Q + q_i\}, \quad \forall i \in N,\, k \in K \tag{14.43}$$

$$x_{ijk} \in \{0,\, 1\}, \quad s_{ik},\, Q_{ik} \ge 0 \tag{14.44}$$

The objective function (14.32) minimizes the total travel cost. Constraint (14.33) ensures that each pickup node is served by assigning exactly one outgoing node for the pickup node. Note that (14.33) is not defined for a delivery node. Service to a delivery node is guaranteed by Constraint (14.34), which states that the same vehicle must serve both the pickup and delivery of a request. Specifically, for each vehicle, the total outflow of a pickup node i must equal the total outflow of its corresponding delivery node $i + n$. Constraint (14.35) requires that each vehicle must depart from the depot. Constraint (14.36) is the flow conservation constraint, where for each non-depot node the total outflow must equal the total inflow of the node. Constraint (14.37) requires that each vehicle must return to the depot. The proper timing to serve each node based on the sequence of nodes in the route is satisfied by the big-M constraint (14.38). Specifically, when $x_{ijk} = 1$, i.e., vehicle k travels from node i to node j, the time s_{jk} to serve j must be no less than the completion time of service at node i ($s_{ik} + d_i$) plus the travel time τ_{ij} between i and j; when $x_{ijk} = 0$, (14.38) is always satisfied due to subtracting a big M on the left-hand-side. Constraint (14.39) is the big-M constraint to express the vehicle capacity in an incrementally way similar to Constraint (14.19) in the formulation for the CVRP. Constraint (14.40) satisfies the precedence relationship between the pickup and delivery of the same request: the time to deliver at node $i + n$ must be no less than the completion of pickup at node i plus the travel time from i to j. The time window of each node is met by Constraint (14.41). Constraint (14.42) starts each vehicle from the depot at time zero. Constraint (14.43) specifies the lower and upper bounds of the cumulative loads of a vehicle at each customer.

14.5 Periodic VRP

Many applications in transportation require services to be performed recurrently during multiple time periods. For instance, waste collection vehicles visit locations in a certain region on weekdays, such that each location is served a certain number of times during a week. Homecare workers are scheduled to visit their patients at different locations certain times of a week, following some visit-pattern based on the healthcare needs and patients' preferences. In the food and beverage industry, food products are delivered to grocery stores, restaurants and food shops on certain days of a week to replenish their inventory. Repair and maintenance services in the utility and telecommunication industries often require supply of products, equipment and parts to be delivered to operating centers/sites at certain frequencies. These call for a rich and versatile variant of VRP known as the Periodic VRP (PVRP).

Figure 14.5 shows a schematic illustration of the PVRP with three customers, one depot and two days in the planning horizon. Suppose Customer 1 must be served twice, and Customers 2 and 3 only need to be served once. A solution consists of routes planned for both days, e.g., Day 1: $0 \rightarrow 1 \rightarrow 2$, and Day 2: $0 \rightarrow 1 \rightarrow 3$.

A Periodic VRP with Time Windows (PVRPTW) can be formally described as follows. A set $N = \{1, 2, \ldots, n\}$ of customers need to be served by a set K of heterogeneous vehicles over planning horizon of $1, 2, \ldots, T$ periods. Let node 0 and $n + 1$ denote the departure from and return to a single depot, respectively, and $V = \{0, 1, \ldots, n + 1\}$ be the set of all the nodes. A customer $i \in N$ must be served a

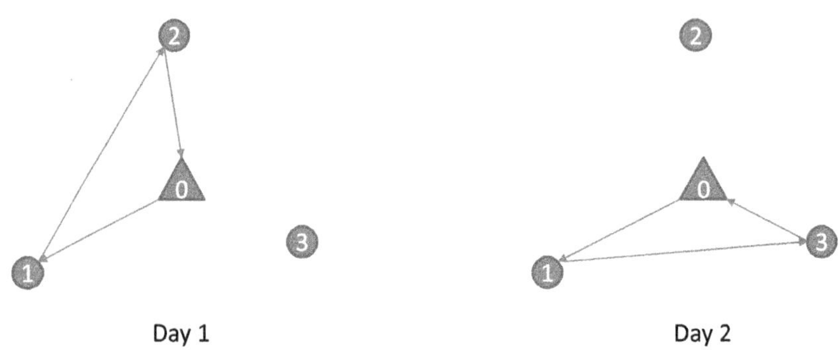

Figure 14.5. A schematic illustration of the PVRP.

minimum of θ_i times during the planning horizon on certain days according one visit-pattern in the list of available patterns denoted by R. A visit-pattern $r \in R$ can be described by a_{rt}, such that $a_{rt} = 1$ means that time period $t \in T$ is covered by pattern $r \in R$, and $a_{rt} = 0$ otherwise. Service at customer $i \in N$ demands a load of q_i, takes a duration of s_i and must satisfy a time window $[e_i, l_i]$ where e_i and l_i are the earliest and latest time to start the service at i, respectively. A vehicle $k \in K$ has a maximum capacity of Q_k and a maximum duration D_k of operation per trip. The travel cost and time of vehicle $k \in K$ from node i to node j are denoted by c_{kij} and τ_{kij}, respectively. The PVRPTW seeks to find a feasible schedule of routes for multiple time periods that minimizes the total travel cost.

There are clearly two layers of decisions in the PVRPTW. The first is the set-covering decision to select a visit pattern for each customer, satisfying the minimum number of visits required. Then given the selected visit patterns of all the customers, thus a fixed set of customers in each time period, a VRPTW is solved, which has both the assignment and scheduling types of decision itself. A full-fledged example of PVRPTW is provided below.

Example 14.3 (PVRPTW). Consider six customers to be served by three vehicles in a three-day horizon. The table below provides information of the customers including minimum number of visits per week θ, load per service q, duration of service time s, earliest service time e and latest service time l.

	1	**2**	**3**	**4**	**5**	**6**
θ	1	2	3	1	3	1
q	2	2	2	2	2	2
s	1	1	1	1	1	1
a	7	10	16	10	0	5
b	12	15	18	13	5	10

Service to a customer can only be performed in certain visit patterns, e.g., Day 1 only, Day 1-Day 2-Day 3, etc. The table below shows a list of all the available visit patterns and which days they cover. For example, pattern 2 covers only Day 2, pattern 5 covers Day 1 and Day 3, etc.

	Day 1	**Day 2**	**Day 3**
1	X		
2		X	
3			X
4	X	X	
5	X		X
6		X	X
7	X	X	X

All the vehicles are homogenous with a maximum capacity of 10, maximum duration of 30 per trip, and matrix of travel cost below.

$$
\begin{aligned}
&[\\
&[0,6,9,8,7,3,6,0],\\
&[6,0,8,3,2,6,8,6],\\
&[9,8,0,11,10,6,3,9],\\
&[8,3,11,0,1,7,10,8],\\
&[7,2,10,1,0,6,9,7],\\
&[3,6,6,7,6,0,2,3],\\
&[6,8,3,10,9,2,0,6],\\
&[0,6,9,8,7,3,6,0]\\
&];
\end{aligned}
$$

An optimal solution with minimum total travel cost of 85 is shown in Figure 14.6(a). The optimal choice of visit pattern for each customer is in the table at the upper-left corner. For instance, pattern 6 is selected for customer 2 to be visited on Day 2 and Day 3, i.e., twice as required; pattern 7 is needed for both customers 3 and 5 to be visited on all 3 days, i.e., three times as required. The visit-pattern solution determines the set of customers on each day. For example, customers 3, 4 and 5 are visited on Day 1 by one vehicle via the route: $0 \to 5 \to 4 \to 3 \to 0$; customers 1, 2, 3, 5 and 6 are visited on Day 3 by two vehicles via two routes: $0 \to 1 \to 3 \to 0$ and $0 \to 5 \to 6 \to 2 \to 0$.

Suppose the maximum vehicle capacity reduces by half to 5. Apparently, no route may serve more than two customers due to

	Day 1	Day 2	Day 3	Pattern
Customer 1			X	3
Customer 2		X	X	6
Customer 3	X	X	X	7
Customer 4	X			1
Customer 5	X	X	X	7
Customer 6		X	X	6

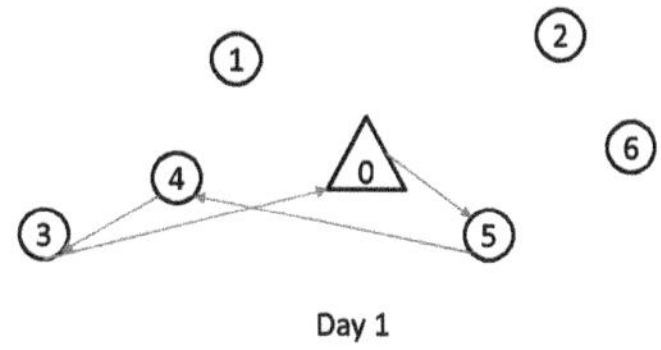

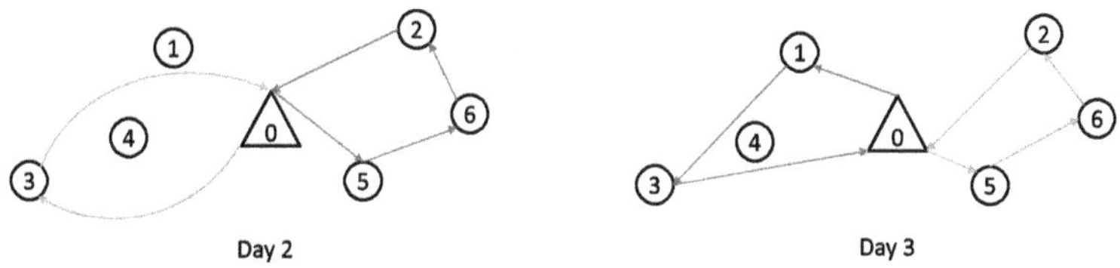

(a) Optimal solution with maximum vehicle capacity of 10.

	Day 1	Day 2	Day 3	Pattern
Customer 1	X			1
Customer 2	X	X		4
Customer 3	X	X	X	7
Customer 4			X	3
Customer 5	X	X	X	7
Customer 6		X		2

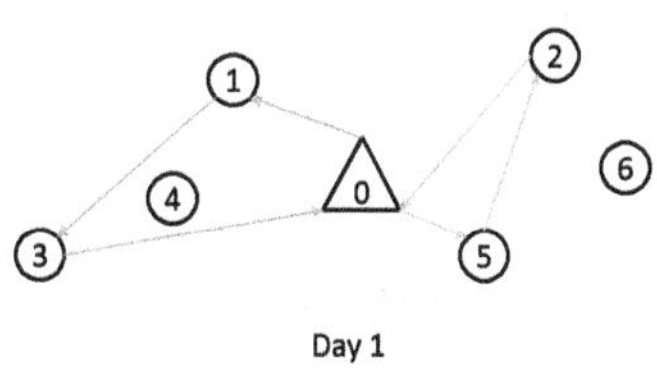

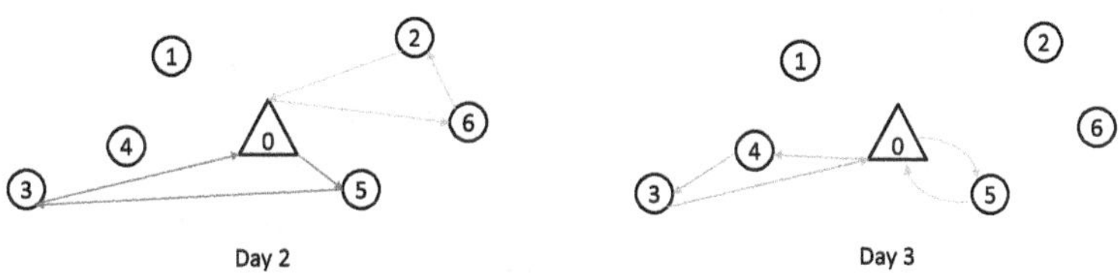

(b) Optimal solution with maximum vehicle capacity of 5.

Figure 14.6. Illustration of optimal solution to Example 14.3.

the reduced vehicle capacity. The new optimal solution is shown in Figure 14.6(b), with the minimum total travel cost increased to 93. The optimal visit patterns for customers change significantly, and so are the route configuration for each day.

Key to Formulation: Following the two-layer decision structure of the PVRP, we first define a two-index binary decision variable to select one visit-pattern for each customer. Using the visit-pattern, the problem is reduced to multiple VRPs, each for one time periods. Thus, the key is to extend the typical binary sequencing decision variable and the continuous starting time decision variable to include another time-dimension for each time period. A new binary decision variable is needed to track whether a vehicle is utilized in a time period. It can then be used to ensure the correct route configurations. Specifically, if a vehicle is utilized in a time period, it must depart from and return to the depot; otherwise, an unutilized vehicle cannot depart from or return to the depot.

Sets and parameters

V: set of all nodes, $V = \{0, 1, 2 \ldots, n, n+1\}$
0: start from the depot, and $n+1$: return to the depot
N: set of customers, i.e., $N = V \backslash \{0, n+1\}$
E: set of edges
K: set of vehicles
T: number of time periods in the planning horizon
c_{kij}: travel cost of vehicle $k \in K$ from node $i \in V$ to node $j \in V$ for $i \neq j$
τ_{kij}: travel time of vehicle $k \in K$ from node $i \in V$ to node $j \in V$ for $i \neq j$
q_i: amount of demand of customer $i \in N$ on each day of the planning horizon
θ_i: minimum number of times to serve customer $i \in N$
s_i: service (processing) time at customer $i \in N$
e_i: earliest time service may start at customer $i \in N$ in a day
l_i: latest time service may start at customer $i \in N$ in a day
Q_k: available capacity of vehicle $k \in K$
D_k: maximum duration allowed for the route of vehicle $k \in K$
R: a list of visit-period patterns
a_{rt}: equals 1 if period $t \in T$ is covered by pattern $r \in R$
M: a large positive number

Decision variables

$x^t_{ijk} = 1$: if vehicle $k \in K$ travels from node $i \in V$ to node $j \in V$ in time period $t \in T$; and 0 o.w.
$y_{ir} = 1$: if pattern $r \in R_i$ is assigned to customer $i \in N$

$z_{kt} = 1$: if vehicle $k \in K$ is employed in time period $t \in T$; and 0 o.w.

$w^t_{ik} \geq 0$: service start time of vehicle $k \in K$ at customer $i \in V$ in time period $t \in T$

Objective function

$$\text{Minimize} \quad \sum_{t\in T} \sum_{(i,j)\in E} \sum_{k\in K} c_{kij} x^t_{ijk} \tag{14.45}$$

Constraints

Subject to:

$$\sum_{r\in R} y_{ir} = 1, \quad \forall i \in N \tag{14.46}$$

$$\sum_{r\in R} \sum_{t\in T} y_{ir} a_{rt} \geq \theta_i, \quad \forall i \in N \tag{14.47}$$

$$x^t_{ijk} \leq z_{kt}, \quad \forall (i,j) \in E,\ k \in K,\ t \in T \tag{14.48}$$

$$\sum_{k\in K} z_{kt} \leq |K|, \quad \forall t \in T \tag{14.49}$$

$$\sum_{j\in N} x^t_{0jk} = z_{kt}, \quad \forall k \in K,\ t \in T \tag{14.50}$$

$$\sum_{i\in N} x^t_{i,n+1,k} = z_{kt}, \quad \forall k \in K,\ t \in T \tag{14.51}$$

$$\sum_{k\in K} \sum_{j\in V:j\neq i} x^t_{ijk} = \sum_{r\in R} y_{ir} a_{rt}, \quad \forall i \in N, t \in T \tag{14.52}$$

$$\sum_{j\in V:j\neq i} x^t_{ijk} = \sum_{j\in V:j\neq i} x^t_{jik}, \quad \forall i \in N, k \in K, t \in T \tag{14.53}$$

$$\sum_{i\in N} q_i \sum_{j\in V} x^t_{ijk} \leq Q_k, \quad \forall k \in K, t \in T \tag{14.54}$$

$$w^t_{ik} + s_i + \tau_{kij} - M(1 - x^t_{ijk}) \leq w^t_{jk}, \quad \forall (i,j) \in E, k \in K, t \in T \tag{14.55}$$

$$e_i \sum_{j\in V:j\neq i} x^t_{ijk} \leq w^t_{ik} \leq l_i \sum_{j\in V:j\neq i} x^t_{ijk}, \quad \forall i \in N, k \in K, t \in T \tag{14.56}$$

$$w^t_{n+1,k} \leq D_k z_{kt}, \quad \forall k \in K,\, t \in T \tag{14.57}$$

$$w^t_{0k} = 0, \quad \forall k \in K,\, t \in T \tag{14.58}$$

$$x^t_{ijk}, y_{ir}, z_{kt}, w^t_{ik} \geq 0 \tag{14.59}$$

The objective function (14.45) minimizes the total travel cost. Constraint (14.46) assigns exactly one visit pattern for each customer. Constraint (14.47) ensures that each customer is visited for a minimum number of times. Note that Constraints (14.46) and (14.47) model the "set-covering" sub-problem of the PVRPTW.

Constraint (14.48) ensures that no customer can be visited by a vehicle in a time period, if the vehicle is not utilized in the time period. Constraint (14.49) limits the number of vehicles utilized in a day to be no more than the total number of available vehicles.

Constraints (14.50) and (14.51) require that a utilized vehicle must depart from and return to the depot, respectively. Note the use of the binary decision variable z_{kt} on the right-hand-side of the two constraints, which effectively forbids an unutilized vehicle to depart from (or return to) the depot.

Constraint (14.52) guarantees that each customer "covered" in a time period (according to the visit-pattern selection decision) must be served by exactly one vehicle. Note the use of the visit-pattern selection decision variable y_{ir} on the right-hand-side of the constraint to identify whether a customer is served in a time period.

Constraint (14.53) is the flow conservation constraint to guarantee that a vehicle entering into a customer must leave the customer and travel to the next node (possibly the depot).

Constraint (14.54) limits the total assigned load of a vehicle not to exceed the maximum vehicle capacity.

Constraint (14.55) maintains the proper relationship between the route sequencing binary decision variable and the timing decision variable to visit each node. Specifically, when $x^t_{ijk} = 1$, i.e., vehicle k travels from node i to node j in day t, the time to visit j, w^t_{jk}, must be no less than $w^t_{ik} + s_i + \tau_{kij}$, i.e., the completion time of service at customer i plus the travel time from i to j; when $x^t_{ijk} = 0$, the constraint is always satisfied due to subtracting a big M on the left-hand-side.

Constraint (14.56) ensures that the time window constraint of a customer in a time period is satisfied by the vehicle that serves the customer.

Constraint (14.57) limits the duration of operation of a vehicle (if utilized) in a day, i.e., the timing for the vehicle to return to the depot, does not exceed its maximum allowed duration. Constraint (14.58) states that each vehicle departs from the depot at time zero.

14.6 Technician Routing and Scheduling

Many applications involve utilizing skilled technicians to serve the right customers at the right location and the right time. This motivates the study of Technician Routing and Scheduling Problem (TRSP). For instance, a telecommunication firm serves customers at different locations in a region, and dispatches technicians with proper skills to serve the customers in certain order on time. A property management company employs a team of skilled workers for maintenance and repairing jobs at houses, buildings and properties located in different places. A common and distinctive feature of these applications is the need for considering the skills of personnel or crew to complete the jobs, which is usually not present in routing vehicles. In addition, these applications often emphasize service level and customer satisfaction, which calls for alternative metrics for the objective function other than the operating cost.

A typical TRSP can be formally described as follows. A set of K of technicians serve a set J of customers in different locations. The technicians are housed at a set D of service centers (depots), and each must depart from and return to the depot he/she belongs to. Let L denote the set of locations of all the customers and depots, i.e., $L = J \cup D$. The travel time from location $i \in L$ to location $j \in L$ is τ_{ij}. The processing time of the job at customer $j \in J$ is p_j, which requires skill $s \in S$ to complete, where S is the set of all the skills. Technicians' skill mix can be described by a binary parameter q_{ks}, such that $q_{ks} = 1$ means technician k possesses skill s, and $q_{ks} = 0$ otherwise. Technician $k \in K$ has a maximum workload capacity W_k of service and travel time during the planning horizon. Depending on the nature of a job (routine maintenance or emergency), and status of the corresponding customer (existing or new), importance of job $j \in J$ can be assessed with a priority score π_j. A job $j \in J$ is assigned to at most one technician who possesses the required skill, starts the service within the pre-specified time window $[a_j, b_j]$, and completes the job before a due date of d_j.

Since the amount of business can exceed the capacities of the available technicians, some jobs may not be fulfilled, and one can be selective in choosing the right jobs to perform, based on their importance (priority score). Suppose not being able to fulfill a job incurs a significant loss due to customer un-satisfaction or potential loss of customer. Another consideration in real world practice is that the arbitrary time windows specified by customers can be too tight to satisfy, and there is often room to negotiate the timing of service. Thus, we assume that the time window can be violated with some loss (penalty), which is less than the loss (penalty) of an unfulfilled job. The TRSP seeks to find a feasible technician-job assignment, route and schedule that minimizes the total loss, i.e., maximizes customer satisfaction.

Example 14.4 (TRSP). A telecommunication company manages seven technicians in two depots: A and B, to serve customers in different locations on a daily basis. The technicians' maximum service capacity, the depots they are housed in, and their skill mix are provided in the following table. For instance, Gina at Depot A is the most versatile technician who is qualified for six out of the seven job types and has a maximum workload capacity of 360 minutes (for service and travel) per day.

Priorities and average durations of all job types are provided below. For instance, Repair-Critical is assessed with the highest priority score of 4, and takes a duration of 60 minutes on average.

	Capacity (mins)	Depot	Equipment installation	Equipment setup	Inspect/Service equipment	Repair-regular	Repair-important	Repair-urgent	Repair-critical
Albert	480	A		1	1				
Bob	480	A		1		1		1	
Carlos	480	B		1	1	1		1	
Doris	480	B	1	1			1		1
Ed	480	A			1	1		1	
Flor	360	B	1			1	1	1	
Gina	360	A	1	1		1	1	1	1

	Equipment installation	Equipment setup	Inspect/Service equipment	Repair-regular	Repair-important	Repair-urgent	Repair-critical
Priority	2	3	1	1	2	3	4
Duration (mins)	60	30	60	60	120	90	60

On a particular day, seven customer orders are received with their job type, time window of service and due time shown below. Assume the day of operation starts at time zero. For instance, the job type for Customer 6 is Repair-Critical, which must start no earlier than 300 minutes (5 hours) into the day, i.e., 1 pm assuming the day of operation starts at 8 am, and no later than 420 minutes (7 hours) into the day, i.e., 3 pm. It must be completed by 480 minutes (8 hours) into the day, i.e., 4 pm.

Orders	**Job type**	**Earliest time to start**	**Latest time to start**	**Due time**
Customer 1	Equipment Setup	0	30	60
Customer 2	Equipment Setup	30	150	180
Customer 3	Repair-Regular	60	180	240
Customer 4	Equipment Installation	120	240	300
Customer 5	Equipment Installation	240	360	420
Customer 6	Repair-Critical	300	420	480
Customer 7	Inspect/Service Equipment	360	480	540

The travel time (in minutes) matrix of all the nine locations: two depots plus seven customers, is given below.

	A	B	Customer 1	Customer 2	Customer 3	Customer 4	Customer 5	Customer 6	Customer 7
A		120	24	50	67	71	88	98	150
B	120		125	85	68	62	45	39	48
Customer 1	24	125		53	74	77	95	106	160
Customer 2	50	85	53		31	35	51	61	115
Customer 3	67	68	74	31		16	36	46	98
Customer 4	71	62	77	35	16		30	40	92
Customer 5	88	45	95	51	36	30		26	80
Customer 6	98	39	106	61	46	40	26		70
Customer 7	150	48	160	115	98	92	80	70	

The optimal solution in Figure 14.7(a) utilizes four out of the seven technicians with an objective value of zero, i.e., all the customers are served within their time windows. Idleness is often needed to satisfy customer-specified time windows.

Suppose all the technicians' capacities are reduced by half, then one customer (customer 4) cannot be served in the optimal solution as shown in Figure 14.7(b). Now five out of seven technicians are utilized, with Bob assigned with two jobs and all the others assigned with only one job each.

The unique feature of the TRSP is the skill-based assignment between jobs and technicians, which necessitates the definition of binary assignment decision variable. The typical route sequencing decision variable is also needed to determine the valid configuration

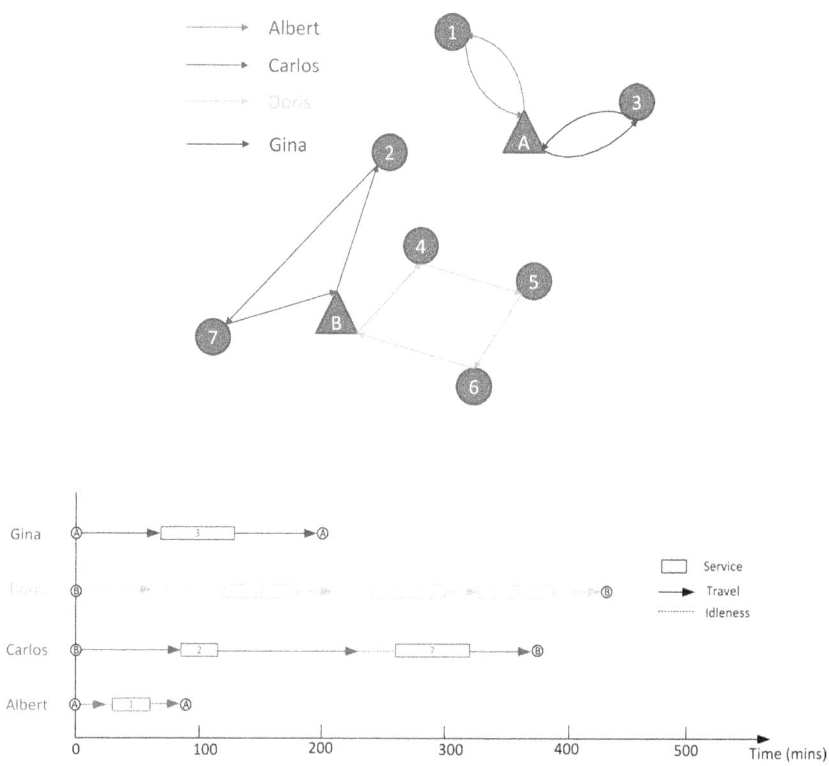

(a) Optimal solution with all the jobs fulfilled within their time

Figure 14.7. Illustration of optimal solution to Example 14.4.

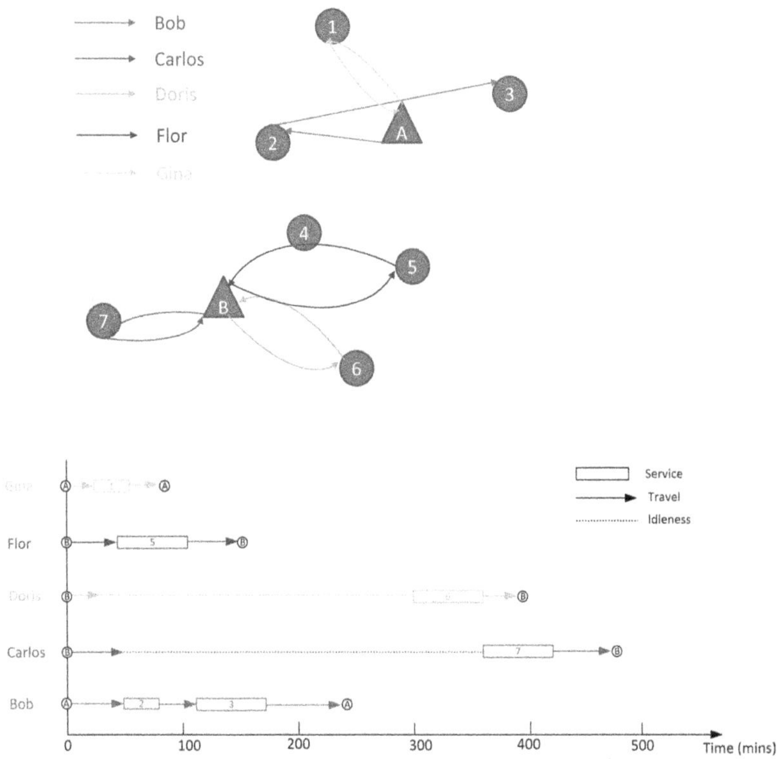

(b) Optimal solution when technicians' capacities are reduced by half.

Figure 14.7. (*Continued*)

of the route. Next, to control whether to utilize a technician (and his/her return to the depot the technician is housed in) requires a binary decision variable to indicate if a technician is utilized or not.

Different from other routing applications we have seen so far, the TRSP considers service-based performance metrics in the objective function. For this purpose, we introduce the idea of "soft constraints" that allow violation of a constraint with some penalty. In particular, one may construct a soft constraint to identify whether a job cannot be fulfilled, i.e., assigned to any technician. Another place where the soft constraint approach can be applied is for the time window requirements. We may allow possible deviation from the customer-specified time window, but with some penalty.

The objective function for the addressed TRSP is to minimize the total penalty, which includes the penalty on not fulfilled jobs and deviation from the customer-specified time windows. The decision maker may come up with business rules to define the proper penalty. For instance, not fulfilling a job can be more severe than deviation from the time window, thus a higher penalty can be imposed for it.

With such an objective function, the optimization model will behave in the following way: (i) utilize as much technician capacity as possible to serve all the customers; and (ii) attempt to find feasible routes and schedule that satisfy the customer-specified time windows, or exploit minimum violation of the time windows in case a complete satisfaction is not possible. Behavior (i) implicitly maximizes utilization of technicians, which is of critical importance for service operations and firms. Since a company's workforce and skilled personnel are often internal and a sunk cost, maximizing their utilization is a practical objective. Behavior (ii) identifies potential infeasibility due to time window requirements, and allows the company to negotiate with the customer for adjustment of the time window. This customer-centered feature enables the company to achieve and maintain customer satisfaction or minimize customer un-satisfaction.

Key to Formulation: Three types of decision variables are defined, including the technician-job assignment (binary), route sequencing (binary) and starting time (continuous) decision variables. A route is maintained only for each technician who is utilized, i.e., assigned to at least one job. An MTZ-type big-M constraint is employed to satisfy the time window, while preventing subtours, similar to the way it works in a VRPTW.

Sets

J: set of n jobs, i.e., $J = \{1, 2, \ldots, n\}$
S: set of skills
K: set of technicians
D: set of m service centers, i.e., $D = \{n+1, n+2, \ldots, n+m\}$
L: set of all locations, i.e., $L = J \cup D = \{1, 2, \ldots, n+m\}$

Parameters

β_{kd}: equals 1 if technician $k \in K$ must depart from and return to service center $d \in D$

p_j: processing time of a node $j \in L$, with $p_j = 0$ for $j \in D$
r_{js}: equals 1 if job $j \in J$ requires skill $s \in S$
q_{ks}: equals 1 if technician $k \in K$ possesses skill $s \in S$
θ_{jk}: equals 1 if job $j \in J$ can be assigned to technician $k \in K$, which can be computed as $\theta_{jk} = r_{js} \cdot q_{ks}$
τ_{ij}: travel time from location $i \in L$ to location $j \in L$
W_k: workload limit of technical $k \in K$ during the planning horizon
π_j: priority weight of job $j \in J$, a larger value means higher priority
a_j: earliest time to start the service at job $j \in J$
b_j: latest time to start the service at job $j \in J$
d_j: due date of job $j \in J$, i.e., latest time to complete the service for job $j \in J$
M: a large positive number

Decision variables

$u_k = 1$ if technician $k \in K$ is utilized, and 0 o.w.
$x_{jk} = 1$ if technician $k \in K$ is assigned to job $j \in J$, and 0 o.w.
$y_{ijk} = 1$ if technician $k \in K$ is travels from location $i \in L$ to location $j \in L$; and 0 o.w.
$t_j \geq 0$: time to arrive or start service at location $j \in L$
$z_j \geq 0$: lateness of completing job $j \in J$
$x_j^{\mathrm{a}} \geq 0$: adjusted earliest starting time of job $j \in J$
$x_j^{\mathrm{b}} \geq 0$: adjusted latest starting time of job $j \in J$
$g_j = 1$ if job $j \in J$ cannot be filled, and 0 o.w.

Objective function

$$\text{Minimize} \quad \sum_{j \in J} \pi_j z_j + 0.01M \sum_{j \in J} (xa_j + xb_j) + M \sum_{j \in J} g_j \qquad (14.60)$$

Constraints
Subject to:

$$\sum_{k \in K} \theta_{jk} x_{jk} + g_j = 1, \quad \forall j \in J, \qquad (14.61)$$

$$\sum_{k \in K} x_{jk} \leq 1, \quad \forall j \in J, \tag{14.62}$$

$$\sum_{j \in J} p_j x_{jk} + \sum_{i \in L} \sum_{j \in L} \tau_{ij} y_{ijk} \leq W_k u_k, \quad \forall k \in K, \tag{14.63}$$

$$\sum_{j \in L} y_{ijk} = x_{ik}, \quad \forall k \in K, \, i \in J, \tag{14.64}$$

$$\sum_{i \in L} y_{ijk} = x_{jk}, \quad \forall k \in K, \, j \in J, \tag{14.65}$$

$$\sum_{j \in L} y_{djk} = \beta_{kd} u_k, \quad \forall k \in K, \, d \in D, \tag{14.66}$$

$$\sum_{i \in L} y_{idk} = \beta_{kd} u_k, \quad \forall k \in K, \, d \in D, \tag{14.67}$$

$$t_j \geq t_i + p_i + \tau_{ij} - M \left(1 - \sum_{k \in K} y_{ijk} \right), \quad \forall i \in L, \, j \in J, \tag{14.68}$$

$$t_j + x_j^{\mathrm{a}} \geq a_j, \quad \forall j \in J, \tag{14.69}$$

$$t_j - x_j^{\mathrm{b}} \leq b_j, \quad \forall j \in J, \tag{14.70}$$

$$z_j \geq t_j + p_j - d_j, \quad \forall j \in J, \tag{14.71}$$

$$x_{ik}, \, y_{ijk} \in \{0, 1\}, \quad t_j, \, z_j, \, g_j, \, u_j \geq 0, \tag{14.72}$$

The objective function (14.60) minimizes the total loss of service, which includes the weighted tardiness (lateness) of all the jobs, penalty on potential violation/adjustment of the time-windows, and penalty on the unfulfilled jobs. Note that the penalty of unfulfilled jobs is set to be larger than that of the time-window adjustment.

Constraint (14.61) assigns each job to one technician who possesses the corresponding skill, or identifies the job to be unfulfilled. Constraint (14.62) ensures that each job is assigned to at most one technician with the corresponding skills required. Constraints (14.61) and (14.62) together ensure that a technician without the required skill of a job cannot be assigned to the job. Constraint (14.63) guarantees that the available capacity of each selected technician is not exceeded by its total assigned workload and travel time. Constraint (14.64) states that if a technician is assigned to a job, then the technician must travel *to* another location (to form a tour). Symmetrically, Constraint (14.65) ensures that if a technician is assigned to a job, then the technician must travel *from* another location to the location of the job (to form a tour). Constraints (14.66) and (14.67) guarantee that a technician, if assigned to any job, must depart from and return to the service center (depot) the technician belongs to, respectively. Constraint (14.68) is the big-M constraint that satisfies the temporal relationship between two consecutive jobs served by the same technician. That is, if a technician travels from job i to job j, then the start of service time at job j must be no less than the completion time of job i plus the travel time from job i to job j. Constraints (14.69) and (14.70) are soft constraints to adjust the earliest and latest start time of each job, respectively. Constraint (14.71) computes the lateness of each job. Since the lateness decision variable z_j is non-negative, there is no benefit to complete a job before its due date; on the other hand, since the objective function minimizes the total weighted tardiness, Constraint (14.71) should always be binding.

14.7 Additional Notes

The VRP and its variants belong to a rich set of optimization problems that have been extensively studied. We refer to [96] for a survey on VRP and [97] for a systematic treatment of variants of VRP and their applications. The MIP formulation and branch-and-cut algorithm for the VRPTW in Section 14.3 are presented in [98]. We refer to [99, 100] for MIP formulations and efficient branch-and-cut and branch-and-cut-and-price algorithms for the VRPPDTW in Section 14.4. A systematic survey of the PVRP in Section 14.5 is available in [101], and an exact method is presented in [102]. The model for TRSP in Section 14.6 is the author's joint work with Gurobi Optimization, which is available at the Gurobi website.[a]

Exercises

14.1. Discuss the classification and variants of the VRP, and show three application examples.

[a]https://www.gurobi.com/resource/webinar-technician-routing-scheduling-problem/.

14.2. Show different MILP formulations for the standard VRP, and discuss their connections, differences, advantages and disadvantages.

14.3. Show and discuss three real world applications of the VRPTW. What could be alternative objective functions and constraints for the VRPTW?

14.4. Explain the model building approach for the VRPPDTW. Show and discuss three real world applications. What could be alternative objective functions and constraints for the VRPPDTW?

14.5. Explain the model building approach for the PVRP. Show and discuss three real world applications. What could be alternative objective functions and constraints for the PVRP?

14.6. Explain the model building approach for the TRSP. Show and discuss three real world applications. What could be alternative objective functions and constraints for the TRSP?

14.7. Consider the ABC Energy utility company in Problem 7.8. The company's outbound logistics operations deliver SKUs (materials, parts and components) from stocking locations to operating centers. The fleet consists of three types of trucks: small, medium and large, with different capacities and operating costs. Every week, each operating center comes up with a list of SKUs for the stocking locations to fulfill. Propose a data-driven optimization approach for ABC Energy to manage its outbound operations efficiently. Elaborate the decision variables, objective function(s), constraints and the input data needed in your approach.

14.8. ABC Logistics Inc. is a company providing third-party last-mile delivery services for small and medium restaurants. In addition to the traditional way of transport via truck, the company implements a team of independent drivers/contractors using motorcycles and bicycles for delivery, which is quite suitable in the urban setting. Given a set of orders, the company needs to determine an optimal way of assigning orders to the available drivers and scheduling their routes. Orders must be delivered within customers' preferred time windows. A driver may have preferences of working hours, areas of service, etc. that need to be satisfied if possible. Propose a data-driven optimization model for ABC Logistics Inc. to manage its delivery operations. Elaborate the decision variables, objective function(s), constraints and the input data needed in your approach.

14.9. Consider the ABC Brewery in Problem 8.8. In addition to its regional and national markets, the company serves fresh crafted beer for a total of over 50 local customers including grocery stores, bars and restaurants, on the weekly basis. Given the weekly demands of a variety of crafted beer of each customer, the company manages its own transportation fleet of six vehicles at two production facilities for the delivery operations. A customer may specify the frequency of replenishment per week, and the specific days of a week for replenishment. Propose a data-driven optimization model for ABC Brewery to manage its delivery operations. Elaborate the decision variables, objective function(s), constraints and the input data needed in your approach.

14.10. Consider the ABC Foodbank in Problem 13.7. One routine operation of the foodbank is to pickup the food items donated by grocery stores, food processors and farmers, then deliver them to its customers, including schools and households. Donors often have strict time windows for food pickup. The perishable foods such as vegetables and fruits must be transported via refrigerated trucks. The foodbank manages its own fleet of five trucks for the pickup-and-delivery operation, including two refrigerated ones and three without refrigeration. Propose a data-driven optimization model for ABC Foodbank to manage its pickup-and-delivery operation. Elaborate the decision variables, objective function(s), constraints and the input data needed in your approach.

14.11. Consider the vaccine delivery application in Problem 13.6. Revise and extend your model to handle the following scenarios.

(1) The delivery operation can be performed by a fleet of vehicles (instead of one vehicle).
(2) Vaccine delivery at remote regions often requires healthcare workers to administrate the shots. Thus, the routing and scheduling of vaccine delivery must be coordinated with that of a healthcare worker. That is, the arrival times of vaccines and healthcare worker are better to be close enough to reduce waiting time and increase efficiency.

14.12. Consider the emergency logistics application in Problem 12.12. Effective and efficient distribution of essential goods, including foods, medical supplies, cloths, etc., is a vital operation in disaster relief. Areas in need may vary in population, severity of damage, and types and quantity of goods. Depending on the development and progress of a disaster event, e.g., hurricane, earthquake, etc., the demands of goods may vary over time. Discuss multiple data-driven decision-support needs involved in disaster relief. Explain multiple performance metrics to optimize, with their applicability in different scenarios. Conceptually describe a data-driven decision-support approach to optimize the routing and scheduling of distribution of essential goods. Elaborate the decision variables, objective function(s), constraints and the input data needed in your approach.

Chapter 15

Credit Term Optimization

15.1 Introduction

Trade credit refers to the delay of payment offered by a supplier to a buyer, which is a common practice of short-term financing. It improves the buyer's working capital and potentially incentivizes them to purchase more. The supplier may benefit from it to maintain long-term supplier-buyer relationship and to lower risk of default on banks.

Among various issues in managing accounts payable, an important decision is to determine the *credit term*, i.e., length of delayed payment granted by the supplier to the buyer. This decision was traditionally approached from a pure financial and accounting perspective by a treasurer or controller. However, since demand is often a function of credit term, which in turn determines the production quantity and inventory level, the credit term decision has an intrinsic effect on the production and inventory decisions. Intuitively, a longer credit term may induce more purchase from the buyer, but at the same time require more products to be produced and more inventory to be held. An optimal decision should explicitly factor in both the benefit of longer credit term and production/inventor cost, and exploit their best tradeoff.

In addition, the credit term decision is often made over multiple time periods in a dynamic fashion. In each time period, given the inventory level, the supplier shall make the credit term and production quantity decisions, which determine the inventory level carried to the next time period. Thus, the decisions made in one period will impact those made in the future. Optimizing decisions for each period in a static way is prone to local optima.

Another important aspect of a real world Credit Term Optimization Problem (CTOP) is the interaction of decisions between supplier and buyer. Specifically, the supplier's demand is how much the buyer purchases, a decision made by the buyer based on its own inventory level and market demand. This calls for a more sophisticated modeling approach that explicitly considers two decision-makers and the interaction between their decisions, which is known as a *game-theoretic* model.

The CTOP belongs to a rich research topic of Supply Chain Finance, which studies the financial transaction and cash flow in the supply chain and operations setting. We shall start with a basic version of the problem with the supplier being the single decision-maker. We then extend it to a game-theoretic model that explicitly considers two decision-makers and the interaction between their decisions.

15.2 The Basic Credit Term Optimization Problem

The basic CTOP can be formally described as follows. A supplier sells one product to a buyer at a constant price of p per unit in T time periods. The length of a time period depends on the frequency of orders, e.g., weekly, bi-weekly or monthly. The demand (order quantity) of the buyer in time period $t = 1, 2, \ldots, T$ is denoted by d_t. The supplier offers a credit term δ_t, representing the number of days of the delayed payment, to the buyer. We assume that demand increases with longer credit term, because longer delayed payment frees more on-hand cash for additional purchase. In particular, assume $d_t = d_{t0} + \theta\delta_t$, where d_{t0} is the nominal demand in period t, and $\theta > 0$ is a constant coefficient of δ_t representing the units of demand increase per day of payment delay. The supplier's production cost is c per unit, the inventory holding cost is h per unit per time period, and the maximum production capacity per period is K. Let r denote the prevalent interest rate, i.e., cost of holding one dollar of account receivable for one day. The supplier determines the credit term and production level in each time period to maximize its total profit.

The problem is an extension of the production planning problem covered in Section 4.7. The main difference is the complication in demand d_t, which is a function of the decision variable δ_t, rather than being a constant as in the standard production planning problem. There is also a new and unique implication from the financial perspective in the cost of delayed payment, i.e., the interest cost of the supplier incurred due to account receivable. Specifically, delaying the payment of pd_t for one time period, for selling d_t units at the unit price p in period t, incurs an interest cost of rpd_t. Thus, a credit term of δ_t in t costs an interest of $r\delta_t pd_t$, which is *nonlinear* due to multiplication of two decision variables.

Key to Formulation: The objective function properly computes the total net profit as the total revenue subtracting the total cost of production, inventory and interest. The flow conservation constraint is needed to link all the decision variables, i.e., those for production, inventory and credit term. A nonlinear programming (NLP) model for the basic CTOP can be written as below.

Parameters

- T: number of time periods in the planning horizon
- K: supplier's production capacity per time period
- p: unit price of the product
- c: production cost per unit
- h: inventory holding cost per unit per day
- d_{t0}: nominal demand in each week $t = 1, 2, \ldots, T$
- θ: units of additional demand generated per time period of delayed payment
- r: interest rate per day

Decision variables

- $\delta_t \geq 0$: the credit term, i.e., number of time periods of delayed payment determined by supplier in time period $t = 1, 2, \ldots, T$
- $x_t \geq 0$: production level of the supplier in time period $t = 1, 2, \ldots, T$
- $I_t \geq 0$: supplier's inventory level in time period $t = 1, 2, \ldots, T$. And define $I_0 = 0$

Objective function

$$\text{Maximize} \sum_{t=1}^{T} [p\,(d_{t0} + \theta\delta_t) - cx_t - hI_t - r\delta_t p\,(d_{t0} + \theta\delta_t)] \quad (15.1)$$

Constraints
Subject to:

$$I_{t-1} + x_t - (d_{t0} + \theta\delta_t) = I_t, \quad \forall t = 1, 2, \ldots, T \tag{15.2}$$

$$x_t \leq K, \quad \forall t = 1, 2, \ldots, T \tag{15.3}$$

$$\delta_t, x_t, I_t \geq 0 \tag{15.4}$$

The objective function (15.1) maximizes the total profit of the supplier, which subtracts three cost terms from the total revenue: product cost, inventory holding cost, and interest cost due to delayed payment. Constraint (15.2) maintains the flow conservation of inventory for each period. Constraint (15.3) limits the production capacity in each period.

15.3 The Bilevel Credit Term Optimization Problem

While the basic CTOP captures the integrated credit term and production/inventory decisions for multiple time periods in a dynamic way, it assumes the buyer's order quantity is given as a constant. In reality, unless the supplier and buyer cooperate, the order quantity is often a decision made by the buyer, which depends on the market demand and the credit term offered by the supplier. Thus, there is a clear interaction between the supplier's and buyer's decisions. This calls for a game-theoretic modeling framework with two decision-makers.

We assume a leader-follower game setting, also known as the Stackelberg game, where supplier is the *leader* who makes the credit term decision first, then buyer determines how much to order as the *follower*, given the credit term offered by the supplier. This assumption applies for a buyer's market where suppliers face competition and are expected to offer an attractive credit term *before* orders are made. It might also apply for the situation where the supplier has more bargain power than the buyer, such that the credit term is given as is when the buyer places an order. In either case, it is viable to assume the supplier to be leader in the game.

The addressed CTOP in the leader-follower game setting can be formally described as follows. A buyer places an order for one product with its supplier to satisfy a market demand of d_t in period $t = 1, 2, \ldots, T$ of a planning horizon. The market price of the product is p per unit, the wholesale price offered to the buyer by the supplier is π. Assume $p > \pi$, so that there is a positive margin for the buyer to resell the product. The supplier grants a credit term of δ_t to the buyer for the purchase in period t, which induces more demand. Following the assumption in Section 15.2, let the total demand $\bar{d}_t$ in period t be a linear function of δ_t, i.e., $\bar{d}_t = d_t + \theta\delta_t$, where θ is units of demand increased per day of delayed payment. The supplier also offers a quantity discount rate β per unit of product ordered. We also assume that the unit production cost reduces at a constant rate of α as production level increases due to economies of scale. The supplier and buyer may each keep maximum Γ of inventory at the end of the planning horizon. The interest rate is r per day and the inventory holding cost is h per unit per time period.

Figure 15.1 shows the game structure of addressed problem. The sequence of events occur as follows. The supplier (leader) determines the optimal credit terms, production quantities and inventory levels to maximize the total profit over all the time periods, while anticipating the buyer's order quantities. Then the buyer (follower), taking the credit term prescribed by the supplier as given, determines the optimal order quantities and inventory levels to maximize its profit for all the time periods. Note that the supplier's and buyer's decisions interact through both the credit terms (from supplier to buyer) and the order quantities (from buyer to supplier), called *linking decision variables* in the sequel. Since the supplier and buyer each solve

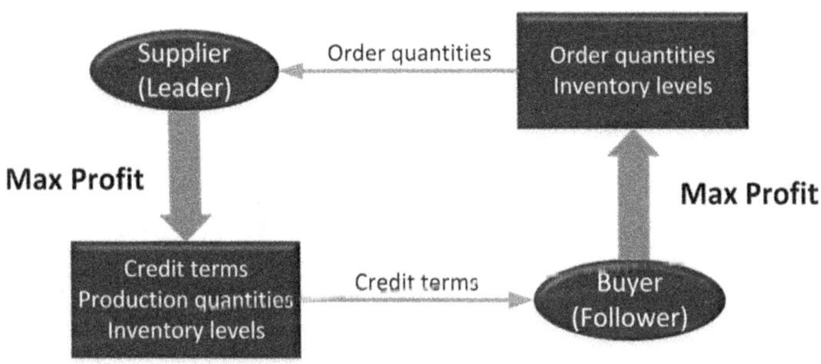

Figure 15.1. The leader-follower game of credit term optimization.

their own profit-maximization problem, we name the addressed problem the Bilevel Credit Term Optimization Problem (BLCTOP). This name is also motivated by the modeling approach we shall present next, which is based on a special type of math programming, namely, bilevel programming.

Key to Formulation: The key to model building for the BLCTOP is to separately model the profit-maximization problems of the supplier and buyer, while indicating the linking decision variables explicitly. Each player's profit-maximization problem can be built upon a standard production planning framework, modeled again by NETFORM. The complete nonlinear (bilevel) programming formulation of the BLCTOP can be written as below.

Sets and parameters

- T: number of time periods in the planning horizon
- K: supplier's production capacity per time period
- Γ: maximum amount of ending stock in the last time period of the planning horizon
- π: wholesale price charged by the supplier to the buyer
- c: production cost per unit
- p: retail market price
- h: inventory holding cost rate per time period
- d_t: market demand in each period $t = 1, 2, \ldots, T$
- θ: units of additional demand generated per day of delayed payment
- r: interest rate per day
- α: coefficient of economies of scale for production cost
- β: rate of quantity discount for wholesale price

Supplier's problem

The supplier's problem contains three decision variables as defined below.

- $\delta_t \geq 0$: the credit term determined by supplier at time period t
- $x_t \geq 0$: production quantity of supplier in time period t
- $I_t \geq 0$: supplier's inventory level in time period t, with I_0 being some initial inventory level

Let y_t denote the order quantity to be determined by the buyer in time period t, then the supplier's objective function and constraints follow.

$$\max_{\delta_t, x_t, I_t} \sum_{t=1}^{T} [\pi(1 - \beta y_t)y_t - c(1 - \alpha x_t)x_t - r\delta_t\pi(1 - \beta y_t)y_t - hI_t] \tag{15.5}$$

Subject to:

$$I_{t-1} + x_t - y_t = I_t, \quad \forall t = 1, 2, \ldots, T \tag{15.6}$$

$$x_t \leq K, \quad \forall t = 1, 2, \ldots, T \tag{15.7}$$

$$I_T \leq \Gamma \tag{15.8}$$

$$x_t, I_t, \delta_t \geq 0 \tag{15.9}$$

The objective function (15.5) maximizes the supplier's total profit by subtracting the production cost, interest cost and inventory holding cost from the revenue of selling the product to the buyer. The first term in the objective function is the revenue of selling y_t units of product, with $\pi(1 - \beta y_t)$ being the wholesale price of the product due to quantity discount. The second term is the cost of producing x_t units of product, with $c(1 - \alpha x_t)$ being the unit production cost considering economies of scale. The third term is the interest cost of granting δ_t days delayed payment for y_t units of product sold to the buyer at the price of $\pi(1 - \beta y_t)$ and interest rate of r. The fourth item is the inventory holding cost.

Constraint (15.6) is the well-known flow conservation constraint, as in the NETFORM, to maintain the total inflow of period $t - 1$'s inventory plus period t's production level, i.e., $I_{t-1} + x_t$, into period t, being equal to the total outflow of products sold to the buyer plus period t's inventory, i.e., $y_t + I_t$. Constraint (15.7) limits the supplier's production level not to exceed the maximum capacity K. Constraint (15.8) ensures that the inventory of supplier in the last period does not exceed Γ.

Note that the buyer's order quantity y_t enters into the formulation of the supplier's problem being a decision to be made by the buyer, but "anticipated" by the supplier.

Buyer's problem

The buyer's problem contains two decision variables as defined below.

$y_t \geq 0$: order quantity of the buyer in time period t

$O_t \geq 0$: buyer's inventory level in time period t, with O_0 being some initial inventory level

As a follower, the buyer's decision is made taking the credit term δ_t, determined by the leader (supplier), as given. We now state the buyer's objective function and constraints.

$$\max_{y_t, o_t | \delta_t} \sum_{t=1}^{T} [p(d_t + \theta\delta_t) - \pi(1 - \beta y_t)y_t + r\delta_t\pi(1 - \beta y_t)y_t - hO_t] \tag{15.10}$$

Subject to:

$$O_{t-1} + y_t - d_t - \theta\delta_t = O_t, \quad \forall t = 1, 2, \ldots, T \tag{15.11}$$

$$O_T \leq \Gamma \tag{15.12}$$

$$y_t \geq 0, \quad \forall t = 1, 2, \ldots, T \tag{15.13}$$

$$O_t \geq 0, \quad \forall t = 1, 2, \ldots, T \tag{15.14}$$

The objective function (15.10) maximizes the buyer's total profit by subtracting the purchasing cost and inventory holding cost from the revenue of meeting customer demand plus the saving due to delayed payment. Note in (15.10), we explicitly specify that the decision y_t and O_t are optimized *given* the credit term δ_t using the notation $|$(reads "given"). The first term is the revenue of selling $(d_t + \theta\delta_t)$ units of product at price p, the second term is the cost of purchasing y_t units of product at the price of $\pi(1 - \beta y_t)$, the third term is the saving due to delayed payment (note it is exactly the same as the third term in the supplier's objective function but with different sign), and the fourth term is the buyer's inventory holding cost.

Constraint (15.11) is the flow conservation constraint requiring that the total inflow of period $t-1$'s inventory plus period t's purchasing quantity, i.e., $O_{t-1}+y_t$, into period t, being equal to the market demand plus period t's inventory, i.e., $d_t + \theta\delta_t + O_t$. Constraint (15.12) limits the buyer's inventory level in the last time period not to exceed Γ.

Unlike the models we have seen so far, a bilevel programming model cannot be solved directly but needs some special solution strategy to tackle. Among various solution approaches, the one we present here is to reformulate the model such that it reduces to an optimization problem of a single player, i.e., the leader (supplier). This is achieved by deriving the Karush-Kuhn-Tucker (KKT) conditions for the buyer to achieve its optimal solution, and augmenting the supplier's problem by adding these conditions as constraints.

Recall that the KKT conditions include the complementary slackness condition and the stationarity condition. Define ρ, v_t and φ_t as the KKT multipliers for Constraints (15.12)–(15.14) in the buyer's problem, respectively. The complementary slackness condition can be written as below:

$$\rho(O_T - \Gamma) = 0 \tag{15.15}$$

$$v_t y_t = 0, \quad \forall t = 1, 2, \ldots, T \tag{15.16}$$

$$\varphi_t O_t = 0, \quad \forall t = 1, 2, \ldots, T \tag{15.17}$$

In order to derive the stationarity condition, we need to define an additional Lagrangian multiplier λ_t to get the Lagrangian dual $\mathcal{L}(\cdot)$ of the buyer's problem:

$$\begin{aligned} \mathcal{L} = & \sum_{t=1}^{T} [p(d_t + \theta\delta_t) - \pi(1 - \beta y_t)y_t + r\delta_t\pi(1 - \beta y_t)y_t - hO_t] \\ & + \sum_{t=1}^{T} \lambda_t (O_t - O_{t-1} - y_t + d_t + \theta\delta_t) + \sum_{t=1}^{T} v_t y_t \\ & + \sum_{t=1}^{T} \varphi_t O_t + \rho(\Gamma - O_T) \end{aligned} \tag{15.18}$$

The stationarity condition can be obtained by taking the first-order partial derivatives of (15.18) with respect to y_t and O_t, and equate them to zero:

$$-\pi + 2\pi\beta y_t + r\delta_t\pi - 2r\delta_t\pi\beta y_t - \lambda_t + v_t = 0,$$

$$\forall t = 1, 2, \ldots, T \tag{15.19}$$

$$-h + \lambda_t + \varphi_t = 0, \quad \forall t = 1, 2, \ldots, T - 1 \tag{15.20}$$

$$-h + \lambda_T + \varphi_T - \rho = 0, \tag{15.21}$$

Now the reformulated model consists of the supplier's objective function (15.5), constraints (15.6)–(15.8), the buyer's constraints (15.11)–(15.12), the complementary slackness condition (15.15)–(15.17), plus the stationarity condition (15.19)–(15.21).

The complete reformulation can be written as below.

$$\text{Maximize} \sum_{t=1}^{T} [\pi(1-\beta y_t)y_t - c(1-\alpha x_t)x_t - r\delta_t\pi(1-\beta y_t)y_t - hI_t] \tag{15.5}$$

Subject to:

$$I_{t-1} + x_t - y_t = I_t, \quad \forall t = 1, 2, \ldots, T \tag{15.6}$$

$$x_t \leq K, \quad \forall t = 1, 2, \ldots, T \tag{15.7}$$

$$I_T \leq \Gamma \tag{15.8}$$

$$O_{t-1} + y_t - d_t - \theta\delta_t = O_t, \quad \forall t = 1, 2, \ldots, T \tag{15.11}$$

$$O_T \leq \Gamma \tag{15.12}$$

$$\rho(O_T - \Gamma) = 0 \tag{15.15}$$

$$v_t y_t = 0, \quad \forall t = 1, 2, \ldots, T \tag{15.16}$$

$$\varphi_t O_t = 0, \quad \forall t = 1, 2, \ldots, T \tag{15.17}$$

$$-\pi + 2\pi\beta y_t + r\delta_t\pi - 2r\delta_t\pi\beta y_t - \lambda_t + v_t = 0, \quad \forall t = 1, 2, \ldots, T \tag{15.19}$$

$$-h + \lambda_t + \varphi_t = 0, \quad \forall t = 1, 2, \ldots, T-1 \tag{15.20}$$

$$-h + \lambda_T + \varphi_T - \rho = 0, \tag{15.21}$$

$$\delta_t, x_t, I_t, y_t, O_t, \lambda_t, \rho, v_t, \varphi_t \geq 0 \tag{15.22}$$

As a numerical example, consider a buyer who purchases from a supplier to meet the market demands of one product in the next five weeks: 60, 70, 65, 80, 100 units. The market price of the product is \$200/unit, and the wholesale price is \$150/unit. Historical data reveals that one day of delayed payment granted by the supplier generates about 0.5 units of demand. The supplier's production cost is \$100 per unit with the weekly capacity of 400 units. The supplier offers quantity discount for the buyer at a constant rate of 0.2%/unit, and estimates an economies of scale rate to be 0.125%/unit. The

Table 15.1. Summary of supplier and buyer's optimal decisions.

		Week-1	Week-2	Week-3	Week-4	Week-5	Total
Supplier's Decision	Credit term (days)	150	150	62	0	0	
	Production (units)	356	400	0	0	0	
	Inventory (units)	104	252	0	0	0	
	AR ($)	18,749	18,749	18,749	0	0	56,246
	COGS ($)	−19,760	−20,000	0	0	0	−39,760
	Interest cost ($)	−62	−562	−234	0	0	−1,359
	Inv. cost ($)	−125	−302	0	0	0	−427
	Net profit ($)	**−1,698**	**−2,116**	**18,515**	**0**	**0**	**14,701**
Buyer's Decision	Purchase (units)	252	252	252	0	0	
	Inventory (units)	117	224	380	300	200	
	Demand (units)	135	70	96	80	100	
	Revenue ($)	27,000	14,070	19,230	16,000	20,000	96,300
	AP ($)	−18,749	−18,749	−18,749	0	0	−56,246
	Interest gain ($)	562	562	234	0	0	1,359
	Inv. cost ($)	−140	−269	−456	−360	−240	−1,465
	Net profit ($)	**8,673**	**−4,385**	**259**	**15,640**	**19,760**	**39,947**

inventory holding cost of $1.2 per unit per week for both the supplier and buyer. The current interest rate is 0.02% per day. To avoid excessive stock, neither the supplier nor buyer may keep more than 200 units of inventory at the end of the planning horizon.

Using the model and solution approach in Section 15.3, one may obtain an optimal solution in Table 15.1. It is optimal for the supplier to grant the buyer 150, 150 and 62 days credit term for the first three weeks, with the buyer ordering 252 units in each of the three weeks. It turns out that the buyer's overall interest gain of $1,359 is about to cover its total inventory cost of $1,465. Through this optimal plan, the supplier and buyer achieve a net profit of $14,701 and $39,947, respectively.

15.4 Additional Notes

The seminal work of [103] simultaneously optimizes a supplier's credit term, production and inventory decisions, assuming that a buyer's order quantity is a function of time, inventory level and credit term. One of the early work that addresses the interdependency of decisions between the supplier and buyer is available in [104]. The bilevel programming model for the CTOP in the leader-following game setting is presented in [105].

Exercises

15.1. Discuss connections and differences of the basic CTOP with the production planning problem.

15.2. Explain the model building approach for the BLCTOP. Show and discuss three application examples.

15.3. What are possible variants and extension of the BLCTOP? Hint: alternative supply chain structure, with or without bank, alternative objective functions and constraints.

15.4. ABC Logistics is a 3PL service provider with its business in multiple industries of manufacturing, food/agriculture, mining and retail. Working with both shipper and carrier, ABC Logistics is in a unique position to help a shipper negotiate discounted shipping rates, while helping a carrier to determine the optimal credit term (delayed payment). For each of the following scenarios, propose a data-driven optimization approach and elaborate the decision variables, objective function(s), constraints and the input data needed.

(a) ABC Logistics collaborates with the carrier to make the credit term decision for the carrier.
(b) ABC Logistics acts as a bank between the carrier and the shipper to make the credit term decision in a centralized way.

15.5. ABC Home is a furniture retailer with both the traditional brick-and-mortar and the online sales channels. It sources most of its products from East Asia with high quality design and craftsmanship, but long shipping lead time. The furniture market is also known for its high variation and seasonality of demand. Thus, ABC Home opts to make bulk orders and shipments to achieve economies-of-scale. It also sees opportunity to negotiate the payment terms, i.e., advanced or delayed payment, with its suppliers to save the total procurement cost. By paying the supplier earlier (than the industry benchmark), it may get a discounted purchasing price; by a negotiating flexible delayed payment, it may better utilize its available funds and save the overall procurement cost. Propose a data-driven decision-support approach to help ABC Home better manage its procurement and supply chain finance. Elaborate the decision variables, objective function(s), constraints and the input data needed in your approach. What else is needed in order to implement your approach in practice?

Appendices

Appendix 1 CPLEX OPL Studio

A1.1 Introduction

Building model formulation is the first and crucial step to approach an optimization problem, but to obtain an optimal solution efficiently is not a trivial task. The good news is that modern optimization software are available for solving mathematical programming models to optimality efficiently. These software often include an *optimization modeling language* which provides a platform to translate the algebraic formulation of an optimization model into computer code, and use *solver(s)* which implements and embeds the solution methods (to be introduced in the subsequent Appendices A.2, A.3 and A.4) to solve optimization models.

Figure A1.1 compares the flexibility and ease of the use of various software and programming languages for optimization applications. The category of commercial software at the top-left corner provides application-specific optimization decision-support. For instance, the MRP and production scheduling modules in SAP, resource planning functions in Oracle, supply chain network design in Llamasoft and i2, and transportation optimization in MercuryGate. These provide predefined functionalities with easy-to-use graphical user interface (GUI), e.g., click-and-drag, without the need for users to build an optimization model from scratch. However, since the model features and functionalities are generic and pre-built, they can be limited in modeling new decision variables, objective function or constraints that are unique to an industry or company.

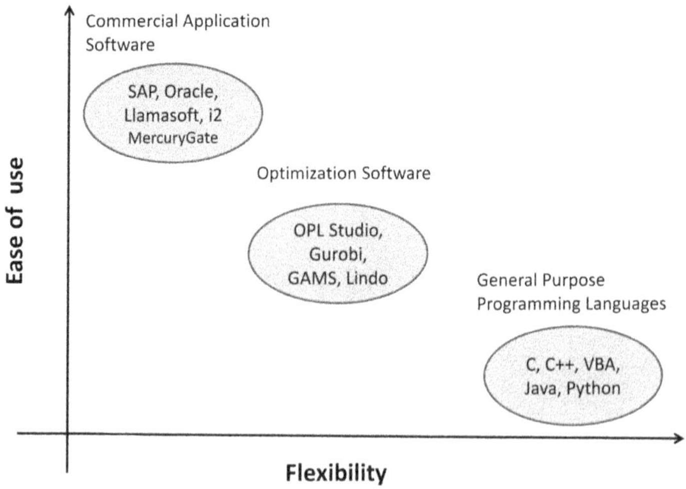

Figure A1.1. Comparison of various software for optimization applications.

The general purpose programming languages at the bottom-right corner are the most flexible and suitable tools for developing and implementing problem-specific algorithms. However, the use of these programming tools for solving optimization models often requires expertise in algorithm design (e.g., heuristics and metaheuristics) and significant coding efforts.

The suite of optimization software at the center bridges the gap between the commercial application software and the general purpose programming languages. On one hand, they are general and flexible enough to implement user-built optimization models with moderate coding efforts; on the other hand, the embedded optimization solvers can be readily employed for solving optimization models, eliminating the needs for users to implement the solution algorithms. The use of optimization software is an efficient way to implement and solve custom-design optimization models, making it possible to deploy and test prototype optimization models for real world applications.

The IBM's CPLEX OPL Studio is a powerful and accessible optimization modeling software for both mathematical programming and CP. It is built upon the Optimization Programming Language (OPL) for expressing the algebraic formulation of mathematical

Table A1.1. Comparison of main features of selected optimization software.

	Math programming	CP	IDE	Script	API	Free to academia*
OPL Studio	CPLEX	Yes	Yes	Yes	C++, .NET, Java	Yes
GAMS	Multiple/ Optional	No	Yes	Yes	C, C++, VBA, C#, Java, Python	No
Gurobi	Gurobi	No	No	No	C, C++, VB, C#, Java, Python, R	Yes
Xpress	Mosek	Yes	Yes	Yes	C, C++, .NET, Java, Python	Yes
Lindo	Lindo	No	Yes	Yes	C++, VB, C#, Java	No

Note: *The full version with no problem size or time limit (renewable).

programming models, including the LP and MILP models introduced in this book, and utilizes CPLEX as the solver. The ILOG Solver and Scheduler are the underlying engine for solving CP models in CPLEX OPL Studio. Table A1.1 compares the main features of CPLEX OPL Studio with other popular optimization software.

All the optimization software in Table A1.1 have modeling capability and solvers for LP and MILP, although their performance may differ significantly.[a] While most software have a dedicated optimization solver, it is worth noting that GAMS is a versatile platform that allows for multiple (optional) solvers for the model at hand, including CPLEX, Gurobi, Xpress and Lindo, as well as a number of nonlinear programming solvers. CPLEX OPL Studio and Xpress stand out in their capability of modeling and solving CP problems. As for the ease of use, most have GUI-based integrated development environment (IDE) and scripting language. For users with the needs for applying optimization models and deploying them in an application tool for real world decision-support, APIs can be used to call

[a]We refer the reader to the website and documentation of each software for detailed information on their performance. There are also third-party evaluation and assessment reports available to compare the performance of different optimization solvers.

and embed the optimization models and algorithms in an application tool developed in other more flexible general-purpose programming languages such as C++, C#, .NET, Java or Python, among others. Finally, note that CPLEX OPL Studio, Xpress and Gurobi are available for academic users for research and teaching purposes for free.

A1.2 A Guided Tour of CPLEX OPL Studio

The CPLEX OPL Studio has a nice and intuitive GUI-based IDE for expressing optimization models in the OPL modeling language, and solving the models with embedded solvers: CPLEX for mathematical programming and ILOG Solver and Scheduler for constraint programming.

Figure A1.2 provides a screenshot of the main windows in the IDE GUI of CPLEX OPL Studio. In the default view setting, the OPL Project Window on the left shows the view of all the projects currently included in the IDE, including the model file (*.mod), data file (*.dat), run configuration, and any other files in a project folder. The OPL Coding Window in the center is the place where the user writes and edits the OPL code for the model, data and scripts (if any) in a project. The Outline Window on the right provides a structured view of the components in an optimization model, including all the

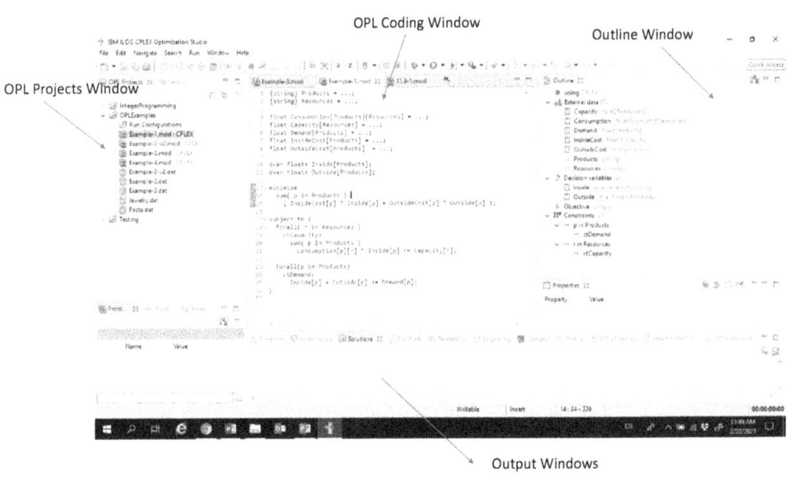

Figure A1.2. Main windows in the IDE of CPLEX OPL studio.

sets and parameters, decision variables, objective function, and constraints, in exactly the same format of the algebraic formulation. The Output Window at the bottom shows the solution and output information after solving the model at hand.

Note that there are multiple tabs in in the Output Window, each for a different type of information. Here we introduce the most commonly used tabs. The Problems Tab shows any issues or errors occurred. The Scripting Log Tab shows the user-specified output information through the script part of the code in a *.mod file, which is optional. The Solutions Tab shows the optimal solution of a model, including the optimal objective function value and the optimal values of decision variables. The Engine Log Tab shows detailed information of the corresponding solver in its solution process, i.e., CPLEX for mathematical programming, and ILOG Solver for CP. Checking and understanding this information is needed for assessing the effectiveness and efficiency of solution process for the problem at hand. For this purpose, the user needs to have some fundamental knowledge of the Simplex Method for LP, Branch-and-Bound and Branch-and-Cut methods for MILP, and the CP methods, which are covered in Appendices A2, A3 and A4, respectively. The Statistics Tab provides information about the model size: number of decision variables (continuous and integer) and constraints, and summary of the solution process with a visualization of the lower bound and upper bound found during the solving iterations. More detailed information about the time and memory usage of the solving process is provided in the Profiler Tab.

A1.2.1 *OPL Project*

An OPL project consists of optimization model files (*.mod) and data files (*.dat) organized in one folder. As we will show later, each *.mod file is associated with a *.dat file, reflecting the fact that the model formulation and data is closely connected, but can be separated. In this way, the same model can be applied for different input data by associating it with different data files.

To create a new OPL Project, go to File → New → OPL Project. Type in the name of your project in the "Project name" field. Then choose the directory in the "Project location" field where you would like to locate the project (folder). You may check "Create Model" and "Create Data", which will automatically create and add an empty *.mod and *.dat file into the project. You may also leave them unchecked, then add the model and data files manually later. Suppose you have checked both, then a new folder with the name being your project name will be automatically created with one *.mod and one *.dat files, both having the same default name being the project name.

To add a new *.mod file, go to File → New → Model. Then you will see a list of projects currently included in the IDE. Choose the project you would like to add the new model file, then type in the name of model file you prefer. A new *.mod file is automatically created with the name you specified. An alternative way is to right click the project in the OPL Project Window, then select New → Model and follow the same steps. A new *.dat file can be created and added in the same way.

Since an OPL project is nothing but a folder of files, one can conveniently move existing model and data files into a project, by copying/pasting *.mod and *.dat files into a project folder (outside the IDE). Right click the project in the OPL Projects Window, select Refresh, then the copied model and data files will show up in the project view.

To load an existing OPL project, go to File → Import → Existing OPL projects. Click Browse and choose the right directory where the project is located. Check the right OPL project in the list of projects shown, then click Finish.

To run a model in an OPL project, one must create a Run Configuration to link an optimization model (*.mod file) with an input data (*.dat file). To do this, right click the project in the OPL Project Window, and choose New → Run Configuration. Leave the default location and name of the new Run Configuration, or type in your preferred name, then click Finish. You will see an empty Run Configuration is shown in the Project Window. To associate a model with an input data, simply drag the corresponding *.mod and *.dat files into the Run Configuration. Right click the Run Configuration and choose Run This.

A1.2.2 *Viewing Optimization Solutions*

When solving a complex model and/or a large size instance, one may view and monitor the solution process in the Engine Log Tab of the Output Window. Otherwise, the model is solved in a matter of seconds with the optimal solution information automatically generated in the Output Window. The Solutions Tap provides immediate information about the solution status, optimal objective function value, and solutions of all the decision variables. One is also recommended to view the detailed log information of the solving process in the Engine Log Tab for solution quality (optimality gap), computational time, and other technical details of the solution process. Advanced users may these information to tune the parameter settings of the solvers, which goes beyond the scope of this text.

A1.3 Basics of OPL Syntax

The OPL is a modeling language based on the algebraic formulation of an optimization model. The coding structure of a *.mod file follows exactly the structure and format of algebraic formulation, i.e., sets, parameters, decision variables, objective function and constraints. OPL code and script are all case sensitive.

A1.3.1 *Sets*

There are two ways to define a set in OPL. The most popular and convenient way is to define the set over generic integer elements/indexes. An example code is provided below, with *italic* words being the keywords in OPL.

int card = . . .;
range SetName = 1..card;

The first line defines an integer parameter "card" as the *cardinality* of the set (number of elements in the set). Then in the second line, a set named "SetName" is defined as a set of integer indexes from 1 to card, i.e., $\{1, 2, \ldots, \text{card}\}$. Correspondingly in the *.dat file, the following code is needed to provide the data for "card", for example:

card = 10;

This assigns 10 to the parameter "card", such that the SetName has 10 elements: $\{1, 2, \ldots, 10\}$.

Sometimes one may need to explicitly identify the name of each element in a set. This can be achieved by an alternative way to define a set as a set of strings.

{*string*} Produce = ...;

The curly bracket { } is used to define a set named "Produce" consisting of strings. Note that the cardinality is not needed in this approach, as it requires the user to explicitly enumerate all the element (names) in the data. For example, to define a set of vegetable products: lettuce, tomatoes, and herbs, the following code is needed in the corresponding *.dat file:

Produce = {lettuce, tomatoes, herbs};

A1.3.2 *Parameters*

To define a single parameter, simply define it in the *.mod file and provide its value in the *.dat file. Use *int* for an integer parameter, and *float* for a continuous parameter. For instance,

float $b = \ldots;$

defines b as a parameter of float type. Then in the *.dat file:

$b = 0.5;$

assigns 0.5 to b.

The following code defines an array of n (integer) elements named "ArrayName" over the set named "SetName" n integer elements: $\{1, 2, \ldots, n\}$.

int ArrayName[SetName] = ...;

Then in the corresponding *.dat file, the following code provides the values of the n integer elements $\mathrm{v_1, v_2, \ldots, v_n}$.

ArrayName = $[v_1, v_2, \ldots, v_n]$;

To define an array of n float elements b_i for $i \in N$, where N is a set of n integers: $\{1, 2, \ldots, n\}$, the following two lines of code are needed in the *.mod and *.dat files, respectively:

$float\ b[N] = \ldots;$
$b = [v_1, v_2, \ldots, v_n];$

OPL supports the use of multi-dimensional array. To define an $n \times m$ two-dimensional array b_{ij} of float elements for $i \in N$ and $j \in M$, where N is a set of n integers: $\{1, 2, \ldots, n\}$ and M is a set of m integers: $\{1, 2, \ldots, m\}$, the following is needed in the *.mod file.

float $b[N][M] = \ldots;$

Then in the corresponding *.dat file, we need the following:

$b = [$
$[v_{11}, v_{12}, \ldots, v_{1m}],$
$[v_{21}, v_{22}, \ldots, v_{2m}],$
$\ldots$
$[v_{n1}, v_{n2}, \ldots, v_{nm}]$
$];$

Each row in the two-dimensional array is a one-dimensional array, ending with a comma. Note that the last row does not need to end with a comma.

A1.3.3 *Decision Variables*

Let N be a set, we now show how to define different types of decision variables over the set N. The following code starting with the keyword *dvar* defines an array of continuous decision variables x_i for $i \in N$:

$dvar\ float + x[N];$

float+ indicates the decision variable is non-negative.

To define an array of binary decision variables x_i for $i \in N$:

$dvar\ boolean\ x[N];$

Or alternatively,

$dvar\ int + x[N]\ in\ 0..1;$

which explicitly specifies that x_i is a positive integer in the domain (range) of $\{0, 1\}$.

To define an array of general integer decision variables $a \leq x_i \leq b$ for $i \in N$, we need the following:

dvar int+ x[N] in a..b;

To define a two-dimensional array of binary decision variables x_{ij} for $i \in N$ and $j \in M$, one can write the following:

dvar boolean x[N][M];

A1.3.4 *Objective Function*

OPL uses the keywords *minimize* or *maximize* for a minimization or maximization objective function, respectively. One also often needs to use the *sum ( )* function to express the summation Σ expression in an algebraic formulation. For instance, the following code minimizes an objective function of $\sum_{i \in N} x_i$, where N is a set.

minimize sum (i in N) x[i];

Note that the keyword *in* serves the role of the "belongs to" notation $\in$ in the algebraic formulation.

To maximize an objective function of $\sum_{i \in N} x_i$, simply write:

maximize sum (i in N) x[i];

One can also express a double summation expression conveniently in the following way:

minimize sum (i in N, j in M) x[i][j];

which minimizes the objective function of $\sum_{i \in N} \sum_{j \in M} x_{ij}$.

A1.3.5 *Constraints*

The component of constraints in an optimization model starts with the keyword *subject to* followed by the block identified by a pair of curly brackets {...};. The *forall* keyword serves the role of "for all" notation $\forall$ in an algebraic formulation. For instance, to express the constraint $\sum_{i \in N} b_i x_{ij} \leq k_j$, $\forall j \in M$, one writes the following:

forall (j in M)
*sum (i in N) b[i] * x[i][j]* $\leq k_j$;

The following code expresses the constraint $b_{ij}x_{ij} = K$, $\forall i \in N$, $j \in M$:

forall $(i\ in\ N,\ j\ in\ M)$
$b[i][j] * x[i][j] == K;$

A1.4 Examples of Mathematical Programming Models

Next, we show three simple but concrete examples to demonstrate how to write OPL code for mathematical programming models.

A1.4.1 *Product Mix Problem*

As your first CPLEX OPL Studio model, consider the simple product mix problem of Example 2.4 in Section 2.3. The algebraic formulation of its LP model was presented in Section 2.4.

<u>Sets</u>

P: set of products
R: set of resources

<u>Parameters</u>

π_i: profit of product $i \in P$
k_j: maximum capacity of resource $j \in R$
r_{ij}: capacity of resource j required by product i

<u>Decision variables</u>

$x_i \geq 0$: units of product $i \in P$ to produce

<u>Objective function</u>

Maximize $\sum_{i \in P} \pi_i x_i$

Constraints

$$\sum_{i \in P} r_{ij} x_i \leq k_j, \quad \forall j \in R$$

$$x_i \geq 0 \qquad \forall i \in P$$

The complete OPL code for the above formulation (in a *.mod file) is below. Note the one-to-one correspondence between each component in the algebraic formulation and the OPL code.

Sets

```
{string} Products = ...;
{string} Resources = ...;
```

Parameters

```
float profit[Products] = ...;
float capacity[Resources] = ...;
float requ[Products][Resources] = ...;
```

Decision Variables

```
dvar float+ x[Products];
```

Objective Function

```
maximize sum(i in Products) profit[i] * x[i];
```

Constraints

```
subject to {
    forall (r in Resources)
       sum(i in Products) requ[i][r] * x[i] <= capacity[r];
}
```

The corresponding *.dat file is below:

```
Products = {Max, Multimax};
Resources = {fabrication, assembly};
profit = [400, 800];
capacity = [5000, 3000];
requ = [
[3, 1],
[5, 4]
];
```

Solving the model with the data yields the following output in the Solution Tab of the Output Window. An optimal solution is found, which recommends to produce 714.29 units of Max and 571.43 units of Multimax, with a maximum profit of 742,847.14.

```
// solution (optimal) with objective 742,857.14
// x = [714.29   571.43];
```

Now consider an alternative product mix problem. ABC Indoor Farm is planning for the next quarter's production of lettuce and herbs. The market price of lettuce is \$3.50/lb and that of herbs is \$12.50/lb. To produce one pound of lettuce requires 0.8 square feet, and one pound of herbs requires 2.8 square feet. The total available space for production is 750 square feet. The maximum available labor hours are 160 hours per month. The average labor hours required by lettuce is 6.5 minutes/lb, and that required by herbs is 40 minutes/lb. What is the optimal production mix of lettuce and herbs to maximize the total monthly revenue?

Although the above clearly has appears to have a different setting in farm planning from the manufacturing setting in the previous example, it turns out that its LP formulation is the same. All we need here is to modify the input data in the *.dat file tailored to the new problem setting. This demonstrates the important feature and advantage in optimization modeling that the model and data can be separated, i.e., the same model formulation can be applied for problems in different settings with the same mathematical structure but different input data.

The new *.dat file for the above product mix problem in farm planning is below:

```
Products = {lettuce, herbs};
Resources = {space, labor};
profit = [3.5, 12.5];
capacity = [750, 9600];
requ = [
[0.8, 6.5],
[2.8, 40]
];
```

Solving it generates the following output in the Solution Tab of the Output Window. An optimal solution is found, which recommends to produce 226.09 lbs of lettuce and 203.26 lbs of herbs, with a maximum revenue of 3,332.06.

```
// solution (optimal) with objective 3332.07
// x = [226.09      203.26];
```

A1.4.2 *Advertising Mix Problem*

Consider the advertising mix problem in Section 2.5.1, with the algebraic formulation of its integer programming model below:

Sets

A: set of advertising media
B: set of different types of budget

Parameters

e_i: expected number of exposures of advertising media $i \in A$
k_b: limit of budget type $b \in B$
c_{ib}: cost of budget type b per spot of advertising media $i \in A$
N_i: maximum number of spots of advertising media $i \in A$ available

Decision variables

$x_i \geq 0$ and integer, number of spots of advertising type $i \in A$

Objective function

$$\text{Maximize} \sum_{i \in A} e_i x_i$$

Constraints

$$\sum_{i \in A} c_{ib} x_i \le k_b, \qquad \forall b \in B$$
$$x_i \le N_i, \qquad \forall i \in A$$
$$x_i \in Z^+, \qquad \forall i \in A$$

In this example, we use a different way to define a set. Instead of enumerating all the elements in a set, we use integers to index elements in a generic way.

The OPL code in the *.mod file is below. As an option, one may label each constraint as shown in the constraint block below.

```
int numAds = ...;
int numBudgTypes = ...;

range Adv = 1..numAds;
range Budget = 1..numBudgTypes;
```

```
int exposure[Adv] = ...;
int spending[Adv][Budget] = ...;
int budgetLimit[Budget] = ...;
int maxSpots[Adv] = ...;
```

```
dvar int+ numSpots [Adv];
```

```
maximize sum(i in Adv) exposure[i] * numSpots[i];
```

```
subject to {

spendinglimit:
    forall (b in Budget)
      sum(i in Adv) spending[i][b]*numSpots[i] <= budgetLimit[b];

maxTVSpots:
    forall (i in Adv)
      numSpots[i] <= maxSpots[i];
}
```

Note that only the TV spot is limited. One may input a large enough number for the maximum available spot for the other two media: Magazine and Sunday Ad. The *.dat is provided below.

```
numAds = 3;
numBudgTypes = 2;
exposure = [1300, 600, 500];
spending = [

[300, 90],
[150, 30],
[100, 40]

];
budgetLimit = [4000, 1000];
maxSpots = [5, 100, 100];
```

Solving it yields the following output in the Solution Tab of the Output Window, which suggests 20 Magazine advertisements, 10 Sunday advertisements and zero TV spot, with a maximum expected exposure of 17,000.

```
// solution (optimal) with objective 17,000
//numSpots = [0 20 10];
```

Since this is an integer programming model, one is recommended to inspect the Engine Log Tab of the Output Window for detailed information on the solution process of the CPLEX solver. While one may not need all the information in the output, here are some important observations to gain in this example.

- Presolve: number of variables and constraints reduced, and the time spent
- Key CPLEX settings: the optimality and feasibility setting to balance the quality of feasible solution and the ability to prove optimality
- Number of cores used in the branch-and-bound and branch-and-cut search
- In the CPLEX log part: Best Integer is the objective value of the best feasible solution found (indicated by * at certain iteration ItCnt), Best Bound is the best possible objective value of the linear relaxation of the original model, Gap is the % of difference between the best objective value found and the best bound. A zero gap indicates optimality is proved. Note that CPLEX may find an optimal solution early, but spend significant more time to prove optimality, especially for large and/or complex integer programming models.

```
Version identifier: 12.10.0.0 | 2019-11-26 | 843d4de2ae
Found incumbent of value 0.000000 after 0.06 sec. (0.00 ticks)
Tried aggregator 1 time.
MIP Presolve eliminated 3 rows and 0 columns.
MIP Presolve modified 2 coefficients.
Reduced MIP has 2 rows, 3 columns, and 6 nonzeros.
Reduced MIP has 0 binaries, 3 generals, 0 SOSs, and 0 indicators.
Presolve time = 0.11 sec. (0.01 ticks)
Tried aggregator 1 time.
Reduced MIP has 2 rows, 3 columns, and 6 nonzeros.
Reduced MIP has 0 binaries, 3 generals, 0 SOSs, and 0 indicators.
Presolve time = 0.00 sec. (0.00 ticks)
MIP emphasis: balance optimality and feasibility.
MIP search method: dynamic search.
Parallel mode: deterministic, using up to 4 threads.
Root relaxation solution time = 0.00 sec. (0.00 ticks)

        Nodes                                         Cuts/
   Node  Left     Objective  IInf  Best Integer    Best Bound    ItCnt     Gap

*     0+    0                         0.0000     34600.0000              ---
*     0     0      integral     0    17000.0000    17000.0000        3    0.00%
Elapsed time = 0.34 sec. (0.02 ticks, tree = 0.00 MB, solutions = 2)

Root node processing (before b&c):
  Real time             =    0.36 sec. (0.02 ticks)
Parallel b&c, 4 threads:
  Real time             =    0.00 sec. (0.00 ticks)
  Sync time (average)   =    0.00 sec.
  Wait time (average)   =    0.00 sec.
                          ------------
Total (root+branch&cut) =    0.36 sec. (0.02 ticks)
```

The Engine Log not only provides useful information about the solution process in terms of solution quality and computational time, it also sheds lights on the need (if any) to fine-tune the solver parameter settings. The reader is recommended to study the Solver Manuals and tutorials on how to fine-tune the parameter settings to improve the performance.

A1.4.3 *Transportation Problem*

Consider the transportation problem in Section 2.5.3, with the algebraic formulation of its LP model below.

Sets

S: set of supply nodes
T: set of demand nodes

Parameters

d_j: demand at demand node $j \in T$
k_i: capacity at supply node $i \in S$
c_{ij}: transportation cost per unit shipped from supply node $i \in S$ to demand node $j \in T$

Decision variables

$x_{ij} \geq 0$: units of goods shipped from $i \in S$ to $j \in T$

Objective function

$$\text{minimize} \sum_{i \in S} \sum_{i \in T} c_{ij} x_{ij}$$

<u>Constraints</u>

$$\sum_{i\in S} x_{ij} \geq d_j \quad \forall j \in T$$

$$\sum_{i\in T} x_{ij} \geq k_i \quad \forall j \in S$$

$$x_{ij} \geq 0 \qquad \forall i \in S, j \in T$$

The OPL code in the *.mod file is below:

```
int numSources = ...;
int numCustomers = ...;

range Sources = 1..numSources;
range Customers = 1..numCustomers;
```

```
float demand[Customers] = ...;
float supply[Sources] = ...;
float c[Sources][Customers] = ...;
```

```
dvar float+ x[Sources][Customers];
```

```
minimize sum(i in Sources, j in Customers)c[i][j] * x[i][j];
```

```
subject to {
  MeetingDemand:
      forall (j in Customers)
        sum(i in Sources)x[i][j] >= demand[j];

  NotExceedingSupply:
      forall (i in Sources)
        sum(j in Customers)x[i][j] <= supply[i];
}
```

The corresponding *.dat file is below.

```
numSources = 3;
numCustomers = 4;

demand = [80, 65, 70, 85];
supply = [75, 125, 100];

c = [
[464, 513, 654, 867],
[352, 416, 690, 791],
[995, 682, 388, 685]
];
```

A1.5 Examples of Network Optimization

Pure network optimization problems that can be modeled as NETFORMs have a generic and unique structure that is amenable to be implemented in OPL Studio. We focus on the generic LP formulation of a NETFORM model presented in Section 4.4, and present its corresponding OPL code.

<u>Sets</u>

V: set of all nodes
S: set of supply nodes
D: set of demand nodes
A: set of arcs, with $(i, j) \in A$ representing arc (i, j)

<u>Parameters</u>

c_{ij}: cost of flow per unit of goods on arc (i, j), i.e. from node i to node j
s_j: supply capacity of node $i \in S$
d_i: demand of node $i \in D$ (need $d_i \leq 0$)
k_{ij}: maximum flow capacity on arc (i, j)
l_{ij}: minimum flow on arc (i, j)

Decision variable

$x_{ij} \geq 0$ as the flow from node i to j

Objective function

Minimize Total Cost $= \sum_{(i,j)\in A} c_{ij}x_{ij}$

Constraints

$$
\begin{array}{ll}
\sum_{j:(i,j)\in A} x_{ij} = s_i; & \forall i \in S \\
\sum_{j:(i,j)\in A} x_{ij} = d_i; & \forall i \in D \\
\sum_{j:(i,j)\in A} x_{ij} - \sum_{j:(j,i)\in A} x_{ji} = 0; & \forall i \in V \backslash S \backslash D \\
x_{ij} \leq k_{ij}, & \forall (i,j) \in A \\
x_{ij} \geq l_{ij}, & \forall (i,j) \in A \\
x_{ij} \geq 0 &
\end{array}
$$

Note that most of the input data are associated with an arc, including the unit transportation cost, upper and lower bounds of flow on the arc, and the node indexes identifying the arc. To efficiently represent and organize such structured data, we introduce a new approach in OPL using the *tuple* keyword. For a NETFORM model, one may define a structure of parameters (data) for an arc in the following way:

```
tuple arc {
   key int fromnode;
   key int tonode;
   float cost;
   float lb;
   float ub;
}

{arc} Arcs = ...;
```

It defines a tuple (structure) called "arc" with five fields: a pair of node indexes ("fromnode" and "tonode") to identify the arc, unit transportation cost called "cost", and "ub" and "lb" for the upper and lower bound of flow on the arc, respectively. Then the last line of the above code defines a set of "arc" tuples called "Arcs", for which the data is to provided in the *.dat file.

The complete OPL code in the *.mod file is below.

```
int NumNodes = ...; // Number of nodes
range Nodes = 1..NumNodes;
```

```
tuple arc {
   key int fromnode;
   key int tonode;
   float cost;
   float lb;
   float ub;
}

{arc} Arcs = ...;

int SupDem[Nodes] = ...;
```

```
dvar float+ Flow[a in Arcs] in a.lb..a.ub;
```

The above one line of code efficiently defines the flow decision variable x_{ij} on an arc (i, j) with its lower bound "lb" and upper bound "ub". Note that the two keywords *in* have different meanings and serve different roles. [a in Arcs] identifies "a" as a member in the arc set called "Arcs", while in a.lb..a.ub specifies the lower and upper bounds of the decision variable. Note the use of "." to retrieve a field in a tuple.

```
dexpr float TotalFlow = sum (a in Arcs) a.cost * Flow[a];
minimize TotalFlowCost;
```

The statement *dexpr float* TotalFlowCost defines a mathematical expression called "TotalFlowCost", which is minimized as the objective function in the next line. The use of *dexpr* is often helpful to track or compute an expression (function) of decision variables in the model.

```
subject to {
   forall (i in Nodes)
     ctFlowConservation:
      sum (<i,j,c,lb,ub> in Arcs) Flow[<i,j,c,lb,ub>]
   - sum (<j,i,c,lb,ub> in Arcs) Flow[<j,i,c,lb,ub>] == SupDem[i];
}
```

The three forms of flow conservation constraints, i.e., for the supply nodes, demand node, and the transshipment nodes, can be efficiently expressed by just one generic constraint as shown above in OPL. Note the use of identifier $<$ `i,j,c,lb,ub` $>$ to index each member in the set Arcs.

It is often helpful to add some script code at the end of the *.mod file to print the optima solution in a customized way. For instance, the follow block of script prints only non-zero flow of an arc with the corresponding nodes of the arc. Note that the syntax of OPL scripts is similar to but differs slightly from the OPL code.

```
execute DISPLAY {
   writeln("\n<from node,to node,Flow[a]>\n");
   for(var a in Arcs)
      if(Flow[a] > 0)
         writeln("<",a.fromnode,",",a.tonode,",",Flow[a],">");
}
```

Next, we show two examples to demonstrate how the same OPL *.mod file can be applied for different pure network optimization problems modeled as NETFORM, with properly prepared input data (in the corresponding *.dat file) tailored to the problem at hand.

A1.5.1 *Minimum Cost Flow Problem*

Consider Example 4.1 in Section 4.3 with the following NETFORM model diagram. Note that the node indexes are re-numbered in a generic way to facilitate the implementation in OPL Studio.

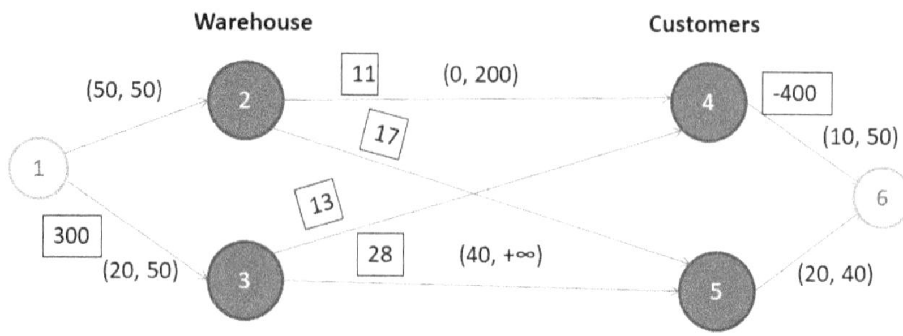

Note that there is no definite amount of supply into the dummy supply node (Node 1), nor definite amount of demand out of the dummy demand node (Node 6). Thus, there is no need for any constraint associated with the two dummy nodes. A minor change in the *forall* statement of the constraint code is needed to limit the constraint for only the non-dummy nodes.

```
subject to {
   forall (i in Nodes: i > 1 && i < card(Nodes))
     ctFlowConservation:
      sum (<i,j,c,lb,ub> in Arcs) Flow[<i,j,c,lb,ub>]
   - sum (<j,i,c,lb,ub> in Arcs) Flow[<j,i,c,lb,ub>] == SupDem[i];
}
```

The statement forall (`i` in `Nodes`: $i > 1$ && i < card(Nodes)) limits the scope of the constraint for non-dummy nodes with indexes $2, 3, \ldots,$ and card(Nodes) — 1, where card(Nodes) is the cardinality of the set "Nodes". The corresponding *.dat file is provided blow.

```
NumNodes = 6;

Arcs = {
   <1, 2, 0, 50, 50>,
   <1, 3, 300, 20, 50>,
   <2, 4, 11, 0, 200>,
   <2, 5, 17, 0, 10000>,
   <3, 4, 13, 0, 10000>,
   <3, 5, 28, 40, 10000>,
   <4, 6, -400, 10, 50>,
   <5, 6, 0, 20, 40>
};

SupDem = [0, 0, 0, 0, 0, 0];
```

The following output is obtained in the Scripting log tab of the Output Window. The negative objective function value indicates a maximum profit of 6,330.

```
// solution (optimal) with objective -6330
<from node, to node, Flow[a]>
<1,2,50>
<1,3,40>
<2,4,50>
<3,5,40>
<4,6,50>
<5,6,40>
```

A1.5.2 *Shortest Path Problem*

Consider the shortest path problem presented in Section 4.5.3, and the following NETFORM diagram as an example. Recall that the shortest path problem is a special case of the minimum cost flow problem by fixing both supply of the source node and demand of the destination node to be one. The lower and upper bound of flow on an arc are 0 and 1, respectively.

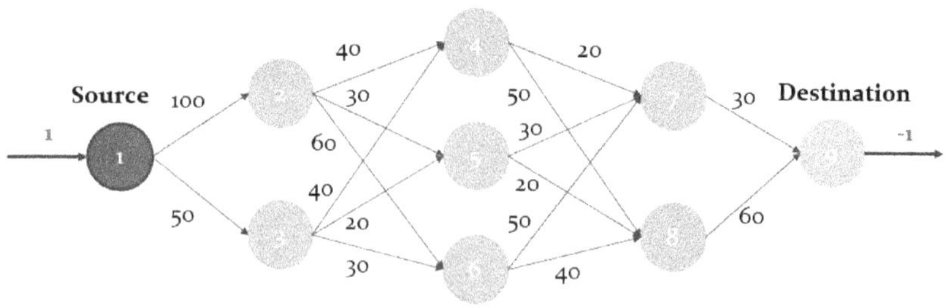

The corresponding *.dat file is:

```
NumNodes = 9;

Arcs = {
<1, 2, 100, 0, 1>,
<1, 3, 50, 0, 1>,
<2, 4, 40, 0, 1>,
<2, 5, 30, 0, 1>,
<2, 6, 60, 0, 1>,
<3, 4, 40, 0, 1>,
<3, 5, 20, 0, 1>,
<3, 6, 30, 0, 1>,
<4, 7, 20, 0, 1>,
<4, 8, 50, 0, 1>,
<5, 7, 30, 0, 1>,
<5, 8, 20, 0, 1>,
<6, 7, 50, 0, 1>,
<6, 8, 40, 0, 1>,
<7, 9, 30, 0, 1>,
<8, 9, 60, 0, 1>
};

SupDem = [1, 0, 0, 0, 0, 0, 0, 0, -1];
```

The following output is generated in the Scripting log tab of the Output Window, which make it easy to identify the optimal shortest path: 1→3→5→7→9 with the shortest distance of 130.

```
<from node, to node, Flow[a]>

<1,3,1>
<3,5,1>
<5,7,1>
<7,9,1>
```

A1.6 Examples of Constraint Programming Models

OPL provides powerful constructs to express constraint programming (CP) models in a compact and expressive way.

A1.6.1 *Send More Money*

We start with a simple example of the Send More Money riddle presented in Section 6.1. While the constraint is explicitly given, one needs to infer the domain of each variable: all can take integers in the range $[0, 9]$, except S and M which can only take integers in the range $[1, 9]$ as they appear in the first digit of a number. The OPL code for its CP model is below. The statement using CP specifies the choice of CP solver.

```
dvar int S in 1..9;
dvar int M in 1..9;
dvar int E in 0..9;
dvar int N in 0..9;
dvar int D in 0..9;
dvar int O in 0..9;
dvar int R in 0..9;
dvar int Y in 0..9;

using CP;

subject to {
              1000*S + 100*E + 10*N + D
  +           1000*M + 100*O + 10*R + E
  == 10000*M + 1000*O + 100*N + 10*E + Y;
}
```

A1.6.2 *N-Queen Problem*

The N-Queen problem of Example 6.2 in Section 6.1 demonstrates the use of unconventional relational operators, such as != (not equal) for efficiently expressing the constraints.

```
int numQueens = ...;
range QueenRange = 1..numQueens;

dvar int queens[QueenRange] in 1..numQueens;

using CP;

subject to {

   forall (i in QueenRange, j in QueenRange: i < j) {

      queens[i] != queens[j];
      queens[i] + i != queens[j] + j;
      queens[j] + i != queens[i] + j;
   }
}
```

A1.6.3 *Magic Series*

The Magic Series problem of Example 6.3 in Section 6.1 demonstrates the use of high-order constraints, i.e., complex constraints that embed logical tests, which is usually not available in mathematical programming.

```
int n = ...;
range Range = 0..n-1;

using CP;

dvar int s[Range] in 0..n;

subject to {
   forall (i in Range)
      s[i] == sum(j in Range) (s[j]==i);
}
```

A1.6.4 *Project Scheduling*

OPL provides special constructs to model various scheduling problems, which makes the model descriptive, compact and easy to read. A job, task or activity in a scheduling problem can be declared as an *interval* in OPL in a generic way:

dvar interval activityName *size p*;

Specifically, it defines an interval variable called "activityName" with duration (processing time) of p time units. The start time of an interval can be conveniently expressed as: *startOf*(activityName), and in a similar way for the finish time: *endOf*(activityName).

OPL provides a comprehensive suite of functions to express various temporal relationships among tasks. Let a and b be two interval variables with durations p_a and p_b, respectively; and S_a and S_b denote the start time (decision variable) of intervals a and b, respectively. A constant time lag $\delta \geq 0$ can be considered in these temporal constraints. Table A1.2 lists the functions for modeling temporal constraints with illustrations. The default value of δ is zero if it is provided.

Table A1.2. OPL functions for temporal constraints.

Functions	Meaning	Illustration
startBeforeStart (**a**, **b**, $\boldsymbol{\delta}$)	$S_a + \delta \leq S_b$	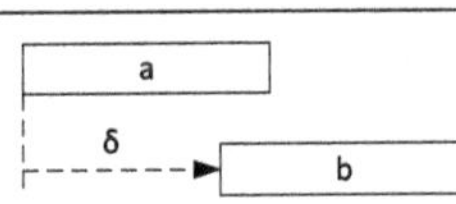
startBeforeEnd (**a**, **b**, $\boldsymbol{\delta}$)	$S_a + \delta \leq S_b + p_b$	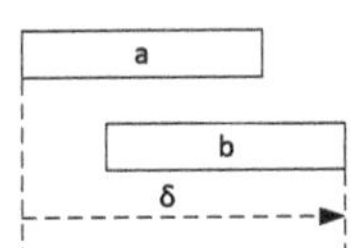
endBeforeStart (**a**, **b**, $\boldsymbol{\delta}$)	$S_a + p_a + \delta \leq S_b$	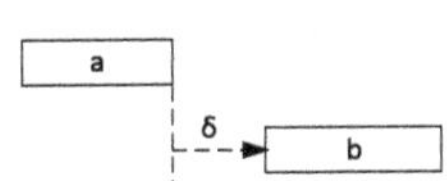
endBeforeStart (**a**, **b**, $\boldsymbol{\delta}$)	$S_a + p_a + \delta \leq S_b + p_b$	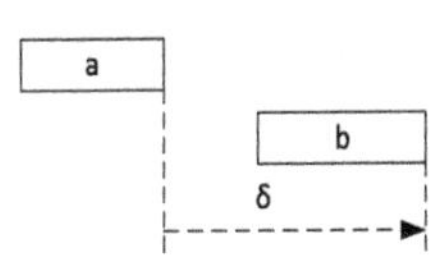

The most popular type of temporal relationship, i.e., precedence constraint, is just a special case of the above. For instance, *startBeforeStart* (a, b, δ) reduces to the precedence constraint between a and b, i.e., a precedes b, when δ equals p_a (the duration of a). Or alternatively, *endBeforeStart* (a, b, δ) is equivalent to requiring a precedes b when $\delta = 0$.

Consider the construction project scheduling problem of Example 6.4 in Section 6.3.1. We first present a *.mod file that combines model with data. The function *maxl* (x, y) take the maximum between x and y.

```
using CP;

dvar interval masonry size 35;
dvar interval carpentry size 15;
dvar interval plumbing size 40;
dvar interval ceiling size 15;
dvar interval roofing    size 5;
dvar interval painting   size 10;
dvar interval windows    size 5;
dvar interval facade     size 10;
dvar interval garden     size 5;
dvar interval moving     size 5;
minimize 200 * maxl (25 - startOf (masonry), 0) +
         300 * maxl (75 - startOf (carpentry), 0) +
         100 * maxl (75 - startOf (ceiling), 0) +
         400 * maxl (endOf (moving) - 100, 0);

subject to {
  endBeforeStart (masonry, carpentry);
  endBeforeStart (masonry, plumbing);
  endBeforeStart(masonry, ceiling);
  endBeforeStart(carpentry, roofing);
  endBeforeStart(ceiling, painting);
  endBeforeStart(roofing, windows);
  endBeforeStart(roofing, facade);
  endBeforeStart(plumbing, facade);
  endBeforeStart(roofing, garden);
```

```
    endBeforeStart(plumbing, garden);
    endBeforeStart(windows, moving);
    endBeforeStart(facade, moving);
    endBeforeStart(garden, moving);
    endBeforeStart(painting, moving);
}
```

The above code is descriptive and easy to read, but requires enumerating every precedence constraint. Next we present more efficient way to use *tuple* for organizing all the input data, which is separated from the model. The *.mod file is below. The tuple called "Task" has seven fields, with the first field being the *key*, which can be used as a unique identifier of a member in a set. Note that the last field is a set of integers called "succ", representing the set of indexes of the immediate successors of the task.

```
using CP;

tuple Task {
   key int id;        //task index
   int duration;      //task duration
   int release;       //earliest start time
   int duedate;       //latest finish time
   float costearly;   //penalty cost per day starting early
   float costlate;    //penalty cost per day finishing late
   {int} succ;        //set of immediate successors
};

{Task} Tasks = ...;

dvar interval task [t in Tasks] size t.duration;

minimize sum (t in Tasks) t.costearly*maxl(t.release -
         startOf(task[t]), 0) +
         sum (t in Tasks) t.costlate*maxl(endOf(task[t])-
         t.duedate, 0);

subject to {
  forall (t1 in Tasks, t2id in t1.succ)
     endBeforeStart(task[t1], task[<t2id>]);
};
```

The corresponding *.dat file is below.

```
Tasks = {
        <1, 35, 25, 1000, 200, 0, {2, 3, 4}>,
        <2, 15, 75, 1000, 300, 0, {5} >,
        <3, 40, 0, 1000, 0, 0, {8, 9}>,
        <4, 15, 75, 1000, 100, 0, {6}>,
        <5, 5, 0, 1000, 0, 0, {7, 8, 9}>,
        <6, 10, 0, 1000, 0, 0, {10}>,
        <7, 5, 0, 1000, 0, 0, {10}>,
        <8, 10, 0, 1000, 0, 0, {10}>,
        <9, 5, 0, 1000, 0, 0, {10}>,
        <10, 5, 0, 100, 0, 400, {}>
};
```

A1.6.5 *Job Shop Scheduling*

In addition to the precedence (and general temporal) constraints, more complex scheduling problems often have resource constraints to be handled. Resources can be classified to two general classes: *unary* resource and *cumulative* resource. A unary resource has *one* unit available during the scheduling horizon, such that no job processed by the resource can overlap. Most machine scheduling problems involve unary resources, as a machine can typically process only one job at a time.

Consider the job shop scheduling problem presented in Section 11.4.2 with the following example of six jobs and six machines. Each row represents a job, and each column represents the (ordered) operations in the corresponding job. Each entry in the matrix $a(b)$ means the index of machine required is a, and the corresponding processing time is b (minutes). For instance, the 5-th operation in Job 1 requires Machine 0 and takes 1 minute.

	Operation 1	**Operation 2**	**Operation 3**	**Operation 4**	**Operation 5**	**Operation 6**
Job 1	5(4)	1(3)	4(3)	3(2)	0(1)	2(2)
Job 2	1(3)	0(8)	5(7)	2(2)	4(9)	3(3)
Job 3	3(1)	4(9)	1(9)	0(7)	5(5)	2(5)
Job 4	3(8)	4(2)	1(1)	5(7)	2(8)	0(9)
Job 5	1(6)	3(2)	4(5)	5(5)	0(3)	2(1)
Job 6	4(10)	2(4)	0(4)	3(3)	1(2)	5(3)

Since no jobs can overlap on a machine, all the operations must be properly sequenced on it. OPL has readily available constructs to model such constraints. One may define a *sequence* decision variable for each machine with its domain being the index of operations associated with the machine. The first step is to define a two-dimensional array of interval variables over all the job-operation pairs, with "Jobs" and "Mchs" being pre-defined set of jobs and operations, and "Ops" being the processing time of the corresponding job-operation pair.

```
dvar interval itvs[j in Jobs][o in Mchs] size Ops[j][o].pt;
```

Next, the sequence decision variables can be defined with their proper domains. The following code defines an array of *sequence* decision variables called "mchs" for each machine, with the intervals processed on the machine being the domain.

```
dvar sequence mchs[m in Mchs] in all(j in Jobs, o in Mchs :
Ops[j][o].mch == m) itvs[j][o];
```

Then one constraint we need for the model is to ensure no jobs may overlap for each sequence decision variable using the *noOverlap* function.

```
forall (m in Mchs)
   noOverlap(mchs[m]);
```

The complete OPL code in the *.mod file is below. The set "Mchs" is used to both index the machines and to represent the order of operations of a job. The *tuple* "Operation" does not include any precedence information because it is already implicitly considered via the operation index. That is, the $(o-1)$-th operation always precedes the o-th operation. It is important to note that the "Ops" data should be defined and organized as an *array* (two-dimensional) instead of a *set* (as in the project scheduling example in the previous section), because the order of operations (columns) matters here.

One may use OPL scripts to change/control the parameter setting of the CP algorithm to solve the model. For example, the script in the middle limits the maximum number of fails during the CP search to be 10,000. Appendix 4 provides a primer in the CP solution methods. The block of scripts at the end prints the solution in customized way, i.e., the start time of each operation of all the jobs.

```
using CP;

int nbJobs = ...;
int nbMchs = ...;

range Jobs = 0..nbJobs-1;
range Mchs = 0..nbMchs-1;

tuple Operation {
  int mch; // Machine
  int pt; // Processing time
};

Operation Ops[j in Jobs][m in Mchs] = ...;

dvar interval itvs[j in Jobs][o in Mchs] size Ops[j][o].pt;
dvar sequence mchs[m in Mchs] in all(j in Jobs, o in Mchs :
Ops[j][o].mch == m) itvs[j][o];

execute {
       cp.param.FailLimit = 10000;
}

minimize max(j in Jobs) endOf(itvs[j][nbMchs-1]);

subject to {

  forall (m in Mchs)
    noOverlap(mchs[m]);

  forall (j in Jobs, o in 0..nbMchs-2)
    endBeforeStart(itvs[j][o], itvs[j][o+1]);
}

execute {
  for (var j = 0; j <= nbJobs-1; j++) {
    for (var o = 0; o <= nbMchs-1; o++) {
      write(itvs[j][o].start + " ");
    }
    writeln("");
  }
}
```

The corresponding *.dat file associated with the above *.mod file is below.

```
nbJobs = 6;
nbMchs = 6;

Ops = [
  [ <5,4>, <1,3>, <4,3>, <3,2>, <0,1>, <2,2> ],
  [ <1,3>, <0,8>, <5,7>, <2,2>, <4,9>, <3,3> ],
  [ <3,1>, <4,9>, <1,9>, <0,7>, <5,5>, <2,5> ],
  [ <3,8>, <4,2>, <1,1>, <5,7>, <2,8>, <0,9> ],
  [ <1,6>, <3,2>, <4,5>, <5,5>, <0,3>, <2,1> ],
  [ <4,10>, <2,4>, <0,4>, <3,3>, <1,2>, <5,3>]
];
```

A1.6.6 *Resource-Constrained Project Scheduling*

Consider the resource-constrained project scheduling problem presented in Section 12.4, where a *cumulative* resource may process multiple jobs at a time as long as its maximum capacity is not exceeded. Cumulative resource is also involved in a special class of machine scheduling problem called flexible machine scheduling, where each machine can process multiple jobs simultaneously.

The key is to define a resource profile, using the function *cumulFunction*, which computes the resource usage during the scheduling horizon. The *pulse* function can be used to track the resource usage of an activity at time points depending on whether the activity is active or not. The following code

```
cumulFunction rsrcProfile[r in Resources] =
  sum (t in Tasks: t.dmds[r]> 0) pulse(itvs[t], t.dmds[r]);
```

defines a *cumulFunction* called "rsrcProfile" over the "Resources" set, which is computed as the summation of resource usage of all the active activities at each time point of the scheduling horizon, tracked by the *pulse* function. This one statement effectively computes the left-hand-side of Constraint (12.18) in the time-indexed integer programming formulation in Section 12.4.1.

Then one may simply enforce the resource profile to not exceed the available capacity of each resource as follows:

```
forall (r in Resources)
    rsrcProfile[r] < = Capacity[r];
```

The complete OPL code in the *.mod file is below. Note that the *tuple* called Task includes an array for the resource requirement of the task, and a set of integers representing the index of the task's successors.

```
using CP;

int NbTasks = ...;
int NbRsrcs = ...;

range Resources = 0..NbRsrcs-1;

int Capacity[r in Resources] = ...;

tuple Task {
  key int id;
  int     pt;
  int     dmds[Resources];
  {int}   succs;
}

{Task} Tasks = ...;

dvar interval itvs[t in Tasks] size t.pt;

cumulFunction rsrcProfile[r in Resources] =
  sum (t in Tasks: t.dmds[r]>0) pulse(itvs[t], t.dmds[r]);

execute {
  cp.param.FailLimit = 30000;
}
```

```
minimize max(t in Tasks) endOf(itvs[t]);

subject to {
  forall (r in Resources)
    rsrcProfile[r] <= Capacity[r];

  forall (t1 in Tasks, t2id in t1.succs)
    endBeforeStart(itvs[t1], itvs[<t2id>]);
}

execute {
  for (var t in Tasks) {
    writeln("Task " + t.id + " starts at " +
itvs[t].start);
  }
}
```

The corresponding *.dat file of the example in Figure 12.2 in Section 12.4 is below.

```
NbTasks = 6;
NbRsrcs = 1;

Capacity = [ 4 ];

Tasks = {
  < 1, 2, [ 3 ], { 4 } >,
  < 2, 3, [ 1 ], { 4, 5 } >,
  < 3, 1, [ 2 ], { 5 } >,
  < 4, 4, [ 2 ], { 6 } >,
  < 5, 2, [ 3 ], { } >,
  < 6, 1, [ 3 ], { } >
  };
```

Appendix 2 Simplex Method for Linear Programming

A2.1 Graph Method for Two-Variable LP

We start with a simple LP model with only two decision variables, which can be conveniently handled by the graph method: iso-profit line method for a maximization model, and iso-cost line method for a minimization one. Grasping the graph method will shed lights on understanding the general Simplex Method.

The iso-profit line method for a maximization problem includes the following five steps. The iso-cost line method for a minimization problem is the same except that in Step 4, the moving direction should reduce the objective value.

Step 1: Plot the straight line associated with each constraint. If the constraint is an inequality, identify one side of the line that satisfies the inequality.

Step 2: Identify the feasible region, i.e., the polygon, that satisfies all the constraints by locating all the feasible corner points.

Step 3: Pick an initial (feasible) objective value and plot its corresponding straight line.

Step 4: Move the initial objective function line to the direction that improves (increases) the objective value as much as possible, until reaching a corner point where no more improvement can be made (without going outside of the feasible region).

Step 5: Solve a system of two equations to find the solution (coordinate) for the optimal corner point found in Step 4.

We will use the product-mix problem in Example 2.4 of Section 2.3 to demonstrate the iso-profit line method. Recall that its extended LP formulation is below.

$$\text{Maximize } 400x_1 + 800x_2 \tag{A2.1}$$

Subject to:

$$3x_1 + 5x_2 \leq 5,000 \tag{A2.2}$$

$$x_1 + 4x_2 \leq 3{,}000 \tag{A2.3}$$

$$x_1, x_2 \geq 0 \tag{A2.4}$$

Figure A2.1 shows the iso-profit line method. In Step 1, two straight lines are plotted for the boundaries of Constraints (A2.2) and (A2.3). Plug the origin (0,0) to the original constraints to see (0,0) is feasible for both constraints, thus should be within the feasible region. Step 2 identifies the feasible region described by the four feasible corner points OABC. An initial objective value of 320,000 is picked in Step 3 and its corresponding straight (dashed) line is plotted. In Step 4, move the initial objective function line following the direction indicated by the blue arrow to increase the objective value. The series of parallel lines obtained are called "iso-profit lines". Improvement can be achieved by moving the iso-profit lines all the way to the

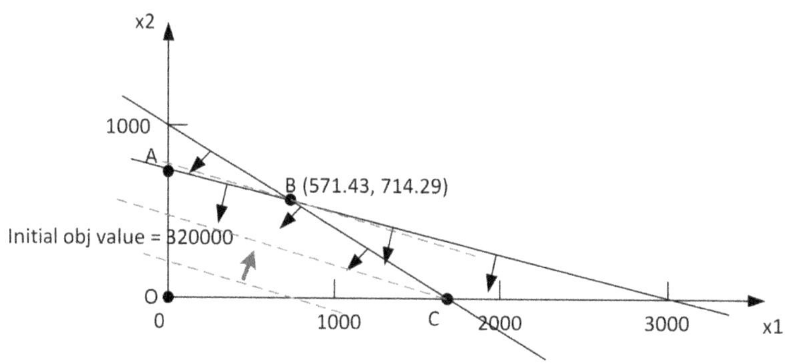

Figure A2.1. Iso-profit line method for Example 2.4.

corner point B, which is the optimal point. Step 5 solves a system of two equations (the two lines associated with the two constraints) to obtain the optimal solution (coordinates of B): $x_1^* = 571.43$, $x_2^* = 714.29$ with a maximum profit of 742,857.14.

A2.2 The Simplex Method

The Simplex Method is an algorithm for solving a general LP model with arbitrary number of decision variables and constraints. The fundamental idea in the graph method, i.e., starting with an initial solution, identifying the right direction to move, and moving to improve the feasible solution, is also the key underlying mechanism of the Simplex Method. The algorithm is an iterative procedure as we now need to search over a multi-dimensional polyhedron, instead of a two-dimensional polygon.

The Simplex Method can be sketched by the flow chart in Figure A2.2. It starts with an initial feasible solution, then iteratively improves it until either an optimal solution is found or the problem is proved to be unbounded.

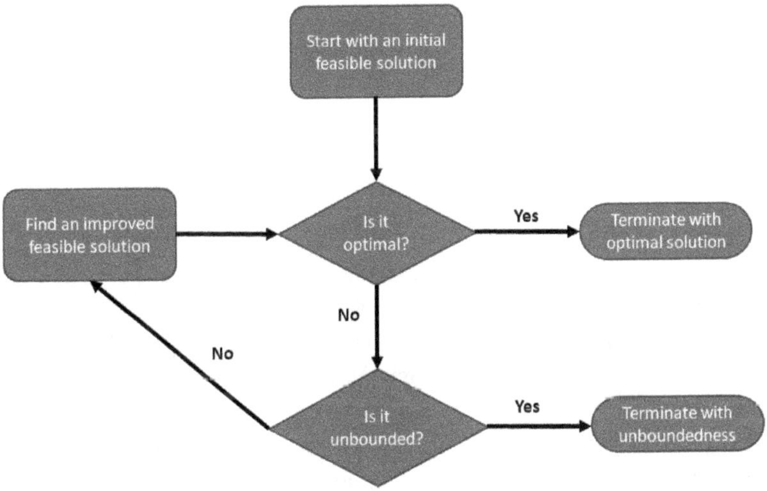

Figure A2.2. Flow chart of the simplex method.

Consider the following general LP model with n decision variables and m constraints:

$$\max \sum_{j=1}^{n} \pi_j x_j$$

Subject to:

$$\sum_{j=1}^{n} a_{ij} x_j \leq b_i, \quad \forall i = 1, 2, \ldots, m$$

$$x_j \geq 0, \quad \forall j = 1, 2, \ldots, n$$

Step 0: Transform the LP to its *canonical* form, which contains only equality constraints with non-negative right-hand side constants, and non-negative decision variables. Introduce non-negative auxiliary (slack) decision variables $x_{n+1}, x_{n+2}, \ldots, x_{n+m}$, for constraint $1, 2, \ldots, m$, to turn the inequalities to equations:

$$\sum_{j=1}^{n} a_{ij} x_j + x_{n+i} = b_i, \quad \forall i = 1, 2, \ldots, m$$

Rearrange terms and introduce a new decision variable ξ to represent the objective function:

$$\xi = \bar{\xi} + \sum_{j=1}^{n} \bar{\pi}_j x_j \tag{A2.5}$$

$$x_{n+i} = \bar{b}_i - \sum_{j=1}^{n} \bar{a}_{ij} x_j, \quad \forall i = 1, 2, \ldots, m \tag{A2.6}$$

The system of equations A2.5 and A2.6 is the initial *dictionary*, which provides a structured framework to identify the *basic variables* (also called dependent variables) on the left, except the ξ variable, and the non-basic variables (independent variables) on the right. The solution obtained by setting the non-basic variables to zero is called *basic feasible solution* (bfs). The Simplex Method iteratively searches the solution space by moving from one dictionary to another to obtain an optimal solution. $\bar{\pi}_j$, $\bar{a}_{ij}$ and $\bar{b}_i$ are used to indicate that their values will change during the solution process.

Step 1: Optimality Test. Let $\mathcal{B}$ and $\mathcal{N}$ denote the set of indexes of basic variables and non-basic variables, respectively. If the coefficients of all the current non-basic variables are non-positive, i.e., $c_j \leq 0$ for all $j \in \mathcal{N}$, the current bfs is optimal, the algorithm terminates with an optimal solution. Otherwise, there exists at least one $c_j > 0$ for $j \in \mathcal{N}$, increasing the value of the corresponding non-basic variable can improve (increase) the objective value, then proceed to Step 2.

Step 2: Picking the entering variable. Exactly one variable moves from non-basic to basic (*entering variable*), and exactly one other variable moves from basic to non-basic (*leaving variable*), which is called *pivoting*. When there are multiple non-basic variable coefficients being positive, one may pick variable k with the largest coefficient, i.e., $k = \text{argmax}_{j \in \mathcal{N}}\{c_j : c_j > 0\}$. Proceed to Step 3.

Step 3: Pivoting. Improvement through the entering variable can be *greedy*, meaning that it is increased as much as possible, on the condition that all the current basic variables maintain non-negative. The leaving variable can be identified using the following *minimum-ratio rule*. As the entering variable x_k increases, the basic variable will decrease until it reaches zero. In other words, we require that: $x_i = \bar{b}_i - \bar{a}_{ik}x_k \geq 0$ for $i \in \mathcal{B}$. Clearly, x_i can only become zero if $\bar{a}_{ik}$ is positive. If all $\bar{a}_{ik}$ are negative or zero, the algorithm terminates with the proof of unboundedness, i.e., x_i can be increased with no limit.

Otherwise, the x_k value that leads x_i to be zero equals $\bar{b}_i/\bar{a}_{ik}$. Because no basic variable can be negative, x_k can only be raised to the smallest of all these values, i.e., $x_k = \min_{i \in \mathcal{B}:\bar{a}_{ik}>0} \bar{b}_i/\bar{a}_{ik}$. Thus, the leaving variable x_l is chosen such that $l = \text{argmin}_{in \in \mathcal{B}:\bar{a}_{ik}>0} \{\bar{b}_i/\bar{a}_{ik}\}$. Proceed to Step 4.

Step 4: Updating the dictionary. Replace the leaving basic variable x_l by the entering non-basic variable x_k via the arithmetic operation of Gaussian elimination, to obtain an updated dictionary. Go to Step 1 of the next iteration.

Next, we use a tableau to facilitate the Simplex Method iterations with a small example to demonstrate how it works. Consider the following LP.

$$\text{Maximize } 4x_1 + 5x_2 + 2x_3$$

Subject to:

$$x_1 + 3x_2 + 2x_3 \leq 6$$
$$4x_1 + 2x_2 + x_3 \leq 12$$
$$3x_1 + 4x_2 + 2x_3 \leq 14$$

Step 0: The initial dictionary in the canonical form. The current bfs is: $x_1 = 0$, $x_2 = 0$ and $x_3 = 0$ with Objective value = 0.

$\xi =$		$+4x_1$	$+5x_2$	$+2x_3$
$x_4 =$	6	$-x_1$	$-3x_2$	$-2x_3$
$x_5 =$	12	$-4x_1$	$-2x_2$	$-x_3$
$x_6 =$	14	$-3x_1$	$-4x_2$	$-2x_3$

Iteration 1: Step 1 — The current bfs is not optimal because there exist positive coefficient in the objective function. Step 2 — Choose x_2 as the entering variable with the largest (positive) coefficient. Step 3 — Using the minimum ratio rule: the increase Δ of $x_2 = min\left\{\frac{6}{3}, \frac{12}{2}, \frac{14}{4}\right\} = \min\{2, 6, 3.5\} = 2$, with x_4 becoming zero (the leaving variable). The objective value increases from 0 to 10 by 10. Step 4 — Gaussian elimination operation to express the new dependent variables x_2, x_5 and x_6 as functions of the new independent variables x_1, x_4 and x_3.

$\xi =$	10	$+7/3x_1$	$-5/3x_4$	$-4/3x_3$
$x_2 =$	2	$-1/3x_1$	$-1/3x_4$	$-2/3x_3$
$x_5 =$	8	$-10/3x_1$	$+2/3x_4$	$+1/3x_3$
$x_6 =$	6	$-5/3x_1$	$+4/3x_4$	$+2/3x_3$

Iteration 2: Step 1 — The current bfs is not optimal because there exist positive coefficient of the non-basic variables. Step 2 — Choose x_1 as the entering variable as it is the only choice. Step 3 — Using the minimum ratio rule: the increase Δ of $x_1 = \min\{6, 2.4, 3.6\} = 2.4$, with x_5 becoming zero (the leaving variable). The objective value

increases from 10 to 15.6 by 5.6. Step 4 — Gaussian elimination operation to express the new dependent variables x_2, x_1 and x_6 as functions of the new independent variables x_5, x_4 and x_3.

$\xi =$	15.6	$-0.7x_5$	$-1.2x_4$	$-1.1x_3$
$x_2 =$	1.2	$+0.1x_5$	$-0.4x_4$	$-0.7x_3$
$x_1 =$	2.4	$-0.3x_5$	$+0.2x_4$	$+0.1x_3$
$x_6 =$	2	$+0.5x_5$	$+x_4$	$+0.5x_3$

Iteration 3: Step 1 — The current bfs is optimal because all the coefficients of the non-basic variables are negative. Terminate with optimal solution found: $x_1^* = 2.4$, $x_2^* = 1.2$, and $x_3^* = 0$, with an optimal objective value of 15.6. Note that the procedure also obtains optimal solutions of the slack variables: $x_4^* = 0$, $x_5^* = 0$, and $x_6^* = 2$. They indicate that the first two constraints are binding, and the third constraint has a slack of 2 in the optimal solution.

A2.3 Transformations to the Canonical Form

Several types of transformations are often useful to obtain the initial dictionary in the canonical form.

A2.3.1 *Minimization Problem*

A minimization problem with objective function: Minimize ξ, can be transformed to a maximization problem by Maximize $-\xi$.

A2.3.2 *Converting the $\geq$ Constraint*

For $\geq$ constraints as below, equality can be obtained by subtracting non-negative surplus variables on the left-hand-side.

$$\sum_{j=1}^{n} a_{ij}x_j \geq b_i, \quad \forall i = 1, 2, \ldots, m$$

Introduce non-negative surplus variables $x_{n+1}, x_{n+2}, \ldots, x_{n+m}$ and subtract them on the left-hand-side to get:

$$\sum_{j=1}^{n} a_{ij}x_j - x_{n+i} = b_i, \quad \forall i = 1, 2, \ldots, m$$

A2.3.3 *Converting the Right-hand-side Constant*

In case the right-hand-side of a constraint is negative, we may simply multiply both sides by -1.

Appendix 3 Exact Methods for Integer Programming

A3.1 Introduction

A bounded integer programming model has a finite number of feasible solutions, thus it is tempting to *enumerate* all the feasible solutions and identify the optimal one. However, this naïve enumeration approach only works for tiny toy problems, but is computationally intractable for problems with reasonably large size. For instance, a facility location problem with n candidate locations has 2^n possible network configurations; a machine scheduling problem with n jobs has $n!$ possible job sequences; and a TSP problem with n nodes has $n!$ possible routes. These problems are all *combinatorial* in nature, whose solution space grows rapidly with the problem size. Even for a well-designed exact algorithm seeking to find optimal solutions, it can be proved that the number of steps required grows following a non-polynomial function of the problem size, which is known as *NP-hard*.

Many combinatorial optimization (integer programming) problems presented in this text are NP-hard, including the set-covering, set-packing, set-partitioning, GAP and bin-packing problems in Chapter 3, facility location problems in Chapter 7, the MPS, MRP and MRP II in Chapter 8, the SCCP in Chapter 10, machine scheduling problem in Chapter 11, the RCPSPs in Chapter 12, the TSPs in Chapter 12, and the VRPs in Chapter 14.

An intelligent algorithmic strategy is needed for finding optimal solutions to NP-hard combinatorial optimization problems efficiently. Recall that the pure network flow models automatically guarantee integer solutions due to the unimodularity property of the LP formulation in Section 4.3. This means that solving a pure network flow problem with integral requirement of the flow decision variables is equivalent to solving its LP formulation *without* the integral requirement. This is good news, but it only applies for problems/models with the pure network structure.

Nevertheless, the above observation sheds lights on a general solution strategy to solve the *LP relaxation* of an integer programming model. One may not expect to obtain an optimal (feasible) integer solution in one round, but will need an iterative procedure, called *branch-and-bound*, to systematically search the solution space to find an optimal solution and prove optimality.

A3.2 Linear Programming Relaxation

We first provide a geometric interpretation for the feasible region of an integer programming model. Consider the following integer programing model:

$$\min \{\boldsymbol{c}^T\boldsymbol{x} : \boldsymbol{x} \in S\}, \quad \text{(IP)} \tag{A3.1}$$

where $\boldsymbol{x}$ is a (column) vector of n integer decision variables, $\boldsymbol{c}$ is a (column) vector of coefficients, and S is the feasible region of $\boldsymbol{x}$ described by the following constraints:

$$S = \{\boldsymbol{x} \in \mathbb{Z}^n : \boldsymbol{A}x \geq \boldsymbol{b},\ \boldsymbol{x} \geq \boldsymbol{0}\}, \tag{A3.2}$$

where $\boldsymbol{A}$ is an $m \times n$ matrix, $\boldsymbol{b}$ is a n-vector. S can be re-written as:

$$S = \mathbb{Z}^n \cap P = \{\boldsymbol{x} \in \mathbb{R}^n, \boldsymbol{A}x \geq \boldsymbol{b},\ \boldsymbol{x} \geq \boldsymbol{0}\}, \tag{A3.3}$$

where P is the polyhedron of the feasible region with the integral requirement relaxed. Thus, the linear programming relaxation (LPR) of the original model IP is:

$$\min\{\boldsymbol{c}^T\boldsymbol{x} : \boldsymbol{x} \in P\}, \quad \text{(LPR)} \tag{A3.4}$$

Since $P \subset S$, any feasible solution for IP must be feasible to LPR, thus the optimum objective value of LPR is a lower bound of the optimum objective value of IP.

A3.3 Branch-and-Bound Method

The branch-and-bound method relies on two key concepts, namely, *branch* and *bound*. Branching is a technique to deal with any decision variable with fractional values in the optimal solution to the LP relaxation of the original integer programming model. Recall that if all the decision variables have integral values, the optimal solution to LP relaxation is optimal to the original model, thus working with fractional values in the LP relaxation solution is the main task for solving an integer programming model. In general, suppose a decision variable in the LP relaxation solution $x = a$, where a is a fractional number. Then two sub-problems can be created, each of which includes all the constraints in the original model plus one of the two constraints: $x \leq \lfloor a \rfloor$ and $x \geq \lceil a \rceil$, where $\lfloor \bullet \rfloor$ and $\lceil \bullet \rceil$ are *floor* and *ceiling* functions, respectively. Two *branches* are thus created correspondingly.

Let Z^* and $\bar{Z}$ denote the optimal objective value of an integer programming model $\mathcal{P}$, and the optimal objective value of its LP relaxation $\mathcal{P}'$, respectively. Since $\mathcal{P}'$ has larger solution space than $\mathcal{P}$, any feasible solution to $\mathcal{P}$ must be feasible to $\mathcal{P}'$. Therefore, for a minimization problem, $\bar{Z}$ is no larger than Z^*, i.e., $\bar{Z} \leq Z^*$; and for a maximization problem, $\bar{Z}$ is no smaller than Z^*, i.e., $\bar{Z} \geq Z^*$. In this way, $\bar{Z}$ provides a *bound* on Z^*: a lower bound for a minimization problem, or an upper bound for a maximization problem. For convenience, we shall describe the branch-and-bound method assuming a maximization problem.

Having bounds on the optima objective value available makes it possible to *prune* a sub-problem, which may significantly reduce the search space and computational effort. Let $\underline{Z}$ be the current best feasible solution, called *incumbent*, to the original (maximization) problem $\mathcal{P}$. Since $\underline{Z}$ is not necessarily optimal, we have $\underline{Z} \leq Z^*$, thus $\underline{Z}$ is a lower bound of Z^*. Clearly, the relationship $\underline{Z} \leq Z^* \leq \bar{Z}$ holds.

Suppose the optimal objective value $\bar{Z}$ of the LP relaxation of a sub-problem is no greater than the incumbent $\underline{Z}$, then we know that further branching from this sub-problem will *never* generate a solution that improves the incumbent. Thus, this sub-problem can be pruned. Other conditions under which a sub-problem can be pruned include: it is infeasible, or, all the integral decision variables in the optimal solution have integral values.

The branch-and-bound method is a general divide-and-conquer approach that iteratively solve LP relaxations of a sub-problem, which are easier to handle. It can also be viewed as an implicit enumeration method to search the solution space in a systematic and more intelligent way than the naïve enumeration. Its procedure can be conceptually described as follows.

Step 0: Initialization and solve the root problem. Set the incumbent $\underline{Z} = -\infty$ and upper bound of the original problem $\bar{Z}^0 = +\infty$. Solve the LP relaxation of the original problem, i.e., the *root problem* (indexed by 0). If there is no feasible solution, terminate: the original problem is infeasible. Else if an optimal solution is found with integral decision variables having integer values, terminate: the optimal solution to the root problem is an optimal solution to the original problem. Otherwise, update $\bar{Z}^0$ and proceed to Step 1.

Step 1: Main iterations.

1.1 Branching: Among the remaining sub-problems, select one according to certain rule, e.g., the one has the largest upper bound. Then select an integral decision variable with fractional value to be the branching variable. Let x_j be the branching variable with fractional value a. Branch from the sub-problem to create two sub-problems by adding two constraints: $x_j \leq \lfloor a \rfloor$ and $x_j \geq \lceil a \rceil$.
1.2 Bounding: For each new sub-problem i, solve its LP relaxation with objective value $\bar{Z}^i$ being an upper bound of the optimal integer solution to sub-problem i.
1.3 Pruning test: prune the current sub-problem i if one of the following three criteria is met:
    (i) The upper bound of the sub-problem $\bar{Z}^i \leq \underline{Z}$.
    (ii) The LP relaxation of the sub-problem has no feasible solution.
    (iii) The optimal LP relaxation solution to the sub-problem has integer values for all the integral decision variables. It is a

feasible solution to the original problem, and if it is better than the incumbent $\underline{Z}$, update $\underline{Z}$.

1.4 Optimality test: Terminate with an optimal solution if there is no remaining sub-problem, the current incumbent is optimal; Otherwise, perform another iteration.

Some heuristic method can be used to restore feasibility of an optimal solution to a sub-problem with fractional values, which is helpful to improve the incumbent (lower bound). The rules for selecting which sub-problem to branch (branching rule), and that for selecting which decision variable to branch (variable selection rule), are problem-dependent and can be tuned to improve the performance of branch-and-bound.

Next, we use a small example to demonstrate how the branch-and-bound method works. A simple rounding heuristic is employed to obtain a feasible solution from an optimal LP relaxation solution (with fractional values).

$$\text{Maximize } 4x_1 - 3x_2 + 5x_3 - 2x_4$$

Subject to:

$$x_1 + 2x_2 + 3x_3 \leq 12$$
$$2x_1 + x_2 - x_3 \leq 4$$
$$5x_1 - 3x_2 \leq 2$$
$$-x_1 + 2x_3 - 3x_4 \leq 4$$
$$x_1, x_2, x_3, x_4 \geq 0 \text{ and integer}$$

Step 0: Initialize $\underline{Z} = -\infty$ and $\bar{Z}^0 = +\infty$. Solve the LP relaxation of the original problem (root problem) below:

$$\text{Maximize } 4x_1 - 3x_2 + 5x_3 - 2x_4$$

Subject to:

$$x_1 + 2x_2 + 3x_3 \leq 12$$
$$2x_1 + x_2 - x_3 \leq 4$$
$$5x_1 - 3x_2 \leq 2$$
$$-x_1 + 2x_3 - 3x_4 \leq 4$$
$$x_1, x_2, x_3, x_4 \geq 0$$

An optimal solution is found: $x_1 = 0.4$, $x_2 = 0$, $x_3 = 3.87$, $x_4 = 1.11$ with $Z = 18.71$. Update the upper bound $\bar{Z}^0 = 18.71$. Apply the simple rounding heuristic to get feasible solution (to the original problem) $x_1 = 0$, $x_2 = 0$, $x_3 = 3$, $x_4 = 1$ with an objective value of 13, and update $\underline{Z} = 13$. Proceed to Step 1.

Iteration 1:

1.1. Branching: Select x_1 to branch with the following two sub-problems.
Sub-problem 1: original model with $x_1 \leq 0$ added
Sub-problem 2: original model with $x_1 \geq 1$ added
1.2. Bounding: Solve the LP relaxation of Sub-problem 1 to get an optimal solution $x_1 = 0$, $x_2 = 0$, $x_3 = 4$, $x_4 = 1.33$ with $\bar{Z}^1 = 17.33$. Apply the rounding heuristic[a] to obtain a feasible solution $x_1 = 0$, $x_2 = 0$, $x_3 = 4$, $x_4 = 2$ with an objective value of 16, which improves the incumbent $\underline{Z}$ of 13. Thus update $\underline{Z} = 16$.
Solve the LP relaxation of Sub-problem 2 to get an optimal solution $x_1 = 1$, $x_2 = 1$, $x_3 = 3$, $x_4 = 0.33$ with $\bar{Z}^2 = 15.33$.
1.3. Pruning test: Sub-problem 1 is not pruned and needs to branched further. Sub-problem 2 is fathomed, because its bound $\bar{Z}^2 = 15.33 < \underline{Z} = 16$.
1.4. Optimality condition is not met, thus proceed to Iteration 2.

Iteration 2:

2.1. Branching: Select Sub-problem 1 to branch (it is the only remaining sub-problem) with the following two constraints on top of Sub-problem 1.
Sub-problem 3: Sub-problem 1 with $x_4 \leq 1$ added.
Sub-problem 4: Sub-problem 1 with $x_4 \geq 2$ added.
2.2. Bounding: Solve the LP relaxation of Sub-problem 3 to get an optimal solution $x_1 = 0$, $x_2 = 0$, $x_3 = 3.5$, $x_4 = 1$ with $\bar{Z}^3 = 15.5$.
Solve the LP relaxation of Sub-problem 4 to get an optimal solution $x_1 = 0$, $x_2 = 0$, $x_3 = 4$, $x_4 = 2$ with $\bar{Z}^4 = 16$.

[a]In this case, x_4 needs to be rounded up instead of being rounded down to restore feasibility.

2.3. Pruning test: Sub-problem 3 is pruned since $\bar{Z}^2 = 15.5 < \underline{Z} = 16$. Sub-problem 4 is also pruned since its LP relaxation has integer values for all the integral variables.
2.4. Optimality test: no more sub-problem remains. Terminate with an optimal solution being the incumbent: $x_1^* = 0$, $x_2^* = 0$, $x_3^* = 4$, $x_4^* = 2$ with optimal objective value of $Z^* = 16$.

The corresponding search tree of the branch-and-bound solution process is illustrated in Figure A3.1. Each node represents a sub-problem with its index on top. A grayed node indicates that it is pruned. The criterion for pruning is highlighted in blue. For instance, Sub-problem 2 (SP2) is pruned because its upper bound of 15.33 is less than the incumbent of 16; SP4 is pruned because all the integer variables have integer values in the LP relaxation solution.

Note the role and benefit of using a heuristic to find feasible solutions (incumbent) during the branch-and-bound search. Both SP2 and SP3 are pruned with their upper bounds being less than the incumbent, which avoid further branching.

A3.4 Cutting-Plane Method

Consider an MILP model: $\max\{\boldsymbol{c}^T\boldsymbol{x} + \boldsymbol{d}^T\boldsymbol{y} : (\boldsymbol{x},\boldsymbol{y}) \in S\}$, where $S := \{(\boldsymbol{x},\boldsymbol{y}) \in \mathbb{Z}_+^n \times \mathbb{R}_+^r : \boldsymbol{A}\boldsymbol{x} + \boldsymbol{H}\boldsymbol{y} \leq \boldsymbol{b}\}$. Let P_0 be the linear programming relaxation of $\mathcal{S}$. Solving the linear program: $\max\{\boldsymbol{c}^T\boldsymbol{x} + \boldsymbol{d}^T\boldsymbol{y} : (\boldsymbol{x},\boldsymbol{y}) \in P_0\}$ with its optimal objective value z^0 and optimal solution $(\boldsymbol{x}^0, \boldsymbol{y}^0)$. Assume $(\boldsymbol{x}^0, \boldsymbol{y}^0)$ is a *basic* optimal solution.

This section presents an alternative strategy to handle the case when the linear programming relaxation solution $(\boldsymbol{x}^0, \boldsymbol{y}^0)$ is not in S. The key idea is to find an inequality $\boldsymbol{\alpha}^T\boldsymbol{x} + \boldsymbol{\beta}^T\boldsymbol{y} \leq \gamma$ that is satisfied by every point in $\mathcal{S}$ and is violated by $(\boldsymbol{x}^0, \boldsymbol{y}^0)$, i.e., $\boldsymbol{\alpha}^T\boldsymbol{x}^0 + \boldsymbol{\beta}^T\boldsymbol{y}^0 > \gamma$. A valid inequality $\boldsymbol{\alpha}^T\boldsymbol{x} + \boldsymbol{\beta}^T\boldsymbol{y} \leq \gamma$ for $\mathcal{S}$ that is violated by $(\boldsymbol{x}^0, \boldsymbol{y}^0)$ is a *cutting plane* separating $(\boldsymbol{x}^0, \boldsymbol{y}^0)$ from $\mathcal{S}$.

Let $P_1 := P_0 \cap \{(\boldsymbol{x}, \boldsymbol{y}) : \boldsymbol{\alpha}^T\boldsymbol{x} + \boldsymbol{\beta}^T\boldsymbol{y} \leq \gamma\}$. Since $S \subseteq P_1 \subset P_0$, the linear programming relaxation of the MILP model based on P_1 is tighter than that based on P_0. The *cutting plane method* successively generates and adds valid inequalities to tighten the linear relaxation, which can be conceptually described as follows.

Step 0: Initialization. Set $i := 0$.

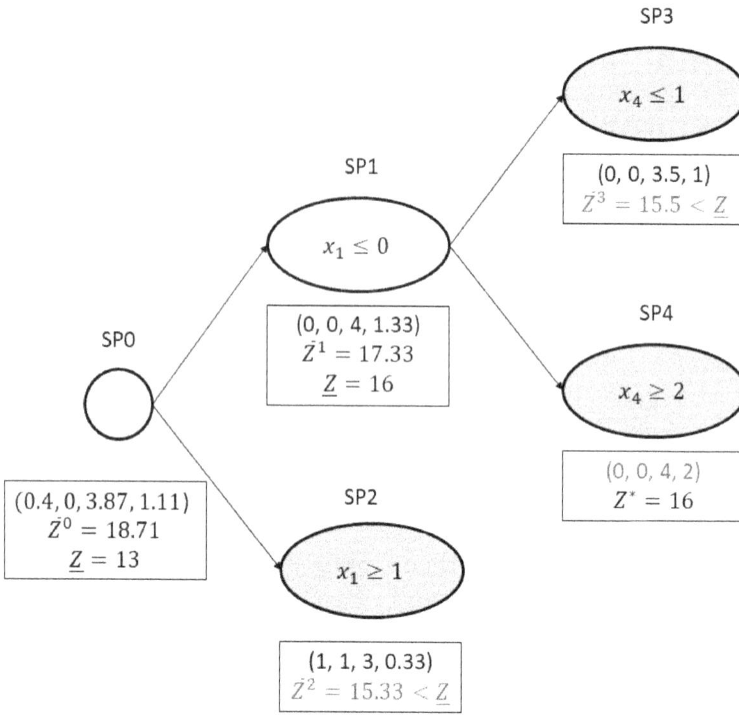

Figure A3.1. Illustration of branch-and-bound method.

Step 1: Main iterations.

1.1 Solve the linear program $\max\{\boldsymbol{c}^T\boldsymbol{x} + \boldsymbol{d}^T\boldsymbol{y} : (\boldsymbol{x},\boldsymbol{y}) \in P_i\}$.

1.2 If the optimal basic solution $(\boldsymbol{x}^i, \boldsymbol{y}^i)$ satisfies S, terminate (an optimal solution to the original MILP model is found).

1.3 Otherwise, solve the *separation problem*: Find a cutting plane $\boldsymbol{\alpha}^T\boldsymbol{x} + \boldsymbol{\beta}^T\boldsymbol{y} \leq \gamma$ separating $(\boldsymbol{x}^i, \boldsymbol{y}^i)$ from S.

1.4 Set $P_{i+1} := P_i \cap \{(\boldsymbol{x}, \boldsymbol{y}) : \boldsymbol{\alpha}^T\boldsymbol{x} + \boldsymbol{\beta}^T\boldsymbol{y} \leq \gamma\}$, and $i := i + 1$.

The key step in the cutting plane method is the way to generate cutting planes. In general, there are infinite number of cutting planes existing to separate $(\boldsymbol{x}^i, \boldsymbol{y}^i)$ from S, and there is a tradeoff between the quality of a separation procedure and its computational time. Generating effective and efficient cutting planes is a central topic in the theory and practice of Integer Programming. Below we introduce the well-known Gomory fractional cut, which has been widely applied in the existing off-the-shelf solvers.

If non-negative integer decision variables $x_1, \ldots, x_n$ satisfy the equation: $\sum_{j=1}^{n} a_j x_j = a_0$, where $a_0 \notin \mathbb{Z}$, the Gomory fractional cut is:

$$\sum_{j=1}^{n} (a_j - \lfloor a_j \rfloor) x_j \geq a_0 - \lfloor a_0 \rfloor, \tag{A3.5}$$

where $\lfloor a \rfloor$ denotes the largest integer that is no greater than a. Since $\sum_{j=1}^{n} a_j x_j = a_0$ implies that $\sum_{j=1}^{n} (a_j - \lfloor a_j \rfloor) x_j = a_0 - \lfloor a_0 \rfloor + \theta$ for some positive integer θ, any $\boldsymbol{x} \in \mathbb{Z}_+^n$ satisfying $\sum_{j=1}^{n} a_j x_j = a_0$ also satisfies (3.5).

Next, we present an example with two decision variables to demonstrate the cutting plane method with the Gomory fractional cuts.

$$\text{Maximize } 4.4x_1 + 3.1x_2$$

Subject to:

$$-2x_1 + 2x_2 \leq 6$$

$$8x_1 + 3x_2 \leq 21$$

$$x_1, x_2 \geq 0 \text{ and integer}$$

Introduce a variable z to represent the objective function, and slack variables x_3 and x_4 to turn the inequality constraints into equalities. The original problem becomes maximizing z subject to:

$$z - 4.4x_1 - 3.1x_2 = 0$$

$$-2x_1 + 2x_2 + x_3 = 6$$

$$8x_1 + 3x_2 + x_4 = 21$$

$$x_1, x_2, x_3, x_4 \geq 0 \text{ and integer}$$

Note that both x_3 and x_4 must be integers because the coefficients and right-hand-side of the constraints are all integers.

Iteration 1. Use the Simplex method to solve the linear programming relaxation, with x_3 and x_4 being the slack variables. An optimal tableau is:

$$z + \frac{29}{55}x_3 + \frac{15}{22}x_4 = 17\frac{13}{27}$$

$$x_2 + \frac{4}{11}x_3 + \frac{1}{11}x_4 = 4\frac{1}{11}$$

$$x_1 - \frac{3}{22}x_3 + \frac{1}{11}x_4 = 1\frac{1}{11}$$

The optimal basic solution is $x_3^0 = x_4^0 = 0$, $x_1^0 = 1\frac{1}{11}$, $x_2^0 = 4\frac{1}{11}$, with an objective value of $z^0 = 17\frac{13}{27}$, which is an upper bound to the original optimal objective value. Since x_1^0 and x_2^0 are not integers, it is not feasible to the original problem. Apply the Gomory fractional cut to $x_2 + \frac{4}{11}x_3 + \frac{1}{11}x_4 = 4\frac{1}{11}$ to obtain a valid cut: $\frac{4}{11}x_3 + \frac{1}{11}x_4 \geq \frac{1}{11}$, or $4x_3 + x_4 \geq 1$. Transforming it in the space of (x_1, x_2) by replacing $x_3 = 6+2x_1-2x_2$ and $x_4 = 21-8x_1-3x_2$, we get $x_2 \leq 4$. A graphical illustration of the above is shown in Figure A3.2(a). Adding the valid cut $x_2 \leq 4$ (Cut-1) leads to the next iteration.

Iteration 2. The original problem becomes:

$$\text{Maximize} \quad 4.4x_1 + 3.1x_2$$

Subject to:

$$-2x_1 + 2x_2 \leq 6$$

$$8x_1 + 3x_2 \leq 21$$

$$x_2 \leq 4$$

$$x_1, x_2 \geq 0 \text{ and integer}$$

Adding slack variables x_3, x_4 and x_5, we have:

$$z - 4.4x_1 - 3.1x_2 = 0$$

$$-2x_1 + 2x_2 + x_3 = 6$$

$$8x_1 + 3x_2 + x_4 = 21$$

$$x_2 + x_5 = 4$$

$$x_1, x_2, x_3, x_4, x_5 \geq 0 \text{ and integer}$$

An optimal tableau for its linear programming relaxation is:

$$z + 0.55x_4 + 1.45x_5 = 17.35$$

$$x_3 + 0.25x_4 - 2.75x_5 = 0.25$$

$$x_1 + 0.125x_4 - 0.375x_5 = 1.125$$

$$x_2 + x_5 = 4$$

The optimal basic solution is $x_4^1 = x_5^1 =$, $x_1^1 = 1.125$, $x_2^1 = 4$, $x_3^1 = 0.25$, with an optimal objective value of $z^1 = 17.35$, which improves over the upper bound of $17\frac{13}{27}$ in the first iteration. Since x_1^1 is not an integer, it is not feasible to the original problem. Applying the Gomory fractional cut to $x_3 + 0.25x_4 - 2.75x_5 = 0.25$, we have $0.25x_4 + (-2.75 - \lfloor -2.75 \rfloor)x_5 \geq 0.125$, thus $0.25x_4 + 0.25x_5 \geq 0.25$. Transforming it in the space of (x_1, x_2) by replacing $x_4 = 21 - 8x_1 - 3x_2$ and $x_5 = 4 - x_2$, we get $2x_1 + x_2 \leq 6$. A graphical illustration of the above is shown in Figure A3.2(b). Adding the valid cut $2x_1 + x_2 \leq 6$ (Cut-2) leads to the next iteration.

Iteration 3. The original problem becomes:

$$max\ 4.4x_1 + 3.1x_2$$

Subject to:

$$-2x_1 + 2x_2 \leq 6$$

$$8x_1 + 3x_2 \leq 21$$

$$x_2 \leq 4$$

$$2x_1 + x_2 \leq 6$$

$$x_1, x_2 \geq 0 \text{ and integer}$$

Adding slack variables x_3, x_4, x_5 and x_6, we have:

$$z - 4.4x_1 - 3.1x_2 = 0$$

$$-2x_1 + 2x_2 + x_3 = 6$$

$$8x_1 + 3x_2 + x_4 = 21$$

$$x_2 + x_5 = 4$$

$$2x_1 + x_2 + x_6 = 6$$

$$x_1, x_2, x_3, x_4, x_5, x_6 \geq 0 \text{ and integer}$$

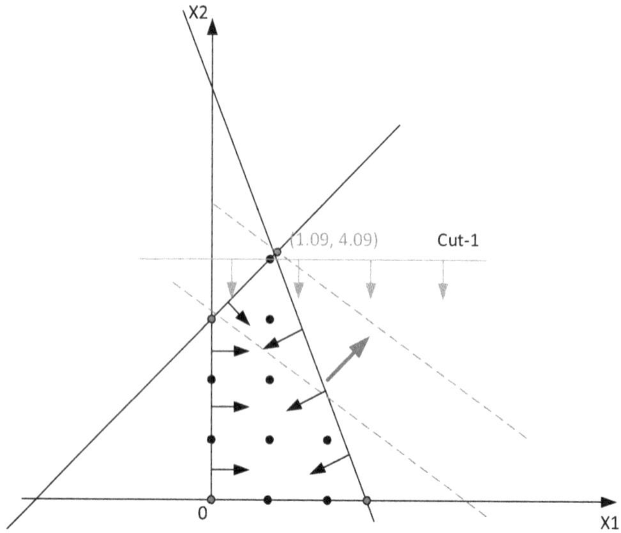

(a) Iteration 1

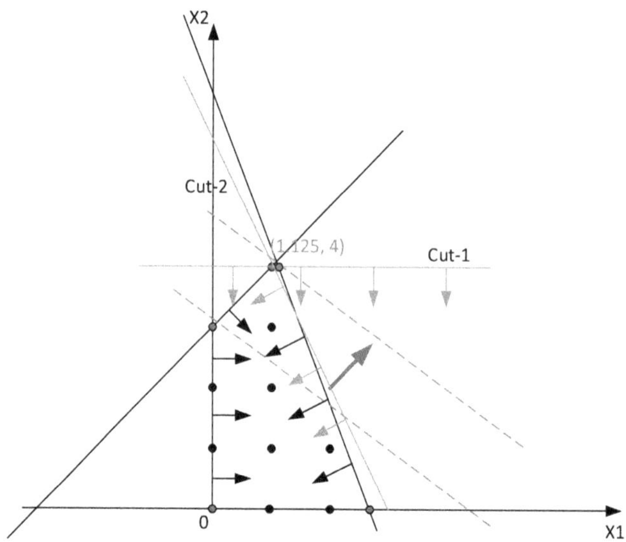

(b) Iteration 2

Figure A3.2. Illustration of cutting-plane method.

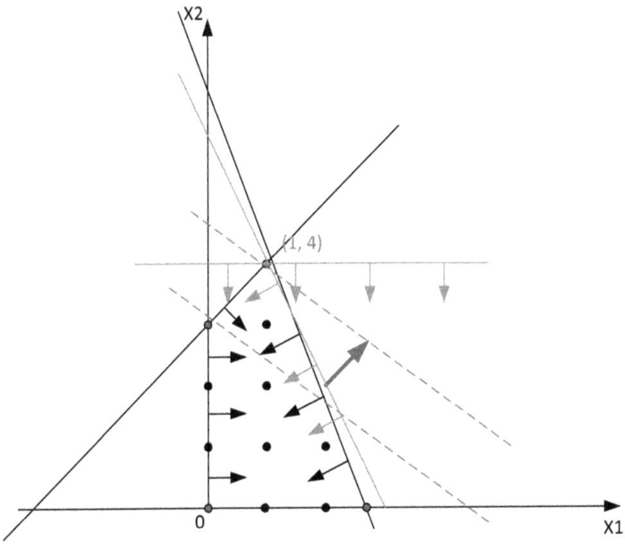

(c) Iteration 3

Figure A3.2. *(Continued)*

An optimal tableau for its linear programming relaxation is:

$$z + 0.9x_5 + 1.2x_6 = 16.8$$

$$x_3 - 3x_5 + x_6 = 0$$

$$x_1 - 0.5x_5 + 0.5x_6 = 1$$

$$x_4 + x_5 - 4x_6 = 1$$

$$x_2 + x_5 = 4$$

The optimal basic solution is $x_5^2 = x_6^2 = 0$, $x_1^2 = 1$, $x_2^2 = 4$, $x_4^2 = 1$, with an optimal objective value of $z^1 = 16.8$, which improves the upper bound of 17.35 in the second iteration. Since both x_1^2 and x_2^2 are integers, the solution is optimal to the original problem. This step is illustrated in Figure A3.2(c).

The cutting-plane method can be embedded in the branch-and-bound procedure to form the well-known branch-and-cut method, which is the main algorithm behind the scene of many commercially available optimization solvers for integer linear programming, including Cplex, Gurobi and Xpress, among others.

Appendix 4 A Primer in Constraint Programming Methods

A4.1 Overview of Constraint Programming Methods

Constraint programming (CP) was originated in AI to solve the Constraint Satisfaction Problem (CSP), which seeks to find a feasible solution to a system of constraints. Formally, a CSP can be defined as follows. Consider a set $\boldsymbol{x}$ of decision variables $x_1, x_2, \ldots, x_n$, each of which has its domain $D_1, D_2, \ldots, D_n$ described by a system of m constraints $f_i(\boldsymbol{a}_i\boldsymbol{x}) \leq \boldsymbol{b}_i$ for $i = 1, 2, \ldots, m$. The goal is to find a feasible assignment of values to each decision variable from its domain that satisfies all the constraints. Note that different from an optimization problem, a CSP does not have an objective function to optimize.

Example A4.1. Consider a CSP with $x \in \{1, 2\}$, $y \in \{1, 2\}$, $z \in \{1, 2\}$ and a system of constraints: $x = y$, $x \neq z$, $y > z$. A feasible solution to the CSP is: $x = 2$, $y = 2$ and $z = 1$.

CP relies on two main solving techniques: *constraint propagation* and *search*. Constraint propagation reduces the domain of decision variables in a systematic way, thus is also known as *domain reduction*. Specifically, when the domain of one decision variable is modified (reduced), the domain of all variables that are related to the decision variable through constraints will be modified (reduced). Ideally, one would like to reduce the domain of decision variables to singleton, such that a feasible solution to the original model can be conveniently identified. However, reducing the domain of decision variables to singleton is itself computationally demanding, i.e., NP-hard in general. Therefore, to find feasible solution to a CSP often requires a systematic procedure to search the solution space.

A4.2 Constraint Propagation

There are various constraint propagation techniques for domain reduction, ranging from the basic version to more computationally involving ones. To facilitate understanding of these techniques, we first introduce graph representation of a CSP. Let a graph $G(V, E)$ denote a CSP, where V is a set of nodes representing the decision variables, and E is a set of edges denoting the constraints. We limit our treatment to the CSP with a constraint involving no more than two decision variables. The more complex constraints with each involving more than two decision variables goes beyond the scope of this text.

Example A4.2. The graph representation of the CSP in Example A4.1 is shown below.

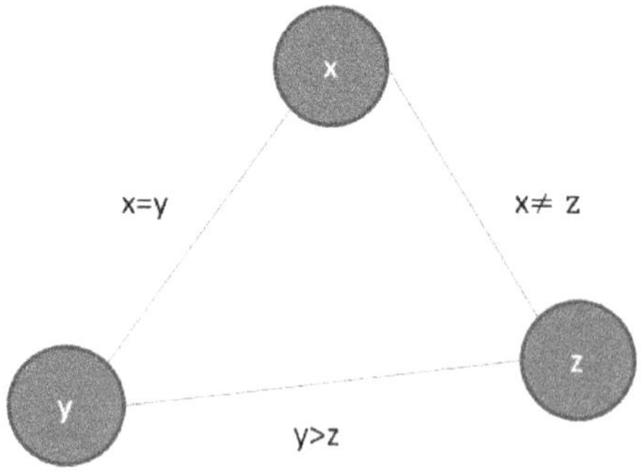

In principle, a constraint propagation procedure works in a way that iteratively removes inconsistent values from the domain of each decision variable to maintain *local consistency*. Two basic local consistency techniques are node consistency and arc consistency.

A constraint over only one decision variable is called *unary constraint*. A unary constraint C over the decision variable x with domain D_x is *node consistent* if and only if $\forall a \in D_x$, a satisfies C, i.e., all the values in D_x satisfy C. A CSP is node consistent if all of its constraints are node consistent.

Example A4.3. Consider $x \in D_x = \{2, 4, 6\}$, then the unary constraint $even(x)$ is node consistent. Consider $x \in D_x = [2, 3, \ldots, 12]$, then the unary constraint $x > 6$ is not node consistent.

A constraint over two decision variables is called *binary constraint*. A binary constraint C over the decision variables x and y with domain D_x and D_y, respectively, is *arc consistent* if and only if: (i) $\forall a \in D_x$, $\exists b \in D_y$ such that (a, b) satisfies C; and (ii) $\forall b \in D_y$, $\exists a \in D_x$ such that (a, b) satisfies C. A CSP is arc consistent if all of its constraints are arc consistent.

Example A4.4. Consider $x \in D_x = \{1, 3\}$ and $y \in D_y = \{2, 4\}$, then the binary constraint $x + y = 5$ is arc consistent; Consider $x \in D_x = \{1, 2\}$ and $y \in D_y = \{1, 7\}$, then the binary constraint $x = y$ is not arc consistent.

A local consistency procedure seeks to achieve both node consistency and arc consistency by examining each constraint in a CSP in an iterative fashion.

Example A4.5. Consider a CSP described by the set of constraints: $\{y > 1, x < z, x = y, y > z - 2; x, y, z \in \{1, 2, 3\}\}$. Apply the node consistency and arc consistency techniques to reduce domains of the decision variables.

The CSP can be represented by the following graph. We then iteratively examine and maintain node consistency on each node and arc consistency on each edge.

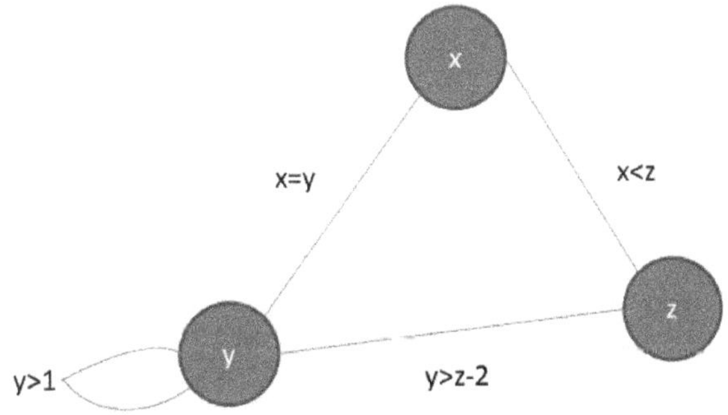

Iteration 1: Node consistency for y reduces D_y to $\{2, 3\}$.

Iteration 2: Examine $x < z$ to achieve arc consistency between x and z reduces D_x to $\{1, 2\}$ and D_z to $\{2, 3\}$.

Iteration 3: Examine $x = y$ to achieve arc consistency between x and y reduces D_x to $\{2\}$ and D_y to $\{2\}$.

Iteration 4: Re-examine $x < z$ to further reduce D_z to $\{3\}$.

Since the domains of all the decision variables are singleton now, a feasible solution is found: $x = 2$, $y = 2$, $z = 3$.

A4.3 Search

A search procedure is needed in general to find feasible solution(s) to a CSP. Among many different algorithms, the depth-first-search (DFS) is a popular one widely applied in constraint programming. In a DFS, each node (decision variable) is explored as far as possible in each branch, with the possible values in its domain, before backtracking. The procedure incrementally searches and builds candidate partial feasible solutions, and *backtracks* (abandons) a candidate as soon as it determines that the candidate cannot be extended to a complete feasible solution.

Example A4.6. Consider a CSP with x, y, $z \in \{1, 2\}$ and a set of constraints: $x = y$, $x \neq z$, $y > z$. Use DFS and backtracking to find a feasible solution. The search procedure is shown in the table on the left, and the search tree is illustrated on the right.

x	y	z	Feasible
1	1	1	No
		2	No
	2		No
2	1		No
	2	1	Yes

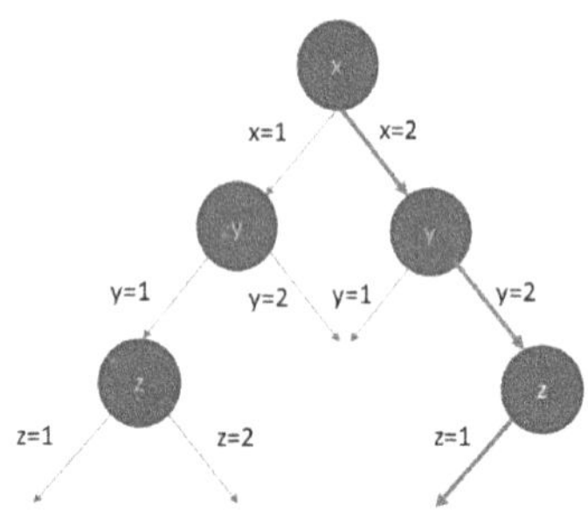

In practice, a CP algorithm simultaneously performs constraint propagation and search to solve a CSP. That is, the domains of decision variables are iteratively being reduced during the search procedure.

Instructions for Downloadable Electronic Slides

Included with this publication are downloadable electronic slides of each lecture for students and teachers around the world to be better able to understand and present climate change. These supplementary materials may be retrieved by using the following access Token:

https://www.worldscientific.com/r/12930-SUPP

The Token may be either clicked on (for eBook only), or manually copied/typed into the address bar of your internet browser.

If you purchased the eBook directly from the World Scientific website, your access token would have been activated under your username.

Users will be directed to the sign in page, and prompted to either sign in or register an account with World Scientific.

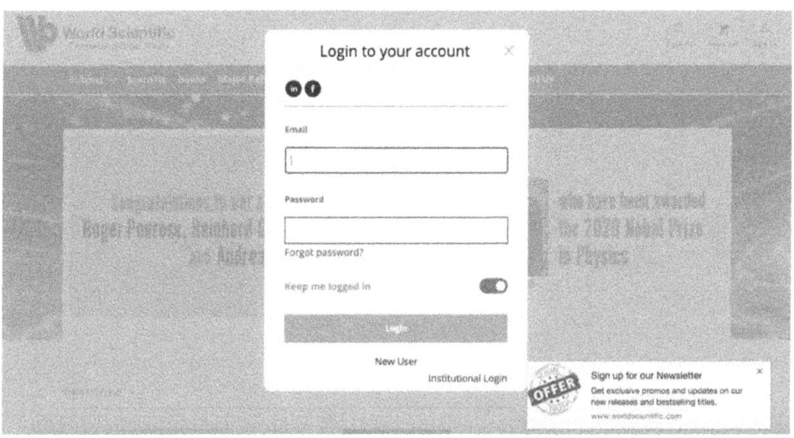

Upon successful login, you will be redirected to the book's page; click on the 'Supplementary' tab (see screenshot below) to locate the .zip file containing the sample IBM Cplex Studio codes. Click on the 'Electronic Slides' hyperlink to commence downloading.

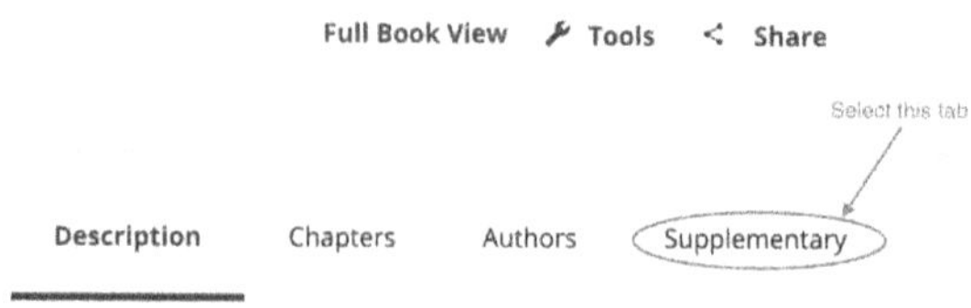

For subsequent access to the supplementary materials, simply login with the same username.

For any enquiries on access issues, please email sales@wspc.com.sg.

References

[1] Myerson, P.A., *Supply Chain and Logistics Management Made Easy.* 2015, New Jersey: Pearson.
[2] Wisner, J.D., K.-C. Tan, and G.K. Leong, *Principles of Supply Chain Management: A Balanced Approach.* 2018, Boston, Massachusetts: Cengage.
[3] Heizer, J. and B. Render, *Operations Management.* 2013, New Jersey: Pearson.
[4] Hopp, W.J. and M.L. Spearman, *Factory Physics.* 2008, New York: McGraw Hill.
[5] Hopp, W.J., *Supply Chain Science.* 2008, New York: McGraw Hill.
[6] Chopra, S. and P. Meindl, *Supply Chain Management: Strategy, Planning, and Operation.* 2014, New Jersey: Pearson.
[7] Dantzig, G., *Linear Programming and Extensions.* 1963, Princeton, New Jersey: Princeton University Press.
[8] Chvatal, V., *Linear Programming.* 1983, New York: Freeman.
[9] Vanderbei, R.J., *Linear Programming: Foundations and Extensions.* 2014, Berlin: Springer.
[10] Hillier, F., *Introduction to Operations Research.* 2014, New York: McGraw-Hill.
[11] Korte, B. and J. Vygen, *Combinatorial Optimization: Theory and Algorithms.* 2006, Bonn, Germany: Springer.
[12] Garey, M.R. and D.S. Johnson, *Computers and Intractability: A Guide to the Theory of NP-Completeness.* 1979, San Francisco: W. H. Freeman.
[13] Williams, H., *Modeling Building in Mathematical Programming* (4th ed.). 1999, New York: Wiley.
[14] Nemhauser, G. and L. Wolsey, *Integer and Combinatorial Optimization.* 1988, New York: John Wiley.

[15] Bertsimas, D. and R. Weismantel, *Optimization over Integers*. 2005, Belmont: Dynamic Ideas.
[16] Conforti, M., G. Cornuejols, and G. Zambelli, *Integer Programming*. 2014, Switzerland: Springer.
[17] Gonzalez, T.F. (ed.), *Handbook of Approximation Algorithms and Metaheuristics*. Computer and Information Science Series, S. Sahni (ed.). 2007, Chapman & Hall/CRC.
[18] Glover, F. and G. Kochenberger, *Handbook of Metaheuristics*. 2005, Dordrecht: Springer.
[19] Glover, F., D. Klingman, and N.V. Phillips, *Network Models in Optimization and Their Applications in Practice*. 1992, New York: Wiley-Interscience.
[20] Ahuja, R.K., T.L. Magnanti, and J.B. Orlin, *Network Flows*. 1993, Englewood Cliffs, New Jersey: Prentice Hall.
[21] Glover, F., G. Kochenberger, R. Hennig, and Y. Du, Quantum bridge analytics I: A tutorial on formulating and using QUBO models. *Annals of Operations Research*, 2022. https://doi.org/10.1007/s10479-022-04634-2.
[22] Punnen, A., *The Quadratic Unconstrained Binary Optimization Problem*. 2022, Switzerland: Springer.
[23] Guillaume, A., E.Y. Goh, M.D. Johnston, B.D. Wilson, A. Ramanan, F. Tibble, and B. Lackey, Deep space network scheduling using quantum annealing. *IEEE Transactions on Quantum Engineering*, 2016, **4**. https://10.1109/TQE.2022.3199267.
[24] Carugno, C., M.F. Dacrema, and P. Cremonesi, Evaluating the job shop scheduling problem on a D-wave quantum annealer. *Scientific Reports*, 2022, **12**. https://doi.org/10.1038/s41598-022-10169-0.
[25] Ding, Y., X. Chen, L. Lamata, E. Solano, and M. Sanz, Implementation of a hybrid classical-quantum annealing algorithm for logistic network design. *SN Computer Science*, 2021, **2**(68). https://doi.org/10.1007/s42979-021-00466-2.
[26] Date, P., D. Authur, and L. Pusey-Nazzaro, QUBO formulations for training machine learning models. *Scientific Reports*, 2021, **11**. https://doi.org/10.1038/s41598-021-89461-4.
[27] Tsang, E., *Foundations of Constraint Satisfaction*. 1993, Norderstedt: Academic Press.
[28] Van Hentenryck, P., *Constraint Satisfaction in Logic Programming*. 1989, Cambridge: MIT Press.
[29] Baptiste, P., C. Le Pape, and W. Nuijten, *Constraint-Based Scheduling: Applying Constraint Programming to Scheduling Problems*. 2001, New York: Springer.

[30] Brucker, P., Scheduling and constraint propagation. *Discrete Applied Mathematics*, 2002, **123**(1-3): pp. 227–256.

[31] Van Hentenryck, P., *The OPL Optimization Programming Language*. 1999, Cambridge: MIT Press.

[32] Hooker, J., Logic, optimization and constraint programming. *INFORMS Journal on Computing*, 2002, **14**(4): pp. 285–321.

[33] Milano, M. (ed.), *Constraint and Integer Programming: Toward a Unified Methodology*. 2004, New York: Kluwer Academic Publishers.

[34] Jain, V. and I. Grossmann, Algorithms for Hybrid MILP/CP Models for a Class of Optimization Problems. *INFORMS Journal on Computing*, 2001, **13**(4): pp. 258–276.

[35] Li, H. and K. Womer, Project scheduling with multi-purpose resources: A combined MILP/CP decomposition approach. *International Journal of Operations and Quantitative Management*, 2006, **12**(4): pp. 305–325.

[36] Li, H. and K. Womer, Scheduling projects with multi-skilled personnel by a hybrid MILP/CP Benders decomposition algorithm. *Journal of Scheduling*, 2009, **12**(3): pp. 281–298.

[37] Li, H. and K. Womer, Optimizing the supply chain configuration for make-to-order manufacturing. *European Journal of Operational Research*, 2012, **221**(1): pp. 118–128.

[38] Daskin, M.S., *Network and Discrete Location: Models, Algorithms and Applications*. 2013, New York: Wiley.

[39] Glover, F., M. Amini, and G. Kochenberger, Parametric ghost image processes for fixed-charge problems: A study of transformation networks. *Journal of Heuristics*, 2005, **11**: pp. 307–336.

[40] Eksioglu, S.D., P.M. Pardalos, and H.E. Romeijin, A dynamic slope scaling procedure for the fixed-charge cost multi-commodity network flow problem, in *Financial Engineering, E-commerce and Supply Chain. Applied Optimization*, P.M. Pardalos and V.K. Tsitsiringos (eds.). 2002, Boston: Springer.

[41] Hewitt, M., G.L. Nemhauser, and M. Savelsbergh, Combining exact and heuristic approaches for the capacitated fixed-charge network flow problem. *INFORMS Journal on Computing*, 2010, **22**(2): pp. 314–325.

[42] Ukkusuri, S.V. and G. Patil, Multi-period transportation network design under demand uncertainty. *Transportation Research Part B: Methodological*, 2009, **43**(6): pp. 625–642.

[43] Pimentel, B.S., G.R. Mateus, and F.A. Almeida, Stochastic capacity planning and dynamic network design. *International Journal of Production Economics*, 2013, **145**(1): pp. 139–149.

[44] Alumur, S. and B.Y. Kara, Network hub location problems: The state of the art. *European Journal of Operational Research*, 2008, **190**: pp. 1–21.
[45] Gelareh, S. and S. Nichel, Hub location problems in transportation networks. *Transportation Research Part E: Logistics and Transportation*, 2011.
[46] Farahani, R.Z., M. Hekmatfar, A.B. Arabani, and E. Nikbakhsh, Hub location problems: A review of models, classification, solution techniques, and applications. *Computers & Industrial Engineering*, 2013, **64**: pp. 1096–1109.
[47] Daskin, M.S. and C. Coullard, An inventory-location model: Formulation, solution algorithm and computational results. *Annals of Operations Research*, 2002, **110**: pp. 83–106.
[48] Shen, Z.-J., C. Coullard, and M.S. Daskin, A joint location-inventory model. *Transportation Science*, 2003, **37**(1): pp. 40–55.
[49] Voβ, S. and D.L. Woodruff, *Introduction to Computational Optimization Models for Production Planning in a Supply Chain*. 2006, Heidelberg: Springer.
[50] Pochet, Y. and L.A. Wolsey, *Production Planning by Mixed Integer Programming*. 2006, New York: Springer.
[51] Ahumada, O., J.R. Villalobos, and A.N. Mason, Tactical planning of the production and distribution of fresh agricultural products under uncertainty. *Agricultural Systems*, 2012, **112**: pp. 17–26.
[52] Lee, Y.H., S.H. Kim, and C. Moon, Production-distribution planning in supply chain using a hybrid approach. *Production Planning & Control*, 2002, **13**(1): pp. 35–46.
[53] Bilgen, B. and Y. Celebi, Integrated production scheduling and distribution planning in dairy supply chain by hybrid modelling. *Annals of Operations Research*, 2013, **211**: pp. 55–82.
[54] Kopanos, G., L. Puigjaner, and M.C. Georgiadis, Simultaneous production and logistics operations planning in semicontinuous food industries. *Omega*, 2012, **40**: pp. 634–650.
[55] Geismar, H.N., G. Laporte, L. Lei, and C. Sriskandarajah, The integrated production and transportation scheduling problem for a product with a short lifespan. *INFORMS Journal on Computing*, 2008, **20**(1): pp. 21–33.
[56] He, P., K. Li, and P.N.R. Kumar, An enhanced branch-and-price algorithm for the integrated production and transportation scheduling problem. *International Journal of Production Research*, 2021, https://doi.org/101080/00207543202111876941.
[57] Li, H., C.A. Santos, A. Fuciec, M.T. Gonzalez, S. Jain, C. Marquez, C. Mejia, and A. Zhang, Optimizing the labor strategy for professional

service firms. *IEEE Transactions on Engineering Management*, 2018, **66**(3): pp. 443–458.

[58] Weingartner, H.M., *Mathematical Programming and the Analysis of Capital Budgeting Problems.* 1963, Englewood Cliffs: Prentice Hall.

[59] Fremgen, J.M., Capital budgeting practices: A survey. *Management Accounting*, 1973, **54**(11): pp. 19–25.

[60] Gitman, L.J. and J.R. Forrester, A survey on capital budgeting techniques used by major US firms. *Financial Management*, 1977, **6**(3): pp. 66–71.

[61] Evans, G.W. and R. Fairbairn, Selection and scheduling of advanced missions for NASA using 0-1 integer linear programming. *Journal of Operational Research Society*, 1989, **40**(11): pp. 971–981.

[62] Kira, D.S., M.I. Kusy, D.H. Murray, and B.J. Goranson, A specific decision support system (SDSS) to develop an optimal project portfolio mix under uncertainty. *IEEE Transactions on Engineering Management*, 1990, **37**: pp. 213–221.

[63] Ghasemzadeh, F., N. Archer, and P. Iyogun, A zero-one model for project portfolio selection and scheduling. *The Journal of the Operational Research Society*, 1999, **50**(7): pp. 745–755.

[64] Dickinson, M.W., A.C. Thornton, and S.C. Graves, Technology portfolio management: Optimizing interdependent projects over multiple time periods. *IEEE Transactions on Engineering Management*, 2001, **48**(4): pp. 518–527.

[65] Li, H., M. Vargas, C.A. Santos, L. Ramshaw, I. Lopez, S. Perez, and C. Valencia, Optimizing large-Scale stochastic resource planning, in *Working paper, University of Missouri — St. Louis.* 2018

[66] Santos, C.A., I. Lopez, F. Orozco, D. Ludwig, E. Canaud, and H. Li, Tool to compute the weights of a set of business indices respecting the hierarchy of preferences, in *Technical Report.* 2016: University of Missouri — St. Louis, USA.

[67] Solomon, S., H. Li, K. Womer, and C.A. Santos, Approximate dynamic programming for multi-period stochastic resource planning. *Decision Sciences*, 2019, **50**(6): pp. 1281–1318.

[68] Simpson, K.F., In-process inventories. *Operations Research*, 1958, **6**(6): pp. 863–873.

[69] Eruguz, A.S., E. Sahin, Z. Jemai, and Dallery, A comprehensive survey of guaranteed-service models for multi-echelon inventory optimization. *International Journal of Production Economics*, 2016, **172**: pp. 110–125.

[70] Inderfurth, K., Safety stock optimization in multi-stage inventory systems. *International Journal of Production Economics*, 1991, **24**: p. 103.

[71] Inderfurth, K. and S. Minner, Safety stocks in multi-stage inventory systems under different service measures. *European Journal of Operational Research*, 1998, **106**: pp. 57–73.
[72] Magnanti, T.L., Z.-J. Shen, J. Shu, D. Simchi-Levi, and C.-P. Teo, Inventory placement in acyclic supply chain networks. *Operations Research Letters*, 2006, **34**: pp. 228–238.
[73] Li, H. and D. Jiang, New model and heuristics for safety stock placement in general acyclic supply chain networks. *Computers and Operations Research*, 2012, **39**(7): pp. 1333–1344.
[74] Graves, S.C. and S.P. Willems, Optimizing strategic safety stock placement in supply chains. *Manufacturing & Service Operations Management*, 2000, **2**(1): pp. 68–83.
[75] Graves, S.C. and S.P. Willems, Optimizing the supply chain configuration for new products. *Management Science*, 2005, **51**(8): pp. 1165–1180.
[76] Li, H., D. Jiang, and D. Li, Optimizing the configuration of a food supply chain. *International Journal of Production Research*, 2021, **59**(12): pp. 3722–3746.
[77] Li, H. and K. Womer, Modeling the supply chain configuration problem under resource constraints. *International Journal of Project Management*, 2008, **26**(6): pp. 646–654.
[78] Amini, M. and H. Li, Supply chain configuration for diffusion of new products: An integrated optimization approach. *Omega*, 2011, **39**(3): pp. 313–322.
[79] Li, H. and M. Amini, A hybrid optimization approach to configure supply chains for new products diffusion: A case study of multiple-sourcing strategy. *International Journal of Production Research*, 2012, **50**(11): pp. 3152–3171.
[80] Amini, M. and H. Li, The impact of dual market on supply chain configuration for new products. *International Journal of Production Research*, 2015, **53**(18): pp. 5669–5684.
[81] Nie, D., H. Li, T. Qu, Y. Liu, and C. Li, Optimizing supply chain configuration with low carbon emission. *Journal of Cleaner Production*, 2020, **271**: p. 122539.
[82] Baker, K.R. and D. Trietsch, *Principles of Sequencing and Scheduling*. 2009, New York: Springer.
[83] Pinedo, M., *Scheduling — Theory, Algorithms and Systems*. 2012, New York: Springer.
[84] Leung, J. (ed.), *Handbook of Scheduling: Algorithms, Models and Performance Analysis*. 2004, Chapman & Hall/CRC, Boca Raton: Florida.

[85] Demeulemeester, E.L. and W.S. Herroelen, *Project Scheduling: A Research Handbook.* International Series in Operations Research and Management Science. 2002, Norwell, MA: Kluwer Academic Publishers.
[86] Schwindt, C. and J. Zimmermann (eds.), *Handbook on Project Management and Scheduling.* International Handbooks on Information Systems (Vol. 1&2). 2015, Springer: Heidelberg, Germany.
[87] Klein, R., *Scheduling of Resource-Constrained Projects.* 1999, New York: Kluwer Academic Publishers.
[88] Li, H. and K. Womer, A decomposition approach for shipboard manpower scheduling. *Military Operations Research*, 2009, **14**(3): pp. 1–24.
[89] Dantzig, G., R. Fulkerson, and S. Johnson, Solution of a large-scale traveling-salesman problem. *Journal of the Operational Research Society*, 1954, **2**(4): pp. 393–410.
[90] Miller, C.E., A.W. Tucker, and R.A. Zemlin, Integer programming formulation of traveling salesman problems. *Journal of Association of Computational Machinery*, 1960, **7**: pp. 326–329.
[91] Gavish, B. and S.C. Graves, The travelling salesman problem and related problems, in *Working Paper GR-078-78.* 1978, Cambridge, Massachusetts: Operations Research Center, MIT.
[92] Oncan, T., I.K. Altinel, and G. Laporte, A comparative analysis of several asymmetric traveling salesman problem formulations. *Computers & Operations Research*, 2009, **36**(3): pp. 637–654.
[93] Applegate, D.L., R.E. Bixby, V. Chvatal, and W.J. Cook, *The Travelling Salesman Problem: A Computational Study.* Princeton Series in Applied Mathematics. 2006, Princeton, New Jersey: Princeton University Press.
[94] Ascheuer, N., M. Fischetti, and M. Grotschel, Solving the asymmetric travelling salesman problem with time windows by branch-and-cut. *Mathematical Programming*, 2001, **90**: pp. 475–506.
[95] Li, H. and B. Alidaee, Tabu search for solving the black-and-white traveling salesman problem. *Journal of the Operational Research Society*, 2015, **67**(8): pp. 1061–1070.
[96] Cordeau, J.-F., G. Laporte, M. Savelsbergh, and D. Vigo, Vehicle Routing, in *Handbook in OR & MS*, C. Barnhart and G. Laporte (eds.). 2007, Holland: Elsevier, pp. 367–428.
[97] Toth, P. and D. Vigo, *Vehicle Routing: Problems, Methods and Applications.* 2014, Philadelphia: Society for Industrial and Applied Mathematics.
[98] Bard, J.F., G. Kontoravdis, and G. Yu, A branch-and-cut procedure for the vehicle routing problem with time windows. *Transportation Science*, 2002, **36**(2): pp. 250–269.

[99] Ropke, S., J.-F. Cordeau, and G. Laporte, Models and branch-and-cut algorithms for pickup and delivery problems with time windows. *Networks*, 2007, **49**(4): pp. 258–272.
[100] Ropke, S. and J.-F. Cordeau, Branch and Cut and Price for the Pickup and Delivery Problem with Time Windows. *Transportation Science*, 2009, **43**(3): pp. 267–286.
[101] Campbell, A.M. and J.H. Wilson, Forty years of periodic vehicle routing. *Networks*, 2013, **63**(1): pp. 2–15.
[102] Baldacci, R., E. Bartolini, and A. Mingozzi, An exact algorithm for the pickup and delivery problem with time windows. *Operations Research*, 2011, **59**(2): pp. 414–426.
[103] Schiff, M. and Z. Lieber, A model for the integration of credit and inventory management. *Journal of Finance*, 1974, **29**(1): pp. 133–140.
[104] Kim, J., H. Hwang, and S. Shinn, An optimal credit policy to increase supplier's profits with price-dependent demand functions. *Production Planning & Control*, 1995, **6**(1): pp. 45–50.
[105] Li, H., L. Mai, W. Zhang, and X. Tian, Optimizing the credit timer decisions in supply chain finance. *Journal of Purchasing and Supply Management*, 2019, **25**(2): pp. 146–156.

Index

U

V

W

X

www.ingramcontent.com/pod-product-compliance
Lightning Source LLC
Chambersburg PA
CBHW071440281224
19406CB00020B/64

9 789811 259685